W9-AOQ-329

This book is the first major reinterpretation of the New Deal in almost thirty years. Gordon not only recasts our understanding of New Deal programs but also offers a compelling interpretation of the relationship among those programs, of their roots in the 1920s, and of the way in which they were shaped by powerful, if disorganized economic interests. Gordon assesses both private efforts to deal with cutthroat competition and federated politics and political efforts (spurred by private failure and the Great Depression) to enforce the rules or socialize the costs of trade association, welfare capitalism, and "regulatory" labor relations. Of particular importance is the author's argument that the labor and welfare legislation of the "second" New Deal grew directly from disparate business demands for organization and stability.

New Deals offers both a wide range of new or newly interpreted archival evidence and a conceptual approach that draws upon theories of rational choice and collective action, marxian concepts of exploitation, and ongoing efforts to theorize the relationship between politics and markets. This study will interest not only those seeking to understand the New Deal but also those exploring the workings of democratic capitalism and the way in which it organizes (or disorganizes) economic and political interests.

New Deals

New deals
Business, labor, and politics in America, 1920–1935

COLIN GORDON
University of British Columbia

CAMBRIDGE
UNIVERSITY PRESS

Published by the Press Syndicate of the University of Cambridge
The Pitt Building, Trumpington Street, Cambridge CB2 1RP
40 West 20th Street, New York, NY 10011-4211, USA
10 Stamford Road, Oakleigh, Melbourne 3166, Australia

© Cambridge University Press 1994

First published 1994

Printed in the United States of America

Library of Congress Cataloging-in-Publication Data

Gordon, Colin, 1962–
    New deals : business, labor, and politics in America, 1920–1935 /
Colin Gordon.
        p.   cm.
    Includes bibliographical references and index.
    ISBN 0-521-45122-1. – ISBN 0-521-45755-6 (pbk.)
    1. United States – Economic policy – To 1933.   2. United States –
Economic policy – 1933–1945.   3. New Deal, 1933–1939.   4. Labor
policy – United States – History – 20th century.   5. United States –
Politics and government – 1933–1945.   I. Title
HC106.3.G625   1994   93-34538
338.973′009′043–dc20   CIP

A catalog record for this book is available from the British Library

ISBN 0-521-45122-1 hardback
ISBN 0-521-45755-6 paperback

FOR MY PARENTS

Contents

viii   *Contents*

Acknowledgments

This book has been a large part of my adult life, during which time I have incurred many academic and practical debts. Indeed, my efforts have depended so heavily on the inspiration and assistance and friendship of others that my intellectual creditors could justly lay claim to any merits that this book might have. In the special economy of scholarship, fortunately, such debts can be repaid in kind or (at ten cents on the dollar) in a prefatory testimonial.

In keeping with my own interpretive approach, I'll start with the cash. I am very grateful for the financial support of the University of Wisconsin Graduate School, the Herbert C. Hoover Presidential Library Association, and the Hagley Museum and Library. Special thanks goes to the Social Sciences and Humanities Research Council of Canada, whose doctoral fellowship program supports both individual research and the broader goal of truly public education.

Archivists at the University of Wisconsin Libraries, the State Historical Society of Wisconsin, the Roosevelt and Hoover Presidential Libraries, the Baker Library at Harvard, the Littauer Library at Georgetown, and the New York Public Library guided me patiently through their collections and were quick to help a visiting researcher catch a bus or find lunch. Special thanks to Jerry Hess and Tab Lewis for reducing the National Archives to a human scale. At the Hagley Museum, where I spent a year as a doctoral fellow, I would like to thank Chris Baer, Monique Borque, Gail Petrovich, Marjorie McNinch, and Michael Nash for their friendship and for the delivery of more archival boxes than I'd care to remember.

My friends and colleagues in the Wisconsin history program were a constant source of friendship and inspiration. Roger Horowitz was a thoughtful critic and, on Sunday afternoons, a fairly good third baseman. Kathy Brown, Nancy Isenberg, Marie Laberge, Earl Mulderink, Ted Pearson, Leslie Reagan, Daniel Schneider, and Joel Wolfe were always willing to share ideas and frustrations, and mixed scholarly enthusiasm and fathomless cynicism in such a way that made it possible and enjoyable to write my dissertation. That I did not miss these friends more keenly during a year-long research trip to the East Coast is thanks largely to Pat Cooper, whose tenure at the Hagley happily overlapped with mine.

At York University, Joe Ernst provided friendship and encouragement. Stan Vittoz exchanged ideas on the political economy of the 1920s; my debt to him should be apparent to anyone who has read his fine monograph on New Deal labor policy. And Gabriel Kolko, as a friend and a scholar, inspired and encouraged my work at various stages – including a careful review of the complete manuscript. Those who have had the good fortune to work with Gabriel will appreciate the importance of his critical insight and generosity. At Wisconsin, I would like to thank Allan Bogue and Tom McCormick for their support and interest, and Rogers Hollingsworth for spurring my interest in the 1920s and encouraging me to probe other disciplines. As reviewers of this manuscript for Cambridge, Michael Bernstein and Nelson Lichtenstein provided both penetrating criticism and critical enthusiasm at a crucial stage. Frank Smith and Liz Neal steered me painlessly through the editorial process, and the blue pencils of Claire Huismann and Greg Everitt made this a better book.

I cannot adequately communicate my debt to Joel Rogers. As a friend, adviser, and colleague, Joel read my work with a judicious mix of skepticism and enthusiasm and taught me more than I would care to admit. His political and intellectual commitments helped me focus my energies and anticipate problems and criticisms. Joel usually knew what I was arguing or where I was going before I did – a fact that I think (and hope) says more about his commitment to my work than it does about my own doubts. Only intellectual embarassment and my editor kept Joel's name from leading off every other footnote.

Finally, I would like to thank my brothers and sister for their support and for enduring numerous long-winded verbal versions of my latest chapter. My parents, to whom this book is dedicated, were my first and best teachers. Special thanks to Susan, whose love and companionship has done more to sustain my intellectual energies, and to place them in proper perspective, than she will ever know; and to Isabel, for happy interruptions of unqualified affection.

C.G.

Vancouver, British Columbia
September, 1993

An earlier version of Chapter 7 appeared as "New Deal, Old Deck: Business and the Origins of Social Security, 1920–1935," *Politics and Society* 19 (June 1991). It is reprinted with the permission of Sage Publications.

Abbreviations Used in Text and Notes

JEH: *Journal of Economic History*
JPE: *Journal of Political Economy*
LAB: Labor Advisory Board (NRA)
LH: *Labor History*
MLR: *Monthly Labor Review*
N&S: Name and Subject Files (Strauss Papers)
NAM: National Association of Manufacturers
NBER: National Bureau of Economic Research
NICB: National Industrial Conference Board
NIRA: National Industrial Recovery Act
NLB: National Labor Board
NLMA: National Lumber Manufacturers' Association
NLRB: National Labor Relations Board
NRA: National Recovery Administration
OF: Official Files (FDR Papers)
PAW: Petroleum Administration for War
PF: Presidential Files (Hoover Papers)
POUR: President's Organization on Unemployment Relief
PPF: President's Personal Files (Hoover, FDR Papers)
PPI: Post-Presidential Individual Files (Hoover Papers)
PRA: President's Re-employment Agreement
PSF: President's Secretary's Files (FDR Papers)
SSA: Social Security Act
SCC: Special Conference Committee
SEJ: Southern Economic Journal
SWOC: Steel Workers Organizing Committee
TCB: Timber Conservation Board
TNEC: Temporary National Economic Committee
TPSS: Trade Practice Studies Section (NRA Records)
UAW: United Auto Workers
UMW: United Mine Workers
URW: United Rubber Workers
USWA: United Steel Workers of America

Introduction

The New Deal is the central landmark of the modern U.S. political economy. It marked the culmination of strategies of economic organization and regulation that had increasingly influenced political discussion after the Civil War and dominated public policy after World War I. And it defined the boundaries of politics for the post–World War II era: a domestic welfare state, federal responsibility for economic regulation and labor law, a U.S.-centered world economic system, and (eventually) a commitment to military expenditure that represented both a "Keynesian" floor for the industrial economy and the overhead costs of an interventionist foreign policy. For students of this "big bang" of institutional innovation, one element stands out as an object of enduring interest and debate. For the first time in a notoriously business-dominated polity, public policy seemed to generate real gains for workers and vocal opposition from business. This book offers both a new interpretation of the origins and meaning of the New Deal and a broader interpretation of the ways in which economic and political power are organized (and disorganized) in the United States.

Simply stated, my argument goes something like this: The U.S. political economy is an extraordinarily competitive and fragmented system, a consequence of economic wealth and diversity, and of political federalism. In this atmosphere, business interests thirsted for order but found lasting organization or stability exceedingly difficult; they had a unique stake in public policy and the resources to dominate political debates but were also chronically disorganized, competitive, and shortsighted. Private disorganization made politics necessary, but political solutions were routinely frustrated by the myopia of business demands, the weakness of national political institutions, and the federation of political responsibility. Business's aspirations and frustrations nurtured a wide array of anticompetitive organizational strategies in the 1920s, including experiments with trade association, welfare capitalism, and a pastiche of labor-management accords hopefully dubbed "the new unionism." Attempts to rein in the organizational chaos of the

1

market, however, were only sporadically successful. Discrete initiatives often solved one industry's or one firm's problems at the expense of others. Private agreements were difficult to maintain and impossible to enforce. And many broader problems (such as underconsumption) went unaddressed.

The shaky framework of private regulation collapsed completely in 1929. With the onset of the Great Depression, cooperative labor relations, private welfare plans, and trade organization became unaffordable luxuries and competitive liabilities – especially given the ability of some firms and regions to stay beyond their reach. The question of the early 1930s was whether the economic crisis would erase the managerial experiments of the 1920s or become an opportunity to rebuild those experiments around federal laws and federal institutions. Competitive pressures, social unrest, and political realities pressed business and the Roosevelt administration along the latter path. The New Deal, in an anxious and ad hoc manner, politicized private patterns of business organization, welfare policy, and labor relations – a process that began with the National Recovery Act (NRA) in 1933 and drifted into labor law and welfare policy after 1935.

I trace, as have others, the constituent policies of the New Deal to private precedents in the 1920s. More importantly, I trace the connections between private organization, the regulatory innovations of 1929–33, and the labor and welfare law of 1935 – and argue that the progressive turn of the "second New Deal" was part and parcel of two decades of business strategy and two years of business-driven recovery politics. In historical memory, of course, the New Deal is virtually synonymous with a transformation of labor relations and labor law. Yet the emergence of industrial unionism and a "common law" of labor relations was not (as it is commonly portrayed) simply the product of an emboldened labor movement, an enlightened state, or a momentarily weakened business community. Rather, federal social security and labor law grew directly from the search for competitive order and (after 1929) recovery. Labor, after all, was a major organizational and material liability for most firms and a focal point for political conflict and intervention. Labor standards, given antitrust concerns and constitutional limits on federal power, became an attractive and necessary alternative to other forms of regulation. As some industries had discovered in the 1920s, and as many more would discover during the unhappy tenure of the NRA, union power could be an effective surrogate for private organization or political regulation. And for many, the concessions implied by labor law promised other benefits, including industrial peace and higher levels of aggregate consumption.

In the first four chapters, I survey business conditions and strategies in the decade preceding the New Deal and argue that the crash of 1929 merely set the experience and experiments of the 1920s in sharp relief. Chapter One ("Rethinking the New Deal") outlines the rules and institutions of the U.S. political economy, particularly the ways in which market competition and competitive federalism interact to make political intervention both necessary and extrememely difficult. Chapter Two ("Competition and Collective Action") traces the characteristics (and characteristic problems) of mass-production, resource, and small manufacturing industries from 1920 to the drafting of the NRA codes. Chapter Three ("Workers Organizing Capitalists") does the same for labor-intensive industry, stressing the ways in which workers and managers assessed the regulatory potential of conservative, industrial unionism. Chapter Four ("The Limits of Associationalism") focuses on trade and "peak" business associations and assesses these more formal efforts to address the competitive divisions and collective action dilemmas outlined in Chapters Two and Three. Taken together, these chapters suggest that competitive chaos and market uncertainty were virtually endemic, that business interests understood their respective troubles in narrowly self-interested terms, and that, *with the exception of labor relations*, the associational fetishes of the 1920s did little to organize markets or ameliorate destructive competition.

The latter chapters turn to the origins and legacies of the major legislative initiatives of the New Deal: the National Recovery Act, the National Labor Relations Act, and the Social Security Act. Chapter Five ("The National Recovery Act") portrays the NRA as a sloppy synthesis of long-standing business strategies, a political experiment riddled with contradictions and frustrations. Yet, although the NRA was a dismal failure, it was less of a failure in those industries in which labor unions were able to enforce compliance to code provisions, and it strengthened the increasingly widespread conviction that effective regulation depended upon the disciplinary presence of either the federal state or industrial unionism. Chapter Six ("The Wagner Act") picks up on this point and argues that New Deal labor law was a legacy of both two decades of "regulatory unionism" and two years of chaotic and futile NRA regulation. I suggest that the business response to Wagner was not a simple ideological reaction to the threat of organized labor but a more complex and discrete reaction to the competitive and organizational problems experienced by various interests before and after 1935. Chapter Seven ("The Social Security Act") most clearly captures the contours of competition and federalism outlined in the opening chapter: casting back to the "welfare capitalism" of the 1920s, I argue that federal social security was largely an effort (made more urgent by the Depression) to "even out" the competitive disparities resulting from two decades of private and state-level experimentation with work benefits.

Such solutions, although the product of business demands, raised new questions about the scope and costs and capability of federal power and inspired widespread business opposition – especially after 1935. In the last chapter, I sketch the shape and logic of this opposition. While the New Deal was a creature of business demands, business came to resent its many contradictions, failures, concessions, and unforeseen consequences. Accordingly, business was ambivalent in its support and, as World War II approached, increasingly vocal in its opposition. This chapter also serves as a more speculative survey of the "New Deal system" and its trajectory after 1945.

This study contributes to a broad stream of interpretation that has stressed the primacy of business interests in the formulation of U.S. public policy and the essential conservatism of the New Deal. It does so, however, without confining its sights to the ideological and political power of a few corporate interests or the ascendence of certain types or groups of industries. Perhaps more importantly, it is attentive to the peculiar logic and limits of the U.S. political system. In many respects, the relationship between economic interests and political power is a product not only of the "privileged position" of business but also of the political institutions through which that privilege is exercised. This is, in this sense, both a historical account of the New Deal and a study in business-government relations and the limits of U.S. politics.

This effort, like any reconsideration of the historical record, rests on both new evidence and new ways of looking at evidence. The latter may be an elaborate theoretical framework to be proven or disproven, an interpretive tradition that identifies important problems, or a set of hunches that make it possible to sift through so many linear feet of correspondence in a morning at the archives. These larger ideas give shape to one's research and are in turn shaped by that research. And as both an element and a product of historical inquiry, they serve as bridges to and for the work of others. For these reasons, I think it is important – as I have tried to do in the following chapter – to lay out such assumptions as clearly as possible.

1. Rethinking the New Deal
The Logic and Limits of the U.S. Political Economy

The New Deal was a set of exceptional political choices made under exceptional political, economic, and historical circumstances. The bulk of this study explains these choices. I begin, however, by examining the context within which these choices were made: the rules, institutions, and expectations that shaped the interwar political economy. To that end this chapter serves two purposes. It traces the institutional and historical background of the U.S. political economy, stressing its uniquely competitive and disorganized character. Just as importantly, it lays some methodological cards on the table, sketching a "rational choice" approach to the interplay of individual choice, collective action, economic interest, and social organization. Why do economic actors do what they do? How do we reconcile the Smithian *Homo economicus* with vast disparities in wealth and power, with the fact that some actors have more choices than others? How do interests and institutions shape each other and the larger political economy of which they are a part? And how did economic interests, political and economic institutions, and historical circumstances interact in the making of the New Deal?

My goal here is less to explore or adopt formal explanatory models than to indulge in a bit of theoretical scavenging, to draw upon a range of disciplinary and conceptual insights in an effort to explicate the logic of public and private choice in the U.S. political economy. I focus particularly on the ways in which democratic capitalism frames political choices and the ways in which U.S. democratic capitalism (distinguished by economic wealth and diversity, a peculiarly weak and fragmented political structure, and a unique intersection of political and economic power) creates both immense organizational demands and serious organizational obstacles. Political organization in the United States is costly and difficult, and the degree to which economic interests depend upon political solutions is matched only by their monotonous disenchantment with political outcomes.

My exploration of the insights of rational-choice theory is intended not so much to propose a model for human behavior as it is simply to highlight the explanatory importance of material self-interest and its collective contradictions. This attention to rational interest, in turn, suggests not only the range of interests but also the ways in which unequal stakes and resources shape their importance and influence: more specifically, it underscores the privileged political status of "business" in the United States. Yet, as I stress in the middle sections of the chapter, this conflation of economic and political power is diffused and frustrated by the peculiarly competitive character of markets and politics in the United States. Economic competition and political federalism overlap to both exaggerate competitive disorganization and compound collective (political) solutions. The necessity and costs of political intervention create an abiding tension and ambivalence in business–government relations; business's attraction to politics is matched only by its resentment of the managerial and material costs of political intervention. By way of conclusion, I set these insights against ongoing debates over the New Deal's place in U.S. history and political theory.

Rational Expectations, Collective Illusions

Without some a priori sense of the way in which particular political and economic systems work, it is nearly impossible to give shape or meaning to the behavior and sentiments of historical actors. In other words, it is necessary to appreciate how and why people (or "interests") make choices, the formal and informal constraints under which those choices are made, and the social or collective outcomes that follow from the repetition or aggregation of those choices. Such problems of individual and collective choice – whether understood (according to disciplinary convention) as problems of social organization, historical causation, or economic rationality and optimality – infuse modern social science.

I will start with this modest behavioral assumption: People are rational, motivated in most settings by short-term material self-interest. This expectation of rational choice does not preclude widely varying chances for success, constraints on action, or even more prescient or altruistic decisions. And it should neither be construed as a blanket assumption about human nature nor confused with the sort of disciplinary imperialism, purporting to explain everything from sexual gratification to suicide, waged by some neoclassical economists.[1] My interest is simply in highlighting the importance

1 See Daniel S. Hammermesh and Neal Soss, "An Economic Theory of Suicide,"

of locally rational behavior as an alternative to the cultural or ideological explanations preferred by some historians and the class- or group-based behavior pursued by some social scientists. The rational-choice approach is appropriate for gaining an understanding of capitalism, which makes a point of encouraging and rewarding self-interested behavior. It is particularly appropriate for gaining an understanding of democratic capitalism, which shapes and ranks interests in peculiar ways, granting political equality with one hand while denying economic equality with the other. And it is singularly appropriate to an understanding of U.S. democratic capitalism, an enduring riddle of concentrated power and chronic disorganization.

Close attention to rational and immediate interests avoids the sloppiness of functional forms of explanation and stresses that history is (or should be) explicable in terms of the actions or choices of individuals. Those choices are qualified less by other (ideological, cultural, social, psychological) motives than by the institutional and material constraints under which they are made. This approach, replete with overtones of libertarian individualism and neoclassical economics, has left some radical theorists wringing their hands, yet it simply reaffirms a classical maxim: Women and men make their own history, but not under circumstances of their own choosing.[2] Although this approach recognizes the evidential and logical limits of functional explanation, it does not deny the analytical importance of linking consequence and cause. *"Cui Bono?* is not the only question a historian should pose," as

Journal of Political Economy 82 (1974): 83–98; Richard Posner, *Sex and Reason* (Cambridge, 1991). On the scope and logic of neoclassical economic explanation, see Alan Wolfe, *Whose Keeper? Social Science and Moral Obligation* (Berkeley, 1989), 31–42; Amartya Sen, "Rational Fools: A Critique of the Behavioural Foundations of Economic Theory," *Philosophy and Public Affairs* 6 (1977): 317–44.

2 Jon Elster, "Explanation and Dialectics," in *Making Sense of Marx* (New York, 1985), 5, and *Ulysses and the Sirens: Studies in Rationality and Irrationality* (New York, 1984), 65–68. See also Jon Elster, "Marxism, Functionalism and Game Theory: the case for methodological individualism," *Theory and Society* 11 (1982): 453–82; Joshua Cohen, "Popper, Methodological Individualism, and Situational Logic," (unpublished, 1987); Mancur Olson, *The Logic of Collective Action* (Cambridge, 1965); John Rawls, *A Theory of Justice* (Cambridge, 1971), 258–71; Russell Hardin, *Collective Action* (Baltimore, 1982), 6–89. For the defense of functional explanation and class analysis, see G.A. Cohen, *Karl Marx's Theory of History: A Defence* (Princeton, 1978), 249–96; Andrew Levine, Eliot Sober, and Erik Wright, "Marxism and Methodological Individualism," *New Left Review* 162 (1987): 67–84; Ellen Wood, "Rational Choice Marxism: Is the Game Worth the Candle?" *New Left Review* 165 (1990): 41–88; Ronald A. Kieve, "From Necessary Illusion to Rational Choice: A Critique of Neo-Marxist Rational-Choice Theory," *Theory and Society* 15 (1986): 557–82.

Charles Maier suggests, "but it is a useful one to start with." Political and economic choices can be explained by identifying those with a substantial stake or interest, by dissecting the consequences of such choices, and by gauging the response of others. Functional explanation, in other words, infers interests from consequences. The rational-choice approach identifies interests from immediate objectives and circumstances; whether those interests get what they want is another story altogether.[3]

Individual motives and historical causes, of course, cannot be exclusively attributed to material self-interest. But although farsightedness, altruism, ignorance, faith, or ideology may distort or distract rational choices, it is usually a good idea to exhaust material motives before falling back on "softer" explanations. Ideology, after all, is usually little more than an attempt to lend intellectual order, consistency, or legitimacy to one's interests. How often do historical actors pursue ideological goals that undermine their real interests? And when, as is usually the case, interests and ideas complement each other, which is the causal force and which is merely its reflection? U.S. historiography's predilection for ideological explanation and its common conviction that the burden of proof rests with those offering a material explanation is less the product of critical reflection than an artifact of an often celebratory and conservative academic culture.[4]

All of this is not as neatly cut and dried as it might sound. Self-interest is often difficult to identify. Because the pursuit of interests is not necessarily functional, they cannot be inferred from consequences; what people get is not a good indication of what they want. Self-interested behavior reflects not only what outcomes are desirable but also what is possible or likely. Demands are often exaggerated and overdrawn – a grant applicant might inflate his budget in order to get what he needs, a manager might underreport her unit's production in order to avoid a higher quota. In turn, frustrated interests may be obscured by proverbial "sour grapes," a willingness to rationalize failure by adjusting goals after the fact. Future goals may be obscured by the tendency to assume that one wants what one doesn't have (the "grass is always greener"). And "rational" calculations are complicated by uneven temporal horizons; what is immediately rational may prove ulti-

---

3 Elster, "Explanation and Dialectics," 5; (quote) Charles Maier, "Political Economy and History," *In Search Of Stability: Explorations in Historical Political Economy* (New York, 1987), 7.

4 Colin Gordon, "Crafting A Usable Past: Consensus, Ideology, and Historians of the American Revolution," *William and Mary Quarterly* 66 (October 1989): 671–95; Hardin, *Collective Action*, 11; Douglass North, "Institutional Change and Economic Growth," *Journal of Economic History* 31 (1971): 118–25.

mately irrational, and vice versa. Self-interest depends largely on the knowledge or perception of what others might do and of what impact present choices might have on future interests.[5] The careful historian must be able to walk in the shoes of historical actors (in order to appreciate the limits of choice and perception) and hover above the historical terrain (in order to appreciate the patterns and consequences of individual choice).

In many respects, the circumstances under which choices are made are as important as the choices themselves. Although alternatives may be virtually unlimited for some (consider the numerous opportunities for investment enjoyed by wealthy individuals or firms), institutional and historical factors nearly always narrow or skew the set of feasible options. Choices may lie within certain boundaries; in a capitalist democracy, for example, politicians cannot challenge the premises of economic growth or alienate business investment. Or they may be narrow and equally unattractive: a poorly paid worker can suffer at her current wages or risk the greater suffering of unemployment by confronting her employer. In this sense, 'choice' does not carry the implications of free exchange often inferred by economists. Indeed, circumstances may coerce only one option by disguising, penalizing, or increasing the costs of others. Some are free to choose, others are free to lose.[6] This is, of course, also a central premise of class analysis, although orthodox Marxism inflates this behavioral insight in such a way as to exaggerate the common experience of those with resources and of those without, thus making classes themselves historical actors.

Self-interest does not determine behavior, but it does raise expectations or establish benchmarks against which altruistic, sacrificial, or otherwise "irrational" actions might be understood. In the chapters that follow, for example, I argue that workers will usually pursue individual security at the expense of collective action because the short-term risks of losing one's job outweigh the longer-term benefit of organization. This is a rational choice, shaped by both immediate material and legal constraints and the historical, cultural, and intellectual burden of those constraints over time. Workers' behavior, in other words, is a product not only of the costs and benefits of

5 Jon Elster, *Solomonic Judgements: Studies in the Limitation of Rationality* (New York, 1989), 178–80, 182, and *Sour Grapes: Studies in the Subversion of Rationality* (New York, 1983), 20–26, 123–24; Raymond Boudon, "The Logic of Relative Frustration," in *Rational Choice*, ed. Jon Elster (Oxford, 1986), 178–79.

6 John Roemer, *Free to Lose: An Introduction to Marxian Economic Philosophy* (Cambridge, 1988), 14–27; Samuel Bowles and Herbert Gintis, "Contested Exchange: New Microfoundations for the Political Economy of Capitalism," *Politics and Society* 18 (1990): 170–77; Elster, *Ulysses and the Sirens*, 76–83.

given choices but also of the ways in which workers and managers perceive those choices. Yet even in materially and culturally oppressive circumstances, workers do form unions. The expectation of rational choice underscores the courage and gravity of such a choice. Without directly explaining union activism, the rational-choice approach does focus attention on the willingness or ability of historical actors to sacrifice immediate interests or to look beyond immediate horizons.[7]

Finally, the importance of rational self-interest is secondary to problems of collective action, to problems of social organization, and to the ways in which interests are channeled or encouraged or overcome in (broadly defined) political settings. Politics, in this sense, is both an expression of aggregate self-interest and the rules under which those interests are pursued or organized.[8] More importantly, politics is a form of collective action that rational actors impose upon themselves as a means of minimizing the costs and uncertainty of disorder. By abdicating some freedom of action and committing to certain rules (as Rousseau and others have noted), individual interests may protect themselves from the consequences of both their own myopia and the destructive competition of others. Politics is largely about the method and degree of coercion used to restrict individual interest and the acceptance or legitimacy of public interest and private restraint. This is especially true of democratic capitalism, which sees collective good in both the capitalist pursuit of self-interest and the democratic social contract.[9]

As we turn our attention to the ways in which interests interact in political and economic settings, various dilemmas of collective action or organization begin to emerge. Certainly the most important distinction between the sort

7 As Elster suggests, "The social scientist should always be guided by a postulate of rationality, even if he may end up finding it violated in many particular cases" (*Ulysses and the Sirens*, 116).

8 Politics here is understood as the promotion or regulation of economic activity, just as economics is understood as political activity viewed in a particular way. Put another way, economic considerations dominate the organization and attention of U.S. politics, and political support and intervention is integral to the U.S. economy. See Gabriel Kolko, *Main Currents in Modern American History* (New York, 1984), 1–33; Adam Przeworski, *Capitalism and Social Democracy* (New York, 1985), 133–248; Joshua Cohen and Joel Rogers, *On Democracy: Toward A Transformation of American Society* (New York, 1983), 47–87; Bowles and Gintis, "Contested Exchange," 166–67; Charles Lindblom, *Politics and Markets* (New York, 1977), 8; Fred Block, "Political Choice and the Multiple 'Logics' of Capital," *Theory and Society* 15 (1986): 175–92; Maier, "Political Economy and History," 1–7.

9 Joel Rogers, "Divide and Conquer: Further 'Reflections on the Distinctive Character of American Labor Laws,'" *Wisconsin Law Review* (1990): 11–29; Elster, *Ulysses and the Sirens*, 36–44, 89–92.

of analysis advocated here and the rational-choice models of "free market" fetishists is that the former makes no assumption that individual choices yield optimal social outcomes – indeed, it holds very nearly the opposite. The larger rationality or optimality of unfettered self-interest is routinely frustrated by rules, expectations, or social norms; by chronic shortsightedness; and by imperfect knowledge of what others might do. The world is a complicated place. Unintended consequences, confusion, and ignorance abound, and lasting stability at any level of social, political, or economic organization is elusive. Historical actors, as Jon Elster suggests, are neither fully rational angels nor purely instinctive animals; they are both inclined to pursue shortsighted interests and inconsistently able to confront the consequences.[10] In short, the importance of rational-choice theory lies less in its insights into human behavior than in what it can tell us about the collective efforts of economic interests, their relative political status and influence, and the ways in which they compete or cooperate in markets and politics.

The "Privileged" Status of Business in the United States

In a nation that has confused economic and political freedom from its very inception and that continues to confuse economic prosperity with political genius, it is little surprise that the relationship between economic and political power has remained a source of scholarly confusion and controversy. The very notion that business interests enjoy a unique and privileged position in U.S. politics threatens the foundations of academic and political liberalism. Radical social analysts, while accepting the premise of business influence, have never come close to agreeing how or where that influence is exercised. And radicals and liberals alike usually see business influence, whether systematic or occasional, as an infiltration or perversion of the political process. A closer look at the logic of U.S. politics, however, suggests that the unique influence of business is less a corruption of the system than one of its institutional and philosophical expectations.

Political power is a reflection of one's opportunity, advantage, and stake in politics. Economic power shapes political participation, which demands time and resources, in important ways. The politics of democratic capitalism are premised on free and equal participation, but its economic logic guarantees that some interests will have the incentive, opportunity, and ability

10 Jon Elster, *Nuts and Bolts for the Social Sciences* (New York, 1989), 3–51, 91–100; *The Cement of Society: A Study of Social Order* (New York, 1989), 1–49; and *Ulysses and the Sirens*, 86, 111.

to wield greater influence than the votes they might cast as individuals. By virtue of its control over employment, investment, resource allocation, consumption, and commercialized public discourse, business wields substantial political power. Politicians and voters depend upon economic growth, business investment, and business confidence. Politics, in Charles Lindblom's felicitous metaphor, are imprisoned by the market. Governments can induce, encourage, or punish business behavior, but the rewards must outnumber the penalties. Politicians may restrain or regulate economic affairs but, seeking stability and growth as a bottom line, they cannot challenge the premises of the economy itself. The state's responsibilities are confined, in effect, to that which the market cannot or will not provide and to any consequences of the market that private interests are able to avoid. Tensions in business-government relations arise not from a natural antagonism but from this natural and mutual reliance.[11]

This background influence, a generic characteristic of democratic capitalism, is exaggerated and compounded in its American setting. In a political system premised on constituency service and organized around perpetual but timid partisan competition, economic interests have a unique ability and incentive to exert political influence, which is exemplified by but certainly not confined to direct campaign contributions. Indeed, formal partisan influence (that is, giving cash to candidates) is dwarfed by the background organizational advantages and resources that allow business to command political attention between elections. Perhaps the best example of the way in which business exploits its unique political resources and stakes is its notorious ability (widely noted by conservative and radical analysts alike) to dominate and distort political regulation of its activities. I devote considerable attention to this problem in the chapters that follow; suffice it to say here that business influence reflects its disproportionate access to resources, its relative advantage in a "capital-intensive" political system, and its unique stake in political outcomes.[12]

11 Charles Lindblom, "The Market as a Prison," *The Journal of Politics* 44 (1982): 324–36, and *Politics and Markets*, 154–57, 170–200; Cohen and Rogers, *On Democracy*, 47–51; Anthony Downs, "An Economic Theory of Political Action," *The Journal of Political Economy* 65 (1957): 135–50; Fred Block, "Beyond Relative Autonomy: State Managers as Historical Subjects," *The Socialist Register* (1980): 227–42; Elster, *Ulysses and the Sirens*, 96–97.

12 Thomas Ferguson, "Industrial Structure and Party Competition in the New Deal," *Sociological Perspectives* 34 (1991): 498–500, and "Party Realignment and American Industrial Structure: The Investment Theory of Political Parties in Historical Perspective," in *Research in Political Economy* 6, (1983): 6–11; Michael Goldfield,

In turn, the privileged position of business is both cause and consequence of the much-noted "exceptionalisms" of the U.S. political experience: a poorly organized and historically apolitical labor movement, legal and institutional obstacles to third-party politics, a weak and federally fragmented national state, and a political culture that internalizes business goals and marginalizes others as "special interests." The absence of a social democratic tradition and the weakness of state institutions not only reflect a history of disproportionate business influence but also exaggerate and contribute to it. This exceptionalism has compounded (among other things) the peculiar antiunion belligerence of U.S. managers, the defensive conservatism of organized labor, the glacial growth of the welfare state, and the ease with which established political interests have been able to erect legal and cultural obstacles to the presence or legitimacy of real dissent. Politics, often a synonym for the organization of business interests in the United States, is also a means of frustrating the organization of others.[13]

But just as neoclassical economists routinely exaggerate the ability of the market to generate optimal outcomes, radical theorists too often mistake business's organizational advantages for lasting organizational success. Although politics may reflect economic power, the strategic perspective sketched above also suggests the limited horizons and inefficacy of political solutions. The influence of business *as a class* is undermined by the contradictory demands of key interests, the shortsightedness of the market, and the tensions that pervade any social system based on equal political rights and unequal economic resources. The institutions of democratic capitalism give business a substantial organizational boost, yet neither business (in its position of chronic advantage) nor labor (in its position of chronic disadvantage) betrays any consistent ability to perceive or act upon collective or class

"Worker Insurgency, Radical Organization, and New Deal Labor Legislation," *American Political Science Review* 83 (1989): 1262–64.
13 Rogers, "Divide and Conquer," 43–98; Sanford Jacoby, "American Exceptionalism Revisited: The Importance of Management," in *Masters to Managers: Historical and Comparative Perspectives on American Employers,* ed. Sanford Jacoby (New York, 1991), 173–87; Sean Wilentz, "Against Exceptionalism: Class Consciousness and the American Labor Movement, 1870–1920," *International Labor and Working Class History* 26 (1984): 1–24; Aristide Zolberg, "How Many Exceptionalisms?" in *Working Class Formation: Nineteenth-Century Patterns in Western Europe and the United States,* ed. Ira Katznelson and Aristide Zolberg (Princeton, 1986), 397–455; Elster, *Ulysses and the Sirens,* 96–97. On political exceptionalism, see n.26 below. On cultural exceptionalism, see Louis Hartz, *The Liberal Tradition in America* (New York, 1955); Michael Rogin, *The Intellectuals and McCarthy: The Radical Specter* (Cambridge, 1967), 9–58.

interests. Democratic capitalism precludes some political options and increases the costs of pursuing some others, but it is neither the master of its own fate nor the certain (if unwitting) agent of social change and class solidarity portrayed by Karl Marx and others.

I turn next to the practical and historical reflection of this disorganization, to the intersection of business's peculiar political power with the competitive and institutional disarray of both markets and politics, and to the ways in which the U.S. political economy both encourages shortsighted self-interest and raises obstacles to collective action or organization. "Business" represents a vast array of distinct and often fiercely competitive interests that share only the most abstract political goals. And U.S. federalism fragments political institutions, resources, and jurisdiction in such a way that "politics" itself becomes an arena of competition rather than cooperation. The U.S. political economy is a creature of these intertwined problems of collective action; intense economic competition makes politics necessary, while interstate and regional political competition frustrate political solutions.

Economic Competition and Collective Action

It is ironic that capitalism – a system premised on competitive self-interest – is most commonly understood in terms of aggregate economic performance, the equilibria of supply and demand, or broadly defined class interests. A close analysis of economic self-interest and competition, however, upsets the expectations of both general equilibrium theory and class analysis. Rational choices made by individuals under competitive conditions undermine collective interests, frustrate cooperation, and increase material pressures. Workers compete in the labor market and, under most circumstances, will cling to the relative security of employment at the expense of cooperation. Capitalists compete with labor over the conditions of work, with firms in the same industry for market share, and with other industries and firms for raw materials, labor markets, foreign markets, and political favor. Individuals make decisions not by virtue of the fact that they are capitalists or workers but by virtue of their distinct competitive positions *within* capitalism. Common goals are rare; the conditions under which common goals may be perceived or pursued are rarer still.[14]

14 On problems of aggregation and disaggregation in economics, see Michael Bernstein, *The Great Depression: Delayed Recovery and Economic Change in America, 1929–1939* (New York, 1987), 1–21; Joan Robinson, *Economic Heresies* (New York, 1971); Maurice Godelier, *Rationality and Irrationality in Economics*, trans. Brian Pearce (New York, 1972), 24–46.

Although economic competition is driven by rational self-interest, it fails to yield rational outcomes. A competitive economy, of course, will under-supply public goods (streetlights, roads) and hide or avoid many of the costs of production (pollution, resource depletion). But even on its own terms, market competition has great difficulty finding any happy equilibria. Perfect competition among unfettered buyers and sellers can be achieved only when background conditions and resources are equal; inequality changes the rules from the outset and only gets worse under competitive conditions. And sources of imperfect or "unfair" competition (politics, unions, fixed costs, debt) are so pervasive that business has historically seen competition less as a virtue than as the economy's signal flaw.[15] The result is a central tension in economic interest and perception; without abandoning the freedom of competition, business interests routinely seek private or political organization as an escape from its effects.

The dynamics of competition can be understood by disaggregating the economy in a number of ways. Certain types of industries (capital-intensive or internationalist, for example) may share certain goals, although the unity and longevity of such industrial blocs or coalitions is usually overdrawn.[16] More importantly, we can identify the collective interests of specific industries and the particular interests of competing firms within them. Each firm belongs to an industry with a distinct organizational and competitive logic, a product of history and industrial structure. Each firm is also one of any number of heterogeneous competitors whose interests are distinct from those of other firms (which it would often like to eliminate) and from the collective interest of its industry. Competition is further complicated by diverse pat-

---

15 Lindblom, *Politics and Markets*, 45–51, 76–81; Bowles and Gintis, "Contested Exchange," 170–77; Maurice Dobb, *Welfare Economics and the Economics of Socialism* (New York, 1969), 10–11; Roemer, *Free to Lose*, 72–107; Block, "Political Choice and the Multiple 'Logics' of Capital," 175–92.

16 For an emphasis on "monopoly capital," see Rhonda Levine, *Class Struggle and the New Deal: Industrial Labor, Industrial Capital, and the State* (Lawrence, 1988); G. William Domhoff, "The Wagner Act and Theories of the State: A New Analysis Based on Class-Segment Theory," *Political Power and Social Theory* 6 (1987): 159–85. Thomas Ferguson ("From Normalcy to New Deal: Industrial Structure, Party Competition, and American Public Policy in the Great Depression," *International Organization* 38 (1984): 41–94) focuses on a bloc of "multinational liberal" firms. Ellis Hawley (*The New Deal and the Problem of Monopoly* [Princeton, 1966]) and Stanley Vittoz (*New Deal Labor Policy and the American Industrial Economy* [Chapel Hill, 1987]) stress the political importance of "sick" industries (for example, coal, textiles, and clothing).

terns of integration and investment and invariably involves a number of distinctly situated and motivated firms.[17]

Competition erodes the collective goals of industries in a number of ways. High fixed costs, excess capacity, low barriers to entry, and competitive disorganization often encourage destructive, cutthroat competition and crowd out any rational equilibrium of prices, supply, and demand. Such conditions, as one contemporary study noted,

> [place] producers in situations of urgent difficulty in which they may be forced to adopt a short-run view rather than a long-run view and consider only the immediate consequences of their actions – all of which tends toward more reckless price cutting. If a seller habitually reckons with the likelihood that his rivals will retaliate if he cuts prices, or will at least meet the cut; and asks whether he is likely to be better or worse off after his rivals have responded than he was before he initiated the price cut, he is much less likely to initiate it than if he is looking no farther ahead than the business he may take from his competitors before they retaliate. [18]

The monotonous repetition of such myopically rational but ultimately irrational choices may impress some with the need for anticompetitive organization. "This idea of killing competitors off is for the birds," as one manufacturer complained. "You can't do it. All you do is end up by making less money." But organization is extremely difficult. Distinct competitive profiles and organizational costs determine the form, urgency, and likelihood of cooperative action. And the presence of a vast internal market in the United States has not (as Alfred Chandler and others have suggested) encouraged a unique predilection or capacity for organization but has simply exacerbated competitive disorganization.[19]

---

17 John Bowman, *Capitalist Collective Action: Competition, Cooperation and Conflict in the Coal Industry* (New York, 1989); Alexander Gerschenkron, *Economic Backwardness in Historical Perspective* (Cambridge, 1962), 5–30; David Abraham, "State and Class in Weimar Germany," *Politics and Society* 7 (1977): 263–98; Ferguson, "From Normalcy to New Deal," 41–94; Bernstein, *The Great Depression*, 16–20, 49–89; Josef Steindl, *Maturity and Stagnation in American Capitalism* (New York, 1976); John Bowman, "The Logic of Capitalist Collective Action," *Social Science Information* 21 (1982): 582–87.

18 National Recovery Administration, "Report on the Operation of the Basing Point System in the Iron and Steel Industry," (Washington, 1934), 61.

19 Manufacturer quoted in Charles Cheape, *Family Firm to Modern Multinational: Norton Company, A New England Enterprise* (Cambridge, 1985), 117. Chandler's view of managerial innovation is best summarized in Chandler, "The United States: Seedbed of Managerial Capitalism," in *Managerial Hierarchies: Comparative Perspectives on the Rise of Modern Industrial Enterprise*, ed. Alfred Chandler and Herman Daems (Cambridge, 1980), 9–40. This view is flawed in three important respects:

In an atmosphere of shortsightedness, imperfect knowledge, and cynical suspicion of others, no firm has the incentive to initiate "sucker" strategies of cooperation in which the costs are borne by cooperators and the benefits are enjoyed by recalcitrants or new entrants. All industries hope to escape competition, but the fact that the stability of a given industry does not guarantee the survival of any individual firm reduces the ability of leading firms – and the desire of marginal firms – to cooperate. Business is peculiarly ambivalent about such problems of collective action; one cutthroat competitor can undermine standards, so competitors seek universal cooperation. But because the number of competitors is part of the problem, business interests (unlike other collective actors) have no interest in distributing the costs of organization among as many firms as possible and actually seek to restrict "membership." Paradoxically, this requires the cooperation of those who will be driven from the market; the collective good (sales at higher prices) must come at the expense of some firms.[20] The competitive pressures that make organization necessary, in short, also make it nearly impossible.

Consider the historical pattern of economic competition and organization in the United States. A turn-of-the-century merger movement failed to control competition or costs. Consolidations could neither bar the entry of new firms nor guarantee that large firms would forgo cutthroat tactics. Because competition invariably remained or reappeared, fixed investment (inflated by integration) quickly became a liability and, for many mass-production firms, turned conventional economic wisdom inside out; in order to service fixed charges, firms responded to lapses in demand or price with greater production. Expensive and dedicated plants maintained productive pressure regardless of the success of individual firms. World War I suspended these dilemmas with an explosion of demand but pushed the industrial economy into the 1920s with a virtually universal burden of excess capacity and competition. *Fortune* remembered the two decades after 1900 for "the expanding of production units by men who had little realization of what they were bringing upon themselves, the over-financing of corporations, and a miracle (the War) which temporarily justified everything." The war also made the United States a global creditor, which, along with rapid technological in-

It is derived largely from the literary reflections of "successful" executives in atypical firms, it assumes that a vast internal market muted competition, and it ignores the importance of politics and labor relations to the managerial environment.

20 Bowman, "Logic of Capitalist Collective Action," 572–78, 581–99; Michael Aglietta, *A Theory of Capitalist Regulation: The U.S. Experience,* trans. David Fernbach (London, 1979), 291–92, 381; Olson, *The Logic of Collective Action,* 37–42.

novation and pressure from organized labor, led to mechanization, unprecedented gains in productivity, and even lower barriers to entry.[21]

Integrated and fragmented industries alike responded to postwar conditions and the inefficacy of the market by seeking the means to quell or escape competition, commonly through private agreements on production standards, prices, or market share. Although commonly portrayed as an important shift in business thinking, these "associational" initiatives simply underscored the chronic instability of market competition. More importantly, the organizational clamor produced no solution to the problem of maintaining or compelling cooperation among competitors. Multi-industry associations were unable to organize or educate members, let alone press even limited political goals with any consistency. Trade association was scarcely more successful, as the raison d'etre for organization – excessive competition – destroyed the long-term prospects for its success.[22] As one executive lamented in 1931:

21 Naomi Lamoreaux, *The Great Merger Movement in American Business, 1895–1904* (New York, 1985), 26–38, 50–62, 118–50, 160–61; Alfred Chandler, "The Structure of American Industry in the Twentieth Century: A Historical Overview," *Business History Review [BHR]* 43 (1969): 270; Michael Piore and Charles Sabel, *The Second Industrial Divide: Possibilities for Prosperity* (New York, 1984), 49–63, 76–77; Kolko, *Main Currents*, 1–7; Senate Subcommittee of the Committee on Manufacturers, *Establishment of a National Economic Council* (Washington, 1935), 211, 279, 346–51, 597–98; Steindl, *Maturity and Stagnation*, 5–6, 67–68; Catherine Ellsworth, "Integration into Crude Oil Transportation in the 1930s," *BHR* 35 (1961): 182–86; (quote) "American Woolen Co." *Fortune* 3 (April 1931): 71; John Bowman, "Politics of the Market: Economic Competition and the Organization of Capitalists," *Political Power and Social Theory* 5 (1985): 43, 46–47, 78, and "Logic of Capitalist Collective Action," 593–99; Aglietta, *A Theory of Capitalist Regulation*, 215–72; Robert Cuff, *The War Industries Board* (Baltimore, 1973); Joe Bain, *Barriers to New Competition* (Cambridge, 1956), 1–14, 121–34.

22 Bain, *Barriers to New Competition*, 121–34; Gabriel Kolko, *Railroads and Regulation, 1877–1916* (New York, 1965); George Stocking, *Basing Point Pricing and Regional Development* (Chapel Hill, 1954), 3–155; Harvey Mansfield, *The Lake Cargo Coal Rate Controversy* (New York, 1932), 13, 37–39; Norman Nordhauser, "Origins of Federal Oil Regulation in the 1920s," *BHR* 48 (1972): 53–71; Donald Brand and Phillipe Schmitter, "Organizing Capitalists in the United States: The Advantages and Disadvantages of Exceptionalism," (Paper presented to the American Political Science Association, 1979); Louis Galambos, *Competition and Cooperation: The Emergence of a National Trade Association* (Baltimore, 1966); H.M. Gitelman, "Management's Crisis of Confidence and the Origins of the National Industrial Conference Board, 1914–1916," *BHR* 58 (1984): 153–77; Margeurite Green, *The National Civic Federation and the American Labor Movement, 1900–1925* (Washington, 1956), 245, 428–38; Philip Burch, "The NAM as an Interest Group," *Politics and Society* 4 (1973): 97–130; Alfred Kelly, *A History of the Illinois Manufacturers' Association* (Chicago, 1940); J. Roffe Wike, *The Pennsylvania Manufacturers' Association* (Phil-

Industry, acting as a unit in a single industrial group, is unable to solve its own problems. The units of a group are too competitive, too jealous of fancied advantages or trade secrets to make frank disclosures. Trade associations in industry establish codes of ethics which everyone subscribes to, but to which few conscientiously adhere. All recognize the advantages of cooperative effort but few are willing to sacrifice much to bring it about. No one in the industry is in possession of all the facts because there is a lack of confidence and the feeling that giving such information would result in losing a competitive advantage. Imagination as to what a competitor is doing runs riot and results in harmful retaliatory measures that affect an entire industry.[23]

Competitive pressures undermined even superficially common goals. Those who agreed on the necessity of organization rarely agreed on the scope or form it should take, let alone which competitors should be included or excluded. Pressure to minimize labor costs was often sidetracked into attempts to standardize wages or increase competitors' labor costs or by the sporadic realization that workers (at least *other* firms' workers) were potential consumers. As international competition undermined the effectiveness and increased the risks of national anticompetitive policies, political regulation often rested on a choice between internationally and nationally oriented industries or between multinationals and "independents" in the same industry. And agreement on any political goal was complicated by diverse political experience or expectations and the fact that all firms resisted the costs of political intervention.[24]

In all, competitive and industrial disparity made it virtually impossible for business to articulate or accomplish collective goals. "Business types," noted the American Trade Association Executives in 1922, range from

adelphia, 1960); "Selling the Trade Association Idea to the Business Group – the Problem of Membership," American Trade Association Executives, *Proceedings of the 3d Annual Meeting* (1922): 229–47; "How to Keep Members Sold," American Trade Association Executives, *Proceedings of the 5th Annual Meeting* (1924): 114–26.

23 R. D. Whitehead [New Haven Clock Company] in *National Industrial Conference Board* [NICB] *Proceedings* (17 December 1931), Series I, Box 4, NICB Papers, Hagley Museum and Library, Wilmington, DE.

24 Michael Wallerstein, "The Micro-Foundations of Solidarity: Protectionist Policies, Welfare Policies and Union Centralization," (unpublished, 1986). For divisions in some major industries, see Richard Lauderbaugh, "Business, Labor and Foreign Policy: U.S. Steel, the International Steel Cartel and the Recognition of the Steel Workers Organizing Committee," *Politics and Society* 6 (1976): 433–57; Norman Nordhauser, *The Quest for Stability: Domestic Oil Regulation, 1917-1935* (New York, 1979), 65–95; M. J. French, "The Emergence of a U.S. Multinational Enterprise: The Goodyear Tire and Rubber Company, 1910–1939," *Economic History Review* 40 (1987): 64–79.

"practical idealists. Always the leaders . . . [to] the slippery, foxy, crafty, crooked, dishonest man – 'the one who rocks the boat.' "[25] As a reaction to both boat-rockers and generally stormy seas, business would ask the state to take the helm. Political intervention, however, was complicated not only by dilemmas of economic competition and collective action but also by their reflection in U.S. politics itself.

Competitive Federalism and Collective Action

U.S. politics is historically and institutionally ill-equipped to facilitate or enforce collective action. Since its atypical revolutionary origins, the United States has been premised on practical and intellectual doubts about the concentration, penetration, and centralization of national power. Even as Europeans streamlined state structures, politicians in the United States clung to an intentionally complex and self-limiting political system. A few core concerns made national government necessary; a multitude of regional interests ensured that, especially in domestic economic affairs, it would have little power. Over time, a narrow two–party system served as an organizational substitute for state weakness. Political parties mobilized voters, fueled the patronage system, and became the means through which economic interests confronted politics. As parties filled the institutional vacuum, they foreswore conventional partisanship, abandoned any sense of ideological or programmatic consistency, and stood for nothing but election.

This peculiar partisanship proved a shaky base for democratic organization. Parties hoarded the ties between citizen and state that gave the latter its legitimacy but commanded none of the national institutions (courts and regulatory agencies) that made effective public policy possible. And participation was increasingly determined by the fact that some interests demanded more of politics and commanded more political resources than the average voter. After a hiccup of ethnocultural partisanship in the late nineteenth century, voter turnout declined steadily. Powerful economic interests dominated party affairs; and, as a result, the parties meant less and less to the average voter. As turnout declined, the parties lost interest in even superficial mass appeals, and this indifference was exaggerated by legal and material barriers to the entry of third parties. The absence of cohesive national institutions set the logic of democratic capitalism in stark relief; the costs of participation skewed politics in favor of those with the time and

25 "The Problem of Membership," American Trade Association Executives *Proceedings of the 3d Annual Meeting* (1922): 231.

ability to play the game and away from those who could scarcely afford to learn the rules, let alone match the bets.[26] Yet even those who dominated politics had to confront the weakness of national political institutions. U.S. politics has rarely tried to organize the interests of voters and has consistently tried, but failed, to organize the interests of business.

Alienation and the debilitating commodification of politics are the most serious and widely studied facets of the U.S. political experience, but for present purposes we devote our attention to the disorganizational and competitive implications of a weak and federated state. For the most part, scholars have equated national weakness with "statelessness" or confined their analyses of political fragmentation to sectional, regional, or congressional politics. Although commonly recognized as a source of tension for nation-states in an international economy, little attention has been devoted to the tension between politics and markets intrinsic to U.S. federalism.[27] Municipal, state, and federal governments (each with distinct legal systems, tax regimes, and bureaucracies) replicate the dynamics of economic competition and the dilemmas of economic organization. States and regions compete over regulatory and tax policy, while interstate or federal authorities encounter familiar problems of coercion and collective action. "The gears of politics

---

26 These two paragraphs are drawn from Stephen Skowronek, *Building A New American State: The Expansion of National Administrative Capacities, 1877–1920* (New York, 1982), 19–25; Richard Oestricher, "Urban Working-Class Political Behaviour and Theories of American Electoral Politics, 1870–1940," *Journal of American History* 74 (March 1988): 1274–75; James Wright, *The Dissent of the Governed: Alienation and Democracy in America* (New York, 1976), 257–310; Walter Dean Burnham, *The Current Crisis in American Politics* (New York, 1982), 121–65; Martin Shefter, "Political Parties, Political Mobilization, and Political Demobilization," in *The Political Economy*, ed. Joel Rogers and Thomas Ferguson (Armonk, 1984), 140–47; Rogers and Cohen, *On Democracy*, 43–87; Peter Argesinger, *Structure, Process, and Party: Essays in American Political History* (Armonk, 1992), 43–67, 130–46, 150–64.

27 Skowronek, *Building A New American State*, 23–25, 39–46; Aaron Wildavsky, "Federalism Means Inequality: Political Geometry, Political Sociology, and Political Culture," in *The Costs of Federalism*, ed. Robert Golembiewski and Aaron Wildavsky (New Brunswick, 1983), 55–72; Martin Shefter, "Party, Bureaucracy, and Political Change in the United States," in *Political Parties: Development and Decay*, ed. L. Meisel and J. Cooper (Beverly Hills, 1978), 211–65; Jordan Schwarz, *The Interregnum of Despair: Hoover, Congress and the Depression* (Urbana, 1970), 3–22; Richard Bensel, *Sectionalism and American Political Development, 1880–1980* (Madison, 1984); Elizabeth Sanders, "Industrial Concentration, Sectional Competition, and Antitrust Politics in America, 1880–1980," *Studies in American Political Development* 1 (1987): 146. For the international dilemmas of multiple governance, see Charles Kindleberger, *The World In Depression, 1929–1939* (Berkeley, 1973); Michael Stewart, *The Age of Interdependence: Economic Policy in a Shrinking World* (Cambridge, 1983).

and economics," as Owen Young of General Electric noted, "do not mesh well."[28] This asymmetry between the territorial limits of politics and the looser boundaries of the market is key to the political economy of the interwar years.

The competitive dimensions of American federalism reflect both a formal division of power and resources and the historical pattern of intervention by different levels of government. Individual states pursue policies that reflect local business goals but usually prove destructive and shortsighted in the national context. States treat each other as economic and political competitors. They are usually unwilling to risk business confidence through unilateral regulation but find interstate cooperation impossible to generate or enforce. Whether or not business interests are placed at real competitive disadvantage or driven to relocate by uneven state laws, state efforts to maintain a favorable business climate reflect the willingness and ability of business patrons to oversell the threat of "oppressive" regulation to growth- and job-conscious legislators. Under disparate legislative and competitive conditions, business anxieties increasingly turn to federal politics and its ability to balance the organizational goals of economic interests with the organizational goals of states and regions and the interests that they represent. The federal state is an arena of both competition and organization; it offers neither a distinct autonomy nor capacity for rational intervention but merely the ability to coerce economic and political interests on a national scale.[29]

Consider taxation, the shadow of any political intervention. The states, prohibited from taxing interstate commerce, relied on property and local

28 Owen Young to Herbert Hoover (n.d.), Presidential Personal File [PPF] 207, Herbert C. Hoover Papers, Herbert C. Hoover Presidential Library, West Branch, IA.

29 David Robertson, "The Bias of American Federalism: The Limits of Welfare State Development in the Progressive Era," *Journal of Policy History* 1 (1989): 273–74; W. Brook Graves, "Interstate Cooperation," in *American Intergovernmental Relations* (New York, 1964), 577–611; Northcutt Ely, *Oil Conservation through Interstate Agreement* (Washington, 1933), 166–213, 359–93; Jane Clark, *The Rise of A New Federalism* (New York, 1938), 6–7, 294; Clark, "Interstate Compacts and Social Legislation," *Political Science Quarterly* 50 (1935): 502–24; Clark, "Interstate Compacts and Social Legislation II: Interstate Compacts after Negotiation," *Political Science Quarterly* 51 (1936): 36–60; NICB, *Industrial Progress and Regulatory Legislation in New York* (New York, 1925); William Graebner, "Federalism in the Progressive Era: A Structural Interpretation of Reform," *Journal of American History* 64 (1977): 341–57; Perhaps the single exception to this regional chaos was the rather sharp isolation of the North and South, which were linked by northern capital and crosscut by a few basic industries. See George Tindall, *The Emergence of the New South, 1913–1945* (Baton Rouge, 1967), 433–72; Gavin Wright, *Old South, New South: Revolutions in the Southern Economy Since the Civil War* (New York, 1986), 156–238.

business taxes through most of the nineteenth century. The tax system soon became a focus of intense competition. States could not discriminate among types of property (a safeguard against corruption), and after 1920 they saw local and municipal governments assume much of the prerogative for property taxes. Tax reforms in the early 1930s further slashed property tax revenues and pushed the states to depend upon regressive sales and consumption taxes. As a result, the regulatory responsibilities and revenues of state governments were grossly mismatched, leaving states to compete with municipal and federal governments – and with each other – for tax revenues and business confidence. The resulting bidding wars over tax rates and concessions eroded state and local tax bases, while attempts to maintain revenues were usually hidden and regressive. States framed tax policy not only to meet basic revenue and regulatory objectives but also to minimize the ability of other states to create a more attractive business climate. As long as production is not confined to a single state, uneven legislation worsens competitive conditions and invites firms to exploit interstate anxieties and variations in state law.[30]

States do not compete as equals. One- or two-industry states have simpler economic goals and interests than more diversified states, although their tax or regulatory strategies will hinge somewhat on whether business patrons have located according to geographic considerations (forests, oil fields) or political concessions (tax breaks, "right to work" laws) – and diversity can encourage strategic chaos as easily as broad-based synthetic solutions. In turn, states may direct their regulatory efforts not at their own economies

30 Paul Hartman, *Federal Limitations on State and Local Taxation* (Rochester, 1981), 6, and *State Taxation of Interstate Commerce* (Buffalo, 1953), 22–36; Walter Hellerstein, *State and Local Taxation of Natural Resources in the Federal System* (New York, 1986), 5–27; Philip Wood, *Southern Capitalism: The Political Economy of North Carolina, 1880–1980* (Durham, 1986), 126–33, 137–38; Wade Newhouse, *Constitutional Uniformity and Equality in State Taxation* (Ann Arbor, 1959); Harold Ostertag, "General Possibilities of Interstate Tax Cooperation," *Tax Relations Among Government Units* (New York, 1938), 50–63; James Patterson, *The New Deal and the States: Federalism in Transition* (Princeton, 1969), 92, 99; B. Guy Peters, "The Development of the Welfare State and the Tax State," in *Nationalizing Social Security in Europe and America*, ed. Douglas Ashford and E.W. Kelley (Greenwich, 1986), 219–43; Clarence Heer, "Financing the Social Security Program in the South," *Southern Economic Journal* 4 (1937–38): 292–302; Mark Leff, *The Limits of Symbolic Reform: The New Deal and Taxation, 1933–1940* (New York, 1984); Graves, "Tax Conflicts and the Balance of Power," in *American Intergovernmental Relations*, 437–76; James Cobb, *The Selling of the South: The Southern Crusade for Industrial Development, 1936–1980* (Baton Rouge, 1982); Christopher Grandy, "The Economics of Multiple Governments: New Jersey Corporate Chartermongering, 1875–1929," (Ph.D. diss., University of California–Berkeley, 1987), 4.

but (through interstate cooperation or federal policy) at less-restrictive regulation in competing states. In the interwar era, for example, diversified industrial states pressed the expansion of the federal commerce power, while southern and smaller states attempted to protect or solicit business in a tax-breaking, charter-mongering "race to the bottom." Even those states recognizing the need for uniform legislation, in other words, cannot be counted on to cooperate; some seek the uniformity of unfettered competition, and others seek the uniformity of formal cooperation. And in any attempt to sort this out, state legislatures, the House of Representatives, the Senate, the Executive Branch, and the ubiquitous two-party system all represent regional and state interests in subtly different ways.[31]

State governments serve not only as the first organizational frontiers for most business competitors but also as economic competitors in their own right. The logic of competitive federalism dwarfs any ideological or cultural explanations for the late bloom or weakness of national political institutions in the United States. Federal economic intervention grew as a haphazard response to the regional and competitive disarray in some industries and to the variety of regulatory choices made by other levels of government. National political and economic interests, as Herbert Hoover observed, had to "endure 49 different regulatory systems which are both conflicting and weakening."[32] The chaos and futility of effective economic policy reflects a persistent battle among competing schemes of economic organization: the regional character of industrial development, the national character of investment and consumption, the geographic dispersal of natural resources, the largely urban structure of labor markets, and the state-to-state fragmentation of public policy.

This disarray was the key concern of federal politics in the interwar era. Before 1920, federal attention was limited to tariffs, transportation and banking regulation, and the twin evils of competition and monopoly. Many pressed for greater federal power in the wake of World War I, using federal authority over railroads, government contracts, and the District of Columbia as an entering wedge. Courts gradually refined the "interstate commerce"

---

31 Grandy, "Economics of Multiple Governments," 5, 239–41, 250–79. The regional organization of industry is summarized in National Resources Committee, *The Structure of the American Economy* (Washington, 1939), 33–59.

32 Hoover to Arch Shaw (n.d.), PPF 207, Hoover Papers. See also Graebner, "Federalism in the Progressive Era," 331–57; Franz Neumann, "On the Theory of the Federal State," in *The Democratic and Authoritarian State*, ed. Herbert Marcuse (New York, 1957), 216–29; George Benson, *The New Centralization* (New York, 1931), 20–41.

clause to encompass the national impact of prices, labor disturbances, and (turning the Sherman Act on its head) competitive practices as potential restraints of trade.[33] The New Deal capped a long offensive by economic interests against competitive and inconsistent state regulation. States with stricter or more costly regulatory legislation pressed for federal legislation that would spread the costs of these policies to other regions and firms. Industries organized beyond the boundaries of a single state found stability impossible as long as marginal competition could thrive in "backward" regions. Progressive states found the absence of regulation elsewhere equally corrosive in terms of investment, industrial location, and business confidence.

Finally, U.S. federalism not only encouraged state competition and made the need for federal intervention more urgent but also exacerbated the privileged position of business by exaggerating business anxieties over competitive disadvantage, interstate competition, and state radicalism. Federalism, in this sense, sharply distorted political possibilities and priorities. The market (to return to Lindblom's metaphor) did not simply imprison politics but held it captive in many cells, and in cells within cells. Under most circumstances, competitive federalism simply blunted politics, discouraging solutions that were beyond the jurisdiction of the federal government or the cooperative abilities of state governments. Under exceptional circumstances (as we shall see), competitive federalism encouraged collective action, although such solutions were invariably shaped less by truly national concerns than by the ability of economic interests to broach their competitive troubles through a higher political authority.

The Price of Politics: Collective Action and Reaction

U.S. politics mimics the competitive economy it is charged with regulating. Accordingly, collective solutions are exceptionally difficult to initiate or enforce; provide few guarantees of cooperation or success; result in diverse demands upon the private economy and the state; and benefit firms, indus-

---

33 National Recovery Administration [NRA], Division of Review, "Possibility of Government Contract Provisions as a Means of Establishing Economic Standards," Work Materials #26 (Washington, 1938); testimony of Robert Jackson in U.S. Congress, Senate Committee on Education and Labor, House Committee on Labor, *Fair Labor Standards Act of 1937* (Washington, 1937), 9–88; NRA, Division of Review, "Cases on Intrastate Activities," Work Materials #14 (Washington, 1939); U.S. Senate, *Constitutionality of the National Labor Relations Act,* S. Doc. 51, 75/1 (Washington, 1937).

tries, states, and regions unevenly. Interests vary widely, and all competitors try to pass on the costs of stability by free-riding on the backs of other firms, other industries, or the future. Competitive pressures encourage federal political solutions; the weakness of federal politics encourage a range of other regulatory or coercive solutions.

Economic interests face collective dilemmas at many levels; these range from the generic difficulties faced by groups seeking cooperative solutions to the self-interested behavior of their members to the specific problems associated with certain competitive or industrial settings. As a general rule, business strategies reflect business costs. Each firm seeks to minimize its costs of production and is acutely sensitive to inequities in such costs between itself and its competitors. Labor costs, for example, may predispose a firm to oppose unions or wage legislation unless competitors enjoy lower labor costs, in which case a firm may simply seek a uniform level of expenditure. Capital-intensive firms will be much more concerned with fiscal policy and less sensitive to labor policy. In either case, firms may be indifferent to regulation in areas where cost pressures are minimal, or they may view such areas as opportunities for political experimentation or barter; capital-intensive firms may support progressive labor policy because it promises industrial peace at little direct cost.

For most, this complex array of anxieties revolves around a single problem: Under what conditions will competitors adhere to collective rules or standards of behavior? Broadly speaking, there are two means of accomplishing collective action. Competitors may agree among themselves to an *internal* form of regulation (such as a trade association or trade agreement) or they may surrender organizational responsibility to an *external* agent (such as the state). As I explore in later chapters, the former, in which regulatory policies are defined and enforced by the interests being regulated, is characteristic of the Hoover era; the latter, in which policy is defined by the same interests but enforced by external means, is characteristic of the New Deal. Each has its risks and benefits. Internal forms of organization require little sacrifice but cannot guarantee participation or penalize defection. External forms of organization are more coercive, because external interests have no incentive to defect from agreements and no reason to treat competing interests differently. Yet, for the same reasons, external regulation is also more likely to generate resentment and resistance.[34] As a rule, business seeks the best of both worlds: the freedom of internal agreements and the efficacy of external enforcement.

34　Bowman, "Politics of the Market," 55–58.

Consider the dilemmas of state regulation. Although economic interests appreciate the regulatory prescience and power of the state, they continue to define and pursue their interests narrowly. Political regulation organizes some interests at the expense of others and rarely accords equal weight to competing, consuming, or collective interests. Whether business interests demand, capture, or battle political regulation, that regulation usually bears little relation to either concurrent efforts in other industries or a broader public interest.[35] Business sees little in politics but freedom from competitive self-interest and the resources to compel and enforce organization. "Compared to them I'm a conservative," Secretary of Labor Frances Perkins told *Business Week* in 1933, "They're willing to go to any length of Government regulation if it will get them out of their troubles and take care of their outlaws." Business agreed. "If general adherence to association programs is to be ensured," noted one interwar observer, "they must be enacted into law and enforced by the state." Leading oil firms solicited "the exercise of governmental power in support and defense of their business strategy," while leading lumber firms hoped regulation would "reliev[e] a progressive few from bearing the burden for all."[36]

This said, business interests have great difficulty reconciling the organizational utility of politics with its costs and breadth. They favor the organization of their own industries but oppose state efforts elsewhere.[37] Most

35 I should distinguish here between the "capture" theory of regulation, which sees regulation as a violation of free markets, and a radical critique, which argues that capitalism is inherently political and that regulation is initiated by capitalists. On the former, see Richard Posner, "Theories of Economic Regulation," *Bell Journal of Economics* 5 (1974): 335–58; George Stigler, "The Theory of Economic Regulation," *Bell Journal of Economics and Management* 2 (1971): 3–21. On the latter, see Gabriel Kolko, *The Triumph of Conservatism* (Chicago, 1963), and "Intelligence and the Myth of Capitalist Rationality in the United States," *Science and Society* 14 (1980): 134, n.4. See also James Wilson, "The Politics of Regulation," in *The Politics of Regulation,* ed. James Wilson (New York, 1980), 367–70; Alan Stone, *Regulation and its Alternatives* (Washington, 1982), 65–166; Alfred Marcus, "Business Demand For Regulation," *Research in Corporate Social Performance and Policy* 7 (1985): 25–46; Ellis Hawley, "Three Facets of Hooverian Associationalism," in *Regulation in Perspective,* ed. Thomas McCraw (Cambridge, 1980), 95–103.

36 Perkins quoted in *Business Week,* 17 May 1933, 3; other quotes, in order, from Temporary National Economic Committee, *Competition and Monopoly in American Industry,* Monograph 21 (Washington, 1941), 260; Myron Watkins, *Oil: Stabilization or Conservation?* (New York, 1937), 251; Harold Steen, *The U.S. Forest Service* (Seattle, 1976), 174.

37 David Vogel, "Why Businessmen Distrust Their State: The Political Consciousness of American Corporate Executives," *British Journal of Political Science* 8 (1978): 50–54; Theodore Lowi, "American Business and Public Policy: Case Studies and Political Theory," *World Politics* 16 (1964): 677–715.

interests grumble at the majority of state interventions, resent the associated costs, and demand special treatment. Federalism encourages business to cut its best deal at a number of levels. Inconsistent state regulation presses some to seek federal intervention; others turn first to state governments or exploit inconsistencies in state law. And political organization raises the same specter as private organization; stability comes at the expense of some firms, and these are not likely to knuckle under quietly. As firms, industries, states, and regions seek political solutions, some succeed and some do not – a weeding-out process that by no means suggests that the state has any coherent interest in long-term stability, let alone the ability to achieve it. In practice, political regulation falls far short of coordinated planning and alienates both the marginal regions and firms it purports to discipline and the leading regions and firms it purports to help.

Business interests use politics but have no guarantee that other business interests will not do the same. Perhaps more importantly, most find that even their own political panaceas come with a price tag. Although the state brings a unique capacity for enforcement, the accompanying loss of managerial control is often hard to stomach. The necessity of enforcement alone suggests that some oppose collective solutions from the outset and that others feel precommitment is necessary to guard against future defection. Most hope collective solutions will only regulate the behavior of others and want out when they fail to do so or intrude on their own freedom. Simply put, business surrenders certain prerogatives in the hope that the state will be able to accomplish certain goals; when the state fails, business asks for its prerogatives back. "Businessmen," as V. O. Key notes, "pragmatically advocate state intervention today and nonintervention tomorrow."[38] In this sense, the New Deal incurred business opposition not because federal acts and agencies challenged the premises of a business organization but because

---

38 David Vogel, "Why Businessmen Distrust Their State," 45–78; Phillipe Schmitter and Wolfgang Streeck, "Community, Market, State – and Associations," in *Private Interest Government*, ed. Wolfgang Streeck and Phillipe Schmitter (New York, 1985), 1–29; Joel Rogers and Joshua Cohen, "Secondary Associations in Democratic Governance," *Politics and Society* 20 (1992): 393–416; Leo Panitch, "Theories of Corporatism: reflections on a growth industry," in *Working Class Politics* (London, 1986), 160–86; Claus Offe, "The Capitalist State and the Problem of Policy Formation," in *Stress and Contradiction in Modern Capitalism*, ed. Leon Lindberg (Lexington, 1973), 134; Block, "Beyond Relative Autonomy," 227–42; David Vogel, "The Persistence of the American Business Creed," *Research in Corporate Social Performance and Policy* 2 (1980): 77–102; Key quoted in Vogel "Why Businessmen Distrust Their State," 50.

the stakes were so high and the prospects for unqualified success so slim. Business opposition was little more than business support gone sour.

Although the federal state, with its capacity to coerce both economic and political competitors, is the most obvious agent of external regulation, industrial unions also have the incentive and ability to organize competing interests. I explore the union role in more detail in later chapters, but it deserves some emphasis here. Many labor-intensive firms placed the onus of organizing competition directly on unions, seeking, as one student of labor law notes, "to extend uniform labor agreements to all employers doing the same kind of business in the area of keenest competition." Of course the ability of workers to organize peripheral firms and regions varied considerably. Organizing competition by organizing workers was inconsistently effective as long as union gains and rights were not formally protected.[39] National unions and political institutions are uniquely positioned to appreciate and discipline the excesses of competition, and some combination of their organizational potential – comprehensive political protection of labor's organizing rights, for example – may prove both a politically expedient and effective regulatory tool.

In short, political regulation was both the product of a strikingly competitive political economy and a casualty of the self-seeking behavior and political incapacity created and encouraged by that political economy. What made politics necessary also made politics futile; what drove business to politics also alienated business from politics. New Deal policies reflected the organizational efforts of different firms, industries, industrial coalitions, and regions. But neither these policies nor the voluntarist, associational programs that they echoed had the inclination or ability to synthesize public and private goals or to consistently satisfy business's political demands.

A Disorganizational Synthesis?

This interpretation of the logic and history of the American political economy challenges both our historical understanding of the New Deal and the

---

39 Bowman, "Logic of Capitalist Collective Action," 573; (quote) Jesse Carpenter, *Employers' Associations and Collective Bargaining* (Ithaca, 1950), 237. See also Michael Maloney, Robert McCormick, and Robert Tollison, "Achieving Cartel Profits Through Unionization," *Southern Economic Journal* 46 (1979): 628–34; John Bowman, "When Workers Organize Capitalists: The Case of the Bituminous Coal Industry," *Politics and Society* 14 (1985): 289–327; Grant Farr, *The Origins of Recent Labor Policy* (Boulder, 1959); Vittoz, *New Deal Labor Policy,* 20–45; Przeworski, *Capitalism and Social Democracy,* 133–69; Rogers, "Divide and Conquer," 38–43.

larger theoretical assumptions that have been drawn from the politics of the interwar years. I hope that the following chapters can move the debate beyond simple questions of whether the New Deal was liberal or conservative or of whether the New Deal can be called in as evidence of a certain kind of "state." Although it is not necessary to fully explore other historical and theoretical interpretations (or my disagreements with them) here, I should draw a few distinctions.

Celebrations of the "Roosevelt Revolution" aside, much of the historiography of the New Deal takes a "corporate liberal" approach to interwar reform. This approach stresses an intellectual and political continuity between the associational 1920s and the New Deal and sees the entire interwar era as evidence of the organizational triumph of capitalism.[40] This said, there is sharp disagreement within the corporatist camp over the meaning of the New Deal. For liberal historians, it reflects the managerial imperatives of a society increasingly dominated by large corporations and large state institutions – although, as Ellis Hawley admits, this was less a real organizational revolution than a "vision of a state" or "a mode of social thought, especially associated with certain professions and the political center."[41] For radical historians, the New Deal is less benign, reflecting both the intellectual poverty of American politics and a conspiratorial "campaign to save large-scale corporate capitalism." This view understates the range and diversity of busi-

40 See Ellis Hawley, "The Discovery and Study of a 'Corporate Liberalism'," *BHR* 52 (1978): 309–20; Louis Galambos, "The Emerging Organizational Synthesis in Modern American History," *BHR* 44 (1970): 279–90, and "Technology, Political Economy, and Professionalization: Central Themes of the Organizational Synthesis," *BHR* 57 (1983): 471–93; Robert Cuff, "American Historians and the 'Organizational Factor'," *Canadian Review of American Studies* 4 (1973): 19–31. Important critiques of the corporatist view include Kolko, "Myth of Capitalist Rationality," 130, and *Main Currents*, 100–151, 177–81; Fred Block, "Beyond Corporate Liberalism," *Social Forces* 24 (1978): 352–61. "Corporate liberalism" bears little resemblance to similar themes in European or Latin American scholarship. In the latter, 'corporatism' usually denotes some form of tripartite economic planning. In U.S. corporatist scholarship (which ranges from libertarian critiques of big government and radical critiques of big business to liberal celebrations of technocratic order), the etymological root of 'corporatism' is the *corporation* rather than genuinely corporatist political arrangements. See Panitch, "Theories of Corporatism," 160–63.

41 (Quote) Hawley, "Discovery and Study," 315–16, 319. See also Edward Berkowitz and Kim McQuaid, "Businessman and Bureaucrat: The Evolution of the American Social Welfare System, 1900–1940," *Journal of Economic History* 38 (1978): 120–41; the essays in Joseph Huthmacher and Warren Susman, eds., *Herbert Hoover and the Crisis of American Capitalism* (Cambridge, 1973); and Ellis Hawley, ed., *Herbert Hoover as Secretary of Commerce* (New York, 1978).

ness support for the New Deal and, as a consequence, confuses the contradictions of New Deal policy with some sort of eternal divide between "big business" and everyone else. And in its eagerness to debunk the first generation of Roosevelt-tinted scholarship, this approach does less to explain the New Deal than to simply catalogue the ways in which it falls short of the exaggerated claims of academic admirers or the broader vision of contemporary radical critics.[42]

Their disagreements aside, both liberal and radical variations on the corporatist theme exaggerate the political prescience and power of "corporate capitalists" and confuse organizational rhetoric with organizational strength. As I suggest above (and show in the chapters that follow), the New Deal was driven more by the competitive anxieties of a wide range of business interests than by the prescriptive vision of a ill-defined corporate elite. In all, the corporatist view shuns an obvious question: Were business interests able or willing to forgo immediate profits and pursue collective goals? Visions of organized markets and industrial democracy may have danced in the heads of a few enlightened capitalists, but few corporatist solutions transpired beyond Herbert Hoover's subject files. And while corporate interests were eager to lend a larger intellectual or political importance to their economic solutions, narrow self-interest was never far beneath the surface.[43] Leading firms or reformers had no special knowledge of the requisites for long-term stability (a point made rather decisively in 1929). And even if some mo-

42 Barton Bernstein, "The New Deal: The Conservative Achievements of Liberal Reform," in *Towards A New Past: Dissenting Essays in American History*, ed. Barton Bernstein (New York, 1968), 263–88 (quote, 268). See also Ronald Radosh, "The Myth of the New Deal," in *A New History of Leviathan*, ed. Ronald Radosh and Murray Rothbard (New York, 1972); Howard Zinn, ed., *New Deal Thought* (New York, 1966), xv–xxxvi. This view is, in many respects, an attempt to carry forward the conclusions of a "corporate liberal" interpretation of the Progressive Era and to account for the failure of radical politics during what seemed the golden opportunity of a protracted depression. See James Weinstein, *The Corporate Ideal in the Liberal State* (Boston, 1968); Martin Sklar, *The Corporate Reconstruction of American Capitalism, 1880–1916* (New York, 1988); Stephen Scheinberg, "The Development of Corporation Labor Policy, 1900–1940" (Ph.D. diss., University of Wisconsin, 1966).

43 Consider the case of General Electric. Although some scholars have stressed the personal, liberal influence of GE executives (see Kim McQuaid, "Young, Swope and General Electric's 'New Capitalism': A Study in Corporate Liberalism, 1920–1933," *American Journal of Economics and Sociology* 36 [1977]: 323–34), others have noted the peculiarly corporatist mind-set of electrical manufacturers (see Ronald Schatz, *The Electrical Workers* [Urbana, 1983], 12–14, and "The End of Corporate Liberalism: Class Struggle in the Electrical Manufacturing Industry, 1933–1950" *Radical America* 9 [1975]: 187–205).

mentarily enhanced their positions, they did so not in the interest of general stability but at the expense of others, a fact more likely to increase tensions and divisions than to lessen them.

Recent interest in the New Deal has come via more explicitly theoretical work that, even when it does not take the New Deal as its centerpiece, raises questions about the nature of "the state" and the organization of political and economic power central to the interpretative debate over the New Deal. Much of this literature is a product of (or a response to) the debate among radical theorists over whether the state acts as an instrument of a self-conscious business elite (focusing on the relationship between capitalists and politics) or as an autonomous manager or structure of collective business interests (focusing on the relationship between capitalism and politics). Structuralists see the state as both a functional expression of the immediate needs of capitalism and a repository for its longer-term contradictions (exacerbated by the intervention of the state, an actor charged with both facilitating production and disguising its effects). The most immediate problem with this approach is that these contradictions clearly lack such a causal force. Economic and political competition has not pointed the U.S. political economy in any particular direction, least of all towards its own destruction. By contrast, instrumentalists draw business-government relations on a grand and conspiratorial scale, putting "monopoly capital" in political control. If structuralists exaggerate the autonomy of state institutions, instrumentalists ignore those institutions altogether and lean on an elaborately oppressive notion of cultural hegemony in order to dismiss the political influence of anyone but big business.[44]

Perhaps the sharpest *riposte* to radical state theory has come from a renewed interest in the role and autonomy of political institutions and a "state-centered" account of the New Deal.[45] Yet this view's fascination with state

44 On this debate, see Nicos Poulantzas, "The Problem of the Capitalist State," *New Left Review* 58 (1969): 67–78; Ralph Miliband, "Poulantzas and the Capitalist State," *New Left Review* 82 (1973): 83–92; David Gold, Clarence Lo, and Erik Wright, "Recent Developments on Marxist Theories of the State," *Monthly Review* 27 (1975), 5:29–43, 6:36–51; Claus Offe and Volker Ronge, "Theses on the Theory of the State," *New German Critique* 6 (1975); 137–47; Martin Carnoy, *The State and Political Theory* (Princeton, 1984), 89–127.

45 See Theda Skocpol, "Political Response to Capitalist Crisis: Neo-Marxist Theories of the State and the Case of the New Deal," *Politics and Society* 10 (1982): 155–201, and "Bringing the State Back In" in *Bringing the State Back In*, ed. Theda Skocpol et al. (New York, 1985), 3–37; Theda Skocpol and John Ikenberry, "The Political Formation of the American Welfare State," *Comparative Social Research* 6 (1983): 87–120; Theda Skocpol and Kenneth Finegold, "State Capacity and Economic In-

capacity and independence (based largely on the early and celebratory New Deal histories) ignores the legal and institutional constraints on federal politics, the tremendous background influence of business, and the heterogeneity of economic interests. Proponents of this view are torn between the equally untenable assumptions that state institutions have the means and the motive to remain aloof from economic interest and that any business opposition to state policy is evidence of state autonomy. Curiously, this view also grants considerable autonomy to economic interests, seeing prominent "corporate liberals" or "welfare capitalists" as intellectual reformers rather than representatives of their firms or industries. While correctly stressing that institutions matter, the state-centered account presses the more dubious claim that political or bureaucratic entities had independent and influential interests of their own, assumes autonomy from the absence of formal ties between state and class power, and glosses over the distinct logic of democratic capitalism.[46]

Their limitations aside, I have borrowed from all of these approaches, an eclecticism that admittedly lends itself better to historical explanation than theoretical rigor. Corporatist, structuralist, instrumentalist, and institutional accounts of the New Deal contain important insights; calling attention, respectively, to the unique political importance of business, to the limits and biases of state intervention under democratic capitalism, and to the importance of state institutions and the rules under which interests are pursued. But they also share some fundamental weakness; ignoring, for the most part, both the pervasive competitive disorganization of the business "class" and the peculiarities of a state whose responsibilities and resources are constitutionally and geographically fragmented.

The U.S. political economy, in exceptional and complex ways, rewards and encourages self-interested, competitive behavior. Given the persistence of economic competition and competitive federalism, the state is neither simply the "executive committee of the ruling class" nor a *deus ex machina* that descends periodically to ensure that the pursuit of self-interest never threatens the survival of the system. Economic and political interests, rarely

tervention in the Early New Deal," *Political Science Quarterly* 97 (1982): 255–78; Ann Orloff, "The Political Origins of America's Belated Welfare State," in *The Politics of Social Policy in the United States,* ed. Margaret Weir et al. (Princeton, 1988), 37–80.

46 This debate is neatly summarized in exchanges between Theda Skocpol and her critics. See Michael Goldfield et al., "Explaining New Deal Labor Policy," *American Political Science Review* 84 (1990): 1297–1315; Jill Quadagno et al., "Did Capitalists Shape Social Security?" *American Sociological Review* 50 (1985): 572–78.

able to cooperate for short periods in limited competitive arenas, are scarcely in a position to pursue farsighted class interests or political solutions. The discrete interests of economic competitors and the material anxieties of workers erode class interests – or at least the willingness and ability of individual interests to act upon them. The way in which the state itself is organized shapes and channels the political actions of economic interests. And the relative autonomy of state actors rests less upon the requisites for the ultimate survival of capitalism than upon more immediate and mundane concerns with business confidence and electoral success. Attempts to escape competitive chaos replace old contradictions with new ones, and the discretionary focus and monotonous failure of state intervention alienate business interests that are already leery of political solutions.

A political economy inclined toward organizational chaos does not lend itself easily to historical generalizations or theoretical models. This "disorganizational synthesis" – the interplay of rational self-interest, political and economic competition, and ambivalent business-government relations – is less a theory of U.S. politics than it is a suggestion of characteristic problems and patterns, a benchmark for individual and collective behavior. This understanding of the logic and limits of the larger political economy illuminates the particular dilemmas and dynamics of the interwar political economy. The New Deal stepped up the tempo of long-standing associational efforts and raised the costs of cooperation and defection. In some respects, the Roosevelt administration was bound by the same dilemmas of collective action that had always confounded business and politics; in other respects, the administration was able to change the rules under which individual interests and collective solutions were pursued. The New Dealers, as one trenchant observer noted,

> were not entirely clear as to just what game they were supposed to be playing. Then, too, while it was generally agreed that everyone should quit a winner, there was considerable dispute as to the rules and procedures of play. . . . The game was getting exactly nowhere . . . All of which only proves that so long as the old deck can be re-shuffled, there can always be a new deal.[47]

47 H.B. Smith, "Re-Shuffle and Re-Deal 'Em" (22 May 1934), File 137, Alexander Sachs Papers, Franklin D. Roosevelt Presidential Library, Hyde Park, NY.

2. Competition and Collective Action
Business Conditions and Business Strategies, 1920–1933

Behind their rhetorical embrace of a laissez-faire economy, interwar business interests courted any means of muting existing competition or barring new competition. Faced with the market's persistent inability to rationalize capacity or competition, business turned to collective solutions: trade association, unionism, and political regulation. The form or focus of industrial strategy aside, success hinged on the ability of leading firms to ensure that all competitors either played by the rules or paid for their recalcitrance. Competitive jealousies and federated politics encouraged an anxious, ad hoc range of private and political solutions. Industrial structures, competitive pressures, and organizational prospects varied widely, as did the ability of any industry or firm to gain lasting stability.

This state of rivalry and disarray set the stage for the New Deal. For business, politics was an opportunity to enforce or socialize competitive strategies that had sputtered through the 1920s and collapsed (when they were most needed) after 1929. In this chapter, I highlight the competitive and organizational concerns of key industries and firms before 1933, focusing on the diversity of business interests, the private and public efforts of these interests to escape or regulate competition, and the state of business strategy and thought on the eve of the New Deal. This is less a comprehensive history of the interwar industrial economy than an exploration of characteristic problems of economic strategy and collective action. (Labor relations is traced in greater depth in the following chapter.) I begin, as a backdrop to more detailed discussions of competition and organization in various industries, with a brief survey of some common conditions and trends.

An Overview of the Interwar Economy

World War I accelerated the displacement of labor by capital. Despite a fourfold increase in the value of manufactured product from 1914 to 1929, the workforce stopped growing in 1919 and did not reapproach its previous

35

peak until the 1940s. Although such figures had more meaning in specific industries, aggregate worker-hours per unit of production fell by 35 percent between 1919 and 1939.[1] As the 1920s wore on, however, capital recommited to production declined sharply as new industrial investment fed a vicious circle of excess capacity and plunging profits. In the words of Hugh Johnson, the nation's purchasing power was "congealed in icebergs of unnecessary building and unneeded plants." Commercial banks rescued and reorganized many firms and industries during the 1920–21 downturn but brought with them few new ideas. For industry, indebtedness was yet another fixed cost encouraging cutthroat production. Banks internalized the competitive ethos and, as Alexander Sachs of Lehman Bros. noted, became an "undisciplined horde of investment trusts," buying up large chunks of plant capacity while "maintain[ing] the fiction of 100 percent liquidity upon demand."[2]

This stagnation was reflected, well before 1929, in aggregate industrial capacity and profit. New investment in the early 1920s and the capacity inherited from the war made profitable production increasingly elusive. Barely half of manufacturing capacity was utilized in the immediate aftermath of the war. Although aggregate utilized capacity peaked at a healthy 72 percent in 1923, this obscured serious problems in many sectors. One observer commented that excess capacity stood "like masked batteries of machine guns waiting to lay down a new barrage of production whenever buying reappears." With the exception of a few technological neophytes, industry leaders tried to restrict the creation or entry of new capacity. Profit margins in the 1920s lagged well behind those of preceding decades; this, combined with high rates of business mortality, shuffled capacity within industries but did little to rationalize competition.[3] The number of firms

1 Solomon Fabricant, *Employment in Manufacturing, 1899–1939* (New York, 1942), 9–19, 23–27; Gabriel Kolko, *Main Currents in Modern American History* (New York, 1984), 100–104; Bureau of the Census, *Census of Manufacturers: 1937* (Washington, 1938), 44–45, and *Census of Manufacturers: 1931*, (Washington, 1932) 40–41; Michael Bernstein, *The Great Depression: Delayed Recovery and Economic Change in America, 1929–1939* (New York, 1987), 103–8; Temporary National Economic Committee [TNEC], *The Structure of Industry*, Monograph 27 (Washington, 1941), 3–15; Harry Jerome, *Mechanization in Industry* (New York, 1934), 28–32, 219–20.

2 Michael Piore and Charles Sabel, *The Second Industrial Divide* (New York, 1984), 19–45; (quote) Hugh Johnson, *The Blue Eagle from Egg to Earth* (Garden City, 1935), 159; (quote) "Extracts from [Sachs] Memo" (22 January 1934), Official File [OF] 1983, Franklin D. Roosevelt Papers, Franklin D. Roosevelt Presidential Library [FDRPL], Hyde Park, NY. For broad patterns of ownership, see National Resources Committee [NRC], *The Structure of the American Economy*, Part 1 (Washington, 1939), 160–63, 309–17.

3 Kolko, *Main Currents*, 102; Robert Himmelberg, *The Origins of the National Recovery*

with production valued at greater than $5,000 shrank by one-quarter from 1919 to 1937. Market concentration increased steadily but not dramatically in most industries; this meant substantial economies of scale for some, but concentration actually declined in industries whose growth outstripped attempts to erect effective barriers to entry.[4]

Despite capital intensity and concentration, labor remained an important liability, hovering between 30 and 50 percent of value added in most manufacturing industries. Moreover, high fixed costs often left labor costs as the sole arena of competition. At the end of World War I, employers launched an "open shop" campaign that drove organized labor into a protective shell bounded by a few industries (printing, railroads, coal, and clothing) that pragmatically exploited unions as a surrogate for the organization of firms. In all, declining industries integrated workers and unions into their competitive strategies, mass-production industries marginalized workers even as they employed record numbers, and new, high-technology industries did their best to sidestep industrial conflict by enacting "liberal" wage and welfare policies.[5]

The labor question also infused the problem of consumption. A swing from producer- to consumer-good production after 1920 left aggregate demand and economic growth in the hands of individual consumers who were increasingly unable to meet the economy's expectation of mass-production *and* mass-consumption. Some firms and industries appreciated this problem, but its solution posed a vexing dilemma of collective action; any firm could raise the wages of its workers, but this simply cut into profits or raised prices and left barely a ripple in aggregate consumption. More importantly, the disparate growth of consumer- and producer-goods industries (the former dependent on levels of aggregate income, and the latter dependent on levels of industrial activity) determined how each would experience and respond to the Depression.[6]

Administration (New York, 1976), 83–85; Ralph Epstein, *Industrial Profits in the United States* (New York, 1934), 75–78, 122–23; Edwin Nourse, *America's Capacity to Produce* (Washington, 1934), 296–309, 560–71; (quote) "Report of Committee on Recent Economic Change" (1932), File 456, John J. Raskob Papers, Hagley Museum and Library, Wilmington, DE.

4 TNEC, *The Structure of Industry*, 3–15, 59–62, 407–12.

5 Labor costs calculated from Bureau of the Census, *Census of Manufacturers* (various years, 1921–1937); see also David Montgomery, *The Fall of the House of Labor* (New York, 1987), 395–436; Leo Wolman, *Ebb and Flow of Trade Unionism* (New York, 1936); Melvyn Dubofsky, "Not So 'Turbulent Years': A New Look at the 1930s," in *Life and Labor: Dimensions of American Working Class History*, ed. Charles Stephenson and Robert Asher (Albany, 1986), 205–23.

6 Bernstein, *The Great Depression*, passim, and "Why the Great Depression was Great:

Patterns of consumption, profit, concentration, labor relations, and investment varied from state to state and region to region. Disparate regional resources and sharply federated regulation complicated and exaggerated collective economic problems and solutions. Mixed manufacturing was concentrated in the northeast quarter of the nation (bounded by Boston, Detroit, and Chicago to the north and Baltimore, Cincinnati, and St. Louis to the south), the few industries that dominated southern and western states voiced narrower political programs. This regional variance affected specific industries in specific ways according to the regional or national character of markets; the portability of capital equipment and investment; the political climate of given states; the geography of resource wealth; and regional competition for labor, markets, and political favor.[7]

In international markets, U.S. industry remained overwhelmingly protectionist. Exports slipped from a high of 16 percent of domestic production in 1919 to an average of less than 9 percent through 1923–33. Imports were also limited but included a number of essential minerals and tropical commodities.[8] While trade shrank, overseas investment by U.S. banks and firms grew rapidly, driven in part by the complex pattern of war debts, in part by the unprecedented value of the U.S. dollar in international markets, and in part by the absence of attractive investment opportunities in the domestic economy. Internationalists, such as J.P. Morgan partner Thomas Lamont, argued that "a prosperous Europe is worth more to the United States as a

Toward a New Understanding of the Interwar Economic Crisis in the United States," in *The Rise and Fall of the New Deal Order, 1930–1980*, ed. Steve Fraser and Gary Gerstle (Princeton, 1989), 32–54; NRC, *Structure of the American Economy*, 1:11, 330.

7 A good geographic overview of the economy is provided by the maps in NRC, *Structure of the American Economy*, 1:33–55. On regional and national markets, see TNEC, *The Structure of Industry*, 323.

8 Nash Memo (19 June 1931), File 49, Alexander Sachs Papers, FDRPL; NRC, *Structure of the American Economy*, 1:26, 76–77; Kolko, *Main Currents*, 206–11; Mira Wilkins, *The Maturing of Multinational Enterprise: American Business Abroad, 1914–1970* (Cambridge, 1974), 62–163; Joseph Brandes, *Herbert Hoover and Economic Diplomacy: Department of Commerce Policy, 1921–1928* (Pittsburgh, 1962), 163–66, 192–96; Carl Parrini, *Heir to Empire: United States Economic Diplomacy, 1916–1923* (Pittsburgh, 1969), 203–10; on protectionism, see E.E. Schattschneider, *Politics, Pressures and the Tariff* (New York, 1935); "Chronological Documentation of NAM Positions on the Tariff and Reciprocity since 1895," File 855.3, National Association of Manufacturers Papers, Hagley Museum; for representative views on the tariff, see John Raskob, "A Democratic Business View of the Tariff" (1930), File 765(1), Pierre S. DuPont Papers, Hagley Museum; Raskob to A.H. Geuting (10 November 1932), File 602(12), and Cordell Hull to Raskob (7 November 1931), File 1134, Raskob Papers.

customer than all the debts," but most industries objected to what they saw as investment in European competition and confined their foreign affairs to the security of multinational cartels.[9] For the most part, even "open door internationalists" sought either to exclude European capital from key areas of the world or to strike anti-competitive agreements with potential rivals.[10]

The most pervasive symptom of the interwar political economy's peculiar synthesis of costly concentration and chronic disorganization was cutthroat competition. As Alexander Sachs noted, "Price cutting and aggressive competition for the same business at around or below cost is the general rule." In industry after industry, firms made pricing and production decisions based on short-sighted market conditions and routinely drove industry-wide prices below the break-even point. For many, the premises of laissez-faire competition seemed incompatible with the twentieth century. "The only people who seem to believe in competition," remarked Steven DuBrul of General Motors, ". . . are that small minority in each industry who gain thereby, and the academic economists." In this atmosphere, firms, trade associations, the Department of Commerce, and finally the Supreme Court – all without a hint of irony – began treating competition itself as a potential restraint of trade. As one congressional economist observed, "the tendency appears to be toward denouncing as unfair any effort to compete on the basis of price."[11]

9 See Charles Kindleberger, *The World in Depression* (Berkeley, 1986), 23–69; Frank Costigliola, *Awkward Dominion: American Political, Economic and Cultural Relations with Europe, 1919–1933* (Ithaca, 1984), 100–110, 114–27; Stephen V.O. Clarke, *Central Bank Cooperation, 1924–1931* (New York, 1967); Brandes, *Economic Diplomacy*, 4–7, 63–147; TNEC, *Export Prices and Export Cartels*, Monograph 6 (Washington, 1941), 154–233. "International Finance and World Trade" (1937), File 139–9; "Debt Suspension Matter" (n.d.) file 98–18; Memoranda of conversations between Hoover and Lamont (June 1921), File 98–18; "Confidential Memorandum: The Allied Debt" (1922), File 80–17, Thomas W. Lamont Papers, Baker Library, Cambridge, MA; (quote) "Draft Message," Lamont to Hoover (25 May 1932), Presidential Personal File [PPF] 168; and Owen Young to Hoover (5 January 1926), Commerce File [CF] 719, Herbert Hoover Papers, Herbert C. Hoover Presidential Library, [HCHPL] West Branch, IA.

10 On foreign manufacturing investment (led by trademarked food industries, oil refining, automobiles, aluminum, and electrical manufacturing), see Wilkins, *The Maturing of Multinational Enterprise*, 52–53; George Stocking and Myron Watkins, *Cartels in Action: Case Studies in International Business Diplomacy* (New York, 1947); Herbert Marshall, *Canadian-American Industry: A Study in International Investment* (New Haven, 1936); Cleona Lewis, *America's Stake in International Investments* (New York, 1934), 306–13, 595.

11 (Quote) Sachs, "Note on unprofitableness . . ." (1930), File 101, and (quote) Steven DuBrul to Harry Eaton (9 March 1934), File 28, Sachs Papers; (quote) TNEC,

In general, U.S. industry shared little but uncertainty and anxiety. Disparate regional and industrial development, uneven capitalization, profitless competition, and tentative internationalism not only pressed industries along different strategic and political paths but also turned traditional points of business unity – such as open-shop labor policy or protectionism – into points of contention. Some industries were drawn into tight combinations as a result of market forces or public policy; some fragmented before and after 1929; and some split sharply into two or three camps over regional, national, or international plans of action. In this sense, private and public strategies after 1920 depended much less on what it was that business as a whole wanted and much more on the structural, competitive, and political peculiarities of specific industries.

Automobiles: The Elusive Consumer

The automobile industry led the consumer-goods boom of the interwar years. Consumer industries, especially those that produced durable and expensive goods, traded traditional concerns over competition for a near obsession with the politics and economics of consumption.[12] Especially after World War I, the auto industry, among others, found that mass-production increasingly displaced or impoverished those upon whom it relied to buy their products. In an economy largely isolated from international markets, this disparity between industry's ability to produce and the nation's ability to consume would prove a constant challenge.

The auto industry grew rapidly after the turn of the century. Average annual output in the 1920s (almost 3,000,000 cars) was six times that of 1913, and employment reached 400,000 by 1925. Early auto firms were simple assembly plants that bought on credit from parts firms, sold for cash to dealers, and used both to insulate themselves from the market (dealers failed at a rate of 20 percent annually through the 1920s). Low capital requirements did not, however, nourish competition. Leading firms established economies of scale and used proprietary parts contracts and franchising agreements to bar entry; of 169 new entrants between 1902 and 1920, only 14 remained by

Competition and Monopoly in American Industry, Monograph 20 (Washington, 1941), 7; Himmelberg, *Origins of the National Recovery Administration*.

12 On the economics and culture of interwar consumption, see Lizbeth Cohen, "The Class Experience of Mass Consumption: Workers as Consumers in Interwar America," in *The Power of Culture*, ed. Richard Wightman Fox and T.J. Jackson Lears (Chicago, 1993) 135–62; Martha Olney, *Buy Now, Pay Later; Advertising, Credit, and Consumer Durables in the 1920s* (Chapel Hill, 1991), 22–61, 86–189.

1923 and only 7 by 1930. World War I telescoped concentration and growth, increasing consumer sales fourfold and commercial sales tenfold. Established firms reaped the benefits of wartime demand (Ford built its River Rouge plant at government expense in 1916–17) and abandoned any allegiance to prewar trade agreements and patent pools.[13]

The armistice caught the industry off guard. Ford and General Motors (GM) reconverted to meet pent-up civilian demand but, despite strong sales in the early postwar years, suffered chronic excess capacity. GM had grown recklessly before the war. The company's bankers had squeezed out founder William Durant in 1910 but, with help from DuPont, he reacquired control in 1915. In the next three years, GM's fixed-plant investment more than tripled, and in 1920 the company was again caught short. Durant, almost $30 million in debt, relinquished control to the DuPonts. Ford (which had borrowed $75 million to finance retooling and buy out minority shareholders) was also caught in an unexpectedly profitless 1921. In response, the company ceased all parts purchases, ran through its existing inventory, and then abruptly shut down production and shipped remaining cars to dealers, each of whom "had to pay or forfeit his franchise." The postwar crunch was borne by dealers, their banks, and laid-off employees.[14]

Ford, GM, and Chrysler (which emerged as the third of the industry's "Big Three" following a reorganization of struggling smaller firms) ac-

---

13 Ralph Epstein, *The Automobile Industry* (New York, 1928), 66–77, 93–129, 235–39; James Foreman-Peck, "The American Challenge of the Twenties: Multinationals and the European Motor Industry," *Journal of Economic History* [*JEH*] (1982): 867; Lawrence Seltzer, *A Financial History of the American Automobile Industry* (Clifton, 1973), 39–53, 266; Sidney Fine, *The Automobile under the Blue Eagle* (Ann Arbor, 1963), 6–11; James Flink, *America Adopts the Automobile, 1895–1910* (Cambridge, 1970), 294–97, 318–22; Donald Davis, *Conspicuous Production: Automobiles and Elites in Detroit, 1899–1933* (Philadelphia, 1988), 15–21, 85–86, 142; Robert Thomas, *An Analysis of the Pattern of Growth in the Automobile Industry* (New York, 1977), 174–96, 206–7; William Greenleaf, *Monopoly on Wheels* (Detroit, 1961), 23–75; William McPherson, *Labor Relations in the Automobile Industry* (Washington, 1940), 11–12; John Rae, *American Automobile Manufacturers: The First Forty Years* (New York, 1959), 155–56; Allen Nevins and Frank Ernest Hill, *Ford: Expansion and Challenge, 1915–1933* (New York, 1957), 71.

14 Federal Trade Commission [FTC], *Report On the Motor Vehicle Industry* (Washington, 1939), 421–26; Alfred Chandler, *Giant Enterprise: Ford, General Motors and the Automobile Industry* (New York, 1964), 71–86; John Rae, *The American Automobile Industry* (Boston, 1984), 50–58, and *American Automobile Manufacturers*, 136–37; Alfred Sloan, *My Years With General Motors* (New York, 1963), 19–44; Seltzer, *Financial History of the American Automobile Industry*, 114–18, 145–211; Nevins, *Expansion and Challenge*, 112–13, 164–65; (quote) Kuhn and Loeb Internal Memo (1921), Name and Subject [N&S] File 46, Lewis L. Strauss Papers, HCHPL.

counted for 54 percent of car sales by 1917, 68 percent by 1921, and almost 90 percent by 1933. Ford led the industry in the early postwar era but slowly lost market share to its two rivals. While low price concentration and mine-to-consumer integration undermined Ford's ability to respond to the market, GM's celebrated managerial innovations (many of which existed only on paper) were also futile. The collapse of 1921 cut short GM's attempt to cultivate distinct price markets, and when the market slipped again in 1924, its losses were the largest in the industry. As GM executives admitted, any success in the 1920s "could be attributed less to our own wits than to the improvement in the general economy and the rising demand for automobiles."[15] Despite limited competition and an obsession with managerial structure, the vagaries of the market increasingly determined the industry's performance and strategy.

The industry weathered the early 1920s on the strength of one-time demand for a new product, but markets (despite fairly strong international sales) slipped through the early 1920s.[16] By 1923, 41 percent of U.S. households owned a car, and utilized capacity in the industry had fallen to 65 percent. After 1920 the industry experimented with lower prices, promotion (which, by 1920, absorbed one-quarter of all national magazine advertising), trade-ins,

15 Steve Jeffreys, *Management and Managed: Fifty Years of Crisis at Chrysler* (New York, 1986), 49–51; Davis, *Conspicuous Production*, 67–83, 144–58; Harold Katz, "Decline of Competition in the Automobile Industry" (Ph.D diss., Columbia University, 1970), 59; Chandler, *Giant Enterprise*, 3; Fine, *Automobile under the Blue Eagle*, 2–5; Thomas, *Growth in the Automobile Industry*, 196–225, 239, 268. Concentration confined the industry to Detroit, aiding the industry's organization but limiting its political voice (despite the fact that one Michigan Senate seat was considered the property of the auto giants). On managerial strategies, see Sloan, *My Years at General Motors*, (quote, 170); Alfred Chandler, *Strategy and Structure: Chapters in the History of American Industrial Enterprise* (Cambridge, 1962), 114–62, and *The Visible Hand: The Managerial Revolution in American Business* (Cambridge, 1977); Arthur Kuhn, *GM Passes Ford, 1918–1933* (University Park, 1986).

16 Exports ran at 10 percent through the interwar era. In 1925, the industry exported about 300,000 cars, and foreign assemblies accounted for another 100,000. By the 1930s, Ford's production in Canada, Great Britain, and Latin America was more than double its total exports. GM also moved into Canada (creating GM Canada in 1918) and Europe (purchasing British Vauxhaul in 1925 and German Opel in 1927). Ford and GM also expanded into Japan, but tariffs on parts and production ceilings in the 1930s forced U.S. firms to retreat into joint venture. Chrysler acquired a Canadian subsidiary when it absorbed Maxwell Chalmers in 1925, but its international interests were slight. See George Maxcy, *The Multinational Automobile Industry* (New York, 1981), 69–88; Mira Wilkins and Frank Ernest Hill, *American Business Abroad: Ford on Six Continents* (Detroit, 1964), 436–42; Peck, "Multinationals and the European Motor Industry," 865–69; Automotive Division, "Data and information for Secretary Hoover" (5 January 1927), CF 39, Hoover Papers.

model changes, option packages, and installment plans. Most new features (for example, closed cabs and motorized windshield wipers) were marketing, rather than technical, advances.[17] By the mid-1920s, many potential buyers found the price of new cars, at least as a one-time cash payment, prohibitive. Car owners had little incentive to replace older models. And members of both groups could satisfy themselves in the used car market.

In 1923 new cars outsold used cars three to one, in 1925 the market was evenly split, and by 1927 new cars claimed only a third of the market. Firms tried desperately to prevent past sales from undermining current markets. Chevrolet paid dealers twenty-five dollars for each used car they destroyed, taking 650,000 cars off the market between 1927 and 1930. Ford tried a similar plan, but neither firm was in a position to expect much fealty from dealers, who competed over trade-ins, liquidated used cars as quickly as possible, resold "junked" cars, and collected the disposal fee as many as six times for the same car. In such "schemes advanced for the scrapping of old cars," noted industry consultant Alexander Sachs, "the difficulty lies in finding someone to absorb the loss." And while model changes en–couraged some turnover and new sales, it also created swollen inventories of trade-ins distinguished only by low prices and last year's fashion. The major firms encouraged state and municipal consumer agencies to adopt standard "blue book" prices for used cars, but never solved the "used car evil."[18]

Firms also turned to consumer credit to encourage sales, creating their own financial institutions when commercial banks proved unwilling to offer secured loans. GM formed the General Motors Acceptance Corporation (GMAC) in 1919, and while the elder Ford decried this promotion of consumer debt, his company also introduced it. By 1925, 75 percent of all sales (new and used) were on installment and intense competition drove down

---

17 Robert Thomas, "Style Change and the Automobile Industry During the Roaring Twenties," in *Business Enterprise and Economic Change*, ed. L.P. Cain and Paul Uselding (Kent, 1973); Thomas, *Growth in the Automobile Industry*, 179–204; Davis, *Conspicuous Production*, 6; Bernstein, *The Great Depression*, 60–61, 134–35; Sloan, *My Years With General Motors*, 171–75, 187; Basht Garage to Coolidge (23 April 1924), CF 39, Hoover Papers. After 1923, capacity became difficult to calculate, as the industry moved to a contrived pattern of seasonal "model year" production (Nourse, *America's Capacity to Produce*, 228–35).

18 Thomas, *Growth in the Automobile Industry*, 206–9; Katz, "Decline of Competition," 41–44; FTC, *Report on the Motor Vehicle Industry*, 93; "The Used Car," *Fortune* 17 (June 1938): 116; Paul Nash, "Confidential Report to Lawrence Stern" (26 March 1931), File 49, (quote) "Auto Situation" (3 March 1938), File 92, Sachs Papers; Ward Canady [Willys Overland] to FDR (26 April 1938), OF 102:2, FDR Papers.

payments as low as 10 percent (often satisfied by a trade-in). GMAC executives hoped that trade-ins and installment sales would press car ownership into lower income brackets and create constant (if contrived) markets for new models. GMAC even girded post-1929 markets by offering a refund-and-return policy to installment buyers who lost their jobs (a courtesy not extended to GM workers) and lobbying hard for a veteran's bonus in 1933 (recalling that, for a previous bonus, the company had "put on a collection campaign and virtually followed every veteran around until he got his check").[19]

While struggling to encourage consumption, the auto industry also faced the material and organizational demands of its own workers. As the assembly line displaced skilled workers and employment per unit of production fell steadily, the industry (led by Ford in 1914) tried to minimize unrest by introducing the five-dollar day and other "welfare" programs. The effort was futile and short-lived. Faced with slumping sales and a soft labor market after 1920, auto firms allowed inflation and underemployment to erase the novelty of high wages. Automobile unions suffered the displacement of skilled crafts, a series of setbacks in 1920—22, seasonal "model year" layoffs (which gave employers the opportunity to weed out radicals and activists), and the jurisdictional conservatism of the American Federation of Labor (AFL).[20] Through the 1920s, the industry passed many of its material troubles on to a sharply divided workforce and scrupulously avoided the connection between stagnant markets and its own wage policies.

19 Sloan, *My Years with General Motors*, 353–64; Epstein, *American Automobile Industry*, 115–22; Harold Wright, *The Financing of Automobile Instalment Sales* (Chicago, 1927); Martha Olney, "Credit as a Production-Smoothing Device: The Case of Automobiles, 1913–1938," *JEH* 49 (1989): 377–91; John Raskob to Hoover, CF 291, Hoover Papers; Deane [GMAC] memo for Sachs (7 June 1933), and "GMAC Unemployment Refund Plan," File 28; (quote) "Stimulation of Auto Sales . . ." (May 1933), File 92, Sachs Papers.

20 Stephen Meyer, "The Persistence of Fordism: Workers and Technology in the American Automobile Industry, 1900–1960," in *On the Line: Essays in the History of Auto Work*, ed. Nelson Lichtenstein and Stephen Meyer (Urbana, 1989), 73–99; Nelson Lichtenstein, "Life at the Rouge: A Cycle of Workers' Control," in Stephenson and Asher, *Life and Labor*, 237–41; Stephen Meyer, *The Five Dollar Day: Labor Management and Social Control in the Ford Motor Company, 1908–1921* (Albany, 1981), 196–97; Thomas Klug, "Employers' Strategies in the Detroit Labor Market, 1900–1929," in Lichtenstein and Meyer, *On the Line*, 54–63; Fine, *Automobile under the Blue Eagle*, 4–28, 142–81; Daniel Raff, "Ford Welfare Capitalism in Its Economic Context," in *Masters to Managers: Historical and Comparative Perspectives on American Employers*, ed. Sanford Jacoby (New York, 1991), 90–110; Jeffreys, *Management and Managed*, 53; Roger Keeran, *The Communist Party and the Automobile Workers' Unions* (New York, 1980), 32–35, 49–50, 100–108.

By the early 1930s, the auto industry was reeling. Saturated markets collapsed completely in 1929. "Substantial and progressive recovery of *the whole business community*," pled Walter Chrysler in 1930, "would undoubtedly be accomplished more directly and more extensively by increased auto sales than by any other single factor." The Big Three (especially GM) were increasingly receptive to wage legislation that might jump-start consumption. These sentiments, however, were difficult to reconcile with the industry's own labor relations and sharp internal disagreement over *any* collective efforts, let alone the appropriate response to organized labor.[21] As the New Deal approached, the Big Three were lost in a strategic cul-de-sac; although sensitive to the purchasing power of the nation's workers, the industry was reluctant to consider *its own* workers as potential consumers or to surrender managerial power to broader political solutions.

Rubber, Steel, and Metals: The Crisis in Producer Goods

Although insulated somewhat from fickle consumer demand, the major producer-good industries also struggled through the 1920s. As consumers of basic industrial commodities, rubber, steel, and metals firms were pressed to integrate proprietary domestic supplies or participate in often chaotic international commodity markets. And as producers of basic industrial supplies, they were faced with the potentially destructive buying power of well-organized industrial consumers (especially the auto industry) and the constant threat of substitution (for example, aluminum for steel and synthetics for rubber). These pressures surfaced within producer-goods industries in the form of cutthroat price competition and bitter confrontations with labor.

Demand for automobile tires transformed the rubber industry. Production increased fourfold between 1914 and 1919 to reach over $1 billion in sales. This growth was concentrated in the industry's center, Akron, Ohio, which had extended generous terms to pioneers Frank Seiberling (Goodyear), B.F. Goodrich, and Harvey Firestone. Dependence on specialized tool-and-die shops and foundries and proximity to Detroit kept the booming industry in Akron until the late 1930s, when the exhaustion of Akron's water supply and pressure from chain stores for freight savings encouraged migration south and west. It enjoyed all the trappings of profitable oligopoly – few producers located in a small area (the fourth major rubber firm, U.S. Rubber, was in Detroit), heavy fixed costs, and inelastic demand – and yet suffered

---

21 Bernstein, *The Great Depression*, 58–59; (quote) "Draft of Statement by Chrysler" (17 August 30), PPF 14, Hoover Papers.

savage competition and the worst profit performance of any major U.S. industry.[22] This instability was rooted in international and domestic circumstances and the market power of leading retailers and auto firms.

U.S. tire firms were the principal consumers of raw rubber, most of which came from Dutch- and British-controlled Malaysian plantations. The volatility of international rubber markets and the threat of production restrictions left the tire firms looking constantly for alternate supplies. Encouraged by the Department of Commerce, industry leaders explored the feasibility of plantations throughout Latin America and insular Asia. But a dearth of capital, low rubber prices, the uncertainty of local politics, and the pressures of domestic competition discouraged international ventures. U.S. Rubber surpassed all domestic rivals in agricultural investments but counted on proprietary sources for only one-fifth of its rubber.[23]

After 1920, British interests responded to plummeting prices with the "Stevenson Plan," a system of quotas intended to stabilize prices and block U.S. investments in the largely bankrupt plantation region. The tire firms were divided in their response. Goodyear and the Rubber Association of America (RAA), fearing the inventory losses that could be caused by any precipitous price change and hoping that international stability might spill into domestic markets, sought an accord with the British. Firestone, unable to pass on high prices in its exclusive contracts with Detroit, opposed the British restrictions and withdrew angrily from the RAA. U.S. tire firms were in no position to take advantage of either low prices before 1922 or stable prices under the Stevenson Plan. The industry routinely translated low rubber prices into low tire prices but rarely recovered any increase. In turn, volatile prices and the threat of international restriction forced firms to maintain large raw rubber inventories, putting pressure on production and making it impossible to purchase raw rubber prudently. One observer estimated

22 Ralph Wolf and Howard Wolf, *Rubber: A Story of Glory and Greed* (New York, 1936), 430–33; Maurice O'Reilly, *The Goodyear Story* (New York, 1983), 9; Lloyd Reynolds, "Competition in the Rubber Tire Industry," *American Economic Review* 28 (1938): 459–68; Albert Kress, "The Rubber Industry," in *Industrial Planning Under Codes*, ed. George Galloway (New York, 1935), 261; "Crude Rubber Consumption," CF 209, Hoover Papers.

23 Klein to Hoover (22 October 1923); and "Memorandum on Conference at Lotus Club" (20 May 1924), both in File 82218/34, Department of Commerce Records (RG 40), National Archives, Washington, DC; "Suggestions to Committee on Foreign and Interstate Commerce" (December 1925), CF 209; "Notes on [Rubber] Conference" (May 1924), CF 532; O'Neill [General Tire and Rubber] to Hoover (10 April 1923), CF 209; Klein to Hoover (12 May 1924), CF 209; "Memorandum – Rubber" (n.d.), CF 209, Hoover Papers.

industry losses of over $100,000,000 due to changes in the price of raw rubber and speculative errors alone.[24]

For Secretary of Commerce Hoover and the industry, the logical response to the rubber cartel was a joint purchasing agreement or import cartel. In 1925, Dillon Read and the major tire firms (sans Firestone) sought an accord with Stevenson Plan producers. But Washington cut short negotiations, which threatened to codify international restrictions at the expense of Firestone (a fishing companion of Hoover's). With neither the capital nor the unity to inaugurate an effective buying pool, the tire firms looked to their principal consumers, the auto industry. In 1926 GM underwrote a joint purchasing agreement and lobbied for legislation that would turn the Webb Act inside out, thus allowing import cartels (and legalizing what they had already begun doing). The GM plan tried to bring the pressure of an American purchasing monopoly to bear on domestic prices and British producers. The plan (and the Webb amendment) died in 1928 when domestic markets and the Stevenson Plan collapsed.[25]

Although the Stevenson plan did little to stabilize world rubber markets, it did hasten concentration in the American tire industry. Of 178 firms in 1921, only 32 remained solvent 12 years later, and those that survived the 1920s did so at the pleasure of banks and large retailers. Bankers bailed out debt-laden U.S. Rubber in the early 1920s, after which DuPont acquired

24 Wolf and Wolf, *Rubber*, 238–70; K.E. Knorr, *World Rubber and its Regulation* (Stanford, 1945), 15–37, 94–100; Stocking and Watkins, *Cartels in Action*, 63–117; "Memo: re Firestone Tire and Rubber Company," File 93–23, Lamont Papers; "Analysis of present Crude Rubber Situation" (May 1925), CF 209; Firestone to Hoover (12 December 1925), CF 210; "Memorandum for HH" (29 May 1925), CF 209; Firestone to A.H. Viles [RAA] (3 May 1923), CF 203, Hoover Papers; Glenn Babcock, *History of the U.S. Rubber Company* (Bloomington, 1966), 172–80; Kress, "The Rubber Industry," 261; Michael French, "Structural Change and Competition in the United States Tire Industry, 1920–37," *Business History Review* [*BHR*] 60 (1986): 34–35; Michael French, "The Emergence of U.S. Multinational Enterprise: The Goodyear Tire and Rubber Company, 1910–1939," *Economic History Review* 40 (1987): 64–79; P.T. Bauer, *The Rubber Industry: A Study in Competition and Monopoly* (Cambridge, 1948).

25 "Analysis of Present Crude Rubber Situation" (May 1925), CF 209; Raskob to Hoover (18 August 1926), CF 210; "Memorandum for Mr. Hoover" (27 June 1927); Raskob to Hoover (12 July 1927); Raskob to Special Rubber Committee of the NACC (13 July 1926); "Rubber Situation" (n.d.); "American Rubber Situation" (n.d.), CF 509; M. Paul Seigneur [Belgian Rubber] memorandum (28 July 1930), CF 276, all in Hoover Papers. On U.S. response to the Stevenson Plan, see also Joseph Brandes, "Product Diplomacy: Herbert Hoover's Anti-Monopoly Campaign At Home and Abroad," in *Herbert Hoover as Secretary of Commerce*, ed. Ellis Hawley (Iowa City, 1974), 196–208; Frank Chalk, "The United States and the International Struggle for Rubber, 1914–1941" (Ph.D diss., University of Wisconsin, 1970).

control (an extension of its investments in synthetic rubber and GM). Goodyear fought off creditors but eventually settled with Goldman Sachs and later with Dillon Read and Sears (which had an exclusive cost-plus contract to market Goodyear tires). Goodrich and Firestone lost less financial autonomy but were forced to compete with the Sears/Goodyear pact; Goodrich signed on with Standard Oil and Montgomery Ward, and Firestone established its own retail chain. The four major rubber producers also sought guaranteed markets from the auto firms, but these benefited greatly from the price warfare, were reluctant to grant exclusive contracts, and periodically threw their business to smaller firms in order to keep their suppliers guessing.[26]

Tire firms were unable to organize as either consumers of raw rubber or producers of rubber products. Cutthroat competition reflected the combined effects of slipping and inelastic demand, excess capacity, and the power of retail and industrial consumers. To make things worse, the auto markets upon which the industry had thrived after 1910 were saturated after 1924. Sales of new cars (and with each new car, four tires, and after considerable pressure from tire firms, a spare) dropped off in the mid-1920s. Between 1929 and 1932, demand for original equipment tires fell two-thirds. Retreading and durability eroded the market for replacement tires. Excess capacity and high fixed costs (due especially to inventories and debt) exacerbated falling demand and forced firms to compete fiercely for market share.[27]

Inside the factory gates of Akron and Detroit, rubber producers faced more organizational and managerial challenges. Labor represented only 15 percent of production costs, and the industry saw little connection between wages and consumption. But in a context of brutal competition, the major firms were haunted by the specter of interrupted production. In Akron, turnover was high, and the various companies competed over wages and welfare, including extensive housing programs. These firms weathered a

26 French, "U.S. Tire Industry," 34–36; Alfred Lief, *The Firestone Story: A History of the Firestone Tire and Rubber Company* (New York, 1951), 177–81; O'Reilly, *The Goodyear Story*, 49–67; "Memorandum of conversation with Davis and de Krafft (18 February 1930), N&S File 46, Strauss Papers; Babcock, *U.S. Rubber*, 189–90; "U.S. Rubber I: The Corporate State," *Fortune* (February 1934): 52–55; Wolf and Wolf, *Rubber*, 446–47, 460–62.

27 Donald Anthony, "Rubber Products," in *How Collective Bargaining Works*, ed. Harry Millis (New York, 1945), 635; Charles Pearce, *N.R.A. Trade Practice Programs* (New York, 1939), 165–74; "U.S. Rubber I," 52–55, 124–27; Wolf and Wolf, *Rubber*, 446, 465, 476; Lief, *The Firestone Story*, passim; O'Reilly, *The Goodyear Story*, 3–44; Knorr, *World Rubber*, 52–53; French, "U.S. Tire Industry," 36; Bernstein, *The Great Depression*, 80–81.

radical union drive in 1913 but gradually realized that stability probably rested on the shoulders of conservative unions. Cyrus Ching, industrial relations advisor to U.S. Rubber, conceded that unionization was inevitable and placed great faith in the AFL and the leadership of William Green (who as a state senator had helped rid Akron of radicals in 1913). Industry migration and regional wage competition after 1928 further complicated the labor situation.[28]

The steel industry was spared the international commodity speculation that undercut stability in rubber, but regional competition, uneven integration, and excess capacity upset the price system and the prospects for stability. As the industry struggled, individual firms thrust much of the burden of competition onto the backs of steel workers, a tactic that only created future managerial and organizational dilemmas.

Steel production took place for the most part in large integrated mills in and around Youngstown and Pittsburgh (with captive supplies of coal), newer mills in Cleveland and Chicago (close to Superior-shield ore and the auto industry), and low-wage mills in and around Birmingham, Alabama. Prewar demand for steel was unstable, but the industry's leader, U.S. Steel, exerted enough control over the market to attract the half-hearted attention of antitrust prosecutors in 1911. Both the industry and its productivity grew steadily: capital invested in steel increased fivefold from 1899–19 while employment barely doubled. World War I drove up prices and profits but, with one eye on the peace, established firms were reluctant to invest in new capacity and emerged from the war with a mixed future. The government-industry *entente* of 1915–19 took the air out of the antitrust charges against U.S. Steel, and the defeat of organized labor in the Great Steel Strike of 1919 gave steel producers further freedom to manipulate costs and prices. But collapsing exports, the burden of wartime capacity, and shifts in production and markets left them on thin ice.[29]

28 Daniel Nelson, *American Rubber Workers and Organized Labor, 1900–1941* (Princeton, 1988), 80–83; P.W. Litchfield, *Industrial Voyage: My Life as an Industrial Lieutenant* (Garden City, 1954), 50–76; Hugh Allen, *The House of Goodyear* (Akron, 1936), 166–74, 226, 287–98; Anthony, "Rubber Products," 637–638; Cyrus Ching in *Proceedings of the National Industrial Conference Board* (14 April 1934), File I:7, National Industrial Conference Board [NICB], NICB Papers, Hagley Museum; Wolf and Wolf, *Rubber*, 472.

29 Matthew Josephson, *The Robber Barons* (New York, 1934), 102–9, 255–60; Ben Selekman, *Employes' Representation in Steel Works* (New York, 1924), 45; Melvin Urofsky, *Big Steel and the Wilson Administration* (Columbus, 1969), xxi–xxxi, 1–3, 84–116, 152–247; Carroll Daugherty et al., *The Economics of the Iron and Steel In-*

New competition pressed U.S. Steel to supplement its market power with more formal price-fixing, namely a series of voluntary price agreements that became known as the "Pittsburgh-plus" basing-point price system. Under Pittsburgh-plus, all mills added freight from Pittsburgh to their base prices. This promised to "lessen the rigor of price competition," to slow the entry of new capacity, and to ensure that leading mills (willing to absorb losses on freight) had access to scattered markets. But Pittsburgh-plus was a study in noncompliance and unintended consequences. Price fluctuations, secret discounting, and new entry continued. Prices quoted by non-Pittsburgh mills to local customers included "phantom" freight costs, which were gladly counted as profits. Although U.S. Steel should have been the last to cut prices and the first to raise them (trading profits on both sides of the business cycle for a gradual loss of market share), short-sighted pricing eroded its share of both the market *and* industry profits. New firms began to set their own prices, and the courts threw out the basing-point system in 1924. A regional basing-point system employed after 1924 was even less successful.[30]

U.S. Steel failed to protect itself or the industry from an increasingly merciless pattern of competition. Mill capacity increased steadily after 1920, although utilization approached 60 percent only twice in the decade and sank as low as 25 percent in 1922 and 15 percent in 1932.[31] Industrial consumers took advantage of excess capacity and their own market power to command huge discounts. And as price wars raged below the surface of the pricing system, integrated mills were unable to take advantage of low prices

dustry (New York, 1937) 1:9–41; National Recovery Administration [NRA], "Report on the Operation of the Basing Point System in the Iron and Steel Industry" (Washington, 1934), 12; Richard Lauderbaugh, *American Steel Makers and the Coming of the Second World War* (Ann Arbor, 1976), 121–41; FTC, *Wartime Profits and Costs of the Steel Industry* (Washington, 1925), 28–42; Melvin Urofsky and Robert Cuff, "The Steel Industry and Price Fixing During the War," *BHR* 44 (1970): 291–306.

30 "F.O.B. Pittsburgh," *Nation's Business* (19 November 1926), 26–27, 93; FTC, *Report to the President with Respect to the Basing-Point System in the Iron and Steel Industry* (Washington, 1934), 1–37; NRA, "Report on the Basing Point System," 3, 13, 26–27, 40–43, 69; George Stocking, *Basing Point Pricing and Regional Development* (Chapel Hill, 1954), 42, 60; Marvin Barloon, "Institutional Foundations of Pricing Policy in the Steel Industry," *BHR* 28 (1954): 214–35; Thomas McGraw and Forest Reinhardt, "Losing to Win: U.S. Steel's Pricing, Investment Decisions, and Market Share, 1901–1938," *JEH* 49 (1989): 595–96, 599–610; Maxwell Stewart, *Steel – Problems of a Great Industry* (New York, 1937), 8–9.

31 After its experiences in the panic of 1907 and again at the close of World War I, the steel industry had a virtually pathological fear of new or excess capacity. Major firms remained "gun shy" even with the explosion of demand in 1939–41 and added capacity only with explicit reconstruction guarantees and cost-plus contracts. See Lauderbaugh, *American Steel Makers*, 28–48, 59–62, 77–85, 95–107, 117.

in "captive" ore and coal markets or maintain returns on their underutilized fixed costs. Shifts in demand to lighter grades and alloys and the technological superiority of newer mills further scrambled competition. The new mills also hoarded what little prosperity the industry offered in the 1920s and made further gains with each spurt of recovery after 1929. By the mid-1930s, U.S. Steel's share of capacity and production had slipped considerably, although competition remained confined to a limited circle of firms.[32]

The competitive and financial status of the major steel producers was extremely shaky. Having given up prosecuting U.S. Steel, the government welcomed the rise of National, Midvale, and Bethlehem as competitors. And while many condemned U.S. Steel for its managerial failures, other companies drew constant interest from bankers. Kuhn and Loeb tried to put together a merger of second-tier firms around Tom Girdler's Republic Steel, while Cleveland financier Cyrus Eaton, the Block Brothers of Chicago, and Girdler himself also entertained dreams of creating "a second big steel company." Unstable competition discouraged significant mergers, but the top twelve firms quietly absorbed many smaller mills, making trade association largely unnecessary. The American Iron and Steel Institute was a clearing house for basing-point prices before and after 1924 but otherwise demanded and expected little from its members.[33]

32 "The Corporation," *Fortune* 13 (March 1936): 169; William Hogan, *Economic History of the Iron and Steel Industry in the United States* (Lexington, 1971), 813, 877–78; Josef Steindl, *Maturity and Stagnation in American Capitalism* (New York, 1976), 6; Stewart, *Steel*, 7; "National Steel: A Phenomenon," *Fortune* 5 (June 1932): 31, 35; Daugherty, *Economics of Iron and Steel*, 1:207–14; Bernstein, *The Great Depression*, 54–58; Lauderbaugh, *American Steel Makers*, 140–46; "Memorandum of Information: Iron and Steel," Division of Review (DR) File 267:11, and "Iron and Steel," Code Administration Studies [CAS] File 33:3, NRA Records (RG 9), National Archives; U.S. Steel, *TNEC Papers* (Pittsburgh, 1939), 138–39; Gertrude Schroeder, *The Growth of the Major Steel Companies* (Baltimore, 1953), 197–98; TNEC, *The Structure of Industry*, 20–26, 67–68; James Farrell memo (8 January 1929), File 226–30, Lamont Papers. U.S. Steel privately bemoaned its performance but also cynically paraded market losses as a defense against further antitrust prosecution. See testimony of Benjamin Fairless in TNEC, *Hearings: Investigation of Concentration of Economic Power*, Part 26, *Iron and Steel Industry* (Washington, 1940).

33 "Memo for Myron Taylor" (n.d.), File 226–32, and "Memo for Partners" (1936), File 226–332, Lamont Papers; W.S. Carpenter to I. DuPont (14 February 1927), File J:218, Irenée DuPont Papers, Hagley Museum; "Memo: Chicago Conference" (29 November 1931), N&S File 46; "Memorandum" (24 February 1930, 14 November 1930), N&S File 46; "Memorandum for Mr. Strauss" (22 March 1930), N&S File 46; "Memorandum for Mr. Knowlton" (13 July 1934), N&S File 47; "Memorandum for Lawrence Richey" (6 January 1930), N&S File 63, Strauss Papers; "Facts about Republic Steel Corporation" (1937), OF 407B:11, FDR Papers;

Internationally, the industry was threatened by European mills but attracted by European-led cartels. Before 1917, U.S. Steel attempted to press its competitive advantage by allying with European firms, but its efforts were cut short by the antitrust suit and the war. After the war, Europe no longer bought U.S. steel and by 1922 began to challenge U.S. export markets. Steel firms abandoned both the export associations formed in 1918 and any thoughts of investing in European mills (an option also discouraged by U.S. banks with stakes in European steel and overall economic recovery); instead, they sought international agreements that would control prices, entry, and competition but leave domestic markets protected. In 1928, U.S. Steel and Bethlehem joined the tube-steel division of the International Steel Cartel (ISC). Although the ISC was uniquely important to U.S. Steel and Bethlehem (whose coastal markets were vulnerable to imports and whose domestic position was slipping), the industry's involvement grew to include 20 other products and limited membership for 10 smaller U.S. firms. By the late 1930s, U.S. Steel and Bethlehem were responsible to the ISC for maintaining U.S. exports at certain levels, a quota that firms who had not signed the agreement gleefully filled.[34]

With prices either fixed by the basing-point system or falling in the latest competitive scramble, labor bore the brunt of the industry's troubles; wages fell steadily after 1920 and abruptly after 1929. Steel firms flirted briefly with welfare capitalism while using "company unions" (especially during World War I and after 1932) and violence to stem real organization. Neither craft unions nor the AFL maintained a foothold in the wake of the 1919 strike. Employers manipulated internal labor markets, mechanized and deskilled the remaining steel crafts, and divided workers along racial and ethnic lines. In an industry confined to domestic markets, uniform labor agreements were

Hogan, *Economic History of the Iron and Steel Industry*, 878–990. The AISI was more prominent after 1932 when, under former Commerce Secretary Robert Lamont, it served as the industry's NRA code authority. See Daugherty, *Economics of the Iron and Steel Industry*, 1:213–16.

34 Hogan, *Economic History of the Iron and Steel Industry*, 1092–93; Lauderbaugh, *American Steel Makers*, 128–38, 158–68; Paul Tiffany, "Opportunity Denied: The Abortive Attempt to Internationalize the American Steel Industry, 1903–1929," *Business and Economic History* 16 (1987): 229–40; Parrini, *Heir to Empire*, 209–10, 266; FTC, *Report on International Steel Cartels* (Washington, 1948), 3–19; "Study of the Effect of European Steel Consortium . . ." (1926), CF 575, Hoover Papers; Lauderbaugh, "Business, Labor, and Foreign Policy: U.S. Steel, the International Steel Cartel, and Recognition of the Steel Workers Organizing Committee," *Politics and Society* 6 (1976): 433–57; Ervin Hexner, "American Participation in the International Steel Cartel," *Southern Economic Journal [SEJ]* 8 (1941–42): 54–79.

not unheard of; mills had used craft union contracts early in the century and hours restrictions during the war to mute competition. In the absence of strong unions or wartime regulation, however, labor relations deteriorated steadily.[35]

Most other U.S. metal industries, including tin, lead, zinc, and nickel, were largely dependent on international cartels or overseas mining and smelting investments. Although the United States was easily the largest consumer of all nonferrous metals, only aluminum, copper, and brass were domestically processed on any significant scale.[36] Patterns of organization and price competition in these industries diverged sharply. Producers of aluminum enjoyed monopolistic control, growing markets, low labor requirements, and relative international security, which combined to remove almost all competitive pressures. By contrast, the older copper industry suffered chronic labor difficulties, chaotic regional and international competition, and stagnant postwar markets.

The Mellon-owned Aluminum Company of America (ALCOA) used its monopoly on domestic bauxite to dominate its fledgling industry. As the sole source of raw aluminum, ALCOA fleeced independent fabricators and attempted to extend its monopoly to manufacturing, and competitors monotonously filed predatory pricing complaints with the Federal Trade Commission (FTC). ALCOA's monopoly was also girded by patents and the investment in hydroelectric capacity needed to enter the industry. Before World War I, ALCOA joined an international aluminum cartel through its Canadian subsidiary. Although it attracted the attention of the Justice Department in 1912, the cartel only encouraged new international entry and collapsed in 1915–16. After 1920 (with Andrew Mellon now secretary of the treasury), ALCOA sold off its foreign holdings and dug in behind protective tariffs. With only 11,000 workers in a company whose assets totalled $223 million (1937 figures) labor relations remained a minor concern.[37]

35 David Roediger and Philip Foner, *Our Own Time: A History of American Labor and the Working Day* (London, 1989), 204–38; Hogan, *Economic History of the Iron and Steel Industry*, 873–74, 1167; Gerald Eggert, *Steelmasters and Labor Reform, 1886–1923* (Pittsburgh, 1981); Dennis Dickerson, *Out of the Crucible* (Albany, 1986), 85, 114–21; David Brody, *Steelworkers in America: The Non-Union Era* (New York, 1960); Katherine Stone, "The Origins of Job Structures in the Steel Industry," *Review of Radical Political Economics* 6 (1974): 61–97; Charles Gulick, *Labor Policy of the U.S. Steel Corporation* (New York, 1924).

36 Lewis, *America's Stake in International Investments*, 246–63.

37 *New York World* clippings, CF 21, Hoover Papers; George David Smith, *From Monopoly to Competition: The Transformation of ALCOA, 1888–1986* (New York,

Before World War I, the copper industry was centered in Northern Michigan and dominated by Anaconda, Kennecott, Phelps-Dodge, and Calumet-Hecla. After 1919, collapsing world copper prices, deteriorating ore quality in Michigan mines, and the rise of low-cost mines in Montana upset domestic competition and undercut U.S. participation in international agreements. Michigan interests formed an Export Association to dispense of wartime stocks but could not compete with Canadian, African, Mexican, and Chilean mines. The Michigan mines, technologically backward and stripped of high-return copper (which required less smelting and yielded precious metal byproducts) were not only at a competitive disadvantage but also faced constant labor strife and, as wages in Detroit rose, labor shortages. The mining companies also dominated processing and manufacturing (except for those in the brass industry, composed primarily of small firms in Connecticut's "brass valley"). In all, copper and brass manufacturers had overgrown during the war and were desperate for new markets after 1920. But major consumers (autos, utilities, construction, and appliances) had extensive stocks on hand when the war ended and were able to keep pressure on prices throughout the 1920s.[38]

Especially after 1929, the power of industrial consumers drove rubber, steel, and metal (excepting aluminum) firms into tedious, destructive price

1988), 43–190; Charles Carr, *ALCOA: An American Experience* (New York, 1972), 173–78; "FTC Material," Trade Practice Studies Section [TPSS] File 287:2, NRA Records; Louis Marlo, *The Aluminum Cartel* (Washington, 1947), 9–51; Donald Wallace, *Market Control in the Aluminum Industry* (Cambridge, 1937), 24–69, 474–79. Some profit-flush firms in other industries considered entering the aluminum market: Ford envisioned aluminum plants in connection with a lease of the federal Muscle Shoals hydroelectric complex, but a series of sketchy deals fell through. James Duke (looking to invest two decades of tobacco trust profits) came close to threatening the monopoly but, after buying a hydroelectric site in Quebec and scouting for bauxite in the Canadian shield, quietly sold out to Mellon (John Winkler, *Tobacco Tycoon: The Story of James Buchanan Duke* [New York, 1942], 269–74).

38 Harold Barger and Sam Schurr, *The Mining Industries, 1899–1939* (New York, 1944), 59–93, 222–39, 280, 345; William Gates, *Michigan Copper and Boston Dollars* (Cambridge, 1951), 143–69, 188–232; C.B. Glasscock, *The War of the Copper Kings* (New York, 1935), 205; Copper and Brass Research Committee to Hoover (26 April 1921), CF 168, Hoover Papers; "Notes on Composite Views of the American Metal Co.," File 125; "Material Bearing on the Copper Industry," File 125, Sachs Papers; "Provisions in Proposed Copper Code," File 3, Leon Henderson Papers, FDRPL; "Code Authority Minutes . . . Copper Industry," CD File 172:8; "History of the Code of Fair Competition for Copper," DR 267:401; "Brass Products," CD file 172:5 (Industry Reports), NRA Records; F.H. Cooney [Gov. Montana] to FDR (18 October 1933), OF file 401, FDR Papers; Lamont to St. George (25 May 1915), File 88–17; Lamont to W. Mershon (10 September 1926), File 89–2; E. Converse to Lamont (18 Feb. 1911), File 88–17, Lamont Papers.

wars. The rubber industry's dependence on world markets, the steel industry's complex regional growth, the copper industry's anxieties about regional competition and world prices, and the efforts of all concerned to extract competitive losses from their workers only exacerbated their bloodthirsty rivalry. As the Depression wore on, the rubber industry – "which has failed to cope with its problems," as economists in the Commerce Department noted, "[and] for which the National Recovery Act itself might well have been written" – sought control over prices and distribution. The steel industry sought a renewal of regulated prices and production restrictions. Other metal industries, with varying prospects, simply sought stable prices and demand.[39]

Oil and Lumber: Conservation as Collective Action

Complex and often arcane questions of geography, resource depletion, property law, and taxes infused competition in natural resource industries. While the unique nature of their product made private regulation of resource industries exceedingly difficult, it also enabled industrial strategists to appeal to a public or national interest in stability and profitability. In their pursuit of "conservationist" solutions to competitive crises, the oil and lumber industries built on long-established relationships with state and federal politics.

The modern oil industry was born with the auto boom. Ballooning demand, the easy entry of new wells, and complex patterns of integration combined to leave the industry fat in the middle (large refiners and pipeline companies) and ragged at the edges (wildcat drillers and independent retailers). After the legal dissolution of Standard Oil in 1911, other large firms dominated the industry. In 1930, there were over 16,000 producers of oil but barely 100 refineries. Between 1920 and 1940, the top 10 refiners' share of capacity rose steadily. These leading firms deflected competitive pressures to the industry's margins by buying from independents when prices fell, using their own reserves when prices were high, and controlling sales to retailers.[40]

39 "Memo on the Rubber Institute" (23 May 1928), CF 532, Hoover Papers.
40 See George Gibb and Evelyn Knowlton, *History of the Standard Oil Company (New Jersey): The Resurgent Years, 1911–1927* (New York, 1976), 166–78, 411–12, 632–64; Arthur Johnson, *Petroleum Pipelines and Public Policy, 1906–1959* (Cambridge, 1967), 120–30, 185–206; Kendall Beaton, *Enterprise in Oil: A History of Shell in the United States* (New York, 1957), 173–74, 207, 271–73; Catherine Ellsworth, "Integration into Crude Oil Transportation in the 1930s," *BHR* 35 (1961): 180–210;

Despite concentration, competition intruded on the industry in a number of ways. New discoveries, regionally complex markets and growth, and constant fears of excess production in the shadow of ultimate shortages upset business strategies. Established firms (for whom the cost of unsuccessful drilling was an incentive to continue) and wildcatters (for whom the dream of one big well offset any concern for industry-wide stability) combined to sink an average of 25,000 new wells a year between 1910 and 1930. Major discoveries in California (1920), Oklahoma (1926), and Texas (1930) scrambled competitive conditions. The latter came at the worst possible time; markets were languishing in the trough of the Depression, and because geological peculiarities had led the major firms to ignore the field until the first well was "brought in," it was staked out by independents with little incentive to restrain production. "If some arch enemy of the petroleum industry had sought to do it the greatest possible injury," lamented Standard's Walter Teagle, "he could scarcely [have] hit upon a more diabolical scheme than to bring upon it this new field."[41]

In Texas and elsewhere, the industry was incapable of controlling production. Individual producers simply pumped as much oil as they could in as little time as possible. The root of this dilemma was the "rule of capture," a legal peculiarity (drawn from colonial hunting law) that rewarded oil to whomever pumped it to the surface. Amidst a patchwork of private claims,

Myron Watkins, *Oil: Conservation or Stabilization? A Case Study in the Organization of Industrial Control* (New York, 1937), 22–23; Henrietta Larson and Kenneth Wiggins Porter, *History of the Humble Oil Refining Company* (New York, 1976), 143–44; August Giebelhaus, *Business and Government in the Oil Industry: A Case Study of Sun Oil, 1876–1945* (Greenwich, CN, 1980), 86–87; Marquis James, *The Texaco Story: The First Fifty Years, 1902–1952* (The Texas Co., 1953), 54; John McLean and Robert Haigh, *The Growth of Integrated Oil Companies* (Norwood, 1954), 82–114, 181–288; Joseph Pratt, "The Petroleum Industry in Transition: Antitrust and the Decline of Monopoly Control in Oil," *JEH* 40 (1980): 815–37; Melvin de Chazeau and Alfred Kahn, *Integration and Competition in the Petroleum Industry* (New Haven, 1959), 121–67; "Petroleum," *Fortune* 1 (June 1930): 48; Disney telegram to Hoover (3 June 1931), File 82231/17, and Report of the Federal Oil Conservation Board (October 1932), File 82219/27, Department of Commerce Records; W.D. Egolf to Hoover (23 September 1927), CF 452, and "Oil Matters – 1931, March–May," Presidential File [PF] 217, Hoover Papers.

41 David Prindle, *Petroleum Politics and the Texas Railroad Commission* (Austin, 1981), 21–28; Federal Oil Conservation Board [FOCB] Report (October 1932), File 82219/27, Department of Commerce Records; "Minutes of meeting with mid-continent producers . . . in Mr. Teagle's Office" (May 1927), File 9, Petroleum Administration for War [PAW] Records (RG 232), Federal Records Center, Suitland, MD; (quote) Norman Nordhauser, *The Quest for Stability: Domestic Oil Regulation, 1917–1935* (New York, 1979), 70. The major firms were eventually able to buy up half of the Texas field (Giebelhaus, *Sun Oil*, 200–202).

producers tried to drain the field through their own claims, often by spacing or angling wells to reach beneath neighboring properties. In turn, each producer tried to utilize the field's natural gas to propel oil to the surface, an unregulated scramble that wasted much of the potential low-cost "flush" production. Many claimants paid conventional property taxes, a burden that made prudent pumping impossible. Refinery and pipeline investments encouraged large firms to seek even profitless sales. And the wellhead "pumping contest" forced many refiners to bear the costs of storage in an effort to "capture" oil *and* hold it off the market. In short, oil recovery through private claims depressed prices and undercut the efficiency and profitability of the entire field.[42]

Industry leaders, indifferent to physical waste but concerned with the economic waste of profitless production, pushed "conservation" as a means of quelling competition. Rival firms, however, disagreed sharply over the scope of conservationist efforts. All agreed that "unit" operation of fields would allow firms to regulate gas/oil ratios and accomplish a less-frantic rate of recovery. But large refiners equated unit operation with central ownership of all claims, whereas the independents, which were leery of the refiners, leaned towards some system of mandated cooperation or legislation. To complicate matters further, conservationism waxed and waned with market conditions. Standard supported unit operation whenever earnings and stock values dipped, and national conservation attracted serious attention only after the Oklahoma discovery flooded the market in 1927. "Price," as Walter Teagle admitted, "is the controlling factor in conservation." Conservationists also acknowledged that any effective restrictions were impossible without "a force which compels" cooperation but found again and again that "the difficulties in securing voluntary adherence are manifest and one dissenter can set the producing pace."[43]

42 Prindle, *Petroleum Politics*, 23–25; Nordhauser, *Quest for Stability*, 11–12; Donald Brand, "Corporatism, the NRA, and the Oil Industry," *Political Science Quarterly* 98 (1983): 106; Gibb and Knowlton, *Resurgent Years*, 413; Larson and Porter, *History of Humble Oil*, 184–86; Codsden Oil to Board of Directors (19 October 1933), File 494, Raskob Papers; FOCB Report (October 1932), File 82219/27, Department of Commerce Records; untitled memorandum, File 3:73, Sun Oil Papers.

43 Nordhauser, *Quest for Stability*, v, 27–31; Watkins, *Conservation or Stabilization?*, 14–16, 34–35, 44; Gibb and Knowlton, *Resurgent Years*, 434–35, 665; Report of the Committee of Nine to Secretary [of the Interior] (28 January 1928), and Farish and Teagle to FOCB (2 May 1927), File 9; Committee of Nine Meeting (10 December 1927), File 8; "Digest of Replies [from oil executives]" (1926), File 26, PAW Records; FOCB, Public Hearing (10 February 1926) File 1D:27, (quote, 19); [W.H. Gray] Study of Oil Conservation, File 7:9, Sun Oil Papers; American Petroleum

One possible source of industry discipline was trade associations, the most important of which was the American Petroleum Institute (API). Mark Requa and A.C. Bedford of Jersey Standard formed the API in 1919, and a core group of about 40 refiners, half of whom contributed over $10,000 annually, dominated its deliberations. The API accomplished very little. Although the Federal Oil Conservation Board (FOCB) gave the API free reign over federal policy by relying on it for production targets and reserve estimates, API leaders cynically distorted the figures ("whistling to keep up their courage," as G.O. Smith of the Geological Survey put it) to justify immediate political or market concerns. Reviewing the API's record, Henry Doherty of Cities Services concluded that "[v]oluntary cooperation is a pure myth" and that even "the withdrawal or modification of the Sherman antitrust law will not cure the ills of the oil industry." A conference of oil companies and representatives from oil-producing states held in Colorado Springs in 1929 highlighted the limits of the API and the industry's chronic reluctance to bear the costs of cooperation. As Requa complained: "voluntary effort went to smash. There is no blinking the fact that in the background somewhere there must be the power of the State . . . available at the call of industry."[44]

As the promise of voluntary agreements evaporated, stability became inextricably tied to legislation in the oil-producing states. In 1932, the FOCB pinpointed two problems peculiar to the U.S. oil industry: wasteful "rule of capture" production and the fact that cooperation among firms "must pass through two sieves – the barriers of Federal and State [law]." Early regulatory efforts focused on property tax reform but soon evolved into a system of production quotas or "prorationing." Yet any single state, as the FOCB noted, was unwilling to enforce prorationing "in the absence of assurance

Institute, "Confidential Memorandum . . . Conservation of Oil and Gas" (1927), CF 452, Hoover Papers; FOCB Report (October 1932), File 82219/27, Department of Commerce Records.

44 Giebelhaus, *Sun Oil*, 117–20, 130–34, 137–40; Joseph A. Pratt, "Creating Coordination in the Modern Petroleum Industry: The American Petroleum Institute and the Emergence of Secondary Organizations in Oil," *Research in Economic History* 8 (1983): 185; "Memorandum to John Elliot" (1932), File 43, PAW Records (for API contributions); Smith quoted in *NICB Proceedings* (15 May 1930), Files I:2, NICB Papers; Victor Ross to J.E. Pew (13 June 1925), File 7:37; FOCB Public Hearing (27 May 1926), File 1D:27, Sun Oil Papers; "Only Uncle Sam . . ." (May 1927), File 10; (quote) Doherty telegram to Rochester (22 January 1928), File 8; (quote) Mark Requa to Earl Oliver (9 July 1929), File 6, PAW Records; Requa, "Memorandum of Meeting in Sante Fe" (September 1929), PF 217; Requa, "Memorandum re: Colorado Springs Conference" (13 June 1929), PF 217, Hoover Papers.

by its neighbors that the market thereby relinquished would not be absorbed by *their* unrestricted production." States were unable to balance internal stability with their thirst for a greater share of national markets. Prorationing proved impossible in fields that crossed state lines, and the entire patchwork of state prorationing law unravelled in East Texas; the Texas Railroad Commission prohibited the shipment of "hot" oil, (production exceeding state quotas), but never came close to controlling the interstate flow in that region. When a federal court struck down the commission's authority, troops were needed to put down a "production insurrection." The situation in other states was not much better. The major firms admitted that the establishment and the enforcement of statewide proration agreements were two very different tasks and pled for relief from "voluminous . . . dangerous and ignorant State laws."[45]

Eager for order but fearing political control, oil firms turned to a mix of private and interstate cooperation. An Oil States Advisory Committee proposed and drafted an Interstate Oil Compact in 1928–31. But state laws leaned on federal prohibition of interstate commerce in hot oil, and the committee "concluded that only federal action could solve the dilemmas of the oil industry." While other industries exhausted private, state, and interstate regulation in that order before turning to federal politics, the oil industry juggled all simultaneously and grasped at federal solutions when others proved impossible to enforce. The focus of these efforts was the FOCB, formed in 1924 with the hope (as expressed by President Coolidge) that "the oil industry itself might be permitted to determine its own future."[46] The FOCB finessed constitutional control over federal reserves, war

45 (Quote) Report of the FOCB (October 1932), File 82219/27, Department of Commerce Records, Nordhauser, *Quest for Stability*, 28–30, 63–95; John Frey to Wilbur (6 July 1932), File 12; FOCB "Conference with Committee of Oil Company Executives" (23 May 1927), File 9, PAW Records; J.R. Pearson to FDR (27 July 1935), OF 56:1, FDR Papers; Teagle to Hoover (7 December 1929), PF 217, Hoover Papers; McLean and Haigh, *Growth of Integrated Oil Companies*, 82–90, 186–88, 232, 289–301; Wallace Lovejoy and Paul Homan, *Economic Aspects of Oil Conservation Regulation* (Baltimore, 1967), 33–47; de Chazeau and Kahn, *Integration and Competition in the Petroleum Industry*, 121–26; Samuel Pettengill, *Hot Oil: The Problem of Petroleum* (New York, 1936); Prindle, *Petroleum Politics*, 30–37; Giebelhaus, *Sun Oil*, 200–202; Extracts from Hearings on Thomas Bill (April 1935), File 4:3; M.E. Croom to the Board of Directors (15 December 1934), File 7:11, Sun Oil Papers; Larson and Porter, *Humble Oil*, 318–324; (quote) Doherty telegram to Rochester (22 January 1928), File 8, PAW Records. State laws summarized in FOCB, "State and Federal Conservation Laws and Regulations" (1931), File 5, PAW Records; Blake Murphy, *Conservation of Oil and Gas: A Legal History, 1948* (Chicago, 1948), 19–529.

46 Gary D. Libecap, "The Political Economy of the Establishment of the Interstate

powers, and interstate commerce to gird the industry's organizational efforts. But the industry itself remained skeptical, and firms leapt off the federal bandwagon whenever their interests were threatened. An FOCB-sponsored trade practice code fell apart in 1928 "because it lacked enforcement powers and minority interests were able to disregard its rules at will." Although designed to overcome private and political collective action dilemmas, the FOCB only highlighted (as Sun Oil executives complained) "the nearsightedness, selfishness and brigandage of men in the industry." In 1931, Henry Doherty agreed that "until such time as the Federal Government takes action regarding oil, our industry will, in my opinion, remain in a state of chaos . . . wallowing around helplessly, impotent and without a sound idea in [its] head of how to make a fundamental correction of [its] troubles."[47]

Some escaped the persistent turmoil of the domestic market by expanding abroad, supplanting the British and Dutch in the Middle East, South America, Asia, and eastern Europe. Under the aegis of the State Department (Secretary of State Hughes would later become general counsel for the API), direct investment in foreign oil increased from $143 million to $854 million

Oil Cartel, 1933–1940," in *Emergence of the Modern Political Economy*, ed. Robert Higgs (Greenwich, 1985), 53–81; "Memorandum for Secretary Wilbur" (19 March 1929), File 20, Ray Wilbur Papers, HCHPL; J.S. Cullinan to Representative of the Industry in California" (11 April 1928), File 10; "Memorandum on Interstate Oil Conservation Compacts" (1931), File 21; "Preliminary Draft of an Interstate Oil Conservation Compact" (14 April 1931), File 4; J.S. Cullinan to Work (20 December 1927), File 12, PAW Records; (quote) "Confidential Report . . . Committee of Nine" (January 1928), CF 453, Hoover Papers; National Committee of Commissioners on Uniform State Laws, "Second Report of Oil and Gas Resolution" (1926), File 20, Nathan MacChesney Papers, HCHPL; Nordhauser, *Quest for Stability*, 19–58, 76–77; Oil States Advisory Committee to Wilbur (9 April 1931), File 82231/17, Department of Commerce Records; Gerald Nash, *United States Oil Policy, 1890–1964* (Pittsburgh, 1968), 125–26; Northcutt Ely, *Oil Conservation through Interstate Agreement* (Washington, 1933); McLean and Haigh, *Growth of Integrated Oil Companies*, 109–10; Coolidge quoted in Watkins, *Conservation or Stabilization?*, 42.

47 Murphy, *Legal History of Conservation*, 599–709; Doherty to FDR (12 May 1933), OF 56:1, FDR Papers; (quote) Myron Taylor to Hoover (11 November 24), CF 29, Hoover Papers; "Letters from the Oil Industry," File 14; Mark Requa to Earl Oliver (9 July 1929), File 6 ("Colorado Springs"); Committee of Nine Meeting (10 December 1927), File 8; Rochester to Wilbur (26 September 1930), File 11; (quote) "Transcript of Code Hearing" (n.d.), File 53, PAW Records; Raoul Desverne to Raskob (6 March 1931), File 602(6), Raskob Papers; Rochester, "Memorandum for Secretary Ickes" (1 April 1933), File 20, Wilbur Papers; API to Hoover (4 February 1931), PF 217, Hoover Papers; Himmelberg, *Origins of the NRA*, 95–103; "Some Underlying Principles Controlling the Solution to the Problem of Oil and Gas Conservation" (n.d.), File 7:9, Sun Oil Papers; Wilbur to Lamont (30 October 1931), File 82218/27; (quote) Doherty to Lamont (26 October 1931), File 82218/28; Doherty to Ely (18 Nov. 1931), File 12, PAW Records.

between 1914 and 1929, and imports of refined oil tripled. But foreign expansion was complicated by a pastiche of international rationing and concession agreements (such as the 1928 "Red Line Agreement" among British and U.S. firms in the Middle East), the competition of other oil powers, and the threat of nationalization.[48] Multinationals pressed for domestic restrictions and a free flow of imports, while independents that relied on midcontinental fields and import-threatened coastal markets sought import quotas in tandem with conservation laws. In turn, many multinationals were so desperate for domestic stability that they were willing to voluntarily restrict imports (which would raise prices anyway). Federal politicians were torn between alienating oil-producing states by leaving oil unprotected and threatening lucrative prospects in Latin America and the Middle East. In short, oil interests could not decide whether imports were a threat that depressed prices and undercut domestic conservation or a savior that conserved American reserves and pressed marginal wells out of production.[49]

48 John DeNovo, "The Movement for an Aggressive American Policy Abroad, 1918–1920," *American Historical Review* 61 (1956): 854–76; Stephen Randall, *United States Foreign Oil Policy, 1919–1948* (Kingston and Montreal, 1985), 14–42, 62–77; Stephen Rabe, *The Road to OPEC: United States Relations With Venezuela, 1919–1976* (Austin, 1982), 15–42; Mira Wilkins, "Multinational Oil Companies in South America in the 1920s," *BHR* 48 (1974): 414–46; Gibb and Knowlton, *Resurgent Years*, 278–408; "Memorandum Regarding Foreign Oil Policy of the United States" (1921), "Oil Supplies" (1921), "The International Petroleum Situation" (1922), and miscellaneous documents on specific countries, CF 452, Hoover Papers. On Mexico, see Lorenzo Meyer, *Mexico and the United States in the Oil Controversy, 1917–1942*, trans. Muriel Vasconellos (Austin, 1972), 44–172; Stephen Kane, "Corporate Power and Foreign Policy: Efforts of American Oil Companies to Influence United States Relations with Mexico, 1921–1928," *Diplomatic History* 1 (1977): 170–98; Thomas Lamont to Charles Hughes (16 August 1921), File 197–4; Teagle to Lamont (18 August 1921), File 197–9; Oil Producers to Hughes (18 August 1921), File 197–11, Lamont Papers. On eastern Europe, see Standard Oil Company, *Standard Oil Company and Oil Production in Hungary by Maort, 1931–1948* (New York, 1949); George Gibb and Bennett Wall, *Teagle of Jersey Standard* (New Orleans, 1974), 184–220. On Asia, see David Wilson, "Principles and Profits: Standard Oil Responses to Chinese Nationalism, 1925–1927," *Pacific Historical Review* 46 (1977): 625–47; Peter Reed, "Standard Oil in Indonesia, 1898–1928," *BHR* 32 (1958): 311–37; Irvine Anderson, *The Standard Vacuum Oil Company and United States East Asian Policy, 1933–1941* (Princeton, 1976), 3–34.

49 Telegram from Governors of Texas, Kansas, New Mexico, and Oklahoma (n.d.), PF 217, and Teagle to Work (17 April 1925), CF 453, Hoover Papers; Teagle to Lamont (23 March 31), and Farish to Lamont (20 June 1931), File 82231, Department of Commerce Records; E.S. Rochester [FOCB], "Confidential Memorandum for Secretary Wilbur" (28 January 1931), File 20; Feiker Memo on Oil Tariff [Texaco] (13 January 1932), File 21, Wilbur Papers; "Digest of Replies" (1926), File 26; Rochester to Wilbur (26 January 1931), File 11; Rochester to Wilbur (7 February

Although easily the most serious, the domestic-internationalist dispute was not the only rift among oil producers. Firms squared off over a myriad of organizational, regional, and political issues. Some, trusting their influence in local politics, wanted to confine regulatory solutions to the states; others, seeing state solutions as futile, lobbied for federal action. And even those that recognized the necessity of regulation were divided over the threat posed by state and federal solutions ("A little federal control," spat an executive of Sun Oil, ". . . is like being a little pregnant") that might outlast their immediate utility.[50]

Like the oil industry, the lumber industry suffered from cutthroat competition, disorganization, and inconsistent state regulation; however, it could not lean on growing markets, foreign expansion, or a politically influential corporate core. The lumber industry, as one executive noted, "was on the toboggan slide long before the stock market crashed." Sales lagged through the 1920s with the substitution for wood of cement, steel, and brick in construction and of paper in packing. Production, however, was driven by the weight of fixed investment and intense competition over slipping markets; timber consumption fell over 60 percent from 1915 to 1935, but investment ballooned from $2 billion to $10 billion. "Circumstances which sharpened the degree of competition also handicapped the chances for success in regulating the industry," as one observer noted. "The spread of the industry into new regions and the increasing numbers of mills gave lumbermen the desire to diminish competition artificially; yet the ease of making agreements and maintaining them was thereby lessened." High fixed costs, debt, and excess capacity encouraged industry combination "but by their nature [also] conspired to force continued production in many mills even when operations were conducted at a loss."[51]

1931), File 11; Oklahoma Company to Wilbur (15 January 1931), File 11, PAW Records; J.E. Pew to C.B. Ames [Texaco] (10 May 1932), File 3:7; Extracts from Hearings on Thomas Bill (April 1935), File 4:3, Sun Oil Papers.

50 Nordhauser, *Quest for Stability*, 7–11, 29–30, 44–56; Giebelhaus, *Sun Oil*, 112–16; Gibb and Wall, *Teagle of Jersey Standard*, 259; U.S. Senate, Committee on Finance, *Investigation of the National Recovery Act* (Washington, 1935), 1483–1525; Ridell to Hoover (3 February 1925), CF 453, Hoover Papers; Wirt Franklin "Requa's Conservation Policy" (June 1929), File 10; J.S. Cullinan to B.O. Mahaffey (5 March 1928), File 10, PAW Records; J.E. Pew to J.H. Pew (26 May 1927), File 1D:31; Pew Memo (12 July 1935), File 3:7; J.E. Pew to J.H. Pew (25 November 1925), File 7:37; (quote) Thompson address (15 July 1939), File 3:40; FOCB, Public Hearing (27 May 1926), File 1D:27, Sun Oil Papers.

51 "Analysis of Production, Wages and Employment . . . Forest Products," File 1173–2, Pierre DuPont Papers; Fabricant, *Employment in Manufacturing*, 31; History of

Lumber markets were scattered and disorganized. Independent whole-salers and jobbers handled distribution, and many different varieties and grades of wood were sold through local, regional, and national networks. Lumber was produced by both permanent mills, which located near large stands of timber and portable or railroad-based mills (especially in the South), which were able to enter and exit the industry easily. The industry was migratory, exhausting natural and human resources in one area and then moving on, in words of one lumber baron, like "a large army in disorderly retreat." Between 1890 and 1930, the share of production held by the north-eastern and Great Lakes states fell from 55 to 15 percent, while the South peaked at 40 percent in 1910 and the Northwest grew steadily to 25 percent in 1920 and 35 percent in 1930. By the mid-1920s, lumbering in the north-eastern and Great Lakes states was confined to specialty woods and pulp from second-growth forests. Small hardwood mills and a pine industry (par-tially exhausted by a rush of demand in World War I) dominated the south-ern industry. In the Northwest, large corporate mills (for example, Weyer-hauser and Bloedel) created a more permanent pine, spruce, and fir industry and invested heavily in land.[52]

the Code of Fair Competition for Lumber and Timber, DR File 267:9, NRA Re-cords; John Blodgett quoted in "Transcript of Second Executive Meeting" (1931), File 1977, Timber Conservation Board [TCB] Records, Bureau of Foreign and Domestic Commerce, RG 151, National Archives; (quote) Lee James, "Restrictive Agreements and Practices in the Lumber Industry, 1880–1939," *SEJ* 13 (1946–47): 117.

52 Wilson Compton, *The Organization of the Lumber Industry* (Chicago, 1916), 3–7, 54, 61, 128; Walter Mead, *Competition and Oligopsony in the Douglas Fir Industry* (Berke-ley, 1966), 6–7, 21–22, 39; Alfred Van Tassel, *Mechanization in the Lumber Industry* (Philadelphia, 1940), 1–22, 40–77, 93, 112; Robert Ficken, *The Forested Land: A History of Lumbering in Western Washington* (Seattle, 1987), 168–70; Joseph Zaremba, *Economics of the American Lumber Industry* (New York, 1963), 18; Ruth Allen, *East Texas Lumber Workers* (Austin, 1961), 37; James, "Restrictive Agreements," 120–21; Blodgett, "A Survey of the Lumber Industry," Chamber Of Commerce [CoC] Minutes 13 (1925), Chamber of Commerce Papers, Hagley Museum; *Report of the National Lumber Manufacturers Association* (Chicago, 1925), 61–65 (quote, 63); Ver-non Jensen, *Lumber and Labor* (New York, 1945), 8–18; Richard Judd, *Aroostook: A Century of Logging in Northern Maine* (Orono, 1988), 173–99; James Fickle, *The New South and the "New Competition": Trade Association Development in the Southern Pine Industry* (Urbana, 1980), 1–9, 79–105; Archer Mayor, *Southern Timberman: The Legacy of William Buchanan* (Athens, 1988), 120–32; Robert Maxwell and Rob-ert Baker, *Sawdust Empire: The Texas Lumber Industry, 1830–1940* (College Station, 1983), 194–99. On mergers in the Northwest, see Charles Twining, *Phil Weyerhau-ser: Lumberman* (Seattle, 1985), 94; Robert Ficken, *Lumber and Politics: The Career of Mark E. Reed* (Seattle, 1979), 154–55; William Robbins, *Lumberjacks and Legis-lators: Political Economy of the U.S. Lumber Industry, 1890–1940* (College Station,

Migration and regionalism undercut the industry's political power and exposed it to inconsistent patterns of regulation and taxation. As a safeguard against corruption, most states prohibited tax discrimination among types of property. Lumber firms paid conventional property taxes whether or not land was being logged. As a result, mills (especially in the Northwest, where a shortage scare had spurred huge speculative land purchases) liquidated resources with little regard for markets or the land. Taxes encouraged exploitation of immature stands and discouraged private responsibility for cutover land. Counties and states were reluctant to reform an often lucrative tax system but, under industry pressure, many introduced optional yield taxes on cut lumber. In the Midwest, yield taxes applied only to small holdings, and most mills preferred to pay property taxes for the few years of logging they had left. In the South, large firms opposed yield taxes (which favored small competitors) and resisted granting new tax authority to the states. In the Northwest, most mills appreciated the logic of the yield tax but also balked at the prospect of tax-gouging by state legislatures. And wood-using industries (including the politically potent building trades) lobbied for maintenance of property taxes (which kept timber prices down).[53]

Some states toyed with interstate compacts in an attempt to escape the competitive logic of state law, but as forester E.T. Ealen observed, this was "representative of a very amateurish understanding of the function of state legislation, which can never be depended upon to further a consistently nation-wide policy." The only federal attempt to provide relief was the Clarke-McNary Act of 1924, which provided matching funds for fire protection and encouraged studies of state tax law. In all, state tax reform was minimal, and excess production continued unabated. "Lumber companies owning forest land almost all expect to go out of business within a few years," noted the Virginia Forest Service; "they are afraid of carrying charges and

1982), 148–49; "Problems and Needs of the West Coast Lumber Industry," File 87338, Department of Commerce Records; Lumber Division to Hoover (5 February 1927); 1 July 1927), CF 376, Hoover Papers.

53 Wilson Compton, "Recent Tendencies in the Reform of Forest Taxation," *Journal of Political Economy* [*JPE*] 23 (1915): 971–74; Robbins, *Lumberjacks and Legislators*, 57–64; James, "Restrictive Practices," 116–19; Harold Steen, *The U.S. Forest Service* (Seattle, 1976), 190–91; "Problems and Needs of the West Coast Lumber Industry" (1931), File 87338; "Economic Conditions of the Southern Pine Industry," (1930), File 87338; Comptom to Lamont (23 July 1932), (1931), File 87338; Fred Fairchild, "Progress Report of the Forest Taxation Inquiry" (1931), File 87338; TCB, "Taxation of Timberlands" (1932), File 87338; "Yield Tax on Timber" (1932), File 87338, Department of Commerce Records; R.C. Hall, "Forest Land Taxes" (1931), File 1985, TCB Records; NICB Minutes 86 (18 December 1924), NICB Papers.

taxes laid on young timber." The federal Timber Conservation Board agreed that the "annual burden of taxation on mature standing timber . . . is the most important single factor forcing sale or cutting of timber." Excess capacity and heavy fixed charges, in turn, transformed any perk in demand into a competitive price war. "There are two things you will seldom find in the lumber industry," observed *Fortune* in 1933, "a Democrat and a man who won't cut prices."[54]

Lumber firms and lumber states pursued "conservationist" solutions which, as in oil, were aimed not at saving resources for future use but at curtailing current exploitation enough to raise prices, dampen competition, and pass the costs of resource management on to consumers and taxpayers. Industry-promoted conservation focused on reforestation; with new growth 50 or 100 years from commercial potential, responsibility for forested land posed a classic free-rider problem. Lumber interests lobbied for state purchase of cut-over land, efforts that critics dismissed as "a skin game to fool people" and "a big scheme to try and sell land that was not worthwhile for agriculture" to unsuspecting farmers. Many stump-ridden tracts became "parkland" under the Clarke-McNary Act; in Texas alone, lumber companies reaped $3 million from such sales. The industry also sponsored state and federal legislation of fire protection, a public good that all needed (although firms with large land holdings needed it more) but for which no one firm was willing to pay.[55] Such laws were often little more than good forestry

54 (Quote) E.T. Ealen to D. Meyers (27 June 1932), File 1974; "Taxation Letters," File 1983, TCB Records; TCB, "Taxation of Timberlands," File 87338; Arthur Hyde to Lamont (10 September 1932), File 87338, Department of Commerce Records; Kentucky Forest Service, "Forest Fire Protection in Kentucky" (1926), File V:251; Richard Jones, "The Forest Resources of Virginia" (1919), (quote 9), File V:321, Papers of the Pennsylvania-Virginia Corporation, Westmoreland Coal Papers, Hagley Museum; NICB Minutes 88 (19 February 1925), NICB Papers; William Condrell, "How Has Taxation Affected the Growth of Forest Products Industries?" in *Proceedings of the First National Colloquium on the History of the Forest Products Industries* (New Haven, 1967), 144–63; Steen, *Forest Service*, 173–91; Maxwell and Baker, *Sawdust Empire*, 176; Ficken, *The Forested Land*, 169–71, 176; Catherine Baldwin, *Making the Most of the Best: Willamette Industries' Seventy-Five Years* (Portland, 1982), 33–35; "Economic Conditions in the Southern Pine Industry," File 87338, Department of Commerce Records; Clair Wilcox, *Competition and Monopoly in American Industry*, TNEC Monograph 20 (Washington, 1941), 23–24; (quote) "Democrats in Big Business," *Fortune* 7 (January 1933): 21.
55 Axel Oxholm to Lamont (8 October 1931), File 82219/7; J. Blodgett to TCB (17 November 1931), File 87338, Department of Commerce Records; Mayor, *Southern Timberman*, 116–17; (quote) Fickle, *The New South and the "New Competition"*, 242; "Public Requisition of Forest Lands," File 1974, TCB Records; Maxwell and Baker, *Sawdust Empire*, 207–9; Steen, *Forest Service*, 174–76, 194. The NLMA, Weyer-

practices already followed by larger mills and whose imposition on smaller mills might drive them out of business.

Alongside "conservation" and tax reform, the industry also organized privately. The National Lumber Manufacturers' Association (NLMA) had come under FTC scrutiny before 1920, but allegations of price-fixing confused industry anxieties with monopolistic outcomes. The NLMA promoted open pricing and standardization with little success. Although the industry (in the *Hardwood Manufacturers* and *Maple Flooring* decisions) became a test case for "associationalism," its unfounded faith in private regulation simply discredited the voluntarist path promoted by Hoover's Department of Commerce. The futility of private organization turned the industry toward political solutions. Hoover held a lumber conference in 1922, out of which a Central Committee on Lumber Standards was formed; recast as the National Committee on Wood Utilization (NCWU) in 1925, it blithely encouraged wood use and conservation in an effort to raise the value of standing timber "to a point where reforestation [would become] a profitable industry." The NLMA staffed and directed the NCWU and badgered its members to underwrite NCWU efforts. After 1930, the NLMA hoped a new Timber Conservation Board might give "governmental sanction to [its] ideas of industry stabilization."[56]

The lumber industry was fiercely protectionist, although its anxieties had more to do with the state of the industry than any import threat. Southern

hauser, and California lumberman T.B. Walker each contributed $100,000 toward a Chair of Fire Protection at the Yale School of Forestry; when appropriations for the state fire warden lapsed in Washington, the companies picked up the tab (Steen, *Forest Service*, 135, 174).

56 Ralph Bryant, *Lumber: Its Manufacture and Distribution* (New York, 1922), 305–62; James, "Restrictive Practices," 116–19; Robbins, *Lumberjacks and Legislators*, 35–55, 82–83, 134–37; Fickle, *The New South and the "New Competition"*, 12, 33–64; "National Hardwood Lumber Association," CF 430; Southern Sash, Door and Millwork Manufacturers' Association to Hoover (12 April 1922), CF 166, Hoover Papers; Ellis Hawley, "Three Facets of Hooverian Associationalism: Lumber, Aviation, and Movies, 1921–1930," in *Regulation in Perspective*, ed. Thomas McGraw (Cambridge, 1981), 102; (quote) "National Committee on Wood Utilization," File 1971; "Final Meeting of [TCB] Advisory Committee," (1932), File 1973; Compton to Bowman (17 December 1931), File 1974, TCB Records; "National Committee on Wood Utilization: Its Organization and Work" (1925), File 82219/27; F.W. Willard to Roy Chapin (10 January 1933), File 82219/27; (quote) Axel Oxholm to Lamont (25 Jan. 1933), File 82219/27; Peebles memo for Feifer (11 May 1933), File 87338; Feiker memo for Lamont (13 Aug. 1932), File 87339; TCB Release (1 August 1932), File 87338; Compton to Kerlin (28 February 1933), File 87338; Memo for Chapin (20 August 1932), File 87338; Department of Commerce Records.

and midwestern firms lobbied for higher tariffs, and after losing ground in 1913, they regained high rates with the Fordney-McCumber Tariff of 1922 (Representative Fordney of Michigan owned a lumber mill). The fact that many large firms had extensive holdings in Canada complicated international strategies; protectionism often hinged on the accessibility and profitability of standing timber on either side of the border. "Pressure to admit the cheap Canadian product . . . will be exerted by the very American lumber interests which at present insist on protection," one Canadian observer predicted, "for, having cut all the stumpage on their own side of the line in which there is reasonable profit, they will undoubtedly move over to the Canadian side." In turn, tariff battles were often fought between those who owned Canadian timber and those who did not, although multinationals went along with import restriction in the early 1930s because, as Secretary of Commerce Lamont noted drily, "they can buy it from Texas cheaper." Despite hopes of dumping surpluses through export combinations, sales abroad were never significant.[57]

Although lumbering was labor-intensive, labor relations only became an important concern after the industry settled in the Northwest. In the South, employment was sporadic and seasonal, wages were low and contracted on dismal terms, and work benefits were rare. Southern mills also exploited racial divisions and vagrancy laws to ensure a cheap and quiescent work-force.[58] Northwest mills provided sustained employment and marginally better conditions, but workers still bore the brunt of industry instability. "Price reductions are coming out of labor and labor only," admitted one employer during a 1929 price war, noting that some "have cut wages to $1.80 or $2.00 a day" and that one mill was "starting off with $1.35 base wage and putting

57 Steen, *Forest Service*, 176; Fickle, *New South and the "New Competition"*, 35–38; (quote) Arthur Lower, *The North American Assault on the Canadian Forest* (Toronto, 1938), 185, 198, 200; Robbins, *Lumberjacks and Legislators*, 65–67; Lamont to R.W. Mercer (23 July 1931), File 82231, Department of Commerce Records; Lamont quoted in "Transcript of Second Executive [TCB] Meeting" (1931), File 1977, TCB Records; on export associations, see Oxholm to Hoover (2 September 1925), CF 376, Hoover Papers.
58 Allen, *East Texas Lumber Workers*, 35–40, 98–119, 142–90; Jensen, *Lumber and Labor*, 73–93; Jerrel Shoffner, "Forced Labor in the Florida Forests, 1880–1950," *Forest History* 25 (1981): 14–25; John Howard, *The Negro in the Lumber Industry* (Philadelphia, 1970); Fickle, *New South and the "New Competition*," 287–329; Charlotte Todes, *Labor and Lumber* (New York, 1931), 75–101, 170–78; Mayor, *Southern Timberman*, 60; "Economic Conditions in the Southern Pine Industry," File 87338, Department of Commerce Records.

its men on a profit sharing plan when they know in advance there aren't going to be any profits."[59]

The Industrial Workers of the World (IWW) made some progress after 1913, but under the pretext of guaranteeing spruce for the war effort, Secretary of War Baker broke a 1917 strike with federal troops (and the blessing of the AFL). Baker and the industry installed the Loyal Legion of Loggers and Lumberman (the 4L) as an industry-wide "company union," and wages fell steadily (from $4.60 to $2.40 a day in Puget Sound mills). Meanwhile, the IWW and the AFL battled over jurisdiction in the Northwest through the 1920s and early 1930s, and although the former would never regain a foothold, its presence forced the AFL along a more progressive path than it might otherwise have followed. For their part, a few large firms hoped that either the 4L or AFL unions would take wages out of competition and drive out smaller mills, but they did little to encourage them.[60]

Both the oil and lumber industries approached the New Deal with a clear sense of what they needed and an even clearer sense of the frustrations of private and state-level solutions. Regulation "must have teeth in it and be administered by the federal government," argued oil executive Frank Craven; "the States have proven that . . . they cannot handle it." Lumber industry leaders hailed the opportunity to draft a National Recovery Administration (NRA) code as the culmination of a "continually exerted effort to fix prices and to buttress such prices by control of production."[61] While lumber interests looked to the federal government as the sole source of stability, some oil interests considered international investment as an escape from domestic competition and regulation. Neither industry paid much attention to labor, which was of little cost or concern in oil and disorganized in lumber.

59 Jensen, *Lumber and Labor*, 104–8, (quote, 152); William Robbins, *Hard Times in Paradise: Coos Bay, Oregon, 1850–1986* (Seattle, 1988), 54–79.

60 Jensen, *Lumber and Labor*, 12–34, 104–61; Jerry Lembcke, "Uneven Development, Class Formation and Industrial Unionism in the Wood Products Industry," *Political Power and Social Theory* 4 (1984): 184–204; Ficken, *The Forested Land*, 140–63; Twining, *Phil Weyerhauser*, 118–20; Robbins, *Hard Times in Paradise*, 50–51; Edward Mitelman, "The Loyal Legion of Loggers and Lumbermen," *JPE* 31 (1933): 313–41.

61 (Quote) Frank Craven to Johnson (4 August 1933), File 40, PAW Records; History of the Code of Fair Competition for Lumber and Timber, DR File 267:9, NRA Records (quote, 3); "Memorandum for Chief Counsel," File 7, Henderson Papers.

Chemicals: Politics and Protection

The chemical industry was a strategic peculiarity. Like the auto industry, it emerged from the technological and economic watershed of World War I as one of the leaders of the interwar economy, its products central to the consumer-goods boom. Like the rubber and steel industries, however, the chemical industry competed in chaotic producer-goods markets. And like the oil industry, rapid postwar growth and consolidation made the chemical industry an important (if ambivalent) international player. As a result, the chemical industry was both intensely involved in politics and chronically leery of political intrusions. While most industries were entwined in complex patterns of state and federal law, the major chemical firms had two simple political concerns: international competition and corporate taxation.

Before 1914, the international chemical industry was dominated by British soda firms, German dye firms, and international fertilizer cartels. The U.S. industry was largely an appendage to the paper, textile, glass, tanning, and oil industries and (excepting DuPont) consisted primarily of small firms producing industrial chemicals for local use. World War I changed all that. Munitions profits financed postwar expansion and diversification, and U.S. firms counted the fruits of German research as a spoil of victory (courtesy of the Alien Property Custodian). The postwar auto boom led to the commercial development of cellulose and other synthetics as well as constant innovation in oil refining. As long as high protective tariffs guarded profits, large firms exploited old markets and aggressively created new ones. The industry remained profitable even through the Depression, averaging a 28 percent return through 1929–37.[62]

Yet the industry was vulnerable on a number of fronts. The armistice sent prices "tumbling like a spring freshet over a milldam" and underscored excess capacity throughout the industry. While the number of firms fell by half between 1914 and 1933, mergers merely diversified the holdings of large firms, leaving meager barriers to entry in many products. Burdened by high research costs and rapid technological turnover, chemical firms staked out

---

62 "Some Facts Relative to the Chemical Industry," (1921), CF 86, Hoover Papers; L.F. Haber, *The Chemical Industry* (Oxford, 1971), 2–9, 26–29, 174–80, 238–39; William Haynes, *American Chemical Industry* (New York, 1945–54), 2:55–123, 141–81, 277, 332–46, 3:352–68, 4:4–5, 31–53; Manufacturing Chemists' Association, *Chemical Facts and Figures* (Washington, 1945), 3–5; "Chemical Industry: I," *Fortune* 16 (December 1937): 87. On the patent grab, see Gerard Zilg, *DuPont: Behind the Nylon Curtain* (Englewood Cliffs, 1974): 178–97.

market territory and guarded it jealously. Competitive pressures and production costs pressed established firms to consolidate (although some, such
as DuPont, invested outside the already overgrown industry). By the 1930s,
DuPont, Union Carbide, Allied Chemical & Dye, Monsanto, Dow, and
American Cyanimide dominated the industry; of these, DuPont was the most
influential. "The chemical industry has regulated itself in a manner that
would please even a Soviet Commissar," as the editors of *Fortune* noted;
"the industry waltzes decorously, its Grand Marshall, du Pont, viewing it
with a happy and beneficent eye."[63]

On the political front, chemical firms reserved a special enmity for the tax
system. In their eyes, state and federal corporate taxes undervalued depreciation, ignored research costs, and penalized rapid technological change, and
dividend taxes failed to account for the industry's loose diversification, forcing
firms to consolidate or absorb subsidiaries. The industry's fixation with taxes
was hardened by the fact that the DuPonts, unlike established dynasties that
had spirited their fortunes away in trusts and foundations, counted their
wealth as current taxable income. The DuPonts' prominent support for prohibition repeal was largely animated by the hope that controlled liquor sales
might replace income taxes as a source of government revenue.[64]

International competition, in which U.S. firms were often reluctant play-
ers, was an equally troublesome threat. Foreign chemical giants (especially
Germany's I.G. Farben and England's ICI) dominated their markets to a far
greater extent than their U.S. counterparts, which sought both continued
protection and greater access to international markets (a political contradiction routinely encouraged by the Department of Commerce). DuPont, Carbide, and the other major firms pursued export cartelization through the
Webb Act and arranged various technical and market deals with European

63 (Quote) Haber, *The Chemical Industry*, 250; Jules Backman, *The Economics of the
    Chemical Industry* (Washington, 1970), 8–9, 58–77; Haynes, *American Chemical In-
    dustry*, 4:19–32; (quote) "Chemical Industry," 157. The top firms each had a bit of
    a market niche: DuPont in fabrics, fabric finishes, and plastics; Allied in heavy
    chemicals (alkali and coal tar derivatives); Union Carbide in electric furnace products
    (battery metals, carbides, and alloys); American Cyanamid in fertilizers and mining
    chemicals; Dow in brine products (iodines, dyes, aspirin, and insecticides); and
    Monsanto in fine chemicals (especially saccharin) and heavy acids.
64 Haynes, *American Chemical Industry*, 4:28–29; Irenée DuPont to Hoover (21 March
    1921), CF 186, Hoover Papers; P. S. DuPont to American Taxpayers League (10
    June 1932), File 1119; P.S. DuPont to ATL (27 January 1930), File 1119; P.S.
    DuPont to John Pollard (21 March 1932), File 765:1; P.S. DuPont to Alfred Sloan
    (9 May 1932), File 1173; P.S. DuPont to L.D. Staplin (16 January 1936), File 765:2,
    Pierre S. DuPont Papers.

firms. DuPont established ambivalent ties with ICI and I.G. Farben while continuing to oppose reconstruction (underwritten by Standard Oil and U.S. banks) of the German and French chemical industries. The potash, sulphur, and nitrates cartels, in which U.S. presence was minimal, further distorted the international strategies of domestically based firms.[65]

As a result of all this, the industry found itself increasingly isolated from the mainstream of contemporary opinion regarding the relationship between business and government. Although competition was sporadically severe, the major chemical firms did not see political regulation as a realistic or welcome solution. And wage labor, employed to do little more than "keep the plant clean, turn a few valves, [and] weigh final products," accounted for less than 20 percent of costs, although DuPont (reflecting its investments elsewhere) worried constantly about unions.[66] The industry's response to the Depression and New Deal echoed these concerns. Almost alone in the business community, chemical firms desired neither domestic organization nor free trade and opposed any initiatives which contributed to a general tax burden.

Paper: The Tyranny of Fixed Costs

The experience of the paper industry magnified a dilemma confronted, to some degree, by many others – the technical complexity, expense, and scale of modern production discouraged the mobility of resources necessary to "clear" markets and establish an equilibrium of supply and demand. In this industry, fixed costs replaced demand as the arbiter of production and virtually guaranteed destructive competition; in turn, its organizational efforts were confounded by intense regional competition, the economic and political power of its core consumers, and its migration (beyond the reach of state or federal regulators) into Canada after 1920.

The U.S. paper industry consisted of large mills (most with financial ties to lumbering, publishing, or both), which produced their own pulp and manufactured paperboard, newsprint, and kraft, book, and wrapping papers; and smaller "convertors," which purchased pulp and produced specialty

65 Thomas Ferguson, "Critical Realignment: The Fall of the House of Morgan and the Origins of the New Deal" (Ph.D diss., Princeton University, 1981), 456–538; Haber, *The Chemical Industry*, 262–65; Graham Taylor and Patricia Sudnik, *DuPont and the International Chemical Industry* (Boston, 1984): 75–93, 111–41: Haynes, *American Chemical Industry*, 3:420–29, 4:32–60, 390–406; R. Hall to Hoover, (18 April 1928), CF 86, Hoover Papers; Manufacturing Chemists' Association, *Chemical Facts and Figures*, 6–7; "Inevitable Competitor," *Fortune* 5 (May 1932): 58.
66 "Chemical Industry: I," 157.

(stationery, cigarette, sanitary) papers. The top eight firms controlled half of pulp production through the 1920s, and regional concentration (Crown-Zellerbach on the Pacific Coast and Canadian paper and power conglomerates) was even stronger. Principal U.S. firms included newsprint giants Great Northern and International Paper, loosely integrated pulp and paper manufacturers St. Regis and George Mead, sanitary paper mills Kimberley-Clark and Scot Paper, and a few rapidly growing kraft and paperboard firms. The industry's traditional core was in the Northeast and Midwest, but growth was concentrated in Canadian newsprint, southern kraft, and northwestern papers after 1925.[67]

Technically, the pulp and paper industry changed little through the early twentieth century. Mechanically produced groundwood pulp was inexpensive but discolored and perishable, suitable only for newsprint. Fine paper mills used sulfites to break down and bleach pulp fibers; after 1915, mass paper mills began using sulfate pulp to produce a more durable, brownish paper. Initially shunned by older, northern mills, the "kraft" process was widely accepted once chemical tinkering made it possible to use cheap southern pine for kraft paper and kraft-based paperboard became a popular packaging substitute. By the late 1920s, northern bag mills were even tinting sulfite papers to mimic the appearance of southern kraft.[68]

The most important technical and market force in paper production, however, was the fourdrinier, a massive rolling and drying mill in universal use by 1900. The fourdrinier's fixed costs determined industry behavior; they were twice the manufacturing average and were quite literally "fixed" – the fourdrinier weighed over 1,000 tons and measured nearly 400 feet. "You put mills where the forests are, and then you start cutting down the forests," as *Fortune* noted, "but you cannot move your mill: with its great machines it is one of the biggest, most costly, permanent and stationary things in all of industry." As a result, massive streamside mills in rural Wisconsin, New York, or Maine (having exhausted local forests) were soon importing pulp

67 "Fred Hume's Report on the Paper Industry" (22 November 1926), CF 459, Hoover Papers; "Pulp and Paper," CAS File 33:4; Sanitary Napkin Industry Report, Compliance Division (CD) File 172:6, NRA Records.
68 J.H. Lorant, *The Role of Capital-Improving Innovations in American Manufacturing During the 1920s* (New York, 1975), 117–46; Avi J. Cohen, "The Economic Determination of Technological Change: A Theoretical Framework and a Case Study of the U.S. Pulp and Paper," (Ph.D diss., Stanford University, 1982), 3:9–11, 4:4–6, 54–56; John Guthrie, *The Economics of Pulp and Paper* (Pullman, 1950), 25–35; "Union Bag and Paper Corp.," *Fortune* 16 (August 1937): 120–32; "Fifteen Paper Companies," *Fortune* 16 (November 1937): 194–96.

from the Northwest, Canada, and even Europe. Some produced finer papers to compensate for higher pulp costs, but few mills (many of which had been built during a short-lived boom before 1920) ceased production. The cost (often debt-financed) of the fourdrinier pressed even struggling firms into constant production. To makes things even worse, with little adjustment the fourdrinier could be used to produce a wide range of papers, allowing mills to respond quickly to changes in price and swamp profitable lines.[69]

The strategic dilemmas of northern mills were both the cause and the effect of regional shifts in the industry after 1910. As exhaustion of local pulp undermined the turn-of-the-century combinations, only Great Northern (which retained large stands of Maine timber) maintained its market stature. New investment was concentrated in the western and southern states, and especially Canada after the powerful American Newspaper Publisher's Association (ANPA) was able to gain free import of newsprint by 1913. The ANPA also trafficked heavily in editorials at the first hint of high paper prices; making the paper industry the target of constant FTC investigation. The American Pulp and Paper Association (APPA), a relatively weak trade group, fought a losing battle against tariff revision. Converting mills also imported Canadian pulp, and they did not support the newsprint industry in its battle with Canada. And Canadian growth (85 percent of new capacity after 1919) marked not only a regional shift in production but also a profound shift in political and regulatory prospects.[70]

The southern industry also expanded at the expense of its northern counterpart, increasing its share of pulp markets from less than 2 percent in 1916 to almost 40 percent by 1938. The APPA fought southern competition at every turn, including an ill-fated attempt to block Reconstruction Finance Corporation loans in the 1930s. Behind these defensive measures, some large

69 Cohen, "Pulp and Paper," 3:16, 25; Louis Stevenson, *The Background and Economics of American Papermaking* (New York, 1940), 71–91; (quote) "Economics of Pulp and Paper," *Fortune* 16 (September 1937): 113; on the pressure of debt in the early industry, see Naomi Lamoreaux, *The Great Merger Movement in American Business, 1895–1904* (New York, 1985), 42–45, 55–59.

70 Cohen, "Pulp and Paper Industry," 3:8–9, 37–45; Simon Whitney, *Antitrust Policies: American Experience in Twenty Industries* (New York, 1958), 335–40; Max Kossoris, "Paper and Pulp Industry," in *Industrial Planning Under Codes*, 246–47; Herrymon Maurer, *In Quiet Ways: George H. Mead, The Man and the Company* (Dayton, 1970), passim; Ralphy W. Hidy, Frank Ernest Hill, and Allan Nevins, *Timber and Men: The Weyerhauser Story* (New York, 1963), 199–203; Stevenson, *Background and Economics*, 97–101; Guthrie, *Economics of Pulp and Paper*, 39–41, and *The Newsprint Paper Industry* (Cambridge, 1941), 94–95; "Statements Presented at Hearings before the Timber Conservation Board" (10 June 1931), File 87338, Department of Commerce Records.

northern firms also invested in Canadian and southern competition. George Mead and International Paper invested heavily in Eastern Canada, while the latter also owned Southern Kraft, the largest southern mill. As the fourdrinier made it difficult for older firms to shift assets from antiquated northern sites, many adapted their mills to produce finer grades of paper or converted them outright into hydroelectric plants. This expansion and conversion was financed by debt; International Paper alone, after virtual bankruptcy in the early 1920s, owed $330 million by 1935. Outside the South and Canada, growth occurred only in the West, where firms such as Crown-Zellerbach and Weyerhauser thrived on the region's plentiful timber and isolated markets.[71]

Although there were far too many mills in the wake of wartime expansion, some markets (such as paper and paperboard packaging or sanitary papers) grew rapidly, and many larger firms benefited from exclusive contracts with major publishers or institutional consumers. But such stabilizing influences were sporadic. "Whenever consumption rises and prices appear relatively stable, the rush to finance expansion begins again," observed *Fortune* in 1937, ". . . big mills gobble up little mills, and little mills combine to form big mills, and then all of them build in a fine competitive frenzy while the money lasts." New investment invariably came too late to take advantage of the prosperity that encouraged it and just in time to push the industry into another competitive spiral. New capacity after 1926 bore less relation to the market than (as many speculated at the time) to the desire of the bankers in control of the industry to float new securities. Many firms produced at a loss in the hope of recouping at least capital and financial costs, which in turn lowered prices and created more demand for inexpensive paper products. The industry seems "to have a mental illness of its own," concluded *Fortune*, "a sort of manic-depressive cycle . . . by which prosperity immediately creates the first symptoms of disaster."[72]

71 L. Ethan Ellis, *Print Paper Pendulum: Group Pressures and the Price of Newsprint* (New Brunswick, 1948); David Smith, *History of Papermaking in the United States, 1691–1969* (New York, 1970), 391–420; Cohen, "Pulp and Paper," 3:27–28, 50, 5:6–8; Kossoris, "Paper and Pulp Industry," 243; Mauron, *In Quiet Ways*, 98–112; Stevenson, *Background and Economics*, 30–31; Trevor Dick, "Canadian Newsprint, 1913–1930: National Policies and the North American Economy," *JEH* 42 (1982); Guthrie, *Newsprint Paper Industry*, 58, 129–209, and *Economics of Pulp and Paper*, 8–10, 75, 143–64; "Union Bag and Paper," 120–32; "Economics of Pulp and Paper," 178; "International Paper and Power," *Fortune* 16 (December 1937): 134–136.

72 Cohen, "Pulp and Paper," 3:34–53; Whitney, *Antitrust Policies*, 367–69; Smith, *History of Papermaking*, 344–47, 367–69; Stevenson, *Background and Economics*, 135–40; Guthrie, *Economics of Pulp and Paper*, 42, and *Newsprint Paper Industry*, 93–105; (quotes) "Fifteen Paper Companies," 132–35, 137, 194; Nourse, *America's Capacity*

Although the industry employed an average of 120,000 workers, isolation and regional shifts undermined labor organization. Early union strength was concentrated in the newsprint crafts but evaporated in the face of the industry's migration to Canada and an open-shop drive by employers. The International Brotherhood of Pulp, Sulphite, and Paper Mill Workers, which represented unskilled laborers, was moribund through the 1920s. International and Great Northern were the site of bitter strikes in the early 1920s, and while Great Northern settled, International dragged its strike out until 1926, by which time its mills were without unions or markets. Employers instituted welfare programs only in the rapidly growing sanitary paper division. In the labor-starved Northwest, conservative unionists and an employers' association (the latter created at the urging of the union) maintained relatively peaceful industry-wide collective agreements.[73]

Through the 1920s, the paper industry hoped for renewed tariff protection, administered prices, or production restrictions, but it lacked the collective will to accomplish any of these goals. Lasting stability threatened the existence of so many of the industry's debt-laden, regionally distinct, and excess competitors that private cooperation was a mirage. As the industry stumbled into the 1930s, public policy, which required coordinated action on the part of at least forty states, five provinces and two federal governments, held little promise.

Electrical and Industrial Goods: Dilemmas of a Dual Economy

The electrical goods and machinery industries (encompassing industrial and farm machinery, electrical generating and utility equipment, construction and mining equipment, and consumer goods) encapsulated the strengths and weaknesses of the interwar industrial economy. Electrical- and capital-goods firms sought stability, with sporadic success, by either diversifying product lines or retaining monopoly control over specialty products. Electrification,

to Produce, 238–46; Kossoris, "Paper and Pulp," 46–52; "Economics of Pulp and Paper," 111; "Statements Presented at Hearings before the Timber Conservation Board" (10 June 1931), File 87338, Department of Commerce Records.

73 Robert Zieger, *Rebuilding the Pulp and Paper Workers Union, 1933–1941* (Knoxville, 1984), 20–94; James Gross, "The Making and Shaping of Unionism in the Pulp and Paper Industry," *Labor History* 4 (1963): 190–97; "The Crown Zellerbach Corporation and the Pacific Coast Pulp and Paper Industry," *The Causes of Industrial Peace* 1 (Washington, 1948); 34–50; Smith, *History of Papermaking*, 347–51; Stevenson, *Background and Economics*, 50–59; Guthrie, *Economics of Pulp and Paper*, 122–32; Sanitary Napkin Industry Report, CD File 172:6, NRA Records.

rapid technological change, and the growth of consumer-goods industries girded demand for industrial machinery but also exaggerated the chronic instability of consumer and producer markets. Diversification was costly and, especially in consumer markets, usually disappointing. And in the absence of constant demand and enforceable patents, profitable specialization was usually short-lived.

In electrical manufacturing (which included 170 major subdivisions and over 300,000 distinct products), General Electric (GE) and Westinghouse were the only firms with extensive product lines ranging well into consumer goods. Tired of competition and litigation, these two giants pooled their patents in 1896 in an attempt to shut out all but marginal and pirate competition. This partnership dominated some fields; GE and Westinghouse (and AT&T) used the Radio Corporation of America to control the pace and technology of the fledgling broadcasting industry. But in most product lines, competition persisted in the form of bitter and litigious battles between specialty firms and the industry's leaders.[74] In the farm equipment industry, International Harvester faced competition from diversified machinery firms, including Minneapolis–Moline, Case, John Deere, and Allis-Chalmers. As a group, these firms monopolized most product lines.[75] Industrial machinery firms enjoyed high demand and little competition for a variety of specialized products, especially in the context of rapid mechanization and electrification.[76]

74 "G.E." *Fortune* 6 (November 1932), 19–20; Harold Passer, *The Electrical Manufacturers, 1875–1900* (Cambridge, 1953), 350–65; Ronald Schatz, *The Electrical Workers: A History of Labor at General Electric and Westinghouse, 1923–1960* (Illinois, 1983), 4–13; W.J. Donald, "Electrical Manufacturing Industry," in *Industrial Planning Under Codes*, 277–296; Milton Derber, "Electrical Products," in *How Collective Bargaining Works*, ed. Harry Millis (New York, 1942), 744; FTC, *Report on International Electric Equipment Cartels* (Washington, 1948), 2–4; FTC, *Report on the Radio Industry* (Washington, 1923), 2–42; Otto Scott, *The Creative Ordeal: The Story of Raytheon* (New York, 1974), 35–48.

75 Barbara Marsh, *A Corporate Tragedy: The Agony of International Harvester* (New York, 1985), 48; Kenneth Myers, *Marketing Policy Determination by a Major Firm in a Capital Goods Industry* (New York, 1976), 31–34; FTC, *Report on the Manufacture and Distribution of Farm Implements* (Washington, 1948), 12–18, 32–66; FTC, *Report on the Causes of High Prices of Farm Implements* (Washington, 1920), 33–36; Power Farming Bureau to Hoover (5 October 1921), CF 431; National Implement and Vehicle Association to Hoover (17 October 1921), CF 431, Hoover Papers. See also Wayne Broehl, *John Deere's Company: A History of Deere and Company and its Times* (New York, 1984); Robert Ozanne, *A Century of Labor Management Relations at International Harvester* (Madison, 1967); Walter Peterson, *An Industrial Heritage: Allis-Chalmers Corporation* (Milwaukee, 1976); Norman Thomas, *Minneapolis-Moline: A History of Its Formation and Operations* (New York, 1976).

76 On machinery sales, see Lorant, *Capital Improving Innovations*; Jerome, *Mechani-*

The effects of World War I varied widely. In many fields, the war brought technological breakthroughs and demand for new factory equipment. Machine tool and industrial equipment firms lost some overseas markets in 1914 but recovered with extensive sales to Germany and the Allies between 1915 and 1917 and the explosion of domestic demand in 1916–18. Yet established firms could not come close to meeting the demand of war industries, and many high-profit war contracts went to wildcat firms. This peculiar problem of capital-goods industries persisted after 1919. "Business is either feast or famine," noted *Iron Trade Review*, "when times are good, the order books cannot hold all the business offered . . . for to be able to do so would mean a plant investment out of all proportion with [] average needs, . . . when business is dull, the market dwindles to almost nothing." Sales of machine tools (reflecting sporadic capital investment in other industries) fell from $161 million in 1919 to barely $36 million in 1921. Through the rest of the 1920s, capital-goods sales responded slowly and in an exaggerated fashion to the business cycle, surviving largely on the strength of sales to auto firms retooling for model year production after 1925.[77]

Diversification into consumer goods helped fill periodic troughs in demand and, for electrical firms, increased demand for electrical generating equipment. Value-added in electrical goods grew from $121 million in 1909 to $1,389 million in 1929. But patents did little to stem entry, and price competition from single- or limited-product firms was pervasive. Sales of farm implements depended on disposable farm income, which fell from 50 percent to 25 percent of total farm income between 1917 and 1932. For farm implement firms, the Depression began in 1921. Only Deere and International Harvester showed occasional profits, and they increasingly sold on installment or credit or (in some years) for corn rather than cash. International markets were of varying importance. GE and Westinghouse entered numerous manufacturing, patent, and export agreements with foreign firms. Almost one-third of excavating and heavy equipment sales were overseas, but machine tool exports fluctuated wildly with the health of European eco-

zation in Industry; Wayne Broehl, *Precision Valley: The Machine Tool Companies of Springfield, Vermont* (Englewood Cliffs, 1959); Arthur Cox and Thomas Malim, *Ferracute: The History of an American Enterprise* (Bridgeton, 1985); [Cutler-Hammer], *An American Dream: A Commemorative History of Cutler-Hammer* (Milwaukee, 1979); Myers, *Marketing Policy Determination*; Harless Wagoner, *The United States Machine Tool Industry from 1900–1950* (Cambridge, 1968); George Gibb, *The Saco-Lowell Shops* (Cambridge, 1950).

77 Schatz, *Electrical Workers*, 9–10; Breoehl, *Precision Valley*, 87–96, 103–18 (quote, 90); *History of Cutler-Hammer*, 25–32; Myers, *Marketing Policy Determination*, 180–90, 325; Cox and Malim, *Ferracute*, 1–73, 85–104, 122–25.

nomies. Foreign farm implement sales (excepting some shipments to Russia) disappeared after 1917.[78]

Labor relations in capital-goods industries closely reflected market orientation. Large integrated firms selling mass-produced items (GE, Westinghouse, and International Harvester) were models of modern personnel management; they fought unionization, experimented cynically with welfare capitalism, and cultivated ill-deserved reputations as benevolent employers. Employers crushed the remnants of craft control after the war, and despite GE's flirtation with the AFL in the late 1920s, unionization did not succeed until later in the 1930s. Smaller, specialized manufacturers in the machinery and machine tool industries relied more on skilled local labor markets. Workers in these industries labored under fairly good conditions, although few were unionized and employment was unstable.[79]

As the Depression hardened the instability of the 1920s, electrical-goods and machinery firms struggled to create or maintain demand. The competitive picture included so many distinctly motivated interests that constructive trade organization or competitive regulation was virtually impossible. Leading firms, however, were uniquely receptive to the prospect of increased international sales or domestic industrial policy. And larger diversified firms, with investments in a variety of industries and regions, were uniquely receptive to synthetic or "corporatist" solutions.

Food and Tobacco: Competition and Consumer Nondurables

Business strategies in the food and tobacco industries varied widely. New technologies and consumption patterns encouraged the commercialization of food and food preparation. But uneven patterns of growth; the persistence

78 Schatz, *Electrical Workers*, 5–8, 189–90; Marsh, *Corporate Tragedy*, 52–54; Peterson, *An Industrial Heritage*, 198–202, 227, 237; Thomas, *Minneapolis-Moline*, 113–16, 130–32, 147–48, 168, 296–99; FTC, *Report on the Manufacture and Distribution of Farm Implements*, 8, 25–27; A. Legge [International Harvester] to Hoover (7 January 1926), CF 367, Hoover Papers; FTC, *Report on International Electrical Equipment Cartels*, 2; Theodore Geiger, *The General Electric Company in Brazil* (New York, 1976), 40; Stuart Crocker [GE] to Howe (2 August 1933), OF 396, FDR Papers; Owen Young to National Electric Light Association (n.d.), File 602(4), Raskob Papers; Morgan memos on IT&T (1929), File 100–1, Lamont Papers; Broehl, *Precision Valley*, 127–130; Myers, *Marketing Policy Determination*, 18, 188; J.W. Hook [Allied Machinery] to Hoover (10 June 1921), CF 20, Hoover Papers.

79 On GE and Westinghouse, see Schatz, *Electrical Workers*, passim; Montgomery, *Fall of the House of Labor*, 438–52; Memorandum for Hoover (16 December 1921), CF 235, Hoover Papers.

of local production and markets; and disparate links to agriculture, distribution, and retailing complicated competitive strategies. In all, food and tobacco industries experienced a chaotic decade of technological and economic change after 1920.

The tobacco industry grew rapidly after 1920. Cigar production peaked in 1920, but cigarette production grew almost 1,500 percent between 1920 and 1933; this growth reflected wartime demand for a cheap and portable tobacco product, extensive advertising, and the peculiarities of addictive demand. As the *Tobacco Journal* boasted, the industry strove "to sell a man something he doesn't even know he wants." Cigar and cigarette manufacture also mechanized rapidly after 1920. Cigar machinery was slowly introduced as dissolution of the tobacco trust left few with the market or capital to mechanize; by 1930, 50 percent of cigars were made entirely by machine and, between 1921 and 1936, the number of competing firms dropped from 14,500 to 5,000. Once installed, cigar machinery (at $380,000 for installation and upwards of $100,000 in annual royalties) discouraged further entry. By contrast, the cigarette industry was mechanized from the outset. The number of firms fell from 326 in 1919 to 87 in 1935, as the costs of machinery and the advantages of established brands restricted entry.[80]

The interwar history of tobacco industries was rooted in consolidation and antitrust litigation that took place before 1915. James Duke's American Tobacco Company was the target of a prolonged antitrust suit that ended in 1911, according to Duke's biographer, with Duke "asked to unscramble his own omelet." The trust was divided by product among its constituent firms, resulting, as a disgusted Louis Brandeis noted, in "four monopolies instead of one." The dissolution of American Tobacco did not end predatory purchasing from farmers; former American Tobacco directors retained financial control, and the successors (American, Ligget & Myers, Lorillard, and R.J. Reynolds) shared even greater control – 90 percent of the market by 1930.[81]

80 Reavis Cox, *Competition in the American Tobacco Industry* (New York, 1933), 45, (quote, 223), 320; Anthony Badger, *Prosperity Road: The New Deal, Tobacco, and North Carolina* (Chapel Hill, 1980), 16–18; William Nicholls, *Price Policies in the Cigarette Industry* (Nashville, 1951), 7–19; W.D. Evans, "Effects of Mechanization in Cigar Manufacture," *Monthly Labor Review* 46 (May 1938): 11–13; Fabricant, *Employment in Manufacturing*, 39–40; Jerome, *Mechanization in Industry*, 118–19.
81 Nicholls, *Price Policies in the Cigarette Industry*, 12, 17, (quote, 31), 38; Nannie Tilly, *The Bright Tobacco Industry* (rep., New York, 1972), 593; Cox, *Competition in the American Tobacco Industry*, 293–315; (quote) Winkler, *Tobacco Tycoon*, 213–14; Badger, *Prosperity Road*, 17–21.

As cigarette markets grew, leading firms decided to maintain virtually identical prices in the interest of high profits for all. Price competition was of particular concern because aggregate demand was relatively unresponsive to changes in price (a fact that also made tobacco products a fertile ground for revenue taxation). Both cigarette and cigar firms relied heavily on advertising and brand loyalty in place of price competition. Through 1925–31, leading cigarette firms spent between $10 and $20 million on advertising and, by 1930, spent more on billboard advertising alone than they did on raw tobacco. In the cigar industry, distribution contracts and advertising costs also raised barriers to entry. Nonprice competition lasted until "economy brands," appealing to Depression-era smokers, captured 10 percent of the market in the early 1930s. The cigar industry, reflecting a competitive rift between mass-marketed, mechnical production and isolated, individual production was, as the *Tobacco Leaf* noted, "utterly lacking in any semblance of cooperation and cohesion." Through the 1920s, the mechanized "national brands" firms dominated sales through economies of scale, advertising, and exclusive distribution contracts (leading firms even supported Prohibition as a means of combatting local manufacturers who relied on taverns to distribute cigars).[82]

By the 1920s, the industry's international business was largely in its past. American Tobacco's exports accounted for almost one-third of production in the 1890s, but excepting a spurt during the war, these slipped steadily. An agreement between American Tobacco and British-American Tobacco allowed the latter to produce in the United States for export while the firms together sought to exploit prospective markets in China. The Chinese venture slowed in the late 1920s as the Nationalist government moved to support domestic firms. And the British-American–American Tobacco *entente* collapsed when British-American bought controlling interest in Brown & Williamson (an "economy brand" competitor). By the 1930s, international tobacco trade (for American firms) was confined to the import and export of raw leaves.[83]

82 James Stone to Hoover (20 July 1931), PF 303, Hoover Papers; Richard Tennant, *The American Cigarette Industry* (New Haven, 1950), 139–44; Nicholls, *Price Policies in the Cigarette Industry*, 47–97, 111–23; Susan Wagner, *Cigarette Country: Tobacco in American History and Politics* (New York, 1971), 50–59; Patricia Cooper, " 'What This Country Needs is a Good Five-Cent Cigar,' " *Technology and Culture* 29 (1988): 795–800; (quote) Russell Mack, *The Cigar Manufacturing Industry* (Philadelphia, 1933), 4.

83 Cox, *Competition in the American Tobacco Industry*, 71–73; Nicholls, *Price Policies in the Cigarette Industry*, 10; Maurice Corina, *Trust in Tobacco: The Anglo-American*

Labor relations in the cigarette industry, a group of mechanized, southern firms with low labor costs and no tradition of organization, was not a major issue. As a defense against craft unionism and a guarantee against strikes, economy brand firms Axton Fisher and Brown & Williamson recognized AFL unions with little struggle in the early 1930s (these firms would later support New Deal labor legislation as a means of spreading high labor costs to large, nonunion competitors). In the cigar industry, craft production persisted locally while mechanization displaced workers and accelerated the low-wage feminization of work in northeastern factories. Employment in cigar manufacturing dropped from 115,000 in 1921 to 56,000 in 1936. Some small firms experimented with union-management collaboration in hopes of capturing union markets.[84]

Food industries accounted for just under one-fifth of manufactured product between 1919 and 1937 and employed 10 percent of the national workforce. Divisions within the industry by size, influence, and industrial structure were tremendous, ranging from the "big four" meat packers, to the fragmented and seasonal canning industry, to international commodity and processing sectors, to the brewing industry (a strategic curiosity under Prohibition). Generally, food industries processing domestic agricultural products were labor-intensive and mildly competitive; a few major firms competed over national markets and tolerated a large margin of local and regional competition. Stable demand muted rivalry, although strategies in perishable and nonperishable lines diverged sharply. The spread of refrigeration, pasteurization, and trucking widened the distribution of perishable goods and made it possible for large dairies and packers to capture national markets. This technology was expensive, and more capital-intensive lines relied increasingly on chain retailing, packaging innovations, and advertising.[85]

Struggle for Power (London, 1975), 128–30, 152; Sherman Cochran, *Big Business in China: Sino-Foreign Rivalry in the Cigarette Industry, 1890–1930* (Cambridge, 1980), 124–82; Winkler, *Tobacco Tycoon*, 129–31; Deane Malott and Boyce Martin, *The Agricultural Industries* (New York, 1939), 381–98.

84 U.S. Senate, Committee on Education and Labor, *National Labor Relations Board* (Washington, 1935), 212–18; *Wall Street Journal* clippings (May 1936), File 1139:2, Pennsylvania Railroad Papers, Hagley Museum; Mack, *The Cigar Manufacturing Industry*, 72, 85–86; Evans, "Effects of Mechanization in Cigar Manufacture," 11–13; Cooper, " 'What This Country Needs is a Good Five–Cent Cigar,' " 779–807.

85 William Nicholls, *A Theoretical Analysis of Imperfect Competition with Special Application to the Agricultural Industries* (Ames, 1941), 7, 79–81; John Riley, *Organization in the Soft Drink Industry* (Washington, 1946); Piore and Sabel, *Second Industrial Divide*, 57–59; Mary Yeager, *Competition and Regulation: The Development of Oligopoly in the Meatpacking Industry* (Greenwich, 1981); Bernstein, *Great De-*

International policies ranged widely. Exports (excepting grain) were not as crucial as imports. Large processing and marketing firms dominated trade in imported agricultural commodities (for example, coffee and spices), while other internationally traded commodities were subject to the political and economic machinations of domestic producers. The sugar industry, for example, consisted of U.S.-owned cane plantations in Cuba and the Philippines (whose processing was monopolized by the American Sugar Refining Company) and a domestic sugar beet industry closely tied to the beet growers. Competition was complicated by volatile sugar prices after 1919, the contradictory pleas of beet refiners and American Sugar for a tariff policy that would not undercut their investments, and the determination of European beet and cane interests to free-ride on Cuban-sponsored production restrictions. The United States gave slight preference to Cuban imports (a compromise that pleased no one), while Cuban/U.S. interests continued "carrying the [quota] umbrella while other nations walked in the blessed shade."[86]

In meat packing, the Big Four (after the merger of Armour and Morris in 1923) controlled over 70 percent of slaughters, a near monopoly that included control of the supply of meat to independent butchers and processors and of byproducts (fertilizers and hides). In 1920, the FTC settled a long-standing antitrust suit by consent decree, requiring the packers to dispose of proprietary stockyards, terminals, and cold storage. The consent decree did little to alter the competitive picture or stem continued efforts "to rationalize the industry and prevent inordinate competitive practices." In the mid-1920s, refrigerated trucking challenged the Big Four's rail-based monopoly and encouraged smaller firms in the East and Midwest. These

pression, 123–26; William Powell, *Pillsbury's Best* (Minneapolis, 1985), 115–16; Horace Powell, *The Original Has This Signature – "Kellogg's"* (Englewood Cliffs, 1956), 157–93; Ruth Newhall, *The Folger Way* (The Folger Company, [1948]), 50–52; Nourse, *America's Capacity to Produce*, 177–93; Dena Markhoff Sabin, *How Sweet It Is: The Beet Sugar Industry in Microcosm* (New York, 1986), 143–56; TNEC, *Large Scale Organization in the Food Industries*, Monograph 35 (Washington, 1940), 6, 90.

86 FTC, *Report on the Beet Sugar Industry* (Washington, 1917); Thomas Heston, *Sweet Subsidy: The Economic and Diplomatic Effects of the U.S. Sugar Acts* (New York, 1987), 57, 87, 129; Sabin, *How Sweet It Is*, 143–56; John Dalton, *Sugar: A Case Study in Government Control* (New York, 1937), 40–45; Alfred Eichner, *The Emergence of Oligopoly: Sugar Refining as a Case Study* (Baltimore, 1969), 291, 344; TNEC, *Trade Association Survey* (Washington, 1940); Myer Lynsky, *Sugar Economics* (New York, 1938); Malott and Martin, *The Agricultural Industries*, 281–327; O.W. Willcox, *Can Industry Govern Itself?* (New York, 1936), 29–57; (quote) "Mr. Chadbourne Makes a Plan," *Fortune* 4 (1931): 22–29, 112.

"interior" packers cut briefly into the Big Four's market share, but most were bought out by the major firms after 1929. The packers were lukewarm to organizational innovations and twisted their NRA code (which was never enacted) to support continued predatory pricing.[87]

The dairy industry rapidly expanded and concentrated in the interwar era. Although local suppliers and distributors continued to dominate fresh milk markets, National Dairy Products (Kraft), Borden, Beatrice, Carnation, Pet Milk, and the packers (who diversified into dairy goods as part of their control of local cold storage and delivery) took over the production of butter, cheese, canned milk, and ice cream. National dairy interests produced 18 percent of fresh milk, 45 percent of butter, 70 percent of canned milk, and 90 percent of cheese. By 1934, the top three firms controlled a third of all dairy sales, an impressive share considering the novelty of mass-distribution and the persistence of local production.[88]

The canning industry was competitive and divided by region and product. Many canneries drifted in and out of business seasonally or were leased to seasonal users. Competition was severe, although concentration and corporate control varied among products and regions. "The average canner," noted *The Canner*, "couldn't be bothered thinking about anything that promised to rob him of his right to produce more cans of corn or peas or peaches than the market can absorb." Competition lessened somewhat in the 1920s as year-round California canners (including California Packing [Del Monte] and Swift subsidiary Libby McNeil) with close ties to chain grocers pushed many seasonal canners out of business. By 1934, the top three firms controlled one-quarter of all canned goods.[89]

87 Nicholls, *Imperfect Competition*, 69–71; TNEC, *Large Scale Organization in the Food Industries*, 15, 17, (quote 22), Malott and Martin, *Agricultural Industries*, 118–19; Richard Arnould, "Changing Patterns of Concentration in American Meat Packing, 1880–1963," *BHR* 45 (1971): 18–34; R.C. Dougherty, *In Quest of Quality: Hormel's First 75 Years* (Austin, 1966), 120–21; L.D.H. Weld, "The Packing Industry: Its History and General Economics," in *The Packing Industry* (Chicago, 1924), 70–71, 77; Cudahay to Richberg (6 February 1934), OF 577, FDR Papers; "FTC Material," TPSS File 287:2; "History of Negotiations . . . Meat Packing," File 268:62, Code Histories (never approved); "Proposed Code . . . Sausage Products," File 268:66, Code Histories (never approved), NRA Records.

88 TNEC, *Large Scale Organization in the Food Industries*, 25–35; Martin Bell, *A Portrait of Progress: A Business History of the Pet Milk Company* (St. Louis, 1962), 63–79; James Marshall, *Elbridge A. Stuart: Founder of the Carnation Company* (Los Angeles, 1949), 128–51; Eric Lampard, *The Rise of the Dairy Industry in Wisconsin, 1820–1920* (Madison, 1963), 276; Malott and Martin, *Agricultural Industries*, 59, 62; William Nicholls, "Post-War Concentration in the Cheese Industry," *JPE* 47 (1939): 823–45; Nicholls, *Imperfect Competition*, 71–73.

89 Bell, *Pet Milk Company*, 70–71; Nicholls, *Imperfect Competition*, 77; R. Lee Burton,

Milling and baking followed a similar path of concentration and expansion. The introduction of roller milling and air separation in the 1880s raised capital stakes in the industry and shifted its center of operations to the upper Midwest, whose spring wheat crop could be milled commercially for the first time. Consolidation continued through the 1920s; by 1934, General Mills (formed through merger in 1928) and Pillsbury milled over one-third of the wheat crop. Baking continued on a smaller scale (the top four firms controlled 20 percent) but grew later in the interwar era with the rise of chain retailing. In turn, large bakeries put considerable price pressure on millers, dairies, and sugar refineries.[90]

In the 1920s, Prohibition threw the brewing industry into strategic confusion. Although it wiped out small breweries, larger firms had anticipated the spread of state prohibition law and had the resources to diversify operations and wait out the social experiment, producing "near-beer," industrial alcohol, soft drinks, and malt extracts. Pabst and Busch used their large refrigerated plants to produce cheese and store hides and built commercial refrigeration equipment in their machine shops. Because big brewers could not risk cheating the Eighteenth Amendment, they actually financed and encouraged Prohibition enforcement in order to protect their near-beer markets from illegal sales of the real thing. The NRA came on the heels of that amendment's repeal in 1933 and entrenched the large brewers by outlawing the saloon contracts that supported local brewers. The chief beneficiary of Prohibition was the soft drink industry, whose products supplanted beer and liquor and made illegal brews more palatable. Firms such as Coca-Cola, with extensive franchise and distribution networks and heavy investments in vending and dispensing machines and advertising, gradually dominated soft drink production.[91]

Canneries of the Eastern Shore (Centreville, 1986), 38–54; Fred Stare, *The Story of Wisconsin's Great Canning Industry* (Madison, 1949), (quote, 122); Vicki Ruiz, *Cannery Women, Cannery Lives: Mexican Women, Unionization, and the California Food Processing Industry, 1930–1950* (Albuquerque, 1987), 21–39; TNEC, *Large Scale Organization in the Food Industries*, 51; Foodstuffs Division to Mullendore (1923), CF 428; Canners' League of California to Merritt (23 September 1921), CF 458, Hoover Papers.

90 Powell, *Pillsbury's Best*, 113; TNEC, *Large Scale Organization in the Food Industries*, 38–45; History of the Code of Fair Competition for Baking, DR File 267:445, NRA Records; NRA, Division of Review, "The Baking Industry," Evidence Study 26 (Washington, 1935).

91 Thomas Cochran, *The Pabst Brewing Company* (New York, 1948), 329, 332, 368; Ronald Plavchan, *A History of Anheuser-Busch, 1852–1933* (New York, 1976), 154–68, 192; August Busch, "What Else Can We Make?" *Factory and Industrial Man-*

Labor-relations varied widely in the food industries. Employers crushed the AFL packing unions in 1921–22, after which they manipulated welfare programs and exploited racial and ethnic tensions among workers. In the early 1930s, culminating in a drive by the Congress of Industrial Organizations, organizers rebuilt packing unions throughout the Midwest. Milling workers had a shorter history of organization but were swept up in the surge of Minneapolis labor after 1934. Brewery workers had a long craft tradition, and in the 1890s Busch and Pabst competed over recognition of competing Knights of Labor and AFL unions, both of whom threatened to boycott nonunion beer. Nearly three decades of quiet, conservative unionism ended with Prohibition (which cut brewery employment in half and ended the threat of union boycotts). In most agricultural industries, labor was drawn seasonally from migrant labor markets and remained unorganized, underpaid, and badly exploited.[92]

Food industries suffered from the volatility of price and supply that plagued their agricultural base. Depressions destroyed prices but did little to discourage production. Politically, food industries were caught between agriculture and industrial organization. Because each food industry had distinct links to agricultural, industrial, and consumer markets, this political conflict was never realistically confronted or resolved, and New Deal strategies were complicated and confused by the dual impact of the NRA (which allowed some price-fixing) and the Agricultural Adjustment Administration (which raised raw agricultural costs).[93]

Conclusion: Politics and the Crisis of Competition

Throughout the post–Civil War era, established and emerging industries suffered a chronic crisis of competition. The vast internal market that had

agement 78 (1929): 961; John Riley, *A History of the Soft Drink Industry* (Washington, 1948), 139; E.J. Kahn, *The Big Drink: The Story of Coca-Cola* (New York, 1960), 70–78; ? to Teagle (24 October 1934), IAB File 358:13 (correspondence); Riley to Lynch (25 May 1934), in "History of the Code of Fair Competition for Bottled Soft Drink," DR File 267:459 (Exhibit 7), NRA Records.

92 Cochran, *Pabst*, 275–301; Roger Horowitz, "The Road Not Taken: A Social History of Industrial Unionism in Meatpacking," (Ph.D diss., University of Wisconsin, 1990); "Conference of Packers and Packers' Employees," CF 458, Hoover Papers; Powell, *Pillsbury's Best*, 120–34; Ruiz, *Cannery Women, Cannery Lives*, 21–39.

93 James Landing, *American Essence: A History of the Peppermint and Spearmint Industry in the United States* (Kalamazoo, 1969), 72–77; Sabin, *How Sweet It Is*, 169, 207; Malott and Martin, *Agricultural Industries*, 5–6; "General AAA" folder, File 367:3, National Recovery Review Board Correspondence, NRA Records.

encouraged the rapid growth of American industry also proved its undoing as disparate regional growth and federated political responsibility exacerbated market competition. Through the mergers of 1897–1904, older manufacturing sectors had been unable to rationalize their markets; in the aftermath of World War I, excess capacity and competition spread quickly to newer, predominantly consumer-good industries. The rapid growth of these sectors introduced new tensions to the political economy. Although industrial growth before the war had been spurred primarily by technological change and continental expansion, the postwar economy was increasingly dependent on personal standards of living and consumption. Workers marginalized or impoverished by mass-production industry were increasingly important as consumers. The crash of 1929 underscored these twin crises of competition and consumption.

For individual industries and firms, the competitive crisis was rooted in distinct political and economic problems. Before and after 1929, most defined their strategies and objectives narrowly, seeking political sanction for their own organizational solutions but resenting both the similar efforts of others and the costs of broader regulatory experiments. In this atmosphere of almost universal competitive misery and short-sighted political anxiety, the only possible common ground seemed to be a federal law that would give political and legal teeth to industry's organizational efforts but leave the details of those efforts up to the industries themselves: the National Recovery Act of 1933.

The NRA, however, was not a simple culmination of the competitive travail of the 1920s. Against a deep-seated antitrust tradition, the constitutional limits of federal power, the federal government's institutional predilection for piecemeal solutions, and the distrust and dependence that marked business-government relations, the NRA was a fairly exceptional political solution. And even as competitive crises propelled them toward the NRA, firms and industries continued to experiment with other organizational or political solutions. Many sought stability as a byproduct of labor-management relations, hoping that the organization of workers and labor standards would act as a surrogate for the regulatory hand of the state. And many others sought stability in trade or "peak" business association, hoping that formal membership and rules of competitive behavior would make political regulation unnecessary. We now turn to these efforts.

3. Workers Organizing Capitalists
Regulatory Unionism in American Industry, 1920–1932

By the 1920s, labor relations in the United States had reached a watershed. Sharp conflict between employers and unskilled, unorganized workers was increasingly prominent in many industries; skilled workers retained considerable managerial and organizational power in many others. Employers across the industrial economy were able to roll back most of the wartime gains made by the labor movement. At the same time, the success of the open-shop movement also eroded business's sense of political and private organization as employers retreated into their respective corners of the economy and began to regard labor relations as simply a function of industrial structure and competition. Collective bargaining (where it existed) was narrowly defined by employer, employee, and union concerns over industrial competition and organization. And patterns of labor organization were determined not only by workers' activism and management's response but also by the latter's calculus of the costs *and benefits* of organization itself. In short, employers viewed organized labor with the same mix of reactionary antagonism and rational opportunism with which they viewed the state; the promise of competitive order (even advantage) often outweighed less-tangible threats to managerial prerogatives.

In certain circumstances, employers found that the organizational benefits of unionization outweighed its material and managerial costs, that unions and union wages could serve as an important regulatory mechanism. Employers and workers alike saw unionization as a means of regulating labor costs across an industry, building aggregate demand in an underconsuming economy, and rationalizing job structures and job hierarchies within firms. Indeed, alongside the practical and ideological limits of the U.S. labor movement, the organizational utility of unionization allowed it to emerge as a common business strategy. This "regulatory unionism" was a logical organizational option in labor-intensive industries, especially those able to pass increased labor costs on to consumers without encouraging imports or substitution. And it was a necessary or even preferred option in competitively or regionally disorganized industries unable or unwilling to achieve stability through private agreements or political intervention.

Many employers experimented with union-based regulation between World Wars I and II. Their ability to manipulate or exploit labor agreements was, of course, sharply constrained by workers themselves, who obviously saw unionization as a means to a different end. In practice, however, union policies were bound by industrial structure, material constraints, and inconsistent organizational strength. And unions usually shared employers' concerns with short-term stability, competitive status, and profitability. In turn, the form or function of labor agreements rested on the willingness of the state (or states) to define and protect collective and individual rights. These tensions between immediate stability and the broader implications of an organized workforce, between private bargaining and political intervention, underlay the political economy of the New Deal and before 1932 were played out in a number of discrete industrial settings.

In this chapter, I explore the broader logic and impact of regulatory unionism in the interwar industrial economy. My argument has four parts. First, I consider regulatory unionism from the perspective of workers, stressing the material and organizational constraints that encouraged short-sighted strategies of "business" unionism. Second, I turn to employers and trace the constraints and circumstances under which they used unionization as a surrogate for the organization of firms or manipulated existing unions to achieve their own goals. Third, I explore variations in business strategy by sketching patterns of regulatory unionism in a number of industries. Finally, I weigh these experiences against those of persistently antiunion mass-production industries and tie this complex universe of private labor relations to the emergence of a New Deal labor policy.

Workers and the "New Unionism": the Material Bases of Consent

Regulatory unionism went by many names in the 1920s and 1930s. Academic and business celebrants dubbed it "the new unionism," "trade union capitalism," "business unionism," or "job-conscious unionism" and lauded the conservatism of unions that seemed to care as much about profits and production as did their employers. Cynics and progressive unionists preferred the label "class collaboration" and lamented the erosion of a class-conscious labor movement, which had seemed so promising before 1920. Both views, however, underestimated the material pressures faced by workers regardless of their collective strength or ideological radicalism. Workers and unions made real choices under real constraints. Recognizing the immense costs of real social change, organized workers were more likely to champion their corner of capitalism than to challenge it.

This consent was not merely an ideological, cultural, or political concession (as it has usually been portrayed) to either the unique promise or the stifling confines of working-class existence; it was a practical move, given the constraints of working-class life and the unequal distribution of political and economic power. Workers and unions had neither the resources nor the unity to battle prevailing patterns of wage labor, and by simply demanding better wages, they reinforced the background relations of property and power upon which that system was built. The average worker, as one student of labor relations in the 1920s noted,

> sees what he comes in contact with, what is tangible enough to be seen and touched. He knows his employers and other employers, but he knows no employing class. . . . He receives wages as a worker. He thinks of prices as a consumer. To his manner of looking at the world and social relations, "union management cooperation" is but a routine detail of internal shop management. . . . When the union does a bit of thinking, whether collectively or otherwise, it most likely harbors a secret thought that somehow or other the world could very well get along without having to support a class of employers, that the entire institution of employers is a social waste. The union cannot, however, fight and defeat a capitalist system by way of tearing down the business standing of a single company, however large.[1]

This narrowly rational concern with immediate and material issues reflected labor's unsure political footing in the face of fragmented politics and judicial conservatism, the political power and advantage of employers, and sharp divisions among workers by gender, race, ethnicity, and collective power. What was "rational," after all, was a reflection of what was possible. Given limited legal protection, the fierce (if opportunistic) individualism of employers, and little meaningful contact with politics, labor in the United States usually confined issues of workers' control and workers' rights to union publications and union halls. The risks and costs of pursuing more radical claims in the workplace were simply too great.[2]

1 J. Hardman, "Class Collaboration," in *American Labor Dynamics in the Light of Post-War Developments*, ed. J. Hardman (New York, 1928), 146.
2 Sanford Jacoby, "American Exceptionalism Revisited: The Importance of Management," in *Masters to Managers: Historical and Comparative Perspectives on American Employers*, ed. Sanford Jacoby (New York, 1991), 174–86, 191–95; Victoria Hattam, *Labor Visions and State Power: The Origins of Business Unionism in the United States* (Princeton, 1993), 11–16; Jon Elster, *Solomonic Judgements: Studies In the Limitation of Rationality* (New York, 1989), 5–6.

By and large, workers foreswore a burden of political initiative that only academics and ideologues have found realistic. Although objecting to its conditions, workers had a profound interest in stable employment and the continuation of profitable economic growth on capitalist terms. "We cannot wreck the house in which we expect to live," observed Sidney Hillman of the Amalgamated Clothing Workers (ACW); "we have to be for the industry, for law and order in the industry, for science in the industry." Or as David Dubinsky of the avowedly socialist International Ladies Garment Workers Union (ILGWU) admitted, "Unions need capitalism like a fish needs water." This logic of material consent was pervasive after 1920. Workers equated their own future with that of their employers, a fact that infused workers' views of welfare capitalism, labor relations, and the labor movement. Under constant threat of unemployment in an overproducing economy, unionized workers, as David Montgomery observes, simply "sought self-preservation in tight collaboration with those companies that still bargained [with them]."[3]

Indeed, by the early 1920s, the American Federation of Labor (AFL) had internalized the business ethic so completely that most union leaders accepted the core tenets of scientific management, a "productivity theory" of wages, and an antistatist, "voluntarist" approach to social and economic policy. This institutional conservatism was magnified after World War I by the employers' open-shop offensive, the conflation of bolshevism and radical unionism, and the AFL's eager subscription to the litmus test of "Americanism" pressed by Attorney General Palmer, the National Association of Manufacturers (NAM), and others. Not surprisingly, employers came to see the AFL as a means of diffusing more radical threats. "Some things they are standing for . . . will have a tremendously constructive influence," hoped Alfred Sloan of General Motors, adding favorably (if unnecessarily) that the AFL was "an aggressive and potent force against Communism." As progressive unionists lamented and business leaders celebrated, the AFL was

---

3 Hillman quoted in Steven Fraser, *Labor Will Rule: Sidney Hillman and the Rise of American Labor* (New York, 1991), 209; Dubinsky quoted in A.H. Raskin, "The Dubinsky Concept of Unionism," in *Unions and Union Leadership*, ed. Jack Barbash (New York, 1959), 78; (quote) David Montgomery, *The Fall of the House of Labor* (New York, 1987), 409. See also Adam Przeworski, *Capitalism and Social Democracy* (New York, 1985), 133–204; Emily Clark Brown, "The New Collective Bargaining in Mass Production," *Journal of Political Economy* [*JPE*] 47 (1939): 60; David Montgomery, "Thinking About American Workers in the 1920s," *International Labor and Working Class History* 32 (1987): 1–12; Melvyn Dubofsky, "Not So 'Turbulent Years': A New Look at the 1930s," in *Life and Labor: Dimensions of Working Class History*, ed. Charles Stephenson and Robert Asher (Albany, 1986), 205–33.

simply "a business movement selling labor power as if it was selling potatoes [and] striving desperately to prove its devotion to the capitalist system."[4]

The AFL's influence, however, should not be overestimated. Political opportunism and conservatism merely reflected and reinforced patterns of labor relations that were bound by larger constraints of industrial competition and political fragmentation. Many radical unions (especially in the garment trades) also embraced the logic of business unionism. And AFL policies, forged under the leadership of Samuel Gompers, changed little with the succession of William Green in 1925 (although industry-wide pattern bargaining gradually replaced craft-based conservatism as the keystone of union politics.[5]) In practice, neither the AFL nor the distant promises of progressive unionists were able to overcome the material uncertainty of working-class life, the distinct competitive pressures facing (and dividing) workers in different industries, and the short-sighted bargaining that these constraints encouraged.

Although the bulk of this chapter focuses on business strategies of unionization, the logic of workers' interests and choices should not be overlooked. Conservative unionism was neither a pragmatic rejection of labor radicalism nor a simple amalgam of "false consciousness" and employer intransigence. Especially after 1920, "job conscious unionism" was a reflection of organizational weakness and the reliance of workers upon their employers, reinforced by declining wages, unemployment, and job insecurity. This pattern of economic instability, bounded rationality, and material consent did not

4 Sloan to Raskob (23 October 1934), File 310, John J. Raskob Papers, Hagley Museum and Library, Wilmington, DE; Arthur Calhoun, "Labor's New Economic Policy," in Hardman, *American Labor Dynamics*, 322, 325. See also Selig Perlman, "Dynamic Job-Consciousness," in Barbash, *Unions and Union Leadership*, 3–9; Carroll Daugherty, "Functional Aspects of Unionism," *Labor Problems in American Industry* (Boston, 1938), 528–29; H.B. Drury, "Labor and Production," *American Federationist* 22 (February 1920), 237–44. On the AFL, see Montgomery, *Fall of the House of Labor*, 411–64; Hattam, *Labor Visions*, 3–9; Stephen Scheinberg, "The Development of Corporation Labor Policy, 1900–1940," (Ph.D diss., University of Wisconsin, 1966); Jean Trepp McKelvey, *AFL Attitudes Toward Production, 1900–1932* (Ithaca, 1952), 64–78, 93–95; Marguerite Green, *The National Civic Federation and the American Labor Movement, 1900–1925* (Westport, 1973), 133–89; Sumner Slichter, *Union Policies and Industrial Management* (Washington, 1941); Warren Van Tine, *The Making of a Labor Bureaucrat* (Amherst, 1973), 57–58, 77, 82–84; Sanford Jacoby, "Union-Managment Cooperation in the United States: Lessons from the 1920s," *Industrial and Labor Relations Review* 37 (1983): 18–33.

5 For revealing business opinions of Green, see Ralph Easley to George Lockwood (16 April 1925), File 29, National Civic Federation [NCF] Papers, New York Public Library, NY; Cyrus Ching memo, "Activities of the AF of L." (15 October 1926), File 8, DuPont Administrative Papers, Hagley Museum.

preclude a more radical response under different circumstances. It did, however, strengthen the tendency of employers, behind much ideological posturing, to view labor relations in similarly practical and immediate terms.

Behind the Open Shop: Business Strategies of Unionization

Employers never let ideological consistency blind them to the organizational promise of unionization, and they exploited the material anxieties of workers and unions in a number of ways. Unionization allowed firms to discipline marginal competition by unifying labor costs across an industry and restricting the entry of new firms. The fruits of this strategy varied by industry and competitive circumstance. For large competitors in fragmented, labor-intensive industries, unionization was often the key to stability. Where competitive pressures were less severe, employers used unions to guarantee access to skilled labor markets, contain craft-unionist or radical threats, ensure labor's cooperation in the introduction of new technology, and institutionalize internal labor markets and job structures. Some outside this ambit of competitive, labor-intensive industry, saw unionization (albeit among workers other than their own) as a means of inflating aggregate disposable income, as a painless source of social peace, or as a bargaining chip in other political battles. And each of these strategies was reinforced by insulation from international competition; behind a tariff wall, unionism affected only the rivalry among domestic firms.[6]

Even as a business strategy, unionism followed the ability of workers themselves to exact real gains and force the issue. For employers, the ideal world did not include unions. But while an individual firm might favor an open shop, it could not compete for long as one of the few unionized producers in an industry. The managerial threat of labor aside, the first concern of a unionized firm was any disparity in labor costs between itself and its competitors. These differences could be erased by either rolling back union gains or encouraging the organization of the entire industry. A number of considerations pressed employers to choose the latter: open-shop competition was often destructive, the costs of complete unionization could be passed to consumers, and unionization often facilitated other organizational goals that might otherwise have been impossible or prohibitively expensive. These

6 See William Cooke and David Meyer, "Structural and Market Predictors of Corporate Labor Relations Strategies," *Industrial and Labor Relations Review* 43 (1990): 280–93.

were not simple or happy solutions. In most cases, regulatory unionism was a product of economic desperation or opportunism, established union strength, and the exhaustion of political and economic alternatives.[7]

The principal function that employers thrust upon unions was labor cost regulation. Labor-intensive, competitively fragmented industries feared the chaos of both unrestrained, open-shop competition and uneven levels of unionization. As a U.S. Rubber executive observed:

> If we have a situation in our rubber industry where one unit in the industry is paying a wage rate of 86 or 89 or 90 cents an hour, and another unit is paying 45 or 46 cents an hour and that unit is in competition with the other, then the employer interests . . . or some other agency must take hold of that situation and build up the labor rates in that industry beyond what they now are if they are affecting the competitive situation; and if we admit that we are unable to do that, then organized labor is perfectly justified in saying, "We will have to step in and do the job for you."[8]

The point at which unions would be asked to "step in," depending on the business in question, varied considerably. A last resort in the oligopolistic rubber industry, union-enforced regulation occurred much sooner to leading firms in fragmented industries. "Every reduction in labor standards becomes a threat to the entire industry, and an invitation to the other manufacturers to place themselves on a plane of equality with the violator," noted a hat industry unionist, concluding that the union "must be strong in each shop" and "have control over the industry as a whole."[9]

In practical terms, leading firms in labor-intensive industries sought uniform wages but did not care whether wages were uniformly high or low. But such standardization without unionization proved impossible to maintain. Neither marginal competitors with little stake in industry stability nor leading firms anxiously guarding their investments could be trusted to consis-

7 Joel Rogers, in "Divide and Conquer: Further 'Reflections on the Distinctive Character of American Labor Laws' " [*Wisconsin Law Review* 1 (1990): 41], notes, "When it comes to unions, employers still prefer none to some, but a lot to only some, while resisting unions that claim all of the workforce." See also Michael Maloney et al., "Achieving Cartel Profits through Unionization," *Southern Economic Journal* [SEJ] 46 (1979): 628–34; John Bowman, "The Politics of the Market: Economic Competition and the Organization of Capitalists," *Political Power and Social Theory* 5 (1985): 35–88, and *Capitalist Collective Action: Competition, Cooperation and Conflict in the Coal Industry* (New York, 1989), 1–69; Ordway Tead and Henry Metcalf, *Labor Relations under the Recovery Act* (New York, 1933), 131–32, 145–46; Jacoby, "Union-Managment Cooperation in the United States," 31–33.

8 Cyrus Ching in *Proceedings of the NICB*, (14 April 1934), file I:7, National Industrial Conference Board [NICB] Papers, Hagley Museum.

9 Charles Green, *The Headwear Workers: A Century of Trade Unionism* (New York, 1944), 157.

tently respect even minimal standards. The former saw cost-cutting as a source of market share; the latter saw predatory pricing as a means of squeezing out smaller firms. And workers organized against wage wars and won concessions from at least some rival firms. Large firms with economies of scale, unionized firms facing nonunion competition, and virtually all firms in industries suffering ruthless wage competition appreciated the potential of industrial unions to standardize wages and mimic the power of monopoly. "The implications of all of this," reasoned Steven DuBrul of GM, "are that most of us do not like competition and attempt to set up monopolistic controls which will make life easier for us. This is the heart of the union organization plan, as witnessed in the building trades and in the railroads."[10]

Business acceptance or manipulation of union labor was also motivated by the politics of shop-floor organization. Through the early twentieth century, employers in mass-production industries instituted elaborate job hierarchies in an effort to manage their increasingly unwieldy workforces and to create political divisions among workers no longer differentiated by skill or craft. These structures and rules often became a serious managerial burden. Many open-shop firms installed "company unions" to create some aura of collective agreement and participation, only to find that workers were more interested in controlling these bureaucratic regimes than challenging them. Unions often inherited and legitimized work rates, job structures, and grievance or promotion procedures that continued to serve their original "divide and conquer" purpose while imbuing union policies with a managerial ethic. This was a piecemeal process, reflecting attempts by union leadership to "sell" the benefits of collective bargaining and attempts by management to make the most of a bad situation. Although all firms attempted to maximize the managerial utility of their unions, few saw it as a justification for unionization itself.[11]

10 Montgomery, "American Workers in the 1920s," 7; Joe Bain, *Barriers to New Competition* (Cambridge, 1956), 16; (quote) DuBrul to Harry Eaton (9 March 1934), File 28, Alexander Sachs Papers, Franklin D. Roosevelt Presidential Library [FDRPL], Hyde Park, NY. This pattern was not confined to the 1920s. In late 1987, for example, a Cleveland retail workers' union signed a contract that required it to picket its employers' nonunion competitors and commit one hour of wages a month to a general picketing-and-information fund. What rankled the owners of the unionized supermarkets in Cleveland was not the organization of their own workers but the threat posed by unorganized competitors and the failure of the union to regulate wage competition in a given market. See "A Novel Union Role: Picketing For the Boss," *Business Week*, 28 December 1987, 80.

11 David Gordon et al., *Segmented Work, Divided Workers* (New York, 1982), 100ff.; Katherine Stone, "The Origins of Job Structures in the Steel Industry," *Review of*

In turn, employers also pressed unions to share their business anxieties so as to ensure, by innovation or concession, that wage gains would come not from a greater share of industrial profits but as a result of improvements in productivity and the competitive standing of employers. This premise (which leaned heavily on the economic unease of workers) was so pervasive that unions often took the initiative in even labor-displacing productive strategies. Although portrayed by the business press as beacons of industrial democracy, these plans of "union-management cooperation" simply took advantage of the core strategic dilemma facing workers. A union might increase productivity and make material sacrifices in an effort to keep a firm in business and its members employed, but employers were able to bluff the prospect of going out of business and force unions to shoulder the burden of competition.[12]

Finally, consumer-good producers, retailers, and capital-intensive industries saw some promise in unions (and union wages), although less as regulatory tools than as a means of inflating aggregate disposable income or achieving other political goals. Consumer-good firms fought the unionization of their own workers but candidly acknowledged the importance of high wages elsewhere in the economy. "We are interested in labor as an economic factor in the process of wealth production and distribution," noted a furniture manufacturer; "we want fair play for the worker because the employee is also our customer." High-technology and internationally oriented firms adopted a conciliatory stance as early as 1919. The assiduously promoted "liberal" labor policies of Rockefeller, General Electric, and others reflected the absence of labor cost pressures in capital-intensive industry and a sensitivity to broader issues of trade, consumption, economic stability, and public relations.[13] Although "underconsumptionist" or "corporatist" perceptions would not influence national policy until the 1930s, they did influence the private acceptance of unionism in the 1920s.

U.S. business, of course, has always made a great deal of noise about the sanctity of free and unfettered enterprise. This rhetorical individualism

Radical Political Economics 6 (1974): 61–97; Brown, "New Collective Bargaining Policy," 30–66; Sanford Jacoby, *Employing Bureaucracy: Managers, Unions, and the Transformation of Work in American Industry* (New York, 1985), 151–52.

12 Slichter, *Union Policies*, 559; W. Jett Lauck, *The New Industrial Revolution and Wages* (New York, 1929), 270ff.

13 (Quote) Alfred Haake, "The NIRA from the Standpoint of Trade Associations and Code Authorities," 1934 address, File 1644:2, Raskob Papers; Brown, "New Collective Bargaining Policy," 30–42. On the labor policies of capital-intensive industry, see Thomas Ferguson, "Critical Realignment: The Fall of the House of Morgan and the Origins of the New Deal," (Ph.D diss., Princeton University, 1981), 300–14.

served as both the first defence against organized workers or the state and as a self-conscious celebration of the achievements of "self-made men." Furthermore, it reflected a political culture in which employers did not need to think of workers or their demands in political terms. In this sense, certainly most employers in the 1920s were fiercely antiunion, and brutal repression of organized labor was a central feature of the industrial economy. Such sentiments, however, did not blind employers to the fact that organized labor (like the state) was not always a threat to good business. The practical experience of individual employers belied any open-shop consensus. After the 1920 depression destroyed any semblance of unity among employers, many gradually and haphazardly accepted the regulatory potential of conservative unionism and pattern bargaining. "Nationally organized labor," one industrialist urged the Senate in 1931, was essential to the "stabilization of industrial activity." By leaning on unions, employers avoided the legal risks and immense costs of their own organization. "Personally, I would rather deal with the United Mine Workers [UMW]," testified one coal operator, "than with these ruthless price-cutting, wage-cutting operators who are a detriment to the industry."[14]

Although many appreciated the regulatory and organizational utility of unions in discrete competitive settings, such experiments were opportunistic, ambivalent, and often short-lived. Most employers, for example, deeply resented the War Labor Board (especially for the way it encouraged workers to conflate wartime propaganda with the question of industrial democracy at home) and celebrated its dissolution in 1919. Yet most also noted that AFL-enforced wage scales had effectively regulated wartime competition in many industries.[15] After 1920, even the rigidly antiunion NAM had difficulty

14 Jacoby, "American Exceptionalism Revisited," 177; Lloyd Ulman, "Who Wanted Collective Bargaining in the First Place?" *Contemporary Policy Issues* 5 (October 1987): 1–11; Jeffrey Haydu, "Employers, Unions, and American Exceptionalism: Pre-World War I Open Shops in the Machine Trades in Comparative Perspective," *International Review of Social History* 33 (1988): 25–41; Industrialist quoted in U.S. Senate, Subcommittee on Manufacturers, *Establishment of a National Economic Council* (Washington, 1930), 216; Grant Farr, *Origins of Recent Labor Policy* (Boulder, 1959), 28.

15 Joseph McMartin, " 'An American Feeling': Workers, Managers, and the Struggle over Industrial Democracy in the World War I Era," in *Industrial Democracy in America: The Ambiguous Promise,* ed. Howell Harris and Nelson Lichtenstein (New York, 1993), 67–86; George Barnett, "American Trade Unionism and the Standardization of Wages During the War," *JPE* 27 (1929), 670–93; Robert Cuff, *The War Industries Board* (Baltimore, 1973); Walter Drew, "Observations on Bridgeport and Smith & Wesson Cases," File V:11; Drew to J. Emery (19 January 1920), File V:11, NICB Papers.

maintaining enthusiasm among its members for its open-shop drive (which it never saw as much more than a recruiting tool) and finally admitted that antiunion pledges were not likely to affect the labor policies framed by individual firms. During a protracted debate over the meaning of the "open shop" in 1920, one NAM conferee doubted "whether there is an employer here that can say he is consistently carrying out the principles enunciated in that [open shop] plank." Increasingly, the NAM focused its attentions on a small group of firms and industries that still found its open-shop belligerence relevant and useful. The National Industrial Conference Board echoed a "divided opinion as to the value of systems of collective bargaining for the stabilization of industry and the elimination of disputes."[16]

Although often using the language of "efficiency" or "industrial democracy," management sorted out the labor problem on the basis of less-arcane calculations of the material costs and benefits of exploiting, accommodating, or resisting unionization. Many fragmented manufacturing and mining sectors used unions to restrict production and cost competition, and some "growth" industries, particularly after 1936, used them to regulate competition, the threat of entry, and internal structure. Strategies of business unionism were both calculated and chaotic, regulatory and simply reactive. The exact form or function of labor relations, as we shall see in the following sections of this chapter, was determined by the structural and competitive characteristics of specific industries and firms.

Patterns of Regulatory Unionism

Textiles

In the 1920s, the cotton textile industry settled into a pattern of bitter regional competition. After sustained growth in the half-century before World

16 (Quote) "Minutes of a Special Conference of Delegates . . . National Association of Manufacturers [re: Democratic and Republican platforms]," 160–61, Acc. 1412:File 12, National Association of Manufacturers [NAM] Papers, Hagley Museum; Richard Gable, "Birth of an Employers' Association," *Business History Review [BHR]* 33 (1959): 535–45; Allen Wakstein, "The Origins of the Open Shop Movement," *Journal of American History [JAH]* 51 (1964), 462–63, 469, 472; NICB Executive Committee Minutes, Meeting 26 (10 October 1918), File II:2; (quote) NICB Executive Committee Minutes, Meeting 36 (30 October 1919), File II:2, NICB Papers; E.E. Lincoln to Harrington (8 January 1934), File 15, Willis Harrington Papers, Hagley Museum; "How Manufacturing Industries Operate," File 251, NAM Papers; Milton Derber, "Employer Associations in the United States," in *Employers Associations and Industrial Relations*, ed. John Windmuller and Alan Gladstone (New York, 1984), 80.

War I, spindle capacity overwhelmed demand after 1920. Business failure and local rivalries shuffled assets within the industry but, as one observer complained, "bankruptcy again and again proved merely a step for bringing a mill back into cutthroat competition based on the low figures of a bankruptcy sale." After 1923, the North steadily lost spindles to low-wage, technologically superior southern mills. Attempts to curtail excess capacity, regional competition, and volatile prices led to numerous attempts at trade association. Following the failure of a Federal Trade Commission (FTC) experiment, leading southern mills established the Cotton Textile Institute (CTI) in 1926. The CTI pursued industry-wide stability through "open pricing" and statistical exchanges but did so without challenging the southern wage advantage (which might alienate active or potential members in the South). After 1929, the CTI increasingly tried to ration production with wage standards and hours restrictions, but these solutions were undermined by the noncompliance of small and southern mills, state-to-state disparities in legislation, and the difficulty inherent in any attempt to restrain production while industrial capacity remained unchecked.[17]

Mill owners traced excess production and competitive chaos directly to regional inconsistency in wages (which represented over half of value added). Mechanization and a "stretch-out" of the ratio between workers and machines removed some wage pressures, but as southern mills thrived, the wage advantage they enjoyed remained the paramount concern of northern mills. Private attempts to agree on quotas or prices attracted only a minority of

17 (Quote) George Sloan [Cotton Textile Institute] to *New York Times* (12 November 1934), File 1644(2), Raskob Papers; Louis Galambos, *Competition and Cooperation: The Emergence of a National Trade Association* (Baltimore, 1966), 90–107, 126–35; Stanley Vittoz, *New Deal Labor Policy and the American Industrial Economy* (Chapel Hill, 1987), 21–34; Seymour Wolfbein, *The Decline of a Cotton Textile City* (New York, 1944), 126–27; James Hodges, *New Deal Labor Policy and the Southern Cotton Textile Industry, 1933–1941* (Knoxville, 1986), 8–21; A. Henry Thurston, "The Woolen and Worsted Industry," in *Industrial Planning Under Codes*, ed. George Galloway (New York, 1935), 131–43; Thomas Smith, *The Cotton Textile Industry of Fall River, Massachusetts* (New York, 1944), 105–9, 135–38; Archibald M. McIsaac, "The Cotton Textile Industry," in *The Structure of American Industry*, ed. Walter Adams (New York, 1950), 47–65; "History of Code of Fair Competition for Wool Textiles," File 267:2; "History of Code of Fair Competition for Cotton Textiles," Division of Review (DR) File 267:1, National Recovery Administration [NRA] Records, RG 9, National Archives, Washington, DC; Sloan to Hoover (20 September 1932), Presidential File [PF] 857, Herbert C. Hoover Papers, Herbert C. Hoover Presidential Library [HCHPL], West Branch, IA; "Memorandum: Textile Consolidation" (February 1928), Name & Subject [N&S] File 46; Strauss to Sloan (2 July 1930) and Sloan to Strauss (30 November 1930), N&S File 70, Lewis Strauss Papers, HCHPL.

the industry in the 1920s and little serious attention after the crash of 1929. Even the formal trappings of trade association provided no means of enforcing cooperation or compliance. And because business competition was regional, there was little prospect for uniform state legislation; southern states, after all, had as much interest in the low-wage textile economy as southern mills. Southern interests were able to stall federal regulation (such as the Federal Child Labor Law in 1916) initiated and supported by northern mills.[18]

Given the persistent failures of the market, trade association, and sporadic state regulation, large firms in the North (as well as the South) increasingly saw stability and organization as a "function of the union." Despite the chronic weakness of textile unions (southern unions were crushed in the 1920s, and most northern locals were short-sighted "business unions"), northern mills hoped that an industry-wide organizing drive would erase the South's competitive advantage. As tension continued to mount in 1929, *Business Week* thought it "quite possible that [northern] employers [would] let the situation come to a strike in order to assist the union in getting its membership built up." By 1934, even some larger southern firms began to complain that "unless some effective compliance [to National Recovery Administration wage standards] is initiated, we would now like to see the industry 100 percent organized in preference to reverting to the unfair competition of two years ago."[19]

But the likelihood of an industry-wide agreement was slim. In frustration, unionized northern firms turned their labor strategies inward. Under the rubric of "union-management cooperation," northern mills pressed unions and workers to meet southern competition with concessions. A plan at the Pequot Mills in Massachusetts "pledged the Union not only to support management efforts to reduce costs but . . . to initiate adjustments to adverse market conditions and to initiate labor-saving technological developments

---

18 Galambos, *Competition and Cooperation*, 165; Arden Lea, "Cotton Textiles and the Federal Child Labor Act of 1916," *Labor History [LH]* 16 (1976): 485–94.
19 Galambos, *Competition and Cooperation*, 176–202; George Mitchell and Broadus Mitchell, "Cotton Mill Labor," in Hardman, *American Labor Dynamics*, 207–8; (quote) *Business Week*, 12 October 1929, 11; southern firms quoted in Vittoz, *New Deal Labor Policy*, 129. On textile unions, see Jules Backman and M.R. Gainsburgh, *Economics of the Cotton Textile Industry* (New York, 1946), 99–100; Vittoz, *New Deal Labor Policy*, 26–33; McIsaac, "Cotton Textile Industry," 55; Slichter, *Union Policies*, 532ff.; Hodges, *New Deal Labor Policy and the Southern Cotton Textile Industry*, 8–21; Dennis Nolan and Donald Jonas, "Textile Unionism in the Piedmont, 1901–1932," in *Essays in Southern Labor History*, ed. Gary Fink and Merl Reed (Westport, 1977), 48–79; George Mitchell, *Textile Unionism and the South* (Chapel Hill, 1931).

regardless of market conditions." The union introduced wage cuts, systematic layoffs, and the "stretch-out" in the late 1920s. For their part, the rank and file recognized the predicament that southern competition had thrust upon the firm and reserved their wrath for the union, which they had expected to act as something more than an industrial-relations division of management. Strikes in the early 1930s were inspired as much by the prospect of replacing the union as by long-standing grievances.[20] The Pequot experiment would have remained a curious episode in textile unionism had not the AFL used such northern models as the *leitmotif* of its southern organizing strategy; doing so did a great deal to dispel southern employers' endemic fear of unionism but at the cost of any realistic support from workers themselves, for which "the union appeared as yet another agency of exploitation, working hand in glove with the employer."[21]

Employee and employer strategies set strict limits on the course of textile unions; they remained weak and scattered before World War II, and where they did succeed, it was often only as an element of business strategy. While textile workers were among the most active and radical elements of organized labor in the interwar era, harsh management resistance in the South and the defensive cultivation of "business" unions by management and labor leaders in the North combined to distort their efforts. For market-anxious northern employers, industrial unionism promised to remove the competitive advantage of the low-wage South and to slow or reverse industry migration. With an industry-wide agreement a distant possibility, however, northern mills settled on the second-best alternative of forcing plant unions to cut unit labor costs through mechanization and concessions.

The Needle Trades

This industrial sector was an archetype of cutthroat competition. The predominance of small firms and a complex system of subcontracting exerted tremendous downward pressure on wages and perpetuated a rapid turnover of capital and employment. The New York-Philadelphia-Baltimore hub of the industry competed not only internally but also with rural "gypsy" con-

---

20 (Quote) Richmond Nyman, *Union-Management Cooperation in the "Stretch-Out": Labor Extension at the Pequot Mills* (New Haven, 1934), 8–10, 17, 36–37, 83–120, 165–66; Slichter, *Union Policies*, 532–59; "Naumkeag Steam Cotton" file, File 50, Morris Cooke Papers, FDRPL; "World's Largest Mill Profits with Labors' Aid," *Forbes* 26 (15 October 1930).

21 Jean Trepp, "Union-Management Cooperation and the Southern Organizing Campaign," *JPE* 41 (1933): 602–24.

tractors and with low-wage regions in the South and Midwest. Labor costs were the principal business concern of any firm interested in anything beyond a strenuously maintained subsistence. Employers appreciated the utility of unions in regulating costs and entry as early as the "Great Upheaval" of 1909–10, when shirtwaist and cloak-and-suit workers successfully struck in a number of large New York firms. The formerly antiunion employers' association emerged from the strike as an ardent supporter of a union that promised to "protect the legitimate manufacturers from the small fry who are cutting into their trade." A 1912 "Protocol of Peace" recast the role of the garment unions, including the ILGWU. Employers began exploiting the regulatory potential of an organized workforce, and employees slipped into a pattern of narrow, job-conscious unionism.[22]

By 1920 the spirit of the Protocol of Peace infused every branch of the needle trades. In the wake of a 1919 lockout, leaders of the men's clothing industry in New York quickly abandoned the open shop and relied upon the "managerial socialism" of Sidney Hillman's ACW to guarantee competitive stability. For employers the ACW, "run by a small group of autocrats with some understanding in economics," was a model for the new unionism. In discrete urban markets, the ACW lifted wages out of competition and drove marginal firms out of business. "I had a job that I could not do," noted a leading Cincinnati clothier after trying to organize the local industry, "and I just passed the buck to Mr. Hillman." Large firms in Cleveland, Baltimore, New York, Chicago, and Rochester sponsored "authorized strikes" in an attempt to build up membership, and by the early 1930s, New York firms, according to *Business Week*, were "yelling their heads off" at the ACW for its failure to organize gypsy contractors. Under the National Recovery Administration (NRA), leading firms and the garment unions joined forces, using the clothing codes to force smaller firms to recognize the union. "The manufacturers," as Stanley Vittoz notes, "had come to look upon the garment workers as an organizational tool and a competitive weapon indispensable to the purposes of economic control."[23]

22 Vittoz, *New Deal Labor Policy*, 37–41; Theresa Wolfson, "Role of the ILGWU in Stabilizing the Women's Garment Industry," *Industrial and Labor Relations Review* 4 (1950): 33–43.

23 (Quote) Steven DuBrul to Gardiner Means (11 October 1934), File 2, Gardiner Means Papers FDRPL; J. Hardman, "Four Days that Shook Cincinnati," in *American Labor Dynamics*, 149–58 (quote, 150); *Business Week*, 12 October 1929, 22–24, and 11 January 1933, 22; Fraser, *Labor Will Rule*, 146–89; Vittoz, *New Deal Labor Policy*, 34–46 (quote, 45); Gladys Palmer, "Job-Conscious Unionism in the Chicago Men's Clothing Industry," *American Economic Review* [*AER*] 20 (1930): 28–38;

Leading garment firms recognized the potential of unions in regulating wages and as an instrument of order and authority on the shop floor. Large retailers and allied manufacturers saw unions as guarantors of stable supplies, production standards, and (at least indirectly) consistent demand for the industry's product.[24] Large garment firms (such as Hart, Schaffner and Marx of Chicago) and retailers (such as Louis Kirstein of Filene's) spoke fondly of Hillman and the ILGWU's Dubinsky and keenly appreciated their contributions to competitive peace. Wage negotiations between the ACW and employers resembled economic surveys of the industry, and the union not only employed business agents and a "market stabilization department" but often also took the initiative in reforming production and opening new shops.[25] The fact that both the ACW and the ILGWU were nominally socialist unions only underscored the gap between ideology and practice.

Although men's and women's clothing were the most important branches of the industry, the logic of regulatory unionism ran through business strategies in many of the specialty trades.[26] In the hat industries, leading employers

Steve Fraser, "Combined and Uneven Development in the Men's Clothing Industry," *BHR* 57 (1983): 522–47. On union regulation under the NRA, see B.M. Squires [Chicago Clothing Trade Board] to Leiserson (18 August 1933), File 38, William Leiserson Papers, State Historical Society of Wisconsin, Madison; U.S. Senate, Committee on Finance, *Investigation of the National Recovery Administration* (Washington, 1935), 1205–19, 1419; "History of the Code of Fair Competition for Cotton Garments," DR File 267:118; "Industry Report on the Coat and Suit Industry," File 5:7, NRA Records.

24 Steve Fraser, "Dress Rehearsal for the New Deal: Shop Floor Insurgents, Political Elites, and Industrial Democracy in the Amalgamated Clothing Workers," in *Working Class America: Essays on Labor, Community and American Society*, ed. Michael Frisch and Daniel Walkowitz (Urbana, 1983), 213–16.

25 Hart, Schaffner and Marx to Kirstein (25 April 1939), File 26; Kirstein to Members of [Rochester] Clothiers' Exchange (13 November 1911), File 68; "ILGWU" file, File 38, Louis Kirstein Papers, Baker Library, Cambridge, MA; "The Hart Schaffner Marx Labor Agreement," in *Trade Unions and Labor Problems*, ed. John R. Commons (New York, 1920), 534–61; Fraser, "Dress Rehearsal for the New Deal," 218–19; Slichter, *Union Policies*, 393–436, 504–31; Kurt Braun, *Union-Management Cooperation: Experience in the Clothing Industry* (Washington, 1947), 5–76.

26 In the ladies' handbag industry, unions emerged as a more divisive element of competitive relations. "Competition based on unequal labor standards" and industrial migration to Massachusetts, Connecticut, New Jersey, and Pennsylvania induced employers and unions in the established New York core of the industry to force wages up and restrict the employment of skilled handbag workers. Employers outside New York complained bitterly of the restrictive collusion of New York firms and unions, especially when this strategy was sanctioned under the NRA code. See Goldsmith Bros. to NRA (14 February 1934) and Ingbar and Co. to NRA (12 February 1934) in NRA, "The Ladies Handbag Industry," Work Materials #71 (Washington, 1940), 30–31, 34–35, 223–24.

recognized that "the union, by its effective control of working conditions in all important markets, exercises the most potent stabilizing force in the industry." Millinery firms resisted open-shop pressures in the early 1920s, but a dispute over wage cuts left the industry without a collective agreement. In 1930, as one union leader recalled, "a group of manufacturers organized into an association and demanded that the union enter into a collective agreement." The union balked at an agreement while business was bad and did not sign until 1932, after which it struck quickly to organize the remaining shops and, as each settled, "urged upon them that they join the manufacturer's association." This pattern continued through the New Deal, and when the NRA was struck down, the union hurried to call a national millinery conference to ensure that agreements were not threatened.[27]

In full-fashioned hosiery, established Philadelphia firms saw the union as a "white-hope of stabilization in a chaotic industry" and depended upon the American Federation of Full-Fashioned Hosiery Workers (AFFFHW) to organize marginal and migrant competition. The AFFFHW researched the industry's problems (retaining Morris Cooke, an apostle of scientific management), drew on the union's cash reserves to promote the industry's products, and encouraged employers to adopt "a constructive program for the industry." In a 1929 agreement, the union accepted wage cuts and the stretch-out and initiated further wage cuts in 1930 and 1931. According to William Leiserson, "the *industry* wanted and secured a 100 percent closed shop and a [dues] check-off" in order to force employees to honor union-initiated wage cuts and guarantee the financial health of the AFFFHW. The AFFFHW, without a trace of irony, feared further alienating the rank and file by compounding wage cuts with mandatory union dues and unsuccess-

---

27 NRA, "The Millinery Industry," Work Materials #53 (Washington, 1939); Millinery Industry Report, Compliance Division (CD) file 172:6, NRA Records; Green, *The Headwear Workers,* 155, 158–86 (quote, 176), 192–200. Union organization in the hat industry was also a defense against the tremendous market power of large buyers, which made a practice of "holding out the promise of large orders if their prices were met." As Green notes: "All too frequently these prices could be met only at a loss to the manufacturer. But the dream of large orders was ever before him; he hoped that today's loss would be tomorrow's gain. That his dream was rarely realized was natural, for most of his competitors were dreaming the same dream, and there were so many of them that the buyers could move from one to the other, always promising and never fulfilling. And a little extra pressure could always be judiciously applied by financing additional manufacturing units and throwing them into the competitive maelstrom" (187). The background of regulatory unionism in the hat industry is traced in Daniel Ernst, "The *Danbury Hatters* Case" in *Labor Law in America: Historical and Critical Essays,* ed. Andrew King and Christopher Tomlins (Baltimore, 1992), 180–200.

fully resisted the dues check–off. For employers, the AFFFHW was an opportunity rather than a threat, and organized firms frantically sought agreements that would "enable the union to function as an essential instrument for the much-needed stabilization of the industry."[28]

Unfortunately for employers, the regional and competitive fragmentation of the needle trades undermined the regulatory impact of labor agreements. Although, as one student notes, "it made little difference to the employer whether the wage standard of the worker was raised fifty cents an hour or one dollar an hour, as long as the same rule applied throughout the industry," uniform rates and rules proved elusive. Easy entry, migration, and disparate patterns of regional organization in the various trades made regulatory unionism logical but difficult to maintain. Unionized firms were threatened as unions failed to maintain critical levels of organization. A Cleveland firm saw "the sole hope of the industry [resting upon] the union regaining some control," yet, as Sidney Hillman observed, "the 25 percent in the industry which stayed out from under union influence [have] materially interfered with the program which three-fourths of the industry accepted and found workable."[29]

Bituminous Coal

In coal, regional wage competition and an excess of mines constantly upset stability and profits. Labor accounted for 60 percent of costs, and no single firm exerted any palpable influence on the market (the top 300 firms in 1920

28 "Hosiery Strike 1930," File 222, Cooke Papers; (quote) William Leiserson to Benedict Wolf (6 July 1937), File 28, Leiserson Papers; (quote) Lyle Cooper, "Recent National Trade Agreements in the Silk Hosiery Industry," *JPE* 39 (1931): 69–80. In 1931, New Jersey workers walked off the job in disgust with the third union-sanctioned wage cut. The AFFFHW responded by diverting the wildcat strike to a nonunion mill in Reading, Pennsylvania. "The union sent down some pied pipers from its Philadelphia office to lead the excursion," reported *Fortune*, "and most of the 5,000 strikers moved on Reading *en masse*. After an eight-day siege . . . they returned to New Jersey, their indignation safely vented, and went back to work." See "American Federation of Full-Fashioned Hosiery Workers," *Fortune* 5 (January 1932): 49, 52–53, 104, 107.

29 Jesse Carpenter, *Competition and Collective Bargaining in the Needle Trades, 1910–1967* (Ithaca, 1972), 42–43; (quote) Cleveland Garment Manufacturers Association to Morris Cooke (12 October 1926), CGMA to Cooke (1 November 1927), and ILGWU to Cooke (6 November 1929), File 87, Cooke Papers; Hillman quoted in NRA, "Men's Clothing Industry," Work Materials #58 (1936); National Labor Board [NLB], "In the Matter of Full-Fashioned Hosiery Manufacturers . . . (15 December 1933), and "In the Matter of the General Silk Strike" (2 November 1934), *Decisions of the National Labor Board* (Washington, 1934), 7, 9–11.

controlled only 57 percent of production). "Nature has enforced the Clayton Act in the case of the [coal] industry," observed one operator, and *Fortune* agreed that "if coal were a vegetable, the coal producer would greatly resemble the farmer." While leading mines bandied about notions of cartelization and regulation, most others were leery of collective solutions that threatened to "shake out" excess competition. Unionization was a logical regulatory option. "With the opportunity to fix settlements of the largest single factor in operating costs, both over a wide area in the industry and for a definite period," noted one observer, "the purely business value of scale contracts becomes a consideration of prime importance." Since the 1880s, unionism had been a key to stability in the Central Competitive Field (CCF) of Indiana, Illinois, Ohio, and Pennsylvania. Southern operators smelled conspiracy in the collusion of the UMW and the CCF mines, while the latter noted that "entrance of the union may be warranted by conditions in the industry as a whole."[30]

High wartime demand encouraged a flood of new mines that, once the wartime boom had faded, were poised to leap into the fray at the slightest rise in prices. This new competition came primarily from firms or regions beyond the CCF's grasp; coal-using industries established nonunion "captive" mines, and commercial mining expanded into the open-shop pastures of West Virginia and Kentucky. In an atmosphere of collapsing demand, excess competition, and chronic labor strife, the previously cozy agreements between the CCF mines and the UMW were on shaky ground when the principals met at Jacksonville, Florida, in 1924. At Jacksonville, the CCF mines sought sweeping wage cuts, while the UMW hoped to stem concessions, cement its gains in the CCF mines, and flush out excess production. Unfortunately for the union and union mines, the Jacksonville accord eroded their bilateral monopoly. CCF mines that did not shut down were mecha-

---

30 (Quote) W. Barnum [National Coal Association] in NICB Proceedings (15 May 1930), File I:2, NICB Papers; "Code for Coal," *Fortune* 8 (October 1933): 57; Corwin Edwards, "The Dilemma of the Coal Union," in *American Labor Dynamics*, 185; (quote) Labor Policy for Bituminous Coal" (1922), Commerce File (CF) 98, Hoover Papers; A. Ford Hinrichs, *The United Mine Workers of America and the Non-Union Fields* (New York, 1923), 19–21, (quote, 107), 112–25. See also Bowman, *Capitalist Collective Action*, 148–220; Vittoz, *New Deal Labor Policy*, 47–56; William Graebner, *Coal Mining Safety in the Progressive Era* (Lexington, 1976), 72–111; James Johnson, *The Politics of Soft Coal* (Urbana, 1979), 95ff. National Bureau of Economic Research [NBER], *Minimum Price Fixing in the Bituminous Coal Industry* (Princeton, 1955), 10–15, 21–27, and *Report of the Committee on Prices in the Bituminous Coal Industry* (New York, 1938), 5, 13–14, 23; NICB, *The Competitive Position of Coal in the United States* (New York, 1931), 11, 19–27, 37–147.

nized as quickly as possible, and union locals were forced to choose between concessions and jobs. Nonunion southern mines grew rapidly. By 1927, renegotiation of the Jacksonville agreement had become something of a joke, and the industry was competitive on a nonunion basis. In 1920 the UMW counted 400,000 members; by 1929 it collected dues from barely 85,000.[31]

Even as they destroyed the UMW in the 1920s, employers began to appreciate the regulatory role the union had played before 1920 and could play again in the future. Union weakness ushered in a new era of brutal competition and, more troubling to mine owners, a revival of genuinely radical unionism. In 1923, a central Pennsylvania operator wrote UMW President John Lewis that "many operators – both outlaws and *in*laws – are wishing more power to your union." At the same time, southern "outlaw" mines viewed attempts to rebuild the union as "part of an understanding between the union and the bituminous operators . . . that the union will eliminate competition from all independent fields." For its part, the UMW tried to lure CCF mines with a "double contract . . . one contract for consumption by [workers] and the public; another in the form of a letter pledging the union to do certain things." While many mining interests simply shuffled their assets to the South, others longed for the revival of a strong union. "A reestablishment of the United Mine Workers to the position of dominance it held prior to 1920," reasoned *Coal Age* in 1931, "would offer tangible promise of economic betterment to the industry."[32]

31 Lamont to C. Munro (24 October 1928), File 89–2, Thomas W. Lamont Papers, Baker Library; Morton Baratz, *The Union and the Coal Mines* (New Haven, 1955), 60; Waldo Fisher, "Bituminous Coal," in *How Collective Bargaining Works: A Survey of Experience in Leading American Industries*, ed. Harry Millis (New York, 1942), 237–38; Sachs, "Economic Analysis of the Coal Problem," File 112, NRA Records; Hoover to Frank Kellogg (31 August 1922), CF 97; P. Moore to L. Wallace (1 May 1922), CF 98; Memorandum on Coal (August 1922), CF 97; "Coal Conferences: Jacksonville" (1924), CF 101; Peterson and Packer Coal to Hoover (6 June 1921), CF 100; Belaire Ohio Chamber of Commerce to Coolidge (2 May 1925), CF 98; "Coal Conferences: Cleveland" (1925), CF 101; C. White to Hoover (9 February 1927), CF 99, Hoover Papers.

32 Ethelbert Stewart, "Equalizing Competitive Conditions," in Commons, *Trade Unions and Labor Problems*, 525–33; (quote) Melvyn Dubofsky and Warren Van Tine, *John L. Lewis: A Biography* (New York, 1977), 106; John Edgerton in *Open Shop Bulletin* 12 (6 March 1926), File 243, NAM press release (23 September 1930), File 250, NAM Papers; (quote) Van Bittner to W.F. Minton, J.D. Rogers memo (26 October 1933), and (quote) C.B. Neel to Virginia Coal Operators Association (28 October 1933), File II:426, Westmoreland Coal Papers, Hagley Museum; (quote) "Confidential Memorandum for Mr. Green" (1926), CF 98, Hoover Papers; *Coal Age* cited in Vittoz, *New Deal Labor Policy*, 56–69. In 1931, *Coal Age* added: "Direct labor charges are such a major part of the cost of production . . . there can be no

Union-management strategies were complicated by the presence of powerful corporations (including Mellon's Pittsburgh Coal, Rockefeller's Consolidation Coal, and most major steel mills and railroads) among the nonunion outlaws, the uneven willingness of states to safeguard union gains, and the fear that increased labor costs (while bringing order to competition in coal) would undercut the position of coal *vis-à-vis* capital-intensive (oil or hydro) energy industries.[33] Despite these difficulties, major mines promoted the union as an organizational representative for the industry through the 1930s. A Westmoreland Coal executive saw the UMW as "essential if we are not to have conditions which lead to continuous strife and turmoil in the South" but remained "fearful that it will take some time for the United Mine Workers of America to educate its [southern] members into the discipline of the organization." In wage agreements throughout the 1930s, the UMW promised to discipline new entrants and protect union mines "against any lower wage scale in other competing districts." As the New Deal solidified regulatory unionism in coal, the losers were clearly the Progressive Miners of America (who saw the UMW as an antiradical initiative of northern operators) and the nonunion southern mines (which saw UMW gains as a "plot of the union and union operators to force higher labor costs upon them").[34]

hope for price stability and for long term planning without stabilization of wages and standardization of working conditions . . . such stabilization without the interposition of some outside agency representing the workers presents almost insurmountable obstacles" (cited in Farr, *Origins of Recent Labor Policy*, 29).

33 Myron Taylor to FDR (16 October 1933), File 133–4, Lamont Papers; "National Labor Board, Captive Mines Cases," File 1173–5:25, Pierre S. DuPont Papers, Hagley Museum; "Coal Strike," File 860:14, Pennsylvania Railroad [PRR] Papers, Hagley Museum; "1925" folder, CF 98, Hoover Papers; "Notes on meeting of coal operators" (1931), File II:353, Virginia File 258; Southern States Industrial Council press release #105 (1935), File II:353, Virginia File 249, Westmoreland Coal Papers. Mellon underwrote the UMW during a 1922 strike but abandoned it after 1925. Lewis noted: "It is all very well for the administration to say that it has nothing to do with it [the erosion of Jacksonville standards], when Andy Mellon is sitting in the cabinet and Andy dominates the Pittsburgh Coal Company." [Dubofsky and Van Tine, *John L. Lewis*, 87–107; Lewis quoted in J. Leary to Hoover (27 November 1925), CF 101, Hoover Papers.

34 (Quote) R.E. Taggart [Stonega Coal] to T.M. Frazier (3 October 1933); John Lewis to John Saxton (30 September 1935); and (quote) "Virginia District Agreement" (1935), all in File II:426; "Wage Agreement between Southern Appalachian Coal Operators Association and District 19 UMWA" (1933), File II:538; Southern Subdivisional Code Authority to Taggart (23 November 1933), II:399 (VA File 101), Westmoreland Coal Papers; C.E. Pearcy [Progressive Miners of America] to FDR (7 June 1934), Official File (OF) 407, Franklin D. Roosevelt [FDR] Papers, FDRPL;

"What Lincoln once said of the nation applies with poignant force to the coal industry today: It cannot live 'half slave and half free.' " With this characteristic flight of rhetoric, John Lewis captured the basic principle of industrial unionism in coal: partial unionization was far more destructive than full unionization, and a state of no unionization was intolerable. "The United Mine Workers," Lewis added, ". . . in supplying a uniform competitive labor cost for bituminous coal mining has been the only stabilizing force which the industry has ever had." In an industry fragmented by regional politics and the interests of innumerable competing firms, a conservative, national union was the sole source of order. With brutal honesty, mining interests promoted UMW President Lewis as their overwhelming favorite for leadership of the *operators'* association, a position Lewis modestly turned down in 1924.[35]

Trucking

Trucking emerged in a complex competitive environment in which unions were at once a prerequisite for stability. It grew rapidly through World War I and continued to grow after 1929 as Depression-burdened industries turned to flexible inventories and smaller deliveries. The number of vehicles in interstate traffic increased from 1,000 to 70,000 between 1920 and 1938. Through this growth, trucking suffered feverish competition, Byzantine rate and licensing systems, easy entry and exit, rapid capital depreciation, and chronic disagreement among the independents, small firms, and delivery fractions of other trades that made up the industry. Sporadic political regulation did little to ameliorate rate competition or restrict entry. In their "search for stabilizing devices," industry leaders looked increasingly to organized employees and the Teamsters Union. "The strange economic and legal position of the industry, a public utility without monopoly privileges, composed of small businessmen," observed Teamsters official Philip Smith,

(quote) Leverett Lyon, *The National Recovery Administration* (Washington, 1935), 431–33.

35 Dubofsky and Van Tine, *John L. Lewis*, 83–84; Lewis quoted in Baratz, *The Union and The Coal Mines*, 70. Lewis's personal power and national status made the pattern of unionism in coal quite exceptional and strengthened industry support for the UMW. As one operator noted: "John Lewis has such an iron-handed control over the union that when you make a deal with him on a case you know it's settled, because if the men involved revolt against it, he will expel them from the union, and since practically every mine is now unionized . . . as an effective form of employee discipline it is as good as the system of work cards in Germany" (quoted in DuBrul memo [late 1930s?], File 28, Sachs Papers).

"places the union in the position of an umpire to promote fair industry practices and rules which no other instrumentality in the field has been able to accomplish."[36]

In the absence of any viable organization of employers, Teamsters locals became the principal advocates and guardians of wage standards, barriers to entry, rate compliance, and fair trade practices. Especially in the West, Teamsters pursued pricing and competitive strategies and initiated and staffed "employer" associations where employers themselves were unwilling or unable to do so. A Seattle Teamsters leader boasted that, as secretary of a laundry drivers' local, he had eliminated 146 of 380 competing operators. The union's regulatory role broadened after 1933, as the NRA encouraged both union strength and the enforcement of trade practices and, as one observer noted, "produced for the first time an industry-wide consciousness on the part of employers, coupled with a realization of the part which the union could play as a policing or enforcement agency." For employers, the conservative Teamsters also stood out as an oasis of business-minded unionism. After 1933, "firm after firm came into the union without any organizational efforts on the part of the local." Later in the 1930s, the Teamsters (with little cooperation from employers) created and staffed a national Fair Trade Practice Board.[37]

In the long run, the competition and disorganization that made regulatory unionism attractive to trucking employers also undermined the impact of labor agreements. The NRA was an "eye-opener" to the organizational potential of unionization and to the difficulties of such organization in an industry that defied conventional patterns of employment. By NRA estimates, the vast majority of truckers were single-vehicle, single-driver "firms" that lay beyond the scope of union agreements; accordingly, leading firms pressed for a restrictive system of licensing and rate regulation (paralleling the ICC

36 David Garnel, *The Rise of Teamster Power in the West* (Berkeley, 1972), 294–98, 322–23; William Childs, *Trucking and the Public Interest: The Emergence of Federal Regulation, 1914–1940* (Knoxville, 1985), 18–24, 48–57, 73–75; Samuel Hill, *Teamsters and Transportation: Employee-Employer Relationships in New England* (Washington, 1942), 15; Nathan Feinsinger, *Collective Bargaining in the Trucking Industry* (Philadelphia, 1949), 1–15; Philip Smith in *Proceedings of the Fifteenth* [Teamsters] *Convention* (1947): 134.

37 Hill, *Teamsters and Transportation*, 27–29, 226–25; Garnel, *Rise of Teamster Power in the West*, 67–91; Irving Bernstein, "The Politics of the West Coast Teamsters and Truckers," *Proceedings of the Industrial Relations Research Association* 10 (1957): 15; Sterling Rigg, "The Chicago Teamsters' Unions," *JPE* 34 (1926): 17–22; Childs, *Trucking and the Public Interest*, 142ff.; (quote) Feinsinger, *Collective Bargaining in the Trucking Industry*, 33; (quote) Hill, *Teamsters and Transportation*, 76–79, 206–25.

regulation of the railroads) to drive small operators out of the industry and set the stage for a more comprehensive union influence. The industry, as an NRA official observed, was "looking more and more to the rate fixing provisions . . . and anxious to move in that direction." Industry strategies were embodied in the Motor Carrier Act (1935), which ended corrosive rate and wage chiseling by small firms and leaned heavily on the coercive power of the unions to maintain standards.[38]

Glass

The glass industry, like many older manufacturing industries, had a long history of craft unionism, regional competition, and protection from international competition. The importance of skilled labor blurred distinctions between artisan and capitalist, and craft traditions reinforced the employees' interest in production and competition. And employers used unions of skilled and unskilled workers to take wages out of competition, restrict entry, and meet the constant threat of new challenges in a profitable and protected industry. For industry leaders, the power of the established crafts and the tenor of regional competition made stable labor relations necessary; insulation from foreign competition made unionism (and its costs) bearable. As the glass industry adjusted to the technologies, markets, and work regimes of the twentieth century, employers struggled to maintain the regulatory and organizational benefits of union agreements.

In the glass industry as a whole, employment stagnated in the interwar years. New demand (especially from the auto industry) was satisfied by increased productivity. In window glass and bottle glass, the two largest industry sectors, new technology (sheet-drawing machines and automated "feed and flow" bottle machines) led to excess capacity, especially for bottle firms facing Prohibition and the substitution of cans and paper packaging. In an attempt to relieve the pressures of surplus production, glass firms turned to a long-established framework of regulatory unionism. Before 1900, an elaborate stock deal with window glass workers had guaranteed their interest in the competitive health of the industry, and in subsequent years the union even facilitated the introduction of labor-saving machinery. Leading firms and the union renewed this alliance in the 1920s, although em-

38 Trucking Industry Reports, CD Files 172:1, 3, 5, and 6, NRA Records (quote); "Preliminary Report on Trucking," File 14, Leon Henderson Papers, FDRPL; Daniel Tobin [Teamsters] to G. Berry (17 May 1938), OF 4046, FDR Papers; Hawley, *New Deal and the Problem of Monopoly,* 231–34; Meyer Fishbein, "The Trucking Industry and the National Recovery Administration," *Social Forces* 34 (1955): 71–79.

ployers were now more interested in appropriating the organizational power of the unions than the skills they represented.[39]

In the glass bottle industry, employers saw unionization as the key to competitive stability, and the AFL-affiliated Bottle Blower's Union took the profitability of the industry as its primary concern. Union leaders "were very desirous of a similar association of employers" but found that "it was more difficult to hold employers together." When the employers' association ran afoul of the Sherman Act in 1924, the employers, as one contemporary noted, "were upbraided by the union representatives for having submitted to such pressure and were strongly urged to reorganize." The union was both a guarantor of peace (as it only struck in nonunion firms) and the foremost proponent of a tacit agreement to avoid price wars. Indeed, the union straddled the interests of management and workers so carefully that the union president was the final arbiter of industry labor disputes.[40]

Although continued mechanization and the Depression upset labor relations, leading bottlers were fairly receptive to a union resurgence after 1933 and saw the new American Flint Glass Workers' Union as both a defense against the more radical threat posed by the Congress of Industrial Organizations (CIO) and as a promising means of equalizing wages and restricting entry. These regulatory goals were especially important to leading bottlers Owens-Illinois and Hazel-Atlas. Before 1933, Owens and Hazel used proprietary machinery patents to restrict expansion and production. Union-enforced regulation of labor costs made it possible to extend such restrictions beyond the life of the patents. Owens' chief labor negotiator also served thirteen years as president of the union (although one observer noted that "some unionists are resentful when one of their officials transfers to the employer side of the conference table"). Union and management cooperated closely on legislative matters and spoke with one voice at hearings concerning the tariff or Prohibition repeal.[41]

39 U.S. Bureau of Labor Statistics, "Productivity of Labor in the Glass Industry," *Bulletin 441* (Washington, 1927), 15; Pearce Davis, *The Development of the American Glass Industry* (Cambridge, 1949), 184–85, 189; George Barnett, *Chapters on Machinery and Labor* (Cambridge, 1926), 67–115; Daniel James, *Evolution of the Glass Container Industry* (n.p., 1956), 15–17; Window Glass Maunfacturers' Association, "Memorandum for NRA" (30 October 1934), File 5, Henderson Papers; History of the Code of Fair Competition for Window Glass, DR File 267:533; Glass Container Industry Report, CD File 172:6, NRA Records.

40 John Voll, "Collective Bargaining in the Glass Bottle Industry," *The Annals* 90 (1920): 51; (quotes) Carroll Daugherty, "Industrial Disputes in the Glass Bottle Industry," *JPE* 36 (1928): 699, 712; Leo Wolman, "Collective Bargaining in the Glass Bottle Industry," *AER* 6 (1916): 558.

41 Milton Derber, "Glass," in Millis, *How Collective Bargaining Works*, 687–718; His-

In window glass, collective bargaining was "part of a larger arrangement under which the union was to police the operation of output and sales cartels." Labor agreements crafted by the American Window Glass Manufacturer's Association in the late nineteenth century placed the onus of regulation squarely on the union and required it to restrict the supply of skilled workers (a role the union took so seriously that it sent organizers abroad in an effort to control emigration). Employers also expected the union to monitor and restrict output through a punitive piece rate system. As the Commissioner of Labor observed, "The workers, through their organization, have attempted to join with their employers to regulate the total output of the industry according to the varying states of the market." This agreement collapsed just after 1900 when competition between union factions released restrictions on the labor market, and high prices (the result of both union-policed cartel arrangements and the tariff) encouraged expansion and new competition.[42]

While employers lamented the "dissolution of the monopolistic institutions which [had been] erected upon the foundation of union power," they also welcomed the opportunity to mechanize without union resistance. By 1926, only 2 percent of window glass was drawn by hand. Through the 1920s, leading glass firms (Libbey-Owens-Ford and Mellon's Pittsburgh Plate Glass) turned to predatory pricing as a means of driving out marginal firms. On the eve of the NRA, Pittsburgh and Owens led a price war in the hope of destroying competitors before the Glass Code (which outlawed sales below cost) kicked in. Once the code was in place, however, the major firms again turned to the union to discipline the competitive fringe. Because small firms survived by quoting a 5 percent discount on major contracts (particularly to the auto industry), Pittsburgh and Owens were able to use union-enforced uniform wages to regain a competitive advantage.[43]

tory of the Code of Fair Competition for the Glass Container Industry, DR file 267:36; (quote) "Glass Container," Code Administration Studies [CAS] File 33:3; "Glassware Industry," File 112:8, Code Authority Correspondence, NRA Records.

42 (Quote) Lloyd Ulman, *Rise of the National Trade Union* (Cambridge, 1955), 526–29; Davis, *Development of the American Glass Industry*, 138–39, 175–204. In the lamp chimney industry, the union responded to wage cuts in the 1920s by supplementing wages out of union coffers, its dual allegiance to its membership and to the health of the industry plainly requiring a split strategy of maintaining wages while reducing the industry's labor costs (Slichter, *Union Policies*, 348–49).

43 (Quote) Ulman, *Rise of the National Trade Union*, 531; Kane Plate Glass to NRA (3 July 1934), Justice Memo "Re: Pittsburgh Plate Glass, both in History of the Code of Fair Competition for Flat Glass, DR file 267:541, NRA Records; "Memorandum for General Johnson, re Pittsburgh Plate Glass Company" (5 July 1934), File 5,

Despite mechanization, the glass workers of the 1920s and 1930s inherited an established framework of business-conscious unionism. Leading firms and unions continued to serve as the twin guardians of the industry. In the 1930s, the weight of this "bilateral monopoly" fell almost entirely on the union; employers honored contracts only as long as the union maintained the same wages in competing concerns and restricted the mobility and apprenticeship of the remaining skilled workers.[44] Throughout the glass industry, collective bargaining remained a means of barring entry, organizing mechanization, and forging political and economic alliances between union and management as well as a guarantee against wage competition.

Pottery

The pottery industry echoed the structural and competitive characteristics of the glass industry, although the concentration of production in "pottery towns" and the presence of a single national union after 1902 simplified labor policies. In each product line, skilled labor accounted for 50 to 60 percent of costs, and labor relations were marked less by conflict between workers and employers (who found ample ground for cooperation) than by questions of regional competition, union jurisdiction, and industrialization of the various trades.[45]

In the general and hotel ware trades, cooperation between employees and employers and among employers hinged on the tariff. For the union, the National Brotherhood of Operative Potters, high tariffs meant high wages; for employers, wages were not a primary concern as long as they were equitable enough to restrict domestic competition and were reflected in tariffs. And as one observer noted, "the manufacturers were not blind to the strategic importance of having [union] spokesmen support their claims for increased protection." In the sanitary trade, international competition was less important than the inroads of nonunion casting and enameled ironware. As a result, employers broke the sanitary union during an industry-wide strike

Henderson Papers; "Notes on Plate Glass Industry," (21 April 1936), Reel 1, Katherine Pollack Ellickson–CIO Papers (microfilm), FDRPL.

44 Derber, "Glass," 718–36. The Flint Glass Workers' Union incorporated unskilled "miscellaneous" workers in the wake of the Wagner Act; see Richard Slavin, "The Flintglass Workers' Union vs. the Glassware Industry: Union-Management Policies in a Declining Industry," *LH* 4 (1963): 29–31.

45 David McCabe, *National Collective Bargaining in the Pottery Industry* (Baltimore, 1932), 2–4; Marc Stern, "The Potters of Trenton, New Jersey, 1850–1902: A Study in the Industrialization of Skilled Trades," (Ph.D diss., SUNY—Stony Brook, 1986), 753ff.

in 1922, despite the efforts of the Brotherhood "to concede as much as it thought it could persuade its members to give." A year later, the Department of Justice forced the employers' association to disband, leaving the sanitary trade completely disorganized.[46]

For general and hotel ware producers, the union's regulatory role was clearer. Union regionalism undercut uniform wage agreements before 1900, after which time the Brotherhood set out to establish a uniform scale "with or without the cooperation of the manufacturers." Employers welcomed the union initiative and the establishment of uniform wages at an average of going rates in New Jersey and lower-wage Ohio and West Virginia. Union members in New Jersey, who sacrificed high wages for an anticompetitive industry standard, were less enthusiastic. Between 1905 and 1922, union and management cooperated closely in the maintenance of industry standards and shared the chore of presenting the industry's case at congressional tariff hearings.[47]

When conditions in the pottery industry collapsed in 1922, the Brotherhood and employers quickly agreed on a wage cut, showing, as one observer put it, "that the union could give on a large scale as well as take." The workers rejected the wage cut, and the resulting strike found union leaders and management "on the friendliest terms" on one side and disgusted employees on the other. The 1922 strike (the same one that destroyed the union in the sanitary branch) ended with management agreeing to a modest wage increase. Employers clung to the union through the 1920s despite dismal business conditions; they were obviously far more worried about the possible collapse of pattern bargaining than the workers themselves. In the late 1920s, the employers' association even suggested the exchange of $100,000 bonds as a guarantee against violations of the labor agreement. In NRA code negotiations, the major potteries concentrated on continued tariff protection and some guarantee that collective bargaining in the industry would be protected and strengthened.[48]

---

46 McCabe, *Collective Bargaining in the Pottery Industry*, 90, 97, 369–70, 403–5 (quotes 114, 387); Donald Kennedy, "Industrial Relations in the Pottery Industry," *JPE* 35 (1927): 522–42.

47 McCabe, *Collective Bargaining in the Pottery Industry*, 36–38, 43–50, 188–90, (quote 194).

48 McCabe, *Collective Bargaining in the Pottery Industry*, (quote 106), 364–65; Employees of Mansfield Pottery to NLB (3 July 1934), File 28, Official Correspondence, National Labor Relations Board [NLRB] Records (RG 25), National Archives; History of the Code of Fair Competition for China and Porcelain, DR File 267:126, NRA Records.

Printing

The pattern of unionism in printing reflected intense local competition and the peculiar dynamics of a service industry. The bulk of printing employment was in the noncompetitive newspaper branch, in which large chains monopolized local markets and profited from advertising revenue rather than direct sales.[49] By contrast, the commercial "book and job" branch was fiercely competitive. Stenographic and duplicating technology undercut traditional markets by enabling businesses to meet their own printing needs. Large publishing houses (whose role was largely consultative and promotional) and consumer magazines added to competitive instability by subcontracting production to small "bedroom" shops and binderies and engaging in desperate battles for mass markets. In turn, it was often difficult to distinguish employers from employees under the complex contracting system; many were members of the union and the employers' association, the United Typothatae, at the same time.[50]

In this atmosphere, unionism in commercial printing was a mutual and necessary exercise in "joint industrial control." Although the national printing unions were rooted in the newspaper industry, contract printers also saw them as a "a major stabilizing force" essential to organized competition in urban markets (especially New York and Chicago). Employers' associations (the Typothatae and Ben Franklin Clubs) dated to the eighteenth century but had no means of controlling their members and "had banquets as [their] main activity." The Typothatae had little national clout and reflected the ambivalence of employers on the labor question by maintaining open- and closed-shop divisions. Unions, meanwhile, lobbied consistently for "an em-

49 One-sixth of all interwar dailies and over one-quarter of total newspaper circulation were controlled by six chains (Hearst, Gannet, McCormick, Scripps-Howard, Block, and Ridder). National or local monopolies dominated 1,200 of 1,400 cities with daily newspapers. See NLRB, Division of Economic Research, *Collective Bargaining in the Newspaper Industry* (Washington, 1939), 1–26, 68–69, 90, 103; Jacob Loft, *The Printing Trades* (New York, 1944), 9–22, 29–31, 176–79; Robert Burns, "Daily Newspapers," in Millis, *How Collective Bargaining Works*, 103.

50 William Miller, *The Book Industry* (New York, 1949), 3–15, 50–65; John Tebbel, *A History of Book Publishing* (New York, 1978), vol. 3, *The Golden Years Between the Wars*, 5, 8, 55–56, 427–28, 465; O.H. Cheney, *Economic Survey of the Book Industry, 1930–1931* (New York, 1931), 210–310; George Barnett, *The Printers: A Study in American Trade Unionism*, American Economic Association Quarterly 10 (Cambridge, 1909), 3–85; Leona Margaret Powell, *The History of the United Typothatae of America* (Chicago, 1926), 125; Emily Clark Brown, *Joint Industrial Control in the Book and Job Printing Industry*, Bulletin of the United States Bureau of Labor Statistics 481 (Washington, 1928), 1–10.

ployers' association in which they could have confidence." In the absence of such an association, they took it upon themselves to manage the introduction of new technology, regulate cost and price competition, and bar entry by controlling apprenticeship.[51]

The tenor of labor relations changed through the early 1920s as the widespread introduction of Linotype and tape-perforation typesetting displaced skilled workers, increased productivity, and left larger shops with a distinct competitive advantage. The unions were strong enough to demand some say in the introduction of the new technology. A conference of union leaders and employers in 1921 laid the basis for unionism on business terms but also divided employers by reopening the wounds of a prewar battle over the eight-hour day. Although national bargaining deteriorated, the unions maintained a firm regulatory hand on competitive conditions in most major urban markets. And open-shop branches (such as the Baltimore and Boston graphic printing industries) suffered as attempts to stem wage competition or price gouging, without the disciplinary power of a union, lasted only as long as favorable business conditions.[52]

Echoing the experience of other industries, commercial printers reacted to competitive instability and their own disorganization by relying upon the printing unions to restrict entry and regulate costs. After half-hearted confrontations with national printing unions in 1899–1902 and 1920–21, the industry abandoned fleeting agreements among market rivals for union-enforced wage and working standards. Unionization was moderately successful

51 Emily C. Brown, "Book and Job Printing," in Millis, *How Collective Bargaining Works,* 119–25, 125; (quote) Leona Powell, "Typothatae Experiments with Price Maintenance and Cost Work," *JPE* 34 (1926): 84; (quotes) Loft, *The Printing Trades,* 22, 185; Leona Powell, "Typothatae and the Eight Hour Day," *JPE* 33 (1925): 661; Leonard Drake, *Trends in the New York Publishing Industry* (New York, 1940), 15, 31; Clarence Bonnett, *Employers' Associations in the United States* (New York, 1922), 226–83.

52 Loft, *The Printing Trades;* Emily C. Brown, "Price Competition in the Commercial Printing Industry," *JPE* 38 (1930): 204–7; Brown, *Joint Industrial Control,* 11–73. In newspaper labor relations, a stable arbitration procedure established by the ANPA before World War I collapsed in the 1920s with the establishment of an open-shop division. Mediation in the mechanical trades was rebuilt throughout the interwar era, and collective bargaining with newswriters (the American Newspaper Guild) began under the NRA. Despite flirting with the open shop, newspapers remained about 90 percent organized. See Edwin Emery, *History of the American Newspaper Publishers' Association* (Minneapolis, 1949), 62–118, 144–45, 178–81; NLRB, *Collective Bargaining in the Newspaper Industry,* 55; Bonnett, *Employers' Associations,* 207–25.

in "policing the industry" in urban markets. In the absence of strong national organization, however, competition between major printing centers over large consumer and trade contracts and the pressures of the Depression slowly undercut such agreements. Through the 1930s, many employers hoped that the revival of printing unionism (protected by the New Deal) might dampen these competitive pressures.[53]

Construction

The construction "industry" is simply a means of contracting and subcontracting labor, and craft unions representing that labor have always been its organizational focus. Although, as in printing, the contracting system often blurred distinctions between worker and employer, stability clearly hinged on the ability to restrict competitive bidding by controlling wage wars and entry into the trades. Because labor was hired on short-term contracts (a 1919 study noted a laborer who had worked for seventy-six contractors and been hired 108 times in five years), employers wanted to govern the terms of employment before they met with workers. "Labor organizations," noted an observer of the Chicago market, "perform the functions of providing the contractor with men when he needs them *and of taking them off his hands when a particular piece of work is completed.*" Restrictive labor agreements were facilitated by the insulation of local markets, the adoption of a "cost-plus" system (by which consumers paid for increased costs), and the fact that property owners were often more interested in the swift and uninterrupted completion of a project than principles of employment.[54]

Conservative trade unions were dedicated to their own survival through control of apprenticeship and wages, goals that were also applauded by employers (contractors) anxious to drive nonunion competition from contract bidding. Union power, of course, also meant that new machinery or building materials had to be delicately introduced so as not to upset established trades or spark jurisdictional disputes. In such instances, employers had neither the power nor inclination to deal with recalcitrant trades and turned to joint union-management boards (the National Building Trades Council or the

---

53 Brown, *Joint Industrial Control,* 125, 194–95; Brown, "Book and Job Printing," 170; NLRB, *Collective Bargaining in the Newspaper Industry.*

54 William Haber, *Industrial Relations in the Building Industry* (Cambridge, 1930), 3–11, 50; Bonnett, *Employers' Associations,* 170–73; (quote) Royal Montgomery, *Industrial Relations in the Chicago Building Trades* (Chicago, 1927), 4–5, 8 (emphasis added). Through the 1920s, construction employed 2.5 million; by 1926, construction accounted for almost one-third of AFL membership (Louis Stanley, "Prosperity, Politics and Policy," in Hardman, *American Labor Dynamics,* 197).

National Board for Jurisdictional Awards) or the AFL to sort out union politics. To complicate matters, with competition confined to local markets (buildings could not be built somewhere else), local trades had little fealty to national unions although national strikes or jurisdictional disputes were not uncommon.[55]

Overall, contractors proved willing to live with the arcane demands and anxieties of the specialized trades as long as the unions were able to enforce their rules consistently and bar entry. Open-shop advocates seized upon union practices and the gangsterism ingrained in the bidding system, and much of the energy and financial resources for the open-shop drive came from municipal "citizens' committees" composed of business interests offended by the high price of new or renovated commercial property. But employers *in* the industry either had few quarrels with the unions or saw the contracting system as an opportunity to engage in "collective buccaneering" and line their pockets. "Since it is hard to organize the majority of contractors," noted one observer, "employers' associations look with favor upon the union – in fact rely upon it as a policeman to equalize and regulate competition by enforcing uniform labor and wage standards." A New York contractor agreed that profits and stability "can best be accomplished by a bargain with the unions for exclusive employment."[56]

"Since the union will take care of new [contractors] who attempt to chisel into the industry," reasoned one observer, "why should the employers fight such a set-up?" For employers, union recognition was a negligible price to pay for dependable access to skilled labor, guarantees against cutthroat bidding, and contract provisions that prohibited union members from becoming contractors.[57] This pattern of unionism was widespread in northern cities in the 1920s, but it never penetrated southern markets and collapsed everywhere after 1929. Subsisting on government contracts, the industry pressed

55 Haber, *Industrial Relations in the Building Industry,* 127–96; Montgomery, *Chicago Building Trades,* 5; Ulman, *Rise of the National Trade Union,* 345–48.
56 Edgar Heermance, *Can Business Govern Itself?* (New York, 1933), 57; (quote) Haber, "Building Construction," in Millis, *How Collective Bargaining Works,* 206; contractor quoted in Bonnett, *Employers' Associations,* 173. For the construction industry's role as an organizing focus for open shop employers, see Montgomery, *Chicago Building Trades,* 7, 270ff.
57 (Quote) Steven DuBrul to Gardiner Means (11 October 1934), File 2, Means Papers; Ira B. Cross, "The San Francisco Building Trades," in *Trade Unionism and Labor Problems,* 482–83; Arthur Holden, "The Construction Industries," in Galloway, *Industrial Planning Under Codes,* 352–54; Montgomery, *Chicago Building Trades,* 194–208.

for a more comprehensive protection of collective bargaining as a complement to public works programs. The complexity of municipal, regional, and
industrial strategies was readily apparent under the NRA. The construction
unions, fearing the loss of local privileges in a national agreement, opposed
the NRA code and its labor provisions. But among employers, "pressing
need for the application of an external force [was] universally recognized,"
and industry-wide bargaining was the seen as the font of industrial stability.[58]

Electrical Manufacturing

Among mass-production industries, only electrical manufacturing pursued
regulatory unionism without having its hand forced by the Depression or
the New Deal. The liberal labor policies of GE, Westinghouse, Philco, and
other major firms reflected simple structural and material concerns. Electrical manufacturing encompassed almost 200 major subdivisions and
300,000 distinct products. Large firms diversified across a wider range than
their competitors, but with low capital requirements in many product lines,
even the giants were acutely sensitive to price and cost competition. Rapid
growth and the widespread use of electrical products throughout the industrial economy also left major firms singularly sensitive to aggregate consumption and profit patterns and uniquely receptive to "corporatist" political solutions. Through the 1920s, GE and Westinghouse promoted a
"community" wage that recognized their workers' role as consumers and
the regional pattern of skilled labor markets. But few followed this leadership. The competitive necessity of equal labor costs and the practical desire
to displace or discourage craft unionism pressed industry leaders to encourage an industrial union of electrical workers.[59]

58 History of the Code of Fair Competition for Construction, DR File 267:244A; "Construction," CAS File 33:2; (quote) "Construction Industry in California," CD file
172:1, NRA Records. Cost-plus contracting and the absence of regional competition
also gave the industry the flexibility to remove regional wage differentials under the
NRA [Committee on Industrial Analysis, "Report on the Results and Accomplishments of the National Recovery Act," (Washington, 1937), 128].

59 Kim McQuaid, "Young, Swope, and General Electric's 'New Capitalism': A Study
in Corporate Liberalism, 1920–1933," *American Journal of Economics and Sociology*
36 (1977): 323–32; Montgomery, *Fall of the House of Labor*, 438–53; Ronald Schatz,
"The End of Corporate Liberalism: Class Struggle in the Electrical Manufacturing
Industry, 1933–1950," *Radical America* 9 (1975): 190–91; Milton Derber, "Electrical
Products," in Millis, *How Collective Bargaining Works*, 744, 757–58; Ronald Schatz,
*The Electrical Workers: A History of Labor at General Electric and Westinghouse, 1923–
1950* (Urbana, 1983), 12–14; W.J. Donald, "Electrical Manufacturing Industry," in

In late 1926, GE executives attempted just this. Gerard Swope and Owen Young, fearing the "intolerable handicap" of "different and often competing craft unions," hoped that their sponsorship of an industrial union "might make the difference between an organization with which we could work on a businesslike basis and one that would be a source of endless difficulties." Swope recalled his "cordial talk" with the AFL's William Green:

> I began by explaining the methods of industrial relations which we had developed in the General Electric Company. I described the Plans of Representation, which so far had worked well. I thought that this offered a good foundation for a union. I suggested to Mr. Green that he endeavor to enlist the Plans of Representation of the General Electric Company. The first step, I proposed, was that he should seek to win from the membership of our plants a small contribution to the AFL to be used for the workers throughout the electrical industry. This, if successful, would have led to the formal organization of a single union of workers not only in the General Electric Company but in the plants of all electrical manufacturers.[60]

As Young's biographers add: "It was also pointed out to Green that success at GE would strengthen his hand in the industry generally – thus putting pressure on GE's competitors to match its program of benefits."[61]

As recalled by Swope and Young, this episode must be taken with a grain of salt. And, of course, the AFL ignored GE's opening just as it would ignore the requests of rank-and-file unionists in the industry a few years later. Unionism came to electrical manufacturing on starkly different terms, as a consequence of the Depression and the efforts of workers themselves. Yet despite the tenor of the CIO drive, the industry knuckled under quietly. Contracts with the United Electrical, Radio and Machine Workers in the 1930s reflected a decade of regulatory labor policy. An agreement at Philco in 1933 provided that no AFL-chartered radio workers' local would accept lower wages and made wage increases conditional upon the union's ability to have those wages incorporated in the NRA code (thus forcing competitors to follow Philco's lead). Westinghouse executives observed that, with unionization a "going concern," the point was "not merely to 'play ball' with it but to get the greatest possible value from its existence."[62] A decade later, as union contracts failed to bring an end to wage competition and the union's

Industrial Planning Under Codes, 277–96; NRA, "Open Price Filing in the Electrical Manufacturing Industry," Work Materials #53 (Washington, 1938).

60 David Loth, *Swope of G.E.* (New York, 1958), 168–72.

61 Josephine Young Case and Everett Needham Case, *Owen D. Young and American Enterprise* (Boston, 1982), 379.

62 Schatz, *Electrical Workers*, 63–76; James Matles and James Higgins, *Them and Us: Struggles of a Rank and File Union* (Englewood Cliffs, 1974), 63–88; Westinghouse executives quoted in Derber, "Electrical Products," 783, 772, 778.

threat to managerial authority exceeded its regulatory benefits, the industry turned sharply and violently against the union.[63]

Mass-Production Industry and the Logic of the Open Shop

The industries discussed above represented almost one-half of union membership through the 1920s and close to a one-third of the manufacturing workforce.[64] The experience of these industries colored the emergence of federal labor policy in a number of ways. Scattered experiments in regulatory unionism, however, did not inspire consistent business support for collective bargaining. Regulatory unionism remained rooted in the competitive and organizational strategies of specific industries. Those who appreciated the benefits of an organized workforce did not do so for the same reasons, at the same time, or with the same sincerity. Small or regional competitors usually resisted the regulatory labor policies pursued by leading firms, which constantly weighed the regulatory perks of unionism against challenges to managerial authority or the threat of competition from new entrants, substitute products, and foreign firms. In many instances, employers considered the regulatory power of unions without any real collective-bargaining experience; although union density ran at 50 percent in coal, clothing, and construction, barely 3 percent of textile workers were organized before 1930.[65]

63 Schatz, *Electrical Workers*, 167–75.
64 Unfortunately, the statistical record of unionism in the 1920s is incomplete. Although aggregate AFL membership is available, it is difficult to break down membership or union density by industry. There is no statistical source on unionization that corresponds to the information on industrial employment available in the biennial *Census of Manufactures*. The best industry-by-industry data is compiled in Leo Wolman, *Ebb and Flow in Trade Unionism* (New York: NBER Publication 30, 1936), which also serves as the basis for "Labor Union Membership by Industry," Series D 952–969, *Historical Statistics* (Washington, 1971), II:178. These figures combine industries in such a way as to obscure important characteristics and trends, particularly by combining high- and low-density industries (such as chemicals with stone, clay, and glass; mining with oil; or printing with paper). The data can be partially unpacked by breaking down the membership in particular unions within these groups. But these numbers are not strictly comparable with membership at higher aggregates or Bureau of Census employment information. Of the fractions cited in the text, "one-half of union membership" is based on the *Historical Statistics* table cited above; "one-third of the manufacturing workforce" is based on each industry's percentage share as calculated from the *Census of Manufactures* and averaged over 1919–35.
65 The union movement slipped considerably after World War I; by 1933 less than 10 percent of nonagricultural workers were organized, and union strength was confined to the needle trades, coal, construction, and the railroads. The measure of union

Most importantly, there was little interest in regulatory unionism in the mass-production core of the economy. Leading firms in the steel, automobile, rubber, and chemical industries found unionization a less-promising and more dangerous avenue of potential regulation; substantial and fixed capital investments made it costly and difficult for them to drive out smaller competitors (which often responded to market pressure by consolidating or overproducing rather than exiting), or to equalize the costs of production through labor agreements. Excepting the auto industry, mass-production firms sold their products to relatively well-organized industrial consumers who were less likely and able to tolerate the costs of unionization.[66] And the organizational problems posed by immense internal labor markets imbued mass-production employers with a heightened concern over control of the work process and the threat of labor radicalism. Even in situations where unionization might rationalize competition among firms, its costs on the shop floor seemed too high. For these reasons, such firms brutally resisted unionization.

density in this period echoes the statistical uncertainty of the preceding note. The following is adequate for comparative purposes:

Coal	49%
Clothing	47%
Construction	45%
Railroads	44%
Printing	44%
Tobacco products	15%
Leather products	15%
Stone, clay, and glass	13%
Iron and steel	10%
Forest products	10%
Food products	7%
Nonferrous metals	5%

Calculated from Wolman, *Ebb and Flow*, 200–212, 224–30.

66 Among the mass-production industries, labor-intensity varied considerably; in 1939 wages as a percentage of value added were 49 percent in automobile manufacturing, 44 percent in iron and steel, 40 percent in rubber, 35 percent in electrical manufacturing, and 19 percent in chemicals – the latter representing the lowest percentage of labor costs in industry and the others ranging below the industrial high of just over 50 percent in textiles, leather, and lumber [Michael Bernstein, *The Great Depression: Delayed Recovery and Economic Change in America, 1929–1939* (New York, 1987), 131]. On the interindustry flow of goods, see National Resources Committee, *Structure of the American Economy* (Washington, 1939), 364–69. The auto industry consumed almost one-third of the rubber products and one-fifth of the steel produced in the interwar era, while the chemical industry depended on derived demand for petroleum, autos, and other consumer goods.

The most widespread expression of this antiunion sentiment was the company "union." These management initiatives (also known as "shop committees" or "employee representation plans") encompassed candid open-shop offensives, cynical efforts to comply with federal regulations (through World War I and under the NRA), muddling attempts to regulate conduct on the shop floor, and sincere experiments in union-management cooperation. Generally, employers recognized the need for formal (if restricted) representation in order to steal the thunder of outside organizers, solve the organizational difficulties of modern production, turn the workers' attention inward, and enhance the political and moral legitimacy of the corporation. Company unions postponed workplace struggles and became, as David Montgomery notes, "a theater within which struggles for workers' control . . . clashed with employers' efforts to exclude unions from their enterprises, and both clashed with the government's search for a mechanism to mediate industrial disputes and improve productivity."[67]

As the Special Conference Committee stressed, company unions were little more than "an effective means through which management can exercise its normal function of leadership over the working force." Although advocates argued that company unionism "opened a third course" in labor relations, they were also quick to admit that "the majority of plans in operation have involved little or no sacrifice in control on the part of management." Employers found company unions useful in sugarcoating scientific management and wage cuts (especially during 1920–21 and after 1929), but they kept real collective concerns off the table. Bargaining through a company union, as one steelworker remarked, was "like writing a letter to Santa Claus."[68] Company unions more often represented management to the work-

---

67 [Quote] Montgomery, *Fall of the House of Labor,* 411. See also Robert Ozanne, *A Century of Labor-Management Relations at International Harvester* (Madison, 1967), 116–17; William Hogan, *Economic History of the Iron and Steel Industry of the United States* (Lexington, 1971) 866–68; Farr, *Origins of Recent Labor Policy,* 8, 13–19; Glenn Babcock, *A History of United States Rubber Company* (Terre Haute, 1966), 157–60; Ben Selekman, *Employee's Representation in Steel Works* (New York, 1924), 141–42; Bureau of Industrial Research, "American Company Shop Committee Plans," (1919), File 937:4, PRR Papers (surveying 20 company unions in steel, electrical, machinery, and small manufacturing); File 255, NAM Papers [a compilation (circa 1935) of company union plans]; Daniel Nelson, "The Company Union Movement, 1900–1937: A Re-examination," *BHR* 56 (1982): 335–57; Howell Harris, "Industrial Democracy and Liberal Capitalism, 1890–1925," in Harris and Lichtenstein, *Industrial Democracy in America,* 60–65.
68 SCC quoted in Montgomery, *Fall of the House of Labor,* 414; Carroll French, *The*

ers than vice versa and had neither the resources nor the credibility to establish contacts with a wider labor movement.

In all, mass-production firms agreed on only the most abstract platitudes concerning employee representation. Simple antiunionism was qualified by the realities of shop management and business competition. However insincere, company unions gave workers a sense of what real unions might be like, an opportunity for collective action, and an expectation of a certain level of benefits and representation. Perhaps more importantly, company unions forced employers to distinguish between "good" and "bad" labor organizations and left even shrill advocates of the open shop with a large hole in their defences.[69] Capital-intensive firms (for whom labor was a lesser material and managerial threat) were more willing to make concessions; labor-intensive firms tried to ensure that unionization followed its least-destructive path. Those threatened by unionization often hastened recognition in order to avoid the market losses of a strike; those already unionized moved to spread the union to their competitors and press responsibility for the organization of internal labor markets on it.

Rubber and automobile firms both found employee representation essential to industrial peace and, as regionally concentrated industries (rubber in Akron, autos in Detroit), were acutely aware of labor's power in local politics.[70] While auto executives opposed organized labor through the 1930s, they admired the conservatism of the AFL and, once organized, quickly educated the United Auto Workers in the ethos and competitive priorities of the industry. In steel, regulatory unionism was widespread in the aftermath of the turn-of-the-century mergers but collapsed with the weakening of the crafts and their unions. Through the early century, the belligerent National Metal Trades Association took the lead in labor relations, and price regulation became the organizational focus of the industry.[71] Yet steel re-

Shop Committee in the United States (Baltimore, 1923), 9–26, 37–41, 50–64, 86–89; steelworker quoted in Robert Brooks, *As Steel Goes: Unionism in a Basic Industry* (New Haven, 1940), 105.

69 The role of company unionism in softening employer attitudes toward the NRA is argued by Farr, *Origins of Recent Labor Policy*, 18–19, 34–35. On workers in company unions, see Rick Halpern, "The Iron Fist and the Silk Glove: Welfare Capitalism in Chicago's Packinghouses, 1921–1933," *Journal of American Studies* 26 (1992): 172, 177, 182.

70 An attempt by the Industrial Workers of the World to organize Akron workers in 1913 was stemmed by a cooperative effort of a young AFL organizer named John L. Lewis, Governor Cox of Ohio, and a rookie Ohio State Senator and erstwhile United Mine Workers officer named William Green [Daniel Nelson, *American Rubber Workers and Organized Labor, 1900–1941* (Princeton, 1988), 23–43].

71 The National Defense Association, National Founders League, and National Stove

mained susceptible to wage competition, and the regulatory potential of organized labor was the best second bet for at least some firms as soon as cracks appeared in the price front. Although many employers appreciated the promise of pattern bargaining and conservative industrial unionism to impose order, none would actually pursue these strategies until the workers themselves (by organizing some firms) and the Wagner Act (by guaranteeing workers' gains) forced their hand.

The anxieties of mass-production firms were neatly exemplified in the lumber industry. Like its newer counterparts, lumber shied away from any sort of regulatory unionism, in part because other, similarly aimed options (taxes, production standards, or conservation) seemed more promising but primarily because unionism posed a sharp managerial threat. Unlike the essentially bureaucratic craft unions found in older manufacturing industries, lumber unionism was dominated by the radical International Workers of the World (IWW). In other words, lumber workers (with no craft background) had no claim to the labor process, and lumber firms (extremely leery of the IWW) weren't about to hand it to them.[72] As in the newer mass-production industries, the willingness or ability to accommodate unions depended upon both the strength and status of organized labor in the industry and the sort of threat doing so might pose to managerial authority.

Given the importance attached to the organization of work under mass-production, the threat of radical unionization and the promise of its conservative alternative were considerable. Employers fought a constant battle to achieve peace and productivity without sacrificing control. While willing to launder decisions through company unions, mass-production employers rarely considered independent unions as a logical vehicle for shop-floor authority. Once in place, unions often released management from immediate

Founders League broke from union-centered regulation shortly after the turn of the century and became leaders of the open-shop movement. Early steel labor policies reflected the employers' experience with industry-wide trade agreements in the late nineteenth century. The unions' regulatory role and ability to create monopoly conditions were granted, but neither the unions nor the employers were able to maintain fealty to collective agreements as the metal crafts were deskilled. Gable, "Birth of an Employers' Association," 539; Ulman, *The Rise of the National Trade Union,* 489–535; Ulman, "Influences of Economic Environment on the Structure of the Steel Workers Union," *Proceedings of the Industrial Relations Research Association* 14 (1961): 227; Bonnett, *Employers Associations,* 37–61, 98–133; Margaret Strecker, "The National Founders Association," and "The Founders, The Molders, and the Molding Machine," in *Trade Unionism and Labor Problems,* 406–32, 433–57.

72 Simon Knight, "The Pacific Northwest Lumber Industry and its Response to Labor Standards and Union Legislation During the New Deal," (Master's thesis, University of British Columbia, 1993).

responsibility for the details of shop-floor politics and gave some legitimacy to established seniority systems and the division of work. In all, however, the threat posed by even conservative unions to the organization of large, unskilled, internal labor markets discouraged mass-production employers from experimenting with regulatory unionism; they opposed organized labor as long as no firms in their industry were or were about to be unionized. Only later in the 1930s, with the rise of the CIO, would employers scramble to minimize threats to managerial authority and prevent uneven unionization from upsetting competitive conditions. At this point (as we shall see later), full unionization in a protected economy was as logical, at least for unionized firms, as a return to the open shop.

Toward a New Deal Labor Policy

By the late 1920s, labor relations had evolved into a complex pattern of competitive and opportunistic bargaining. Employers often accepted industrial unions in exchange for the costs those unions could force on competitors and just as often resisted them in order to maintain the advantage of open-shop wages. For employers, labor was a mélange of material, managerial, political, and moral liabilities, and different firms and industries juggled them with bewildering variety and inconsistency. Sporadic concessions on benefits and working conditions, self-serving acceptance of unionization, and aggressive open-shop sentiment often existed side by side.

The economic crash scrambled this already dizzying array of private experiments in labor relations. Regulatory arrangements were suddenly both more urgent and much harder to maintain. Under financial pressure, conciliatory or "welfare capitalist" labor relations lost their appeal and credibility. In mass-production industries, the anxiety and intransigence of employers deepened. For workers in all industries, uncertainty and privation overshadowed the costs and risks of organization. And perhaps most importantly, the awakening of organized labor raised the private and political stakes for both workers and managers. Some employers, seeing labor's new legal and political status as a confirmation of their worst fears, simply dug in their heels. Others saw in labor's resurgence a profound shift in politics and political culture and sought accommodation under circumstances in which they could no longer afford the luxury of open-shop belligerence.[73]

The first surge of union organization in the early 1930s began a long and complex dialectic between labor radicalism and public policy that was steered

73 See Ulman, "Who Wanted Collective Bargaining?" 4–8.

by business reaction to the initiatives of workers in more encouraging legal environments, internecine struggles over the interpretation of federal labor law, and the rocky political detour of the NRA. Industries and firms disagreed sharply over the competitive, regional, international, and managerial implications of unionization. Yet the breadth and variety of experiments in regulatory unionism in the 1920s also suggested that New Deal labor policy had important private precedents and that business reaction rested on the scope and administration of that policy rather than on any philosophical quarrel with its premises. With considerable ambivalence, business saw unionization as an alternative to its own organizational efforts; in the face of constitutional challenges, the federal government saw it as an alternative to its frustrated recovery legislation. As I argue in the following chapters, the New Deal's haphazard politicization of regulatory unionism reflected the persistent failure of other organizational efforts, the crucible of the Depression and attendant labor unrest, and the exhaustion of other options.

4. The Limits of Associationalism
Business Organization and Disorganization, 1920–1935

Dilemmas of competitive strategy and industrial organization emerged most starkly in formal efforts at business or trade association. For business interests, such efforts offered a regulatory hand that was neither as unpredictable as the market's nor as heavy as the state's. Scholars have pointed to the professionalization of industrial research and management, the predominance of group bargaining, and the organizational role of the corporation itself as evidence of the increasing influence (and necessity) of coordinated representation in a complex political economy; in this "organizational synthesis," rationalized corporate power dovetails with new state institutions toward an informal, corporatist form of economic governance.[1] Yet although the interwar years were marked by a groundswell of organizational activity, historians have often confused frantic innovation with far-sighted corporate liberalism and the mere existence of industrial and trade organizations with the attainment of their goals. In many respects, this trend was not so much evidence of a new managerial control as it was a symptom of disintegration and instability. The dismal inefficiency of private business organization after 1920 not only underscores the practical and logical dilemmas of private cooperation in a market economy but also suggests the importance that business would attach to the political opportunities of the New Deal.

Through the interwar era, interest in business organization was primarily a response to the strikingly competitive U.S. political economy, in which firms faced both conventional economic competition in a vast and diverse internal market and political competition within a federated patchwork of legislated regulation and responsibility. In this atmosphere, as I suggested

---

1 See Kenneth Boulding, *The Organizational Revolution* (New York, 1953), 3–15, 131–58; Louis Galambos, "Technology, Political Economy, and Professionalization: Central Themes of the Organizational Synthesis," *Business History Review* [*BHR*] 57 (1983): 471–93; and the essays in *Building the Organizational Society*, ed. Jerry Israel (New York, 1972); *Men and Organizations*, ed. Edwin Perkins (New York, 1977); *Institutions in Modern America*, ed. Stephen Ambrose (New York, 1967).

in the opening chapter, many industries suffered from relentless battles for market share, profitless prosperity, price chiselling, or what they considered "unfair" trade practices. What was exceptional about the U.S. experience was not the managerial or organizational revolution itself but the competitive conditions that made private and political efforts to regulate the market so necessary. As various business organizations tried to escape competition, however, they consistently bungled the basic tasks of collective action within or among industries. Given the pressures of the marketplace, business organization was invariably undermined by the very problems it was designed to meet. Members or prospective members were openly skeptical of organizational claims and were unwilling to surrender managerial or competitive prerogative to any shaky collective authority. This tension between the widely perceived need for organization and the inability to enforce such organization infused the interwar experience of both trade associations (which sought to organize competition in a single industry) and peak associations (which sought to represent the political interests of a number of industries).

Organizational Aspirations and Dilemmas

The institutions of capitalist democracy endow business interests with immense responsibility. The organization of work, of production and exchange, and of economic growth itself is left largely to private interests or at least to the mechanisms of "the market." At the same time, the technological and organizational demands of the market encourage producers to apply more formal authority to many previously laissez-faire decisions. In most modern industrial economies, as Alfred Chandler and others have suggested, production is organized by systems of bureaucratic control rather than exchange. A "visible hand" of specialized managerial expertise regulates internal markets for labor, goods, and services and sorts out the technical complexity and transaction costs of modern production.[2] More importantly, of course, the modern firm is a solution to the labor problem, a means of organizing and directing the efforts of workers who are no longer bound by skill or filial ties to the firm.

But the degree to which corporate organization or authority displaced competitive markets in the interwar economy should not be overdrawn. Historians of the "managerial revolution" have ignored the persistent and cha-

2 Alfred Chandler, *The Visible Hand: The Managerial Revolution in American Business* (Cambridge, 1977).

otic impact of labor relations, capital markets, and politics. More to the point, while corporations rationalized their management of "domestic affairs," their conduct of "foreign affairs" (relationships with other firms) remained uncooperative, unorganized, and fiercely competitive.[3] Business, as a general rule, preferred organized competition and stable profits to the vagaries of the market. Yet the ability of private interests to impose order on markets beyond their own gates was minimal. Neither merger and monopoly early in the century nor enlightened management after 1920 were able to control competition with any consistency or durability.

Business organization is a complicated phenomenon. Market competition serves as an immediate arbiter of supply or demand but cannot manage the wider implications of the price system or longer-term problems of economic growth and stability. Indeed, if one looks beyond the setting of a given price for a given product at a given time, the rationality of the market collapses completely. Limited knowledge, technological complexity, and political anxiety encourage producers and consumers to act irrationally, and unintended consequences scramble the logic and incentives of future exchanges. In turn, the day-to-day mechanisms of exchange are ill-equipped to deal with broader threats posed by organized labor, international competition, or politics. At the same time, the very idea of the market is an impressive cultural and political force. In an environment in which competitive self-interest is uniquely encouraged, celebrated, and rewarded, private cooperation is extremely difficult to accomplish or justify. Generic dilemmas of collective action – including limited knowledge and horizons and an unwillingness to bear the costs of cooperation – are exaggerated in market settings.[4]

These paradoxes and frustrations varied with the form and function of business organization. Trade associations focused on standards of competition within an industry and sought to replicate the advantages of merger or monopoly by taking an active, even coercive, interest in the behavior of members. Multi-industry peak associations, by contrast, reflected business

3 Oliver Williamson, "Emergence of the Visible Hand: Implications for Industrial Organization," in *Managerial Hierarchies,* ed. Alfred Chandler and Herman Daems (Cambridge, 1980), 194–99; Edward Herman and Richard DuBoss, "Alfred Chandler's New Business History: A Review," *Politics and Society* 10 (1980): 87–110; William Lazonick, "Organizational Capabilities in American Industry: The Rise and Decline of Managerial Capitalism," *Business and Economic History* 19 (1990): 35–54; Charles Lindblom, *Politics and Markets* (New York, 1977), 11, 36, 38–39.

4 Mancur Olson, *The Logic of Collective Action* (Cambridge, 1965), 5–36; Alan Wolfe, *Whose Keeper?: Social Science and Moral Obligation* (Berkeley, 1989), 27–36; Anthony Downs, "An Economic Theory of Political Action in a Democracy," *Journal of Political Economy* 65 (1957): 135–50.

efforts to organize as a class. Their concerns were more explicitly political but were also less concerned with shaping or mandating the behavior of members; whereas trade associations sought collective action, peak associations sought only a collective voice. Between these extremes, an array of other groups sought to articulate the anxieties of various fractions of the business community; these were organized across industries, between types of industries, within industries, and according to different political targets. Those interested in maintaining regional competitiveness dominated local and state associations; those interested in stabilizing competition among regions dominated national associations.[5] And many saw business organization not as an end in itself but as a more orderly means of political access or influence. At all levels of organization, however, fundamental weaknesses of representation, organization and enforcement were pervasive.

Consider the problem of representation. Business organization usually reflected some crisis of stability or power, of which low profits and the encroachment of organized labor led the list. Yet even the labor problem inspired few collective solutions. At the turn of the century, many employers' associations were designed to facilitate and maintain collective bargaining, as big business and big labor organized in lockstep. In the aftermath of World War I, associationalism was usually aimed at organizing business and disorganizing workers. Ironically, the open-shop movement undermined both unionization and the urgency and coherence of employer organization. As patterns of labor and business organization diverged, the prospects for meaningful agreement among employers shrank. Because employers were often less interested in bargaining principles than they were in the ability of established unions to standardize labor costs and exclude nonunion competition, many were ambivalent about any collective response to the labor problem. Firms looked to peak organizations such as the National Civic Federation or the National Association of Manufacturers for a political defense of their labor policies but not for ideological leadership or practical guidance.[6]

5 Philippe Schmitter and Donald Brand, "Organizing Capitalists in the United States: The Advantages and Disadvantages of Exceptionalism" (paper presented at the American Political Science Association, 1979): 9–10, 17–18, 41—45; J. Roffe Wike, *The Pennsylvania Manufacturers' Association* (Philadelphia, 1960), 54–55; William Smith, *Local Employers' Associations* (Berkeley, 1955).

6 Richard Gable, "Birth of an Employers' Association," *BHR* 33 (1959): 539; Schmitter and Brand, "Organizing Capitalists in the United States," 39–40; Clarence Bonnett, *Employers' Associations in the United States* (New York, 1922), 226–83; Milton Derber, "Employer Associations in the United States," in *Employers Associations and*

Consider the problem of organization. Different firms and industries had vastly different motives, expectations, and stakes in organizing. Trade association set industry against industry and resulted in a profusion of groups that, rather than rationalizing competition, simply politicized regional or competitive divisions. Most were unwilling and unable to distinguish between self-interest and collective interest, especially when the latter required immediate sacrifices or costs. Knowing that others felt the same way, most competitors were leery of any association that would have them as members. Cooperation was elusive as long as economic interests saw organization as an opportunity for exploitation and competitive advantage and flouted it when market conditions changed. Most resisted political solutions that did not promise immediate and tangible rewards. Organization was "reduced to programmatic futility," as Robert Brady notes, "without the wit at the critical moment to make even those half-hearted compromises urged upon it."[7]

Now, consider the problem of enforcement. In some respects, the most serious failure of private business organization lay in its inability to enforce collective goals or collectively-agreed upon standards of competitive behavior. Organized competition required the exclusion or coercion of some competitors and demanded self-discipline of all. Those that did not require some sacrifice on the part of members were either superfluous or ignored. Yet associations were unable to discipline nonmembers – and disciplined members only at the risk of turning them into the former. Trade associationists wanted both free competition and protection from its excesses. Like Ulysses, as Jon Elster has suggested, they wanted to hear the sirens without being lured onto the rocks. By lashing himself to the mast, Ulysses was able to enjoy the sirens' song, but the associational movement lacked this discipline and drifted precariously for most of the interwar era.[8]

Industrial Relations, ed. John Windmuller and Alan Gladstone (New York, 1984), 93; Kenneth McCaffree, "A Theory of the Origin and Development of Employer Associations," *Proceedings of the Industrial Relations Research Association* 15 (1962): 57–63, 65–66; Allen Wakstein, "The NAM and Labor Relations in the 1920s," *Labor History* 10 (1969), 167–69.

7 Robert Brady, *Business as a System of Power* (New York, 1943), 3. See also Herman Kroos, *Executive Opinion: What Business Leaders Said and Thought on Economic Issues, 1920s to 1960s* (Garden City, 1970), 13–15, 124–25; and the correspondence between Wilson Compton [National Lumber Manufacturers' Association] and the National Industrial Conference Board [NICB] (November–December 1925), File V:5, "General Correspondence, 1916–1952," NICB Papers, Hagley Museum and Library, Wilmington, DE.

8 Schmitter and Brand, "Organizing Capitalists," 45; Jon Elster, *Ulysses and the Sirens* (New York, 1979).

The enforcement problem underlined the eccentric and ultimately futile logic of the associational movement. Like all organizations, those in the business world sought the cooperation of the largest possible number of potential members. A broad membership base increased the legitimacy and dispersed the costs of collective action. Unlike other organizations, however, business associations required universal membership; one recalcitrant firm could easily undermine collective goals. And in their attempt to mimic market monopolies, they were also ultimately less interested in distributing organizational costs than in *reducing* the number of members. In short, business organization required the cooperation of competitors that hoped to drive each other from the market. Members of business organizations, after all, wanted increased sales at higher prices, and this could only come at the expense of other members. At the same time, peak and trade associations pursued broader political goals that stood to benefit all members. Most associations were torn by these two logics of collective action: broadening scope and membership in the pursuit of collective political goals and driving members into bankruptcy in the pursuit of organized competition.[9]

These dilemmas were exacerbated by the uniquely competitive dynamics of American federalism. Because political responsibility was fragmented, business often viewed private organization (especially on a national level) as an alternative to federal regulation. At the same time, however, federalism weakened potential support for corporatist solutions. Most industries needed to impose order on themselves beyond the confines of a single state. The federal government was constitutionally prohibited from direct economic organization or regulation and yet was expected to prosecute (through the antitrust laws) any such private attempts. Under such contradictory pressures, organized business remained quite ambivalent about politics. Although such interest groups were institutionalized in the democracies of Western Europe, they found no lasting political voice or role in U.S. politics, in which the uncertain position of such "secondary" associations is a persistent feature, running from the Federalist distrust of "faction" to more recent debates over the evils of "interest group liberalism."[10]

In the interwar era, this uncertainty tended to drag out associational experiments and confuse their relationship to politics. Business associations

9 Olson, *Logic of Collective Action*, 37–42.
10 Joel Rogers and Joshua Cohen, "Secondary Associations in Democratic Governance," *Politics and Society* 20 (1992): 393–416; Phillipe Schmitter and Wolfgang Streeck, "Community, Market, State – And Associations? The Prospective Contribution of Interest Governance to Social Order," in *Private Interest Government*, ed. Wolgang Streeck and Phillipe Schmitter (Beverly Hills, 1985), 1–3.

sat somewhere between the uncertainties of the market and the rigidity of state control; they were both a concession that organization was necessary and a defense against having it dictated from without. Yet associationalism also depended upon political approval or at least freedom from prosecution. As corporate liberals discovered through the 1920s and 1930s, the line between politically sanctioned private organization and political regulation was extremely difficult to draw. Trade and peak associations alike considered themselves both part of the political system and the last line of defense against its encroachment. Some worked closely with government agencies. Others fostered a cultural of opposition to any legally enforced regulation. Most sought some balance of political influence, confrontation, credibility, and independence.

The associational movement was caught between the uncertain freedom of the market and the unwelcome necessity of political intervention. Economic interests resented the private or political constraints that were necessary to successful organization. Organizations that did not make such demands of their members simply distorted the competitive excesses they were designed to prevent. Organization itself, as Charles Lindblom notes, often became "a kind of clumsy market, an unexpected outcome for those who [sought] in the rationalism of formal organizations an escape from the 'chaos' of the market."[11] As a rule, business organizations collapsed when they were most needed; pressed by hard times, trade associationists bailed out of agreements, and members of peak associations stop contributing time or money. Moreover, trade associations could not overcome the dilemma of voluntary enforcement, and peak associations did not show any distinct ability to transform generic business objectives into public policy. A closer examination of the experience of trade and peak associations not only highlights the motives, paradoxes, and failures of private organization but also the ultimate importance – especially after 1929 – of more explicitly political solutions.

The Limits of Trade Association

Trade associations sought to establish and enforce standards of competition among firms in the same industry, typically seeking to discipline or exclude marginal competitors. In the United States this movement was a response to both competitive conditions and antitrust law (the 1890 Sherman Act encouraged associationalism as an alternative to potentially illegal consolidation). Although trade association was sporadic early in the century, the

11 Lindblom, *Politics and Markets*, 65–75 (quote, 67–68).

effective suspension of antitrust law during World War I underscored the promise of cooperative trade agreements. When prices and profits plummeted after 1919, business leaders (the orderly conditions of the war years fresh in their minds) were determined to make the cooperative spirit of the "new competition" a central feature of the postwar economy.[12]

Associationalism itself and its generic goal of antitrust reform were less important than the distinct organizational goals of industries and firms. There were, however, some common patterns and plans of action. Trade association strategies such as uniform cost accounting, open pricing, and product standardization all removed certain production costs from competition and redounded to the benefit of large firms with economies of scale, identifiable product lines, or integral links to consumers or suppliers. Association activities varied considerably according to the number of members, geographic dispersion, financial resources, and the history of the trade group in question. Whether an association chose to couch its goals in the garb of "fair competition," "cooperation" or "efficiency," however, regulating prices and meeting the threat of cutthroat competition were virtually universal concerns. Associationalism was reactive rather than prescriptive, and as Robert Himmelberg has shown, weak profits were a key incentive to organize.[13]

Most associations were constrained by narrow membership and meager incomes. Only half of those surveyed by Congress in 1939 represented a majority of firms in their industry, while 90 percent represented more than half of the volume of business. Although incomes and dues varied widely (average annual income in 1938 was $50,000 and ran as high as $500,000), most associations received more than 40 percent of their revenue from their four largest contributors. In nonmarket political organizations, such lead-

---

12 Schmitter and Brand, "Organizing Capitalists," 54–57; Brady, *Business as a System of Power*, 190–91; NICB, *Trade Associations: Their Economic and Legal Significance* (New York, 1925), 12–13, 17–24, 46–51, 304–07. Because I have traced patterns of competition and collective action in specific industries in some detail in Chapters 2 and 3, this discussion focuses simply on the political and logical dynamics of the associational movement.

13 Temporary National Economic Committee [TNEC], *Trade Association Survey*, Monograph 18 (Washington, 1941), 21–23, 29–33, 46–49, 105ff.; U.S. Department of Commerce, *Trade Association Activities* (Washington, 1927); Simon Whitney, *Trade Associations and Industrial Control* (New York, 1934), 34, 40–45, 62–144; National Association of Manufacturers [NAM], *National Trade Associations* (Washington, 1922); Emmett Naylor, *Trade Associations: Their Organization and Management* (New York, 1921); Robert Himmelberg, *Origins of the National Recovery Act* (New York, 1976), 2, 76–85, 116–24; Louis Galambos, *Competition and Cooperation: The Emergence of a National Trade Association* (Baltimore, 1966).

ership might be a source of strength and cohesion, but in a trade association, whose primary concern was the behavior of nonmembers, this tendency towards oligarchy was debilitating. Industries were torn between those firms interested in organization and those that were not. When a major strategic consideration (such as union recognition or international trade) divided an industry, two or more associations often simply politicized that division. Most large firms spanned a range of trades, a fact that complicated their loyalties; by its own count, the DuPont Company belonged to 102 trade associations ranging from the American Petroleum Institute to the Kansas Association of Ice Cream Manufacturers. Clearly a trade association commanding the allegiance and attention of a majority of representative firms in an industry was a rare occurrence.[14]

Enforcement of antitrust law alternately threatened and encouraged the trade association movement. Business increasingly felt, as Secretary of Commerce Redfield noted in 1919, that it was wrong to enforce "a law intended to prevent combinations in restraint of trade so as to prevent cooperation in promotion of trade." The antitrust issue set the stage for a parade of litigation and a great deal of grandstanding between Secretary of Commerce Hoover and Attorney General Daugherty. Hoover won the political battle by default (Daugherty resigned with the Teapot Dome scandal) and won the legal battle with the *Maple Flooring* decision of 1925, a "friendly suit" pushed through by Hoover and the new Attorney General, Harlan Stone (who also wrote the decision after moving on to the Supreme Court). Although it was good drama, the Hoover-Daugherty controversy did not leave trade associations hanging on its every twist. Hoover used industry conditions rather than constitutional niceties to guide his blessing of restrictive agreements, and his Commerce Department was far more influential in business circles than federal prosecutors or the courts.[15]

14 TNEC, *Trade Association Survey*, 4–6, 359–61, 367; Francis Walker, "The Government's Function in Collecting Business Information," *Proceedings of the American Academy of Political Science* 11 (1925): 616; W.B. Foster to Willis Harrington (5 June 1933), File 15, Willis Harrington Papers, Hagley Museum.
15 (Quote) Redfield in Chamber of Commerce [CoC] Proceedings 7/9 (1919), 108; Chicago lawyer George Buckingham in CoC Proceedings 12/16 (1924), Chamber of Commerce Papers, Hagley Museum; Himmelberg, *Origins of the NRA*, 5–74; NICB, *Trade Associations*, 28–30; M. Browning Carrot, "The Supreme Court and American Trade Associations, 1921–1925," *BHR* 44 (1970): 320–38; "Trade Association Activities" (1922), Commerce File [CF] 177; miscellaneous trade association material, CF 602; Hoover to Arch Shaw (17 February 1933), CF 207, Herbert C. Hoover Papers, Herbert C. Hoover Presidential Library [HCHPL], West Branch, IA. The minutes and proceedings of the Chamber of Commerce are bound in two

The trade association program of the Federal Trade Commission (FTC) was also characterized by legal and political ambivalence. Created in 1913 to nurture the very cooperation the antitrust laws discouraged, the FTC used "consent decrees" and "cease and desist" orders as an alternative to federal prosecution. The FTC ghostwalked through the early 1920s, but after the *Maple Flooring* decision and the appointment of a Washington State lumber lawyer to the "swing" vote on the five-member commission in 1925, it promised renewed attention to industry-sponsored trade practice conferences. "Having opened the shop with a new line of goods and under new management," noted one former official, "the Commission did quite a business." Trade practice conferences were, in effect, an attempt to get individual industries to commit to definitions of what *they* thought constituted fair and unfair trade practices. Given competitive pressures, the fact that trade associations found this task impossible was hardly surprising. Moreover, business found the "unofficial endorsement" of the FTC little comfort and remained confused and skeptical about the effect or legality of the trade practice conferences.[16]

Commerce Department and FTC attempts to abet trade association were undercut by two problems: Neither agency was willing to countenance restrictive agreements *in advance,* and, the blessing of federal regulators notwithstanding, there was no means of coercing or penalizing violators of trade standards. Business interests routinely blasted federal agencies for their failure "to approve in advance of contracts restraining trade [and] . . . grant immunity to the parties thereto from the provisions of the Sherman law." Enforcement problems were even more serious. "We have a code of ethics," noted one trade association official, " . . . something like the Ten Commandments, a nice thing to refer to but something which we do very little about." Another observer recalled: "I have known of cases where a general curtailment was voted with enthusiasm by an industry's representatives. In the midst of the conference, a man would excuse himself for a moment; he

chronological series: minutes of the Board of Directors and Executive Committee and Proceedings of Annual Meetings and Meetings of the National Council. The former is cited as CoC Board or CoC ExComm, followed by a meeting number and date; the latter is cited as CoC Proceedings, followed by the Annual and National Council meeting numbers for that volume.

16 Himmelberg, *Origins of the NRA,* 62–63; NICB, *Trade Associations,* 61–210; Thomas Blaisdell, *The Federal Trade Commission: An Experiment in the Control of Business* (New York, 1932); 80–81; Nelson Gaskill, *The Regulation of Competition* (New York, 1936), 17–72, 110–17; "Round Table Conference: Fair Trade Practice Conferences," CoC Proceedings 17/23 (1929), 364–419, Chamber Papers.

would go to the telephone and wire his factory to start up full blast." Associations were effective only to the point at which it became profitable for someone to ignore them. As *Fortune* mused wistfully on the eve of the New Deal: "It was only the means of enforcing the 'gentlemen's agreement' which lacked."[17]

Successful trade association required some exceptional combination of market power, product identification, and economies of scale. In the abrasives industry, for example, industrial consumers joined leading integrated manufacturers in standardizing grades and wheel sizes and cross-licensing patents. Smaller competitors found quickly that the majors could "put the whiplash on" if any firm tried to increase sales with excessive discounts.[18] Other successful associations were built around proprietary technology, patent pools, or some coercive mechanism unique to the industry in question. In most cases, however, these were little more than market share agreements among two or three firms. And new competition, with no allegiance to the association, rushed in as soon as technological monopolies collapsed or patents expired.[19] With effective barriers to entry, trade association was usually unnecessary; without effective barriers to entry, it was usually futile. No association could enforce industry rules and standards without the ability to keep established competitors in and new competitors out.

Consider the experience of the Cotton Textile Institute (CTI). Encouraged by the *Maple Flooring* decision, southern mills created the CTI as a means of financing (through per spindle assessments) an industry-wide open-price plan. From the outset, the CTI juggled the demands of its southern patrons and the demands of industry-wide stability (which large northern mills tied to competition between north and south). The CTI left political issues to regional associations, refused to challenge the southern wage advantage, and, as a result, became little more than a statistical service. Members used and abused costs and prices filed with the institute but never

17 Rush Butler in CoC Proceedings 7/9 (1919), 213–14, Chamber Papers; trade association officials quoted in TNEC, *Economic Power and Political Pressures*, Monograph 26 (Washington, 1941), 57; Edgar L. Heermance, *Can Business Govern Itself?* (New York, 1933), 19; "The Trade Association Emerges," *Fortune* 8 (August 1933): 39. See also "Codes of Ethics or Business Principles" (1923), CF 84; W.O Vincent to Hoover (24 October 1927), CF 602, Hoover Papers.

18 Charles Cheape, *Family Firm to Modern Multinational: Norton Company, A New England Enterprise* (Cambridge, 1985), 94–99, 117, 171–76.

19 "Round Table Conference: Fair Trade Practice Conferences," CoC Proceedings 17/23 (1929), 364–419, Chamber Papers; Blaisdell, *Federal Trade Commission*, 105–20; TNEC, *Economic Power and Political Pressures*, 59; "The Trade Association Emerges," 40.

escaped their narrowly self-interested competitive perspectives. Although northern and southern mills were better informed, they were no better behaved. "The association's situation was almost hopeless," Louis Galambos concludes; "the Institute could exert no influence on the nonconformers and only slight influence on its own members," and it could accomplish no collective goals "without some kind of binding, government authority."[20]

But even government found it difficult to establish the necessary discipline and enforcement. The moral suasion and threat of a public scolding wielded by the FTC in the 1920s were starkly ineffective. The ability of the Commerce Department to restrain federal prosecutors made little difference to leading firms, which were more interested in punishing recalcitrants than clearing their legal dockets. And antitrust reform could not solve the problem of outsiders and free riders. The vast majority of trade associations stumbled along without any powers of enforcement or persuasion. In many respects, voluntary trade associations only exacerbated the excessive competition they were charged to restrict. Trade and price statistics were of different value to different competing firms and, by revealing market weakness, encouraged competitive gouging. The ill will that followed violation of an industry agreement was often greater than the hostility of unrestricted competition. Without threat of penalty or reprisal, firms remained loyal to associations only as long is they served *both* short- and long-term interests.

Although tallies of interwar trade associations were impressive (between 1,000 and 2,000), they said little about underlying weaknesses and ambivalent allegiance. Fully one-fifth of all trade associations founded between 1900 and 1940 were offsprings of the NRA era (1933–35), and barely one-third of these were still in existence three years later. As one observer noted, most associations "have only meager funds to work with, [and] a cheap secretary whose chief interest is in keeping up the membership so that he might draw his salary."[21] Throughout the interwar era, trade associations lacked both legal assurances and legal teeth. At the risk of running afoul of the Justice Department or allowing outsiders to benefit from industry restrictions, business interests put little faith in cooperation; as a method of organizing capitalists, trade associations generated far more ink than results. Competitors occasionally organized against external threats, a situation in which trade association (other than serving to coordinate lobbying efforts) was superfluous. On questions of internal discipline and competition, the trade associa-

20 Galambos, *Competition and Cooperation*, 90–107, 126–35, (quote) 165.
21 TNEC, *Economic Power and Political Pressures*, (quote) 12, 51–82, 349, 369; Heermance, *Can Business Govern Itself?*, 54.

tion was little more than an organizational placebo, taken to assuage guilt or anxiety but of no lasting effect.

The Limits of Peak Association

Peak associations were burdened by few of the organizational pretensions of the trade associations. They were less concerned with the behavior or loyalty of members and more attentive to issues of broader concern. Some pursued specific political goals and attracted the patronage of those industries and firms for whom these goals were important. Others represented a specific range of industries and firms and adjusted their politics to changing needs. The scope of peak associations varied considerably, but they shared certain fundamental weaknesses. As in any large, loosely knit, voluntary organization, the relationship between the group as a whole and its constituent members was ambivalent and tenuous. The rank and file keenly resented attempts to submerge or dilute their particular interests in a pool of "business" opinion, found it difficult to assess the organization's often intangible influence, and consistently complained that their concerns were secondary to those of leading corporate members or the bureaucratic ethos of the organization itself. Most members seemed to feel that such undertakings, however well-intentioned, had yet to prove their worth.

Although their assessments of peak associations were persistently dismal, business interests clearly felt that these efforts were important and that they might overcome internal differences and strengthen their collective political hand. Most seem to have accepted or ignored this paradox of cynicism and continued support, in large part because the sheer size of peak associations, a source of constant frustration, also dispersed their costs. Participation demanded little time or money, and most members were willing to pay their dues in exchange for an occasional newsletter or press release. More prominent corporate members contributed and demanded more but satisfied themselves with control of association policies, which they hoped might come closer to their political or organizational goals sometime in the future.

The National Association of Manufacturers

The National Association of Manufacturers (NAM) was the most prominent and vocal peak association of the interwar era. Founded in 1895, NAM soon turned its attention to the labor problem. It was not until 1920, however, that NAM took the rigidly antiunion stance which would become its trademark. As the war economy (and wartime labor relations) collapsed into the depression of 1920, a number of municipal and industrial employers' organizations launched open-shop drives. NAM latched on to these movements in the hope of recruiting new members. NAM counsel James Emery argued that the association could promote the open shop "with advantage to itself and benefit to the community." NAM membership reached 5,000 firms in 1920, a level it would not approach again until World War II. During the interwar era NAM was dominated by antiunion southern firms and protectionist northern firms, especially in the metal trades, textiles, and shipbuilding.[22]

The association's character changed markedly after 1929. The Depression forced many small firms to give up active financial support, and the New Deal attracted a new coalition of opponents to public policy. Between 1933 and 1936, the contributions of steel, auto, chemical, domestic oil, food, and tobacco firms grew from 20 to 40 percent of NAM revenue, which increased from under $250,000 in 1933 to almost $1,500,000 by 1937, with virtually all new resources directed toward public relations.[23] The influence of big business was less a New Deal–inspired coup than a reflection of the dynamics and demands of such organizations. As early as 1920, large firms dominated NAM conventions and meetings. Constitutional or policy decisions required a membership quorum of only 5 percent. In 1908 and 1925, directors amended the NAM constitution to insulate themselves "from the likelihood of shifts and changes at the will of the general membership unfamiliar with needs and workings of the association." A core of firms dominated the active membership. "You know as well as I do that NAM is run by the inner

22 Gable, "Birth of an Employers' Assocation," 535–45; Allen Wakstein, "The Origins of the Open Shop Movement," *Journal of American History* 51 (1964): 462–63, (quote) 469, 472; Albion Taylor, *Labor Policies of the National Association of Manufacturers* (Urbana, 1928), 13–20; NAM, "What is NAM?" (Washington, 1944), 9; Albert Steigerwalt, *The National Association of Manufacturers, 1895-1914: A Study in Business Leadership* (Ann Arbor, 1964), 83; John Stalker, "The National Association of Manufacturers: A Study in Ideology" (Ph.D diss., University of Wisconsin, 1950), 3; Kroos, *Executive Opinion,* 12; Philip Burch, "The NAM as an Interest Group," *Politics and Society* 4 (1973): 97–130; NAM, "How Manufacturing Industries Operate," File 251, NAM Papers, Hagley Museum.

23 Burch, "NAM as an Interest Group," 97–102; Richard Tedlow, "The National Association of Manufacturers and Public Relations during the New Deal," *BHR* 50 (1976): 31–32. Contributions calculated from Senate Subcommittee of the Committee on Education and Labor, *Violations of Free Speech and the Rights of Labor,* Part 17, *The National Association of Manufacturers,* 75/3 (Washington, 1938), 7538, Exhibit 3799.

clique," one NAM official confided, adding that "some method is going to have to be established to leave the membership thinking that they are running it."[24]

The NAM was formed in hope "that [business] could and thereafter would speak with one voice," and persistently promoted what it dubbed "unit thinking and unit acting" on the part of U.S. business. In the pursuit of this elusive common denominator, however, NAM found its policies were more often cathartic than constructive. Much of NAM's energy was spent in Washington,D.C., where its lobbyists haunted congressional committees, "preparing something to put in the mouths of prospective legislators," as one employer noted. NAM was a pivotal force in the creation of the Department of Commerce in 1902, the Chamber of Commerce in 1912, the National Industrial Conference Board in 1916, and the National Industrial Council in 1919.[25] These spin-offs allowed NAM to retain its close focus on labor problems. To a large degree, after 1920 NAM was less a representative of manufacturing interests than a source of political pressure and snappy constitutional comebacks in support of open-shop patrons.

Yet even in its pet field, NAM had little influence. Its open-shop argument was refined through the 1920s and served up in press releases, after-dinner speeches, and congressional testimony. But members neither took the NAM stance seriously nor even agreed on what "open shop" actually meant. In 1920, NAM delegates argued testily over an open-shop resolution. Many feared the effect of combative statements on relations with their own employees, and few took it as a guide to labor policy. "I will vote for the resolution," one Virginia manufacturer remarked drily, ". . . but after [we] adopt it, what are you going to do? Put a picture of the Chairman and the Secretary and the Chairmen of the various committees on it and say, 'See

24 Brady, *Business as a System of Power*, 199–200; Bonnett, *Employers' Associations*, 291–94; (quote) NAM, "Amendments to Constitution" (1925), File 42, NAM Papers; Steigerwalt, *The National Association of Manufacturers*, 152–53; Senate, *Rights of Labor*, 17: 7538–41; Optical Manufacturers Association to Robert Wagner (1 June 1933), File 210:1311, Robert F. Wagner Papers, Littauer Library, Georgetown University, Washington; (quote) E.H. Lane to Earl Bunting (7 June 1948), File 851.2, NAM Papers.
25 Gable, "Birth of an Employers' Association," 537; (quote) NAM, "Unit Thinking and Unit Acting," File 40, NAM Papers; Brady, *Business as a System of Power*, 192–194; Bonnett, *Employers Associations*, 344–77; NAM, "What is NAM?" 10; Taylor, *Labor Policies of the NAM*, 12–13; Steigerwalt, *The National Association of Manufacturers*, 156–62; TNEC, *Economic Power and Political Pressures*, 20; NAM, "Milestones Along the Industrial Trail," (1935), File 303; (quote) "Minutes of a Special Conference of Delegates" (3 May 1920), 173, File 1412:12 NAM Papers.

what great work we have done?' " NAM reinforced the belligerency of antiunion employers but had little influence on labor relations in specific firms and industries. Even NAM officials admitted that their task was largely rhetorical, that "to adequately defend existing employee representation plans and to permit the extension of such plans . . . it is necessary to have extensive propaganda concerning the necessity and advantages of the U.S. remaining an open shop country."[26]

By the late 1920s, NAM had painted itself into an intellectual and political corner. With the widespread success of local open-shop movements, NAM lost much of its cohesion. Hoping to patch up internal divisions over labor policy and broaden its appeal, NAM directors tried to balance the bellicosity of the Open Shop Department with attention to some of the newer trends in labor relations, including "welfare capitalism" and the profusion of company unions. These 1926 amendments failed to pass. A core of committed antiunionists had no desire to blunt their best political weapon. Fear of alienating traditional members, uncertainty that such political fine-tuning would attract new members, and simple bureaucratic inertia made it difficult for NAM to adjust its policies.[27] Only the experimentation of the New Deal, which made existing policies more urgent and relevant, would breathe life into it.

Under the pretense of unified business thinking, NAM drifted between pressing positions so abstract they neither offended nor influenced its members and representing only that corner of the business community with which it consistently agreed. NAM positions, as one official admitted, "must always be partly unrealistic and admittedly naive in that they represent the common denominator." NAM officials conceded "we are a fragmentary body. We have officers but we lack numbers"; in 1929 NAM Director Robert Lund added that "the average manufacturer does not know what the association is doing." In the early 1940s, a *Fortune* poll found only 27 percent favorable to NAM, while 30 percent professed indifference and 43 percent were "violently critical." One respondent went so far as to dismiss the association as "just a bunch of top-drawer guys in an ivory tower, stewing in

---

26 TNEC, *Economic Power and Political Pressures*, 17, 102; Stalker, "Study in Ideology"; Taylor, *Labor Polices of NAM*, 35–62; "Minutes of a Special Conference of Delegates" (3 May 1920), (quote) 12, 160–61, 149–207, File 1412:12; (quote) "Memorandum on Open Shop Movement" (1920); "NAM and Industrial Relations" (n.d.); "Status of Open Shop" (1923), File 251; "Special Meeting on Employee Representation" (27 September 1933), File V:1, NAM Papers.

27 Wakstein, "The NAM and Labor Relations," 167–69, 172, 176.

their own juices and issuing feudal and futile pronouncements. They do nothing but talk to themselves."[28]

The Chamber of Commerce

The Chamber of Commerce, as researchers for the Temporary National Economic Committee (TNEC) concluded, was unequalled "as a constant factor in political opinion-forming" or as "organized business' Washington press agent."[29] Certainly no other business organization claimed the Chamber's breadth of membership or close political ties. Its leaders came almost exclusively from elite commercial and banking circles and possessed the combination of economic clout, political savvy, and legal training so crucial in Washington. These attributes, however, also diluted business support and the Chamber's political positions. Like NAM, the Chamber found it difficult to consistently justify its positions to a diverse membership; unlike NAM, it found that its cozy relationship with federal politics (a sharp contrast to NAM's confrontational approach) often undermined its credibility.

The Chamber was inspired by President Taft and Secretary of Commerce and Labor Charles Nagel. Eager to satisfy business patrons but weary of chaotic business representation, Taft called for the creation of a "national clearinghouse for the development and expression of business opinion." A February 1912 meeting under the auspices of the Bureau of Manufactures (with representatives from NAM, and the Boston, Detroit, and San Francisco Chambers of Commerce) set up a national conference in April, seeking a membership of "chambers of commerce, boards of trade, and kindred associations . . . and such trade and industrial organizations as are national in their scope." The fledgling Chamber created a National Council drawn from constituent organizations to nominate directors, run conventions, and advise a board of directors and executive committee (which handled day-to-day administration).[30]

28 Arthur Cleveland, "NAM: Spokesman for Industry?" *Harvard Business Review* (1948): 356 (see also an earlier, more critical draft entitled "Industrial Leadership and NAM" and the response of NAM officials in File 851.3, NAM Papers). On the increasingly cool reception granted NAM lobbyists, see Emery testimony in U.S. House of Representatives, Committee on Labor, *Six-Hour Day, Five-Day Week* (Washington, 1933), 127–54; NAM officials quoted in Tedlow, "The NAM and Public Relations," 37; Bonnett, *Employers' Associations*, 292; D.A. Currie to Weisenberger (10 February 1938), File 303; Lund to Lewis Benton (December 1929), File 851.2, NAM Papers. *Fortune* survey in Kroos, *Executive Opinion*, 12.

29 TNEC, *Economic Power and Political Pressures*, 25.

30 "Minutes of the Meeting of the National Commercial Conference Held at the New

Through World War I, the Chamber struggled to find its role in U.S. politics. Active in tariff hearings and influential in the creation of the Federal Reserve Board in 1913, it initially concentrated on maintaining friendly ties with the federal government and distinguishing itself from NAM. "We are not to be critical," cautioned the Chamber's first President, Chicago lawyer Henry Wheeler, "we are to be cooperative." Secretary Nagel applauded an organization that "government could afford to have relations with," and a postwar president, Chicago lawyer Joseph Defrees, saw the Chamber as "a considerable departure from the precedent and practices of older organizations." Despite close relations with federal agencies during the war, Chamber officials soon felt the pressures and contradictions of representing a complex and competitive business community. In 1919, the Chamber acknowledged the rift between service and manufacturing interests and created separate departments representing industry, trade, distribution, insurance, transportation, and "civic development." Through the 1920s, it reaffirmed its focus on general business problems and its determination not to trespass on the concerns of trade associations.[31]

The Chamber's political positions were tentative. "The Chamber of Commerce is not pioneering," understated one federal official; "it only support[s] a movement when its success has been assured, and then takes credit for accomplishments." Serious consideration of labor relations was notably absent from its proceedings. The Chamber did pass an open-shop resolution in 1920 (amidst the general political fallout from the 1919 Industrial Conference) but said little else on the subject. Capital-intensive commercial, banking, and international interests repeatedly reminded NAM-oriented manufacturers that employers were a minority in the Chamber. When it did consider welfare and labor policies, industrial relations executives associated with Special Conference Committee firms dominated the discussions.[32] Trade association activities were a more consistent concern, but the Chamber provided much less leadership on the question of antitrust revision than

Willard Hotel, Washington, D.C., April 22–23, 1912," (quote) 2, 6, 86–91, bound proceedings, Chamber Papers; CoC, "Seventy Five Years of Achievement" (Washington, 1987): 1–3; TNEC, *Economic Power and Political Pressures,* 25.

31 CoC Board 2 (4 June 1912); Wheeler in CoC Proceedings (first annual banquet), 2/4, (22 January 1913); CoC Board 1 (23 April 1912); CoC Board 51 (20 November 1919); Defrees in CoC Proceedings, 10/14 (1922), 91; CoC Proceedings, 7/9 (1919), 9/11 (1921), 16/22 (1928), Chamber Papers.

32 (Quote) Axel Oxholm [Department of Commerce] to Herbert Hoover (4 November 1927), CF 84, Hoover Papers; CoC Proceedings 17/23 (1929), 876; CoC Board 64 (16 November 1921), Chamber Papers. The labor policies of the Conference Committee are discussed below.

many of its members. It was paralyzed by a fear of counseling violations of the Sherman Act and peppered any discussion of trade practice conferences or cooperative competition with paeans to free enterprise.

A loose coalition of internationalists; shippers; exporters; natural resource industries; and corporate, banking, and railroad lawyers dominated the Chamber.[33] Dues were initially tied to local Chambers of Commerce to cover a budget of $100,000. By 1919, the Chamber's annual income was $500,000 and by 1928 the figure had climbed to over $3,000,000. Although the Chamber tried to avoid the patronage of individual firms (its "associate members"), as early as 1923 it accepted a $10,000 contribution from U.S. Steel. In 1933, the financially strapped Chamber accepted another $10,000 from U.S. Steel; $7,500 from GM; $5,000 each from Standard, AT&T, DuPont, and A&P; $4,500 from oil and utilities tycoon H.L. Doherty; and lesser amounts from the Pennsylvania Railroad, Consolidated Oil, John Deere, Texaco, Pullman, American Tobacco, Beatrice Dairies, Chrysler, Ligget & Myers, and a number of utilities. This dependence on corporate largesse was a product of the Depression, which forced the Chamber to streamline its operations and saw membership fall from 1,739 organizational and 22,529 corporate-individual members in 1928 to 1,319 organizational and 7,356 corporate-individual members six years later.[34]

The Chamber's influence took many forms. Its *Nation's Business* grew quickly from a house organ to a magazine with a circulation of 300,000 by

33 Internationalists included A.C. Bedford and Walter Teagle of Standard, Owen Young of GE, and Morgan partner Thomas Lamont. See "Survey Report #2, American Section, International Chamber of Commerce," File 36–5; and miscellaneous correspondence and memos, Files 18–1, 18–2, 18–4, 37–1 to 37–16, Thomas W. Lamont Papers, Baker Library, Cambridge, MA; miscellaneous ICC Minutes and memoranda, CF 82, Hoover Papers. Leading legal interests in the Chamber included the New York firm of Hines, Rearick, Dorr, and Hammond; Chicago bankers and lawyers Wheeler, Defrees, John O'Leary, and Silas Strawn; antitrust lawyer Gilbert Montague; and Boston utilities czar Henry Harriman. Shipping interests included Julius Barnes, a Chamber president with a heavy investment in Great Lakes shipping; Richard Grant, a Mark Hanna executive, American Iron and Steel Institute pioneer, and coal shipper; and Homer Ferguson of Newport News Shipbuilding. Banking interests included Frank Vanderlip, Fred Kent (also close to the DuPonts and NICB interests), and Lewis Pierson. Corporate affiliations are from CoC Proceedings; *Who Was Who in America*, 8 vols. (Chicago, 1963–85); *The American Dictionary of Biography*, 20 vols. and supplements (New York, 1928–81); see also Julius Barnes file, CF 45, Hoover Papers.

34 CoC ExComm 2 (8 May 1912); ExComm 3 (10 July 1912); ExComm 22 (28 June 1920); Board 56 (5 October 1920), Chamber Papers; income, membership, and contributions are from Board and ExComm minutes (1921–38); CoC Board 75 (29 June 1923); CoC Board 127 (24 June 1932), Chamber Papers; File 18–5, Lamont Papers.

1937. Especially through the Republican 1920s but also under Wilson and Franklin Roosevelt, the Chamber maintained close ties with the Department of Commerce. Charles Nagel served both the Chamber and the Department, and only Herbert Hoover's appointment as secretary of commerce in 1920 prevented him from accepting a vice-presidency in the Chamber (with which he maintained close ties). Rather than support or challenge policy on the basis of immutable principles, the interwar Chamber set its sails to prevailing legislative breezes. During the New Deal, for example, then-President Harriman guided it to support the "better aspects" of National Recovery and Social Security Legislation. This pattern of influence put off many members, few of whom felt that the Chamber consistently represented their interests. The New Deal also eroded the carefully cultivated relationship between the Chamber and government. Commercial and banking interests never reconciled rising federal expenditures and deficit financing with the New Deal's championship of their regulatory and trade strategies.[35]

As a forum for disguising elite corporate and banking opinion as that of "business," the Chamber was superficially effective. As a means of organizing or representing broader interests, it was neither effective nor particularly interested. Although it tried to respect regional and self-interested divisions within the business community, the Chamber suffered the same oligarchic tendencies and loss of broad-based support as NAM. Chamber proceedings merely rubber-stamped policies crafted in peak bargaining among political and business elites. One disgusted delegate to the Chamber's Annual Meeting in 1935 addressed his colleagues as "a flock of sheep" and observed that "we have resoluted on everything from birth control to foreign relations, [yet] we have been sitting here not knowing what we are voting on, and I don't think there has been any resolution presented at this meeting that has received more than fifty or seventy-five votes."[36]

The National Industrial Conference Board

The National Industrial Conference Board (NICB) was founded in 1916 by a group including NAM and metal and textile trade associations. Although the NICB seemed a novel attempt to synthesize the concerns of trade and employers' associations, its private appeals for support were quite familiar.

35 Chamber, "Seventy-Five Years of Achievement," 3–7; on disillusion with the Chamber, see "memo for TWL" (17 February 1933) and reply, File 18–5, Lamont Papers; CoC Proceedings, 9/11 (1921), Chamber Papers; Edward Hunt to Hoover (30 November 1933), File 4, Edward Hunt Papers, HCHPL.
36 CoC Proceedings, 23/30 (1935), Chamber Papers.

As Walter Drew of the Metal Trades Association explained to banker Frank Vanderlip, the NICB sought to nurture "the intelligent class-consciousness of the business man" and to provide "an opportunity for big business interests . . . to [control] wide-spread and effective teaching and dissemination of the fundamental principles most necessary to their maintenance and progress." Like many others, Vanderlip was skeptical: "Neither your letters nor the letters of the other gentlemen leave me clearer in my own mind as to what the Industrial Conference Board proposes to do, how it proposes to do it, and just what in detail it expects to do with the money it is attempting to raise." He added, "I have cooled off in my enthusiasm for a whole lot of things that are organized on the basis of generalities [and] that are officered by men who are busy doing something else."[37] This was a malediction the NICB would never shake.

Although its creators saw the NICB as a "clearing house for discussion" and "a supreme court on industrial matters," it proved impossible to convince business interests that such a venture was worth financing or to overcome internal disputes as to how the NICB might achieve these goals. Founders split immediately over an appropriate response to the 1919 Industrial Conference; most agreed with the open-shop statement issued by the employers group but, trying to distinguish the fledgling NICB in some way, were unsure whether it should "declare itself on the open shop and other controversial questions" or simply adopt "a platform of broad fundamentals [on which] . . . we can safely stand now and always." The NICB chose the latter course, even foreswearing legislative lobbying as a condition of its incorporation as a nonprofit institution in 1924. By 1929, however, NICB members and officials had tired of "objective fact-finding" and began debating the merits of cultivating "opinion."[38] After 1930, the NICB concentrated increasingly on public relations and lobbying – a move that paralleled

37 NICB Executive Committee Minutes 4 (21 September 1916), File III:1, NICB Papers. On the origins of the NICB, see H. M. Gitelman, "Management's Crisis of Confidence and the Origin of the National Industrial Conference Board," *BHR* 58 (1984): 153–77; Clyde Rogers, "Draft History of the Conference Board," [1965] (imprints collection, Hagley Museum), 24; (quote) Walter Drew to Frank Vanderlip (23 January 1917), (quote) Vanderlip to Drew (26 January 1917), Drew to Vanderlip (27 January 1917), File V:11, NICB Papers.
38 (Quote) Drew to H. H. Rice [GM] (13 January 1920), Drew to James Emery (19 January 1920), Magnus Alexander to Drew (16 January 1920), File V:11; (quote) Alexander to Charles Cheney (6 March 1929), Alexander to Charles Nagel (28 February 1931), File VI:1, NICB Proceedings (21 May 1931), 24–25, (16 March 1931), 25–31, File I, NICB Papers.

the shifting focus of NAM, dominated by the same cadre of anti–New Deal executives.

Leading members also gradually played down the NICB's role as an "association of associations," in part because a membership of trade associations proved a shaky financial base. In 1918 it invited state employers' associations to join and in 1924 amended its constitution to allow corporate memberships and (more importantly) contributions.[39] Member associations paid annual dues of $250, but large firms provided the real financial base: $10,000 from GM; $5,000 from GE; $3,000 from Westinghouse; and $2,000 each from International Paper, United Shoe Machinery, John Deere, and American Brass. Through the 1920s the annual assessment averaged $250,000. Contributions evaporated after 1929, bottoming out at $160,000 in 1933. The NICB slashed administrative staff and salaries, borrowed heavily, and contemplated (but ultimately rejected) a merger with the American Management Association. The Depression undercut revenues just as demands on the expertise of the NICB were increasing and erased any vestiges of broad-based business participation. Smaller and regional firms and their associations could not afford the luxury of the NICB amid dismal business conditions, and it emerged from the Depression dominated by a loose clique of top corporations.[40]

The NICB sponsored annual conferences of business leaders (usually held at the Yama Farms Inn in the Catskills) and published research reports. The Yama Conferences were a blend of conventioneering and economic education, although it is easy to exaggerate how seriously those present took the latter (distracted by the amenities of Yama Farms, which included a pond stocked with trout fattened on "chopped fresh beef and wheat pancakes cut

39 NICB Executive Committee Minutes 1 (5 May 1916), File III:1, NICB Executive Committee Minutes 27 (21 November 1918), File III:3, and on incorporation and bylaws, File V:2, NICB Papers; Rogers, "Draft History," 1–3, 16, 80–81; NICB, *Let There Be Light* (New York, 1965), 36, 40.
40 Rogers, "Draft History," 36, 87, 106; NICB, *Let There Be Light*, 25–26, 51; Gitelman, "Management's Crisis of Confidence," 174; NICB, "Treasurer's Report," (annual 1921–36). On early contributions, see also Magnus Alexander to A.B. Daniels (25 October 1916), File V:5; financial distress is noted in Loyall Osborne to Alexander (8 March 1929), and Alexander to Fred Kent (3 September 1929), File VI:1, NICB to Associated Industries of Massachusetts (28 September 1938), American Pulp and Paper Association to NICB (4 March 1930), NICB to American Cotton Manufacturers Association (27 January 1933), and American Gas Association to NICB (26 September 1932), File IV:1, NICB Papers; "National Industrial Conference Board," File H:30, Irenée DuPont Papers, Hagley Museum.

into small squares").[41] Frederick Fish, an NICB pioneer and AT&T lawyer, noted of the first Yama conferees that "their ignorance of and their blindness to the real situation is often astonishing." In 1930, Irenée DuPont observed to NICB President Magnus Alexander that "judging by the Yama Conference, it is going to be difficult to get industrial leaders to take a real interest in the cause of the Depression and its cure." "I personally do not think the Conferences have much point," agreed then–NICB President Virgil Jordan in 1935; "the discussion covers ground which is very familiar to me, and I do not get any of the fun of exercise and alcoholic exhilaration which most of the others enjoy . . . [the conferees] seem to enjoy the affairs. They are mostly golfers."[42]

Members greeted NICB publications with equal cynicism. A rich resource for historians, the NICB's academic efforts had little contemporary impact. Despite their objective gloss, NICB reports were usually commissioned by firms or associations with a particular bone to pick. The Associated Industries of New York paid for a lengthy study of regulatory legislation in their state, and the DuPonts commissioned an analysis of Delaware fiscal policies (although they were so displeased with the finished work that they threatened to renege on their sponsorship). Most business leaders doubted the value of NICB reports, and the NICB itself acknowledged that they went virtually unread. NICB insiders who complained of the "half-baked and cockeyed ideas" of businessmen with "little understanding of economic principles" were also the first to note that the NICB itself would be more useful "if economics were better understood." The NICB maintained an arms-length relationship with its resident academics, who complained repeatedly that it suppressed information that might displease business patrons.[43]

41 "Famous firsts: Shangri-la of the tycoon era," *Business Week*, 3 October 1964, 143.
42 Rogers, "Draft History," (quote) 13; Gitelman, "Management's Crisis of Confidence," 163–164; Jerome Greene to Alexander (11 June 1930), File VI:1, NICB Papers; (quote) Irenée DuPont to Magnus Alexander (13 October 1930), File H:30, Irenée DuPont Papers; Lammot DuPont to Virgil Jordan (6 November 1935), (quote) Virgil Jordan to Lammot DuPont (8 November 1935), File 57, DuPont Administrative Papers, Hagley Museum.
43 NICB Minutes 102 (28 May 1926), File II:3, NICB Papers; Spruance [GM] to Lammot DuPont (18 August 1930), File 56, Lammot DuPont to C. Hodges [NICB] (18 August 1938), Virgil Jordan to Lammot DuPont (24 August 1938), File 57, DuPont Administrative Papers; Irenée DuPont to John Raskob (24 September 1927), File 1644, John J. Raskob Papers, Hagley Museum; E. F. Gay [Harvard Business School] to Lamont (n.d. 1929), File 58–1, Lamont Papers; Alexander memo for Cheney (regarding complaints of Industrial Relations advisors Arthur H. Young and Clarence Hicks), File VI:1, NICB Papers; David Eakins, "The Development of Corporate Liberal Policy Research in the United States, 1885–1965," (Ph.D diss.,

Personality also impinged on the NICB, especially under the "Prussian leadership" of erstwhile GE engineer Magnus Alexander. In 1929, Connecticut silk manufacturer Charles Cheney complained that the president was "intensely individualistic" and an "extremely difficult man to work with." Under Alexander, the NICB alienated open-shop militants among its early supporters, in part due to an ambivalent approach to labor relations, and in part due to Alexander's stormy friendship (which ended over a financial dispute in 1925) with cofounder Walter Drew. As Alexander's health faded in the late 1920s, leading members scrambled to find a successor amenable to their perception of the NICB's role: the dissemination of information as defined by leading corporations, rather than by academics or professional "joiners." A small cadre of executives, including the DuPonts, Cheney, Loyall Osborne of Westinghouse, Marion Folsom of Kodak, Charles Hook of American Rolling Mills, and New York bankers Fred Kent and John Hammond, dominated NICB policy and coaxed one of its economists, Virgil Jordan (who had left for the fledgling *Business Week* in 1929), back to lead it through the 1930s. This group expanded the financial base of the NICB while sharply limiting direct participation in its activities.[44]

The NICB's private and political influence was slight. When solicited for contributions, firms typically dismissed the NICB (if they were aware of its existence at all) as "only a 'paper' affair." Large corporations with the in-

University of Wisconsin, 1966). In 1935, members of the Special Conference Committee asked the NICB to sit on its cost of living figures, noting that "if these got into the hands of some labor leaders and so-called economists [they] . . . will start an agitation which will be quite harmful." See Senate, *Rights of Labor*, part 45, *Memorandum on the Special Conference Committee*, 76/1 (Washington, 1939), 16884–5.

44 Gitelman, "Management's Crisis of Confidence," 154–56, 160–61, 173; Rogers, "Draft History," 1, 20; Charles Cheney to Irenée DuPont (9 August 1929), File H:30, Irenée DuPont Papers; Virgil Jordan memo for Robertson [1930], File V:5, NICB Papers. On the succession of Alexander, see Charles Cheney to Alexander (22 March 1929), Alexander to Executive Committee (6 October 1928), File VI:1, NICB Papers; Loyall Osborne [Westinghouse] to Irenée DuPont (21 August 1929), File H:30, Irenée DuPont Papers; Irenée DuPont to John Raskob (24 September 1927), File 1644, Raskob Papers, Board members also worried about finding a successor to Frederick Fish in 1920; see Walter Drew to H. H. Rice (13 January 1920), File V:11, NICB Papers; NICB telegram to Alexander (31 October 1929), Alexander to Hammond (1 November 1930), File VI:1, NICB Papers. I am grateful to John Rumm for pointing out the importance of this succession debate. On corporate support, see "Confidential List of Subscribers . . . Active and Discontinued" (1932?), File VI:2, NICB Papers; and (for names and contributions) Colin Gordon, "New Deal, Old Deck: Business, Labor, and Politics, 1920–1935 (Ph.D, diss., University of Wisconsin, 1990), 387, n.36.

clination or cash to support the NICB did so, but as Irenée DuPont noted, "immediate returns from our contributions are not apparent." Leery of freeriders, GM made its contributions contingent upon a certain level of total subscription revenue. Smaller firms had fewer pretensions: "In the beginning of my connection I indulged in some rather ambitious intentions," explained a southern cotton mill owner, "but I find that the Board is not well known in these sections and my associates appear to be showing little interest." Thomas Lamont accepted an NICB post after being assured that no demands would be made on his time, and his tenure consisted of little more than five years of turning down invitations.[45] Like the NAM and the Chamber of Commerce, the NICB found it neither possible nor rewarding to represent a plurality of business interests. The NICB's nominal role as the business community's economic theorist and statistician was widely ignored by even its own members, who saw little use for facts and figures that did not support their narrowly self-interested objectives.

The Special Conference Committee

The fiercely private Special Conference Committee (SCC) underlined the need, as perceived by leading corporations, for a peak organization not polluted by the vagaries of a general membership.[46] Formed in 1919, the SCC was a "small group of large employers of labor" (including GE, DuPont, Westinghouse, Goodyear, Bethlehem Steel, Standard [New Jersey], Standard [Indiana], and International Harvester) whose name appeared only in

45 Julius Barnes to Hoover (21 January 1926), CF 431; Joseph Holmes to Hoover (26 October 1925), CF 431, Hoover Papers; Irenée DuPont to John Raskob (10 March 1927), Irenée DuPont to Raskob (17 February 1927), G. Harris [Exposition Cotton Mills, Atlanta] to Irenée DuPont (9 August 1929), Magnus Alexander to Members of NICB Executive Committee (6 October 1928), File H:30, Irenée DuPont Papers; E. F. Gay to Thomas Lamont, file 58–1, Lamont Papers. Charles Hook [American Rolling Mill] had a similar reaction to his appointment at the NICB, see Hook to Raskob (13 February 1933), File 1624, Raskob Papers.

46 The cloak-and-dagger history of the SCC has hindered serious study of its activities. The most extensive published source on the SCC is the LaFollette Committee's *Memorandum on the Special Conference Committee* (Senate, *Rights of Labor*, part 45), which reprints a great deal of routine correspondence but is restricted, with the congressional subpoena, to the period after 1933. Thomas Ferguson, "Critical Realignment: The Fall of the House of Morgan and the Origins of the New Deal" (Ph.D diss., Princeton University, 1981), 309–10, 322–24; and Sanford Jacoby, *Employing Bureaucracy: Managers, Unions, and the Transformation of Work in American Industry* (New York, 1985), 180–82, the latter draws upon documents in the YMCA Papers and sees the SCC as a vehicle of the Rockefeller-King brand of industrial relations.

private correspondence before the late 1930s. Participants cloaked their meetings as informal dinners attended by a "group of gentlemen who have met from time to time to discuss labor matters."[47] The SCC was "a small and congenial group . . . better fitted for frank discussion of the subject of industrial relations than a larger group could possibly be" and "function[ed] solely for the benefit of the companies associated with it." Although members were often indifferent to SCC activities (GE's Owen Young complained that SCC meetings were "not of my making but [are] forced upon me by my friends"), the institution itself was plainly important to them. "I think it is worth a very great deal for a group of big men . . . to have some vehicle for getting together occasionally as they do," argued John Raskob of DuPont, adding that "this alone justifies the [SCC's] existence, [with] all big corporations supporting the effort. The value of having men of big affairs really know each other . . . can be of untold benefit, particularly in emergencies."[48]

The SCC considered all facets of industrial relations but reserved much of its attention for the "company union" movement (of which Standard's served as flagships for the other SCC companies) that accompanied the open-shop drives of the 1920s.[49] But aside from sharing confidential reports and an abstract dedication to the open shop, SCC companies went their own ways on labor policy. Capital-intensive oil, banking, and high-technology interests saw employee representation plans as an attempt "to organize iden-

47 H. F. Brown to Lammot DuPont (16 May 1919), File 27, DuPont Administrative Papers; A.C. Bedford to Hoover (26 February 1923), CF 47, Hoover Papers; Lewis Pierson [Irving Trust] to John Raskob (7 March 1919), File 1827; A.C. Bedford to Raskob (2 Nov. 1922), File 172, Raskob Papers.

48 (Quote) Owen Young to Lammot DuPont (23 February 1927), (quote) Irenée DuPont to Owen Young (1 March 1927), File 8, DuPont Administrative Papers; Clarence Hicks, *My Life in Industrial Relations* (New York, 1941), 52; Senate, *Rights of Labor*, 45:16785–8; "Supplementary Statement of the Special Conference Committee" (1921), File 278, Raskob Papers; Young to Ralph Easley (2 December 1934), File 28, National Civic Federation [NCF] Papers, New York Public Library, New York; (quote) Raskob to Irenée DuPont (27 December 1927), File H:30, Irenée DuPont Papers. With no publishing or lobbying costs, the SCC survived on $15,000 a year (primarily for the salary of general secretary E.S. Cowdrick, who worked initially at Standard and later at the offices of Rockeller lawyers Curtis, Fosdick and Belknap).

49 Bedford to Hoover (26 February 1923), CF 47, Hoover Papers; "Supplementary Statement . . ." (1921), File 278, Raskob Papers; "Minutes of the Annual Meeting of the Special Conference Committee" (1923), "Annual Report of the SCC" (1926), File 8; "Annual Report of the SCC" (1925), File 56, DuPont Administrative Papers; E. M. Herr [Westinghouse] to Owen Young and A. C. Bedford (25 July 1919), File 2528, Raskob Papers. SCC policy and annual reports may be found in Files 6, 12, and 17, Harrington Papers.

tity of interest" with the company, as an extension of the peculiar synthesis of Christian industrialism and public relations that infused Rockefeller labor policies. But for GM, Goodyear, Bethlehem, International Harvester, and DuPont, the company union was simply an antiunion tactic. While capital-intensive Rockefeller interests took a synthetic view, seeing their labor policies as an attempt to steal the high ground from labor leaders and win political concessions elsewhere, labor-intensive mass-production interests viewed labor as a more serious material and managerial liability.[50]

This schism over labor policy underlined the practical and perceptual limits of even such a tightly knit multi-industry association. Although SCC reports consistently reflected a superficial fealty to "industrial democracy," few seem to have taken this position seriously. Raskob complained that members were "so confused in their views they were unable to agree on anything," adding that DuPont and GM executives were "so disgusted with the inability of various so-called big business leaders to get together on anything of value that [they] refused to attend any more meetings . . . [most of which] just resulted in a lot of talk without getting anywhere." Rockefeller consultant Arthur Young maintained his SCC seat (representing Rockefeller's Industrial Relations Counselors) after leaving International Harvester in 1925, but a year later he became the last of the Rockefeller interests to withdraw. By 1934, Standard of Indiana had also withdrawn, and open-shop advocates U.S. Rubber, Union Carbide, and U.S. Steel had joined the club (the latter would soon add Arthur Young as vice-president in charge of labor relations).[51] Despite a concerted attempt to share industrial relations experience and expertise, the companies continued to let material and managerial considerations dictate labor policy.

These basic disagreements aside, members found the SCC to be an important avenue of political power. SCC companies completely dominated the influential Business Advisory Council (BAC), which in turn staffed, formally or informally, the National Recovery Administration's Industrial

---

50 The puzzle in this division is the DuPont company, whose capital intensity would seem to belie its belligerency on the labor issue. Clearly some of this attitude was inherited through its interest in GM. Perhaps more importantly, the fiercely protectionist chemical industry resisted political concessions to organized labor because, unlike oil and banking interests, it was not cultivating political contacts in the hope of liberalizing trade.

51 (Quote) Fahey memo of conversation with Raskob (1932), File 3, John Fahey Papers, Franklin D. Roosevelt Presidential Library (FDRPL), Hyde Park, N.Y.; shifts in membership after 1925 are from "Annual Report of the SCC, 1926"; A.C. Bedford to Irenée DuPont (12 January 1925), File 8, DuPont Administrative Papers; Senate, *Rights of Labor*, 45:16781.

Advisory Board, the Committee on Economic Security, and its forerunner, the President's Organization on Unemployment Relief. Gerard Swope of General Electric appointed Walter Teagle of Standard to chair the BAC's committee on labor and, as a Bethlehem executive recalled, "all the [SCC] members were appointed in their individual capacities to Mr. Teagle's Industrial Relations Committee." The SCC also took it upon itself to ghostwrite BAC reports and seemed only mildly annoyed when the BAC "declined to publish" its more conservative releases on government letterhead.[52] This pattern of influence became apparent in the late 1930s when the LaFollette Committee, in the course of an investigation of antiunion violence, unearthed some scraps of SCC correspondence. The SCC's notoriety, however, was largely undeserved. Its political influence was no greater than that which its members would and could exercise on their own. And its labor policies were a pastiche of private efforts that were scarcely affected by their collection and limited dissemination by SCC secretaries.

By the early 1930s, SCC members had abandoned the notion that leading corporations could simply cooperate and lead by example and considered the positions of its members within the federal government as absolutely crucial to their economic and political objectives. This, of course, came at a time when NAM, the Chamber of Commerce, and the NICB were largely defined by their opposition to the New Deal. That the influence of SCC companies in the New Deal was accompanied by a thinly veiled assertion of control in the NICB (especially over the choice of a successor to Alexander in 1932) and a fairly decisive domination of the NAM after 1933 scarcely bothered SCC leaders – for whom political power and self-interest were greater virtues than consistency.[53]

52 Cowdrick to Willard Jensen (21 May 1934), File 1:11, miscellaneous membership and address lists, Files 1:3 and 1:4, Business Advisory Council [BAC] Records, Records of the Department of Commerce (RG 40) National Archives, Washington, D.C.; "Relief Measures of Special Conference Committee Companies" (October 1931), File 19:5 (and miscellaneous reports, Files 2, 3), Records of the President's Organization on Unemployment Relief, RG 73, National Archives; TNEC, *Economic Power and Political Pressures,* 107; "Notes on Special Conference Committee Meeting of January 11, 1934," File 19, Harrington Papers; membership list, File 1173–2, Pierre S. DuPont Papers, Hagley Museum; (quote) Senate, *Rights of Labor,* 45: 16782; W.B. Foster memo (1 November 1933), File 9, DuPont Administrative Papers; (quote) Swope to Teagle (20 September 1933), File 350:2, National Recovery Administration [NRA] Records (RG 9), National Archives; "In Re Services of the Business Advisory and Planning Council" (August 1934), Official File (OF) 3q, Franklin D. Roosevelt Papers, FDRPL.
53 "Stenographic Record ... Industrial Advisory Board" (June 1934), File 358:12, NRA Records; Draper memo, "To Members of BAC" (5 July 1935), File 1:13, BAC

There was, of course, an almost endless profusion of other peak organizations, most with more specialized or eclectic interests. The American Management Association, a loose affiliate of the SCC, tried to coordinate managerial practices.[54] The Committee for the Nation, a coalition of retailers and silver speculators, lobbied for inflationary monetary policy.[55] The National Civic Federation (NCF), a relic of the Progressive Era, attracted a curious coalition of "progressive" employers and conservative unionists but claimed little business support or political influence.[56] Although of varying

Records; on SCC interest in NICB, see Irenée DuPont to J. Hammond (23 September 1932), Hammond to I. DuPont (29 September 1932), Clarence Hicks to Teagle (27 September 1932), File H:30, Irenée DuPont Papers; on SCC and NAM, see Brady, *Business as a System of Power*, 213–15.

54 The AMA was led by Henry Dennison, Lincoln Filene, and W.J. Donald. Its members included AT&T, GE, Industrial Relations Counselors, Miami Copper, Pennsylvania Railroad, Rand Kardex, Diebold Lock, H.L Doherty, Adolph Lewisohn, Eastman Kodak, Dennison, Hills Bros., Montgomery Ward, Proctor and Gamble, Westinghouse, and the major meat packers. See Jacoby, *Employing Bureaucracy*, 183; "AMA, 1923–1927," File 931:16, Pennsylvania Railroad Papers, Hagley Museum; "AMA," File 2, Henry Dennison Papers, Baker Library; Files 93–20, 93–21, Lamont Papers; Report 25 to ExComm (8 December 1927), Reel 2, Leeds and Northrup Papers, Hagley Museum; Ferguson, "Critical Realignment," 414–16.

55 The Committee for the Nation was led by midwestern retail, financial, and consumer goods interests, including Sears, Zenith, Baird and Warner, Bendix, Continental Illinois National Bank, Oscar Mayer, Borg Warner, Remington Rand, General Mills, and ALCOA. See Robert Wood to Robert Lamont (5 November 1929), File 9; Edward Rumely to Wood (26 July 1935), File 31, Robert E. Wood Papers, HCHPL; Herbert Bratter, "The Committee for the Nation: A Case History in Monetary Propaganda," *Journal of Political Economy* 49 (1941): 531–53.

56 While the NCF has been an object of considerable scholarly interest, after 1920 it was clearly little more than a self-promotional vehicle for founder Ralph Easley. Only a New York City fringe of the AFL retained contact with the NCF through the interwar years, and most business interests were suspicious of Easley's relationship with the AFL and decidedly unappreciative of his attempts to dictate labor relations. Even those more receptive to the AFL–NCF courtship made no connection between Easley's peculiar brand of corporatism and their own labor relations. "I have always been quite willing to discuss," Owen Young reminded Easley, "but even if we did come to an agreement [at the NCF-AFL level], I should not regard that it followed that I should deal with trade unions in our plants." See Easley to John Ames (15 February 1923), File 22, NCF Papers; Marguerite Green, *The National Civic Federation and the American Labor Movement, 1900–1925* (Washington, 1956), 197–99, 272–75, 440–50, 463, 480–81; Easley to John Hammond (16 October 1935), File 41; Tobin to Easley (21 April 1924), File 22; Stone to Easley (6 May 1924), File 28; Easley to Clarence Hicks (12 September 1924), File 27; "New York Industrial Roundtable Lists" (1925), File 50; Owen Young to Easley (2 June 1921), File 22; Easley to John Hammond (16 October 1935), File 41, NCF Papers. I have traced the interwar history of the NCF in greater detail in Gordon, "New Deal, Old Deck," 360–64.

importance and prominence, such organizations echoed the experiences of the NAM, the NICB, the Chamber of Commerce, and the SCC. On paper, peak organizations brought together distinct elements of the business community and tried to maintain an active membership that was both small enough to be coherent and large enough to establish political credibility and underwrite the costs of organization. This was a delicate, and ultimately futile, task. Such organizations were unable to control the behavior of members (let alone nonmembers) and incapable of projecting a consistent "business" consensus on political issues.

These frustrations were often played out in battles over support and status among the major peak organizations. NAM distanced itself from the Chamber on numerous occasions, breaking ties in 1922 over the latter's exclusive support of "commercial and mercantile" interests and sending delegates to a 1934 convention with directions "to prevent the Chamber from pussyfooting and kowtowing to the administration." NAM also waged a war of words with the NCF, at least until the latter abandoned the idealism of its prewar labor policy. And although the NICB and NAM had close hereditary ties, they battled constantly over their respective areas of representation and responsibility.[57] In many respects, peak associations simply cemented the disorganization and diversity of business opinion they were designed to overcome.

Often exaggerated by personal jealousies or ideological rifts, political and jurisdictional spats reflected an ongoing competition for members and income. Each organization cultivated membership, subscription, and mailing lists during the 1920s, but these withered rapidly after 1929. Through the 1930s, NAM, the NICB, and the Chamber of Commerce combined strict austerity with increased dependence on large corporations. Pretensions of broad representation disappeared, and firms that had assumed the financial burden of organization began pressing the NAM, NICB, and Chamber toward a new emphasis on public and political relations (highlighted by the National Business Survey Conference of 1929–30). Members increasingly criticized peak organizations for their inability to represent or influence any meaningful cross-section of their on-paper membership. As the economic

---

57 John Edgerton [NAM] to Chamber of Commerce (18 May 1922), Edgerton to A.B. Farquar (29 May 1922), James Emery to Edgerton (17 May 1922), File 303, NAM Papers; Stalker, "The National Association of Manufacturers," 393, n.18; Green, *The National Civic Federation,* 90–132; Taylor, *Labor Policies of the NAM,* 24–34; NICB ExComm 56 (16 May 1922), File II:3; Noel Sargent [NAM] to J.M. Robertson [NICB] (19 June 1934), File V:5, NICB Papers; "NAM: 1921," CF 427, Hoover Papers.

crisis placed new demands on peak organizations *and* undermined their support, they became little more than forums for the political anxieties of large corporations.[58]

These corporations, however, also had little faith in the organizations that they controlled almost completely by the mid-1930s. "Demands on us for this sort of thing are tremendous," conceded GM's Alfred Sloan,

> [but] . . . I have never thought that we got very much or our stockholders got very much out of the majority of these kind of organizations. We have put, during the past few years, a very considerable sum of money into this activity and, frankly, I cannot see what we have got out of it. . . . we spend our stockholders' money to a large extent because the other fellow does the same thing and he does it because he is told we are doing it . . . [it seems] impossible to do anything different.[59]

This ambivalence was understandable. Firms such as GM, after all, moved to the forefront of these organizations by default rather than design. Most smaller firms were unwilling and unable to support organizational efforts after 1929. Leading firms were simply less sensitive to the costs of organization and more anxious about the political implications of the Depression.

Leading business interests, while consistently skeptical of the promise and costs of organization, were reluctant to abandon any avenue of potential influence. They accompanied their control of NAM, the NICB, and the Chamber with attempts to establish, as NICB President Jordan put it, "more intimate private conferences among a smaller number of important executives." Products of this sentiment included the SCC, banker Fred Kent's 1931 proposal for the creation of a peak "industrial corporation" staffed by the nation's "twenty largest executives," and the "Committee of 12" (which included Sloan, Swope, Robertson of Westinghouse, and Pierre DuPont) organized through the New York Federal Reserve in 1932. These initiatives were girded by the feeling that "the important thing for business men to do is to keep quiet and saw wood, rather than have their pictures in the newspapers . . . [and] lead the man on the street to think that there is something badly out of gear."[60] For most corporate interests, business organization was

58 Gitelman, "Management's Crisis of Confidence," 155; Derber, "Employer Associations in the United States," 109.
59 Sloan to Irenée DuPont (1 March 1929), File H:30, Irenée DuPont Papers.
60 (Quote) Virgil Jordan to Lammot DuPont (7 February 1933), File 57, DuPont Administrative Papers; (quote) Magnus Alexander to Charles Nagel (28 February 1931); Alexander to Charles Cheney (27 December 1929), File VI:1; NICB Papers; on the Committee of 12, see File 189, Irenée DuPont Papers.

a defense against political threats, a rostrum for appeals to consumer and investor confidence, and an index of their own anxiety.

By the monotonous estimation of their own members, peak business associations of the interwar era were starkly ineffective. As one disenchanted member noted, these organizations "do not represent industry – they live off it."[61] A clique of corporate interests did wear many hats in the peak organizations of the interwar era, but they were bound together by little more than deep doubts and the financial ability to experiment in all sorts of quasi-political ventures. Positions taken under the auspices of an organization never strayed from those pursued as private interests. And the same interests experimented in much the same way (with uneven results) with investments in the Democratic and Republican parties, perhaps the preeminent business organizations of the era.[62] By the mid-1930s, peak organizations were satisfied with masquerades of business confidence punctuated by press releases. The industries, firms, and individuals these organizations represented, meanwhile, had long followed their own short-sighted interests and either reacted to the contradictions and failures of the New Deal or threw their energies behind its code authorities and advisory councils.

In all, peak and trade associations were attempts to solve the central riddle of the interwar industrial economy: how to escape economic and political competition without surrendering managerial prerogatives or profits. Yet cooperation with competitors on key aspects of the trade, or with a wider circle of business leaders on matters of broader political or economic interest, accomplished very little. Peak associations found it impossible to faithfully represent their membership with anything but meaningless platitudes. Trade associations found they could never count among their members those firms whose competitive practices were responsible for dismal conditions in the first place. And neither possessed the means of enforcing or coercing cooperation. As a result, peak associations became little more than lightning rods for business opponents of public policy, whereas trade associations became little more than the political arm of leading firms, unable to discipline competitors or, in those instances where all firms might recognize an external threat, to settle on any means of distributing the costs of collective action.

61 E.J. Dant [Oregon Lumber] to Irving Howe (24 May 1933), OF 396, FDR Papers.
62 This point is developed in Thomas Ferguson, "From Normalcy to New Deal: Industrial Structure, Party Competition, and American Public Policy in the Great Depression," *International Organization* 38 (1984): 41–94, and "Party Realignment and American Industrial Structure," *Research in Political Economy* 6 (1983): 1–82; Philip Burch, *Elites in American History*, vol. 3 (Boston, 1981).

The Great Depression and the End of Associationalism

The onset of the Great Depression, of course, only magnified both the urgency and the futility of cooperation. The scale of the downturn defies easy description. From the crash of late 1929 to the trough of 1932, the lives and livelihoods of millions of people fell apart. National income plummeted 40 percent, wages fell over 60 percent, and real weekly earnings (despite deflation) dropped from $25.00 to barely $20.00. These figures meant little to the millions without work. National unemployment, which reached 25 percent by 1933, paled beside joblessness in core industry centers: 50 percent in Cleveland, 60 percent in Akron, 80 percent in Toledo. In the West and South, collapsing prices and near-record production of most staples played havoc with the agricultural economy. Average annual farm incomes fell from a pre-1929 average of $1,000 to barely $300 by 1932, and banks foreclosed nearly 1,000,000 farms between 1930 and 1934. As rural and urban economies collapsed, farmers, workers, miners, and their families joined a desperate migrant community (numbering over 2,000,000 by 1933) that drifted from farm to city and city to farm in a futile quest for security.[63]

The Depression's devastation and persistence challenged the core assumptions of private interests, academics, and politicians. Clearly this was not just another dip in the business cycle. As the immediacy of October 1929 receded, the causes of the Depression became less important than the pervasive obstacles to recovery.[64] The crash had come, as Michael Bernstein has

63 Peter Fearon, *War, Prosperity and Depression: The U.S. Economy, 1917–1945* (Lawrence, 1987), 101–7, 137–40; William Leuchtenberg, *The Perils of Prosperity, 1914–1932* (Chicago, 1958), 247–52; Irving Bernstein, *The New Deal Collective Bargaining Policy* (Berkeley, 1950), 14–15; and *The Lean Years: A History of the American Worker, 1920–1933* (Boston, 1960), 287–311; Alexander Keyssar, "History and the Problem of Unemployment," *Socialist Review* 19 (1989): 15–34; George Tindall, *The Emergence of the New South, 1913–1945* (Baton Rouge, 1967), 354–55; William Leuchtenberg, *Franklin D. Roosevelt and the New Deal* (New York, 1963), 2, 23–30.

64 The causes of the Depression are still a matter of academic controversy. This ideologically charged and often technical debate has concentrated on the merits of a number of short-term economic explanations (the crash itself and business confidence) and political explanations (such as Federal Reserve policies). Whatever weight is given these factors, they clearly explain little more than the timing of a Depression that signalled much more fundamental economic problems. See Michael Bernstein, *The Great Depression: Delayed Recovery and Economic Change, 1929–1939* (New York, 1989), 4–20, and "Why the Great Depression was Great: Towards a New Understanding of the Interwar Economic Crisis in the United States," in *The Rise and Fall of the New Deal Order, 1930–1980*, ed. Steve Fraser and Gary Gerstle (Princeton, 1989): 32–54; John Kenneth Galbraith, *The Great Crash, 1929* (New York, 1961), 25–26, 67; William Leuchtenberg, *The Perils of Prosperity*, 242–43;

pointed out, in the midst of a long swing of disparate industrial growth. A shift to consumer-goods production had occurred without any redistribution of employment or income, making the collapse of capital markets and consumer spending unusually destructive. After 1930, investment recovered primarily in industries (chemicals, oil, food, tobacco) that accounted for relatively small shares of national output and employment. Political efforts to revitalize the industrial economy were at odds with economic pressures that drove employment and investment away from traditional manufacturing and mining sectors. "Something fundamental has happened in respect to the long-term outlook for American business," remarked Alexander Sachs in 1931, ". . . we have become an economically mature country." Although recovery depended on a substantial adjustment to the demands of the emerging consumer economy, it was inevitably understood – by industrial interests and politicians alike – as the rationalization of competition on an industry-by-industry basis.[65]

Although business hoped against hope that the stock market crisis would not affect business conditions, the disappearance of investment in consumer-goods industries and massive unemployment knocked the entire economy off stride. Consumers and producers put off durable-goods orders at the first hint of instability. While aggregate output fell 50 percent, durable-goods output fell almost 80 percent. Industries such as shoes, tobacco, and food were comparatively healthy and quick to recover, but this disparity only distorted regional economies. Southern agricultural and mining were decimated, but the region's largely nondurable, agriculturally based manufac-

Albert Romasco, *The Poverty of Abundance: Hoover, the Nation, and the Depression* (New York, 1965), 24–38.

65 Bernstein, *The Great Depression*, 24–34; Sachs to Paul Nash (7 April 1931), File 49, Alexander Sachs Papers, FDRPL. Domestic dilemmas were compounded by international dilemmas. At the end of World War I, the United States was the preeminent economic power in the world. This status, however, reflected the *weakness* of European economies rather than any conscious sense of power or responsibility in Washington or New York. As Americans and Europeans fought with each other and amongst themselves over European reconstruction, war debts, and trade, the global economy stumbled along without a real center. Through the 1920s, this disorganization skewed global investment, as industrial countries pursued both international markets and traditional protectionism (an approach neatly embodied by Hoover's Commerce Department). After 1929, competitive currency depreciation, tariff retaliation, and the absence of central bank cooperation or an international "lender of last resort" combined to make things much worse and recovery much more difficult. See Charles Kindleberger, *The World in Depression, 1929–1939* (Berkeley, 1986), 288–305; Mira Wilkins, *The Maturing of Multinational Enterprise: American Business Abroad from 1914–1970* (Cambridge, 1974), 169–72; Stephen V.O. Clarke, *Central Bank Cooperation, 1924–1931* (New York, 1967), 15–44.

turing industries thrived on low commodity prices and relatively inelastic demand, and manufacturing bankruptcies ran at about one-third the northern rate.[66] Differences in the way regions, industries, and firms were struck by the crash encouraged a wide array of economic strategies and political demands. The Depression made the prevailing source of instability in an industry more severe and serious, and introduced business to less-familiar problems, including the rumblings of social discontent.

More importantly, the Depression immediately called into question a decade of experiments in union-management cooperation, welfare capitalism, and business organization. Whatever the breadth or experience of these private solutions, business abandoned them quickly and capriciously after 1929. The "new unionism" lost its appeal in a depressed economy, as company and business unions were bombarded by employers seeking concessions and workers seeking meaningful organization and security. Welfare capitalism was a luxury few could afford in bad times. And associationalism foundered as cooperation among competitors, only sporadically successful when sales were brisk, had little chance when sales slowed. In short, the Depression scrambled business strategies, underscored the dilemmas of underconsumption, highlighted the poverty of the social welfare system, and deepened the material anxieties of workers to the point that the promise of collective action began to outweigh its risks.

Hoover responded to the crash by publicly counseling calm and privately hoping that a cold bath would cleanse the economy of inefficiency and excess capacity. When asked for his solution to the Depression, Hoover's Secretary of the Treasury Andrew Mellon suggested, "Liquidate labor, liquidate stocks, liquidate the farmers, liquidate real estate." While not usually stated so harshly, this was essentially the Hoover program. The administration devoted its attention to the problem of business credit, instituting the Reconstruction Finance Corporation as a federal conduit for low-interest, short-term business loans.[67] And Hoover did little to follow through on a

---

66 Kroos, *Executive Opinion*, 116–17; Fearon, *War, Prosperity and Depression*, 92; Tindall, *Emergence of the New South*, 360–61, 371–73.

67 William Barber, *From New Era to New Deal: Hoover, the Economists, and American Economic Policy, 1921–1933* (New York, 1985), 15–27, 53–61, 189; Romasco, *The Poverty of Abundance*, 25 (Mellon quote), 232–33; James Olson, *Herbert Hoover and the Reconstruction Finance Corporation, 1931–933* (Ames, 1977); James Olson, *Saving Capitalism: The Reconstruction Finance Corporation and the New Deal, 1933–1940* (Princeton, 1988); Sachs Memo (n.d.), File 101, Sachs Papers; "Extracts from [Sachs] Memo" (22 January 1934), OF 1983, FDR Papers. For their part, bankers complained that the RFC failed "to remedy the basic evils and maladjustments" of

decade of rhetoric about high wages, industrial organization, and fair competition. The president had "ventured into a legal and economic no-man's
land," as one student notes, "where failure was assured unless everyone
acted honorably and events cooperated." Stasis and confusion were exacerbated by Hoover's testy relationship with a Congress enamored with its
own "potpourri of panaceas." Democrats portrayed Hoover as the "Depression President," while Republicans outside the White House distanced
themselves from the administration.[68]

Business watched the disintegration of the economy and the Republican
party with dismay. Through 1932, most business interests responded to the
Depression by blaming it on others, pretending that misery and privation
constituted a minor "correction" and claiming that recovery was "just
around the corner." With each firm's understanding of the economic crisis
confined to a tangible lack of sales, business urged anyone with cash to "buy
now" and revive the economy. As the Depression deepened and these campaigns failed, business pressed for political intervention to break the competitive and consumptive deadlock. Hard times magnified the conviction that
competition was foolhardy and destructive, and most firms, as TNEC researchers concluded, were "reluctant to accept a competitive price for their
produce if they [could] avoid it." Essentially, as one business consultant
noted, industry wanted legal sanction for organizational efforts that had
"failed in cases where they lacked the power to force the minority to 'play
ball.' " For business interests (many of whom, as Virgil Jordan complained,
seemed "disgustingly crazy to eat out of the President's hand") such demands were a desperate extension 1920s associationalism. For Hoover,
whose faith in the efficacy of an educated market remained intact, such
demands were beyond the pale.[69]

Few held their breath on election night in 1932. As is the rule in U.S.
elections, poor economic conditions destroyed support for the incumbent

a depression that was "structural as well as cyclical" and that RFC funds too often
financed the construction of new and unnecessary plant capacity. See Memorandum
for Mr. Strauss (26 September 1930), Name & Subject File 46, Lewis L. Strauss
Papers, HCHPL.

68 Hoover, *Memoirs: The Great Depression, 1929–1941*, 1–300; Barber, *New Era to New
Deal*, 125–51; (quote) Kendrick Clements, "Herbert Hoover and Conservation,
1921–1933," *American Historical Review* 89 (1984): 75; (quote) Romasco, *The Poverty
of Abundance*, 36; Jordan Schwarz, *The Interregnum of Despair: Hoover, Congress, and
the Depression* (Urbana, 1970), 12–13, 32–33, 46–47, 73–74, 205–29.

69 For a cross-section of business reaction to the Depression, see Kroos, *Executive
Opinion*, 115–58; "Business" Files, Presidential Files 88–91, Hoover Papers; (quote)
TNEC Monograph 25, *Recovery Plans* (Washington, 1939), 10; (Jordan quote) Ralph
Easley to Coffin Van Rensselaer (13 July 1933), File 39, NCF Papers.

president. "You might save yourself the expense of your Western trip," one Senator assured Roosevelt in September, "but the railroads need the money." Business fully appreciated not only the fact that Hoover's policies had failed but also that Roosevelt, however intangible his candidacy, was going to win. Some sent good money after bad in supporting Hoover, many cynically supported both candidates and, in increasing numbers, many more became fair-weather Democrats. Henry Harriman of the Chamber of Commerce had pressed Hoover through 1931 and 1932 to support the Chamber's NRA-like plan; when he balked, as Hoover later recalled, "Harriman told me that Roosevelt had agreed to support the plan, and that highly placed business men would support [him], both financially and by their influence – which they did." As the election approached, the Democrats expanded their traditional business bases among oil, mining, banking, high-tech manufacturing, retail, and southern industry. As *Fortune* noted in a post-election survey: "The Northern businessman is a Democrat for some special reason and the Southern businessman is a Democrat for no reason at all."[70]

The transition from Hoover to Roosevelt was neither as monumental as the latter's hagiographers have suggested nor as inconsequential as his revisionist critics have claimed.[71] Roosevelt drew considerably on business programs of the 1920s and on Hoover's failures. But the novelty of the New Deal rested less on a profound turnover of ideology or personnel than on timid experimentation, persistent failure, and piecemeal attempts by Hoover and Roosevelt to balance the self-interested voluntarism of the business program with the coercion necessary to make it work. It was business interests, and not the incoming administration, that stressed the need to politicize their problems. After a protracted opportunity to voluntarily clean house

70 Senator quoted in Schwarz, *Interregnum of Despair*, 198; Herbert Hoover, *The Memoirs of Herbert Hoover: The Great Depression, 1929–1941* (New York, 1952), 335; "Democrats in Big Business," *Fortune* 7 (Jan. 1933): 16–21, 106.
71 See Ellis Hawley, "Herbert Hoover and Modern American History: Sixty Years After," and Patrick O'Brien and Philip Rosen, "Hoover and the Historians: The Reconstruction of a President," in *Herbert Hoover and the Historians*, ed. Mark M. Dodge (West Branch, 1989), 1–85. Embittered members of the Hoover administration were the first to argue both that the New Deal had looted Hoover's policies *and* that it was a "fascistic" departure from the doctrine of American Individualism. For his part, New Dealer Rexford Tugwell admitted that "the Hundred Days was the breaking of a dam rather than the conjuring out of nowhere of a river." (Quoted in Barber, *From New Era to New Deal*, 195.) See Herbert Hoover, *The Memoirs of Herbert Hoover: The Cabinet and the Presidency, 1920–1933* (New York, 1952); Hoover, *Memoirs: The Great Depression*; Arthur M. Hyde and Ray Lyman Wilbur, *The Hoover Policies* (New York, 1937).

under Hoover, as Jordan Schwarz notes, business now "craved federal assistance regardless of the price on their souls."[72]

Under the New Deal, attempts to organize markets would be more costly and coercive. In order to reap the stable prices and profits that followed from trade agreements, employers had to give something in return – namely the freedom to bail out of agreements on a whim. And trade agreements would not only be binding upon all competing firms but would also ignore regional lines and destroy state and regional competitive advantages. "All efforts at voluntary regulation are completely futile," as one union official reminded Congress in early 1933; ". . . our employers have constantly told us . . . in every [] State where we have attempted to enact measures of State regulation, that they are in favor of Federal regulation. Our point is this: Call their bluff."[73] Of course, many business supporters of New Deal measures were not bluffing. They avidly supported policies that would raise competitive standards, including those involving labor, in such a way as to drive marginally competitive firms and regions from the market. Others held less attractive hands and were not so much bluffing as they were trying to make the most of the cards they held or to protect earlier bets. Others played the game in short-sighted desperation, hoping they could draw new cards at will. And (to exhaust the metaphor) many seemed to feel that they could play without risk, quitting the hand and the game and retrieving all bets if the cards were not there.

The experience of business organization in the 1920s – through the market, labor relations, or formal association – underscored both the debilitating effects of unrestrained competition and the futility of any organization that was unable to articulate or enforce collective goals. The onset of the Great Depression magnified these organizational dilemmas and pushed them to the center of the debate over economic recovery. Beginning with the National Recovery Act of 1933 and continuing with the Wagner and Social Security Acts of 1935, New Deal legislation reflected the organizational demands and ambivalence of U.S. business. Even those who hoped that politics might be able to enforce order where private agreements had failed bridled at the associated costs. And, in the end, governmental efforts to solve the organizational crises of the political economy would be more complex, uneven, and costly than their business proponents ever anticipated.

72 Schwarz, *Interregnum of Despair,* 233.
73 John Edelman of the Hosiery Workers in U.S. Congress, House Committee on Labor, *Six-Hour Day, Five-Day Week* (Washington, 1933), 65.

5. The National Recovery Act
*The Political Economy of Business
Organization, 1933–1935*

The persistence of bitter market competition and the failure of the associational experiments of the 1920s (both compounded by the collapse of 1929) forced leading firms and their political allies to consider more comprehensive and coercive means of effecting collective action. As a result, business strategy after 1929 rested on three premises. First, industry leaders wanted relief from the threat of antitrust law. Hoover had allowed unprecedented cooperation among competitors, but selective prosecution and anxiety over how far associationalism might go (or how long it might last) made antitrust reform preferable to beneficent interpretation. Second, leading firms and trade associations desired not only wider and more precise legal boundaries but assurance that all competitors within those boundaries would be forced to play by the same rules. If trade associations could not compel cooperation, many would never hew to "fair" industry standards and would free-ride on the backs of those who did. Third, coercive organization alone would accomplish little in depressed markets. Industrial self-government had to be accompanied by industrial recovery, some fraction of which it was hoped would end up in the pockets of consumers.

These concerns were synthesized in the National Industrial Recovery Act (NRA), passed in early 1933. Each industry and firm entered the NRA experiment with specific ideas as to what competitive restrictions were desirable or possible; although virtually all interests sought relief from the antitrust laws, they were poised to swim in different directions when the immunity bath was drawn. The political and economic background of the NRA is a familiar story; in the opening section of this chapter, I sketch the NRA's origins and suggest the bewildering variety of business strategies that were drawn into the legislative vortex.[1] The rest of this chapter traces

---

1 I use the acronym *NRA* to represent both the law (the National Industrial Recovery Act) and the agency (the National Recovery Administration). I do not attempt a general history of the NRA and only touch upon its provisions for public works

the NRA's administrative dilemmas, inconsistencies, and contradictions. I focus particularly on the problem of compliance and the NRA's failure to enforce its codes and effectively raise the stakes of capitalist collective action. And I suggest the importance, as perceived by many firms, of labor standards (rather than prices or trade practices) as a focus of regulation, and of labor unions (rather than trade associations or the state) as a means of enforcing regulation.

The Political Scramble: Industry and the Origins of the NRA

In the months after the collapse of the economy in 1929, business interests, academics, and politicians furiously debated the causes of the Depression and the prospects for recovery. Both Hoover and Roosevelt, at least initially, focused their efforts on the financial system – an approach encouraged by the investment crisis, widespread bank closures, and the easy political target of Wall Street. But business knew that its problems ran far deeper than the pattern of debt, consolidation, and speculation that had precipitated the tumble in stock prices. For most, the crash capped a decade of falling profits, ruthless competition, and a widening gap between the economy's ability to produce and its ability to consume. The financial panic was a pale reflection of a more fundamental crisis of industrial stability.

Plans for industrial recovery drew indiscriminately and haphazardly from a wide variety of sources. The trade association movement of the 1920s was a major influence, as were the demands of competitive industries that had found voluntary organization to be problematic. The Federal Trade Commission (FTC) had played with the idea of trade practice codes in the late 1920s but never cleared its efforts with the Justice Department and had to abandon the experiment hastily. In the Hoover administration's last year, business renewed pressure for some form of compulsory trade practice agreements. Notable advocates included the Chamber of Commerce (especially

(Title II). The best account of the NRA remains Ellis Hawley, *The New Deal and the Problem of Monopoly* (Princeton, 1966). See also Bernard Bellush, *The Failure of the NRA* (New York, 1975); Donald Brand, *Corporatism and the Rule of Law: A Study of the National Recovery Administration* (Ithaca, 1988); Daniel Fusfeld, *The Economic Thought of Franklin D. Roosevelt and the Origins of the New Deal* (New York, 1956); Robert Himmelberg, *The Origins of the National Recovery Administration* (New York, 1976); Peter Irons, *New Deal Lawyers* (Princeton, 1982); Stanley Vittoz, *New Deal Labor Policy and the American Industrial Economy* (Chapel Hill, 1987), 73–134.

oil, coal, and lumber firms on its National Resources Committee) and Gerard Swope of General Electric. The "Swope Plan," a sweeping call for trade association–based regulation "under a shadowy government supervision," appealed to frustrated trade associationists, but Hoover advisers dismissed it as "the most gigantic proposal of monopoly ever made in history."[2]

The situation did not change markedly with Roosevelt's election, although the campaign and a large turnover in congressional ranks raised the volume and variety of the recovery debate. By the end of 1932, a number of ill-defined and overlapping currents of thought were prominent. Political progressives, the construction industry, and scattered regional interests favored massive expenditure on public works. Consumer-goods firms and many leading trade associations favored Swope's business planning approach. Fiscal conservatives, bankers, and capital-goods industries leaned toward start-up business loans or guarantees against business losses (usually proposed alongside monetary or banking regulation). And a few labor-intensive industries, conservative unionists, and underconsumptionist theorists (those who saw the Depression as a crisis of consumption rather than production) in the new administration toyed with "share the work" plans for regulating competition and building purchasing power. Although remaining sharply contradictory on a number of points, the Roosevelt administration moved tentatively to synthesize these plans and satisfy the demands they represented – a course determined more by the fear of alienating important interests and the hope of forestalling congressional experimentation than by any prescriptive political vision.[3]

2 John T. Flynn, "Whose Child is the NRA?" *Harper's* 169 (September 1934); Nelson Gaskill, *The Regulation of Competition* (New York, 1936), 120; Miller memorandum for Hoover, Commerce File [CF] 199, Herbert C. Hoover Papers, Herbert C. Hoover Presidential Library [HCHPL], West Branch, IA; Himmelberg, *Origins of the NRA*, 143–45; Chamber of Commerce, *Questions for Consideration* (Washington, 1933), 7; Louis Hacker, "The New Deal is No Revolution," *Harper's* 168 (January 1934); Herbert Hoover, *Memoirs: The Great Depression, 1929–1941* (New York, 1952) 420–32; [Lawrence Richey] Memorandum on Swope-Young Plan (1931), Presidential File [PF] 92, Hoover Papers. On the Swope Plan, see also "Mr. Swope's Insurance Plan," *The New Republic*, 1 April 1931, 202; Draft of "Swope-Young Plan" (1931), PF 92, Hoover Papers; Wilbur Cohen, "The Swope Plan: A Critical Analysis" (14 September 1934), File 17; Committee on Economic Security Records, Records of the Social Security Administration (RG 147), National Archives, Washington, D.C..

3 See Hawley, *New Deal and the Problem of Monopoly*, 19–52; Himmelberg, *Origins of the NRA*, 181–96, 210; Vittoz, *New Deal Labor Policy*, 78–82; Gaskill, *Regulation of Competition*, 129.

During the spring of 1933, a hastily reconvened Congress began sorting through the promises and platitudes of the campaign, and fragments of recovery legislation were drafted in every corner of the new administration. In mid-March, Roosevelt encouraged Senator Wagner to get something started in the Senate and pressed Raymond Moley of his own staff to begin digging through a blizzard of solicited and unsolicited recovery proposals. Moley passed a number of plans (including those of Swope, the Chamber of Commerce, and bankers Fred Kent and Malcolm Rorty) on to New York financier James Warburg, who in turn compared notes with Wagner and brought in Kent, Harold Moulton of the Brookings Institution, and Adolph Miller of the Federal Reserve to hammer out a bill. This group, leaning towards the banking-oriented start-up planners, became bogged down over the targeting of public loans; some favored selective loans to producer-goods firms, whereas others favored guaranteed profit margins for consumer-goods firms. At the same time, business planning proposals were piling up in the office of Undersecretary of Commerce John Dickinson, and Congress was showing renewed interest in the share-the-work wage and hour regulation it had raised in the last session.[4]

For the Roosevelt administration, which was meticulously cautious on such matters, the divided opinion of important economic interests was enough to put everything on hold. In Congress, however, the inertia of the campaign was harder to control. On April 6, the Senate passed the Black Bill, a rigid proposal to limit the work week in industry to thirty hours, and a companion measure (the Connery Bill) was ready to go to the floor in the House. While the administration viewed the Black Bill as one of a number of minor threats, business opposition to the thirty-hour proposal, in the words of a National Association of Manufacturers (NAM) lobbyist, "broke over the Capitol like a bomb." The business position on the Black Bill was simple. Most saw the need for competitive restrictions, but only a few considered the thirty-hour work week realistic or appropriate. As Morris Leeds observed, industry was "not so unanimously opposed to the [Black] Bill as one might expect." Most voiced their displeasure by demanding a different set of wage and hour standards for *their* industry while supporting the general notion of restrictive regulation. The Black Bill was seen, quite accurately, as a measure cut to fit the needs of the textile and clothing trades;

4 Flynn, "Whose Child is the NRA?"; Raymond Moley, *The First New Deal* (New York, 1966), 284–90; Vittoz, *New Deal Labor Policy*, 82–84; William Leuchtenberg, *Franklin D. Roosevelt and the New Deal* (New York, 1963), 55–57.

outside these industries, firms wanted a chance to set their own standards. And labor questioned the impact of what it saw as "share the poverty" legislation that seemed to do little more than "remove the burden of charity from the backs of the rich."[5]

Business anxieties catalyzed the administration's doubts. Roosevelt pulled strings in the House to delay the Connery Bill and frantically pressed his staff to sort out the various objections to the Black Bill and craft an alternative. The House, always more sensitive to regional business interests than the Senate, was happy to scuttle the thirty-hour bill but also appreciated the urgency of finding something to take its place. The administration responded on a number of fronts. Secretary of Labor Frances Perkins explored the possibility of a more flexible hours law during testimony before the House Labor Committee in late April, and the informal caucuses that had studied the recovery problem in March frantically regrouped. Business planners renewed their efforts through the Department of Commerce; General Hugh Johnson (formerly of the War Industries Board, the Moline Plow Company, and the Democratic campaign staff) began studying the same pile of proposals that had passed through Moley's hands a month earlier; and Senator Wagner headed a drafting group that included Moulton, Kent, Rochester banker Meyer Jacobstein, United Mine Workers consultant W. Jett Lauck, Virgil Jordan of the National Industrial Conference Board, and trade association attorneys David Podell and Gilbert Montague. On May 10, Roosevelt asked all those working on recovery plans to "lock themselves in a room" and come up with something, although not before conceding further to business by including the hastily formed Business Advisory Committee in the final deliberations.[6]

5 (Quote) James Emery to Henry Sharpe (16 May 1933), File 851.2, National Association of Manufacturers [NAM] Papers, Hagley Museum and Library, Wilmington, DE; (quote) Leeds to Cooke (28 April 1933), File 79, Morris Cooke Papers, Franklin D. Roosevelt Presidential Library [FDRPL], Hyde Park, NY; Cowdrick Memo (10 April 1933), File 17, Willis Harrington Papers, Hagley Museum; Orra Stone to Emery (11 April 1933); Emery to Stone (12 April 1933), File 851.2, NAM Papers; Solomon Barkin, "NRA Policies, Standards, and Code Provisions," Work Materials #45, B:1 (Washington, 1936), 5–14; Flynn, "Whose Child is the NRA?"; Labor opinion cited in David Roediger and Philip Foner, *Our Own Time* (London, 1989), 245–50.

6 On administration and House response to the Black Bill, see Vittoz, *New Deal Labor Policy*, 85–86; James Emery to Orra Stone (12 April 1933), File 851.2, NAM Papers; The timing and importance of various threads of NRA legislation vary considerably among the recollections of participants and academics. The best account of the drafting process is Himmelberg, *Origins of the NRA*, 195–205. I have also drawn

In late May, the Roosevelt administration sent the National Industrial Recovery Act up the hill. Title I authorized industries to draw up "codes of fair competition" free from the fetters of antitrust law. The labor provisions (Sections 7a, b, and c) embodied an industry-by-industry version of the Black Bill and a gesture toward the rights of workers "to organize and bargain collectively through representatives of their own choosing." Various industries viewed this apparent labor concession quite differently. Open-shop advocates and mass-production firms saw the labor provisions as an annoyance that would not give labor any rights it did not already enjoy. Older manufacturing and mining industries (especially those that had flirted with regulatory unionism) saw Section 7 as the economic core of the act and not just a political expedient to its passage. And many saw Section 7 through the purchasing power arguments of the original Black Bill. The implications of NRA labor policy are examined in the next chapter; suffice it to say here that Section 7 did little to undermine business support, and a basic confusion over federal labor policy remained unresolved. The NRA passed the House easily, and although Senate conservatives tried to strike the labor provisions and progressives railed against the act's embrace of monopoly, it also passed there (by a narrow margin) unchanged. As *Business Week* crowed: "Business gets substantially what it has been asking for ever since Senator Black first confronted it with the threat of rigid control from above."[7]

The NRA was an ad hoc synthesis of disparate industrial or trade association recovery plans, most of which were concerned less with strengthening the economy than with long-standing patterns of competition and disorganization in their respective industries. Few seemed troubled by the act's economic inconsistencies, the legal portent of its intentionally vague anti-competitive and labor provisions, or the looming problem of administration – although one New Deal adviser wrote Johnson that the "multifarious authorship" of the NRA had produced "an omnibus enabling act" which,

upon Vittoz, *New Deal Labor Policy,* 77–93; Irons, *New Deal Lawyers,* 22–24; Arthur Schlesinger, *The Coming of the New Deal* (Boston, 1958), 96–98; Leuchtenberg, *Roosevelt and the New Deal,* 55–57; Hawley, *New Deal and the Problem of Monopoly,* 19–34; Broadus Mitchell, *Depression Decade* (New York, 1947), 234–35; Harold Ickes, *The Secret Diary of Harold Ickes: The First Thousand Days, 1933–1936* (New York, 1953), 36; Flynn, "Whose Child is the NRA?" Donald Brand argues that the NRA was "a progressive measure" over which business had little influence, but he offers as evidence only Senator Wagner's *public* assurance that the Chamber of Commerce's Harriman "had nothing to do with drafting this legislation" (*Corporatism and the Rule of Law,* 83–86).

7 Vittoz, *New Deal Labor Policy,* 91–96; Mitchell, *Depression Decade,* 245; (quote) *Business Week,* 24 May 1933, 1.

"instead of a synthesis [seemed] a conglomeration of purposes, an obfuscation of ends and a stultification of methods." The only common goal was antitrust reform, although this was more a rallying cry than an end in itself. "We had widely varying ideas as to the form and method" of trade regulation, admitted one trade association official, but "to the average trade association secretary, having gone through a period of membership starvation, the National Industrial Recovery Act appeared as a gift from the gods."[8]

The NRA, as one business lobbyist marveled, had "the most widespread and splendid support from industrial groups throughout the country." Important proponents included trade associations in the steel, rubber, textile, paper, lumber, clothing, and leather industries; leading firms (already cooperating closely with the federal government) in oil and coal; and a wide array of larger firms that hoped (with some cause) that the NRA would make it possible to drive out marginal, cutthroat, and regional competitors. While the inconsistencies, failures, and vagaries of the NRA made it difficult to pin down industrial support once the codes were in place, most viewed the NRA as either a golden opportunity or a minor nuisance. "By enlisting the aid of the sheriff to control the other fellow," as Virgil Jordan noted, leading firms simply hoped "they could get some advantage for themselves." Those who had sought such regulatory innovation for the past decade were ecstatic. "The Lumber Code is not an edict handed us by Congress or the President," argued William Greeley of the West Coast Lumbermen's Association; "we went to Washington and asked for it." And those with little need for federal intervention were scarcely threatened. In such cases, as NRA officials admitted of the automobile industry, the code was invariably "very broad and one could do almost anything under it."[9]

8 (Quote) Alexander Sachs to Johnson (20 May 1933), File 123, Alexander Sachs Papers, FDRPL; (quote) Alfred Haake, "The NIRA from the Standpoint of Trade Associations and Code Authorities" (1934), File 1644:2, John J. Raskob Papers, Hagley Museum. See also Temporary National Economic Committee [TNEC], *Recovery Plans*, Monograph 25 (Washington, 1940), 6; Hawley, *New Deal and the Problem of Monopoly*, 15–33, 270; Hawley, "The New Deal and Business," in *The New Deal: The National Level*, ed. John Braeman et al. (Columbus, 1975), 60–61; Himmelberg, *Origins of the NRA*, 160ff.

9 (Quote) James Emery to Henry Sharpe (16 May 1933), File 851.2, NAM Papers; Jordan quoted in Marvin Olasky, "Anticompetitive Strategies by Big Business in the Pre-World War II Era," in *Business Strategy and Public Policy*, ed. Alfred Marcus (New York, 1987), 251; Greeley quoted in Charles Twining, *Phil Weyerhauser: Lumberman* (Seattle, 1985), 120; (quote) "History of the Code of Fair Competition for the Automobile Industry," Division of Review [DR] File 267:17, National Recovery Administration [NRA] Records (RG 9), National Archives. Business support is drawn from the tabular data in Himmelberg, *Origins of the NRA*, Tables I–III. Support for the NRA during its tenure is difficult to gauge, at least in part because

By the early summer (as Secretary of the Interior Harold Ickes recalled), business interests "were crawling to Washington on their hands and knees . . . to beg the Government to run their business for them." Even NAM, which worried that the NRA would penalize small and southern firms or undermine tariff protection, admitted that "while organization under the NRA presents many serious and some almost insurmountable difficulties, we believe that the people of the United States are better served by industry functioning under such a plan than under uncontrolled competition." Leading firms applauded the opportunity for a "final shaking out of the marginal producer" and hoped, as Ickes noted of the large oil firms, "that with the bars let down with respect to the Sherman antitrust law . . . they will be in a position to gobble up their rivals." General Johnson, the director of the NRA's industrial program, argued colorfully that the act would "eliminate eye-gouging and knee-groining and ear-chewing in business."[10]

Administering Business Strategies: The Failure of the NRA

If Congress, the president, and the NRA were willing to ignore the pervasive inconsistencies of promising everything to everyone under the new law, they could not long avoid the prospect of delivering on that promise. Not only did the NRA turn the legal premises of economic competition upside down, but the task of administering the new rules also fell to long-standing or

the NRA itself garnered most of the raw data. See "Tabulation of statements concerning National Recovery Administration," in U.S. Senate, Committee on Finance, *Investigation of the National Recovery Administration* (Washington, 1935), 2907–9; on the budgets of code authorities, see Senate, *Investigation of the NRA*, 2341–42; U.S. Department of Commerce, Trade Association Section, "Code Sponsoring National Trade Associations" (Washington, 1935).

10 Ickes, *First Thousand Days*, 31, 39; Memo on Meeting of Tariff and Foreign Trade Committees (20 November 1933), File 855.3, NAM Papers (on the NAM position, see also Emery to Charles Hook [17 April 1933], File 851.2; "Tariff Memorandum" [20 October 1933], File V:1; Robert Lund to Roosevelt [21 October 1933], File V:1; Emery to Orra Stone [17 April 1933], File 851.2, NAM Papers); Hawley, *New Deal and the Problem of Monopoly*, 30; John Edgerton to Members of Congress (18 Oct. 1934), File II:419, Westmoreland Coal Papers, Hagley Museum; Wasserman to Sachs (n.d.), File 86, Sachs Papers; Johnson quoted in Leuchtenberg, *Roosevelt and the New Deal*, 65. On the business position, see also Gaskill, *Regulation of Competition*, 131; National Industrial Conference Board [NICB], "The National Industrial Recovery Act: Organization of Industry in Light of the German Cartel Experience," *Conference Board Information Service: Domestic Affairs* 8 (1933): 9; A. Berle, Memorandum Report on NRA [1933], File 19, Adolph Berle Papers, FDRPL; U.S. House, Ways and Means Committee, *National Industrial Recovery* (Washington, 1933), 95, 173–274.

hastily formed organizations representing (ideally) every industry and firm in the country and a central, federal administration that did not even exist. From the outset, the NRA was a bureaucratic circus. Charged with writing its rules and implementing them simultaneously, the NRA was persistently unable to grasp the complexity of industrial recovery and was immediately overloaded with information, administrative chaos, and political pressures.

The first problem faced by the NRA was that of writing codes of fair competition for individual industries, a task that involved establishing some precedence and priority for the consideration and application of codes, defining the boundaries of hundreds of industries, and coordinating and refereeing bargaining over code provisions among competitors. The initial emphasis on "pace-setting" codes in large industries had the advantage of bringing the majority of employees under the agreement as rapidly as possible but also threw a very unsure group of NRA officials into the ring with "the cream of the corporate bar" who, as one observer noted, had been "practically invited to find out what they could secure with the trust laws held in abeyance." While the President's Reemployment Agreement (PRA) established basic voluntary standards for firms awaiting formal codes, the drafting process itself devolved, as Johnson put it, into a pattern of "plain horse trading and bare-faced poker playing."[11]

Leading firms, recognizing that the government needed their cooperation as much as they needed the NRA, held most of the cards. Major industries were able to exact huge concessions, including antiunion "merit clauses" in the steel, auto, and chemical codes; provisional duration for the steel and chemical codes; and complete subjugation of the "independent" position in the oil code. And lesser industries soon realized that, for all intents and purposes, their cooperation was voluntary. Only 2 codes (of over 500) were actually imposed by the NRA, and these were summarily rejected by the industries in question (structural steel and artificial limbs). Many smaller industries went without codes entirely, usually by dragging out negotiations until the NRA was on its last legs. The task of drafting codes clearly overwhelmed the NRA, which encouraged endless compromises, turned a blind eye to blatant contradictions within and among the codes, and preferred the ceremonial signing of a code to any equity or consistency in its provisions.[12]

11 (Quote) Irons, *New Deal Lawyers*, 31–32; Johnson quoted in Chamber of Commerce [CoC] Proceedings 23/30 (1935), Chamber of Commerce Papers, Hagley Museum. See also Hawley, *New Deal and the Problem of Monopoly*, 53–56; Committee of Industrial Analysis [CIA], "Report on the Results and Accomplishments of the National Recovery Act" (Washington, 1937), 46; Leverett Lyon, *The National Recovery Administration* (Washington, 1935), 147.
12 Sidney Fine, *The Automobile Under the Blue Eagle* (Ann Arbor, 1963), 54–56; Carroll

Only the cotton textile manufacturers agreed to a code before the PRA campaign of the summer of 1933, but by the time the soft coal industry acquiesced in mid-September, virtually all major industries had signed on, with the notable exception of meat packing (the principal firms insisted on using the code to bring independent processors to heel).[13] Yet with a bewildering variety of provisions and exceptions in the codified industries, the NRA seemed to have accomplished, as banker Charles Dawes noted, little more than "a regrettable stabilization of uncertainty." And months of bargaining with smaller industries (city directories, shoulder pads, bouillon cubes, corset steel, and curled-hair wig manufacturers) threatened to overwhelm the enforcement of those codes that had been signed. By early 1934, when the Burlesque Theatrical Industry proudly announced it had adopted a fair trade practice limiting each production to "four strips," the NRA withdrew from the margins of the economy and exempted "peripheral industries" from the codes.[14]

The process was further complicated by the problem of industrial classification and code jurisdiction. Pressed to sign on industries as quickly as possible, the NRA often solved intra-industry disputes by simply writing a new code for dissenting firms, a practice capitalized on by many as an escape. "If for any reason you are foolish enough to think you are bound to do anything not good for your own pocketbook," the Chemical Alliance advised its members, "merely pull out Article VII [of the chemical code] and call yourself a member of some other handy industry." Diversified electrical firms, such as GE and Westinghouse, sought codified prices and standards, but single-product firms resisted classification as "electrical manufacturers" and fell into a spider's web of overlapping regulations and directives. Having made no provision for industrial classification, NRA administrators were "wholly baffled" by the multiplication of codes which codified rather than solved intra-industry disputes and clashed on the competitive terrain of in-

Daugherty et al., *Economics of the Iron and Steel Industry* (New York, 1937); "Suggested Letter to be Written by the Chemical Alliance . . . the Chemical Manufacturing Code" (1934), File 19, Harrington Papers; Barkin, "NRA Policies, Standards, and Code Provisions," 53; Brand, *Corporatism and the Rule of Law*, 106–7.

13 Cudahay to Richberg (6 February 1934), Official File [OF] 577, Franklin D. Roosevlt [FDR] Papers, FDRPL; "FTC Material," Trade Practice Studies Section [TPSS] file 287:2; "History of Negotiations . . . Meat Packing," TPSS File 268:62, Code Histories (never approved); "Proposed Code . . . Sausage Products," File 268:66, Code Histories (never approved), NRA Records.

14 Charles Dawes to Hoover (31 October 1933), Post-Presidential Individual [PPI] File 2521, Hoover Papers; Code Histories (never approved), DR file 268, NRA Records; "The Business of Burlesque, A.D. 1935," *Fortune* 11 (February 1935): 140; Leuchtenberg, *Roosevelt and the New Deal*, 68.

tegrated firms. Some, such as the major chemical companies, faced the conflicting provisions of literally hundreds of codes; others, such as the larger copper firms, worked with the situation so as to shuffle costs and competitive pressures internally.[15]

The NRA's indifference to competitive and jurisdictional contradictions was best represented (and compounded) by the systematic separation of manufacturing and retail codes. Large retailers wanted the same sort of internal discipline sought by other industries and pressed for an analogous, general code. But consumer-goods firms wanted to wrest control over wholesale and retail prices from large chain stores, which they held largely responsible for ruthless price competition. NRA provisions for industrial control of retail prices proved so controversial and inimical to retailers (represented in the New Deal by Edward Filene and Louis Kirstein of Filene's, Jesse Strauss of Macy's, and Robert Wood and Donald Nelson of Sears) that separate retail codes were drafted for each major industry. The task of maintaining "fair" prices was left to the manufacturer in the form of "customer classification" provisions that prohibited rebates and quantity discounts and introduced the "suggested retail price."[16] In the rubber tire

15 *Industrial Planning under the Codes,* ed. George Galloway (Princeton, 1935), 174–75; "Round Table Conference on the Recovery Program," CoC Proceedings 22/29 (1934), Chamber Papers; (quote) "Suggested Letter to be Written by the Chemical Alliance . . . on the Chemical Manufacturing Code" (1934), file 19, Harrington Papers; History of Code of Fair Competition for Electrical Manufacturing, DR File 267:2; "Electrical Manufacturing," Compliance Division [CD] File 112:6; "Report on the Electrical Manufacturing Industry," CD File 172:4; "Electrical Manufacturing," Code Administration Studies [CAS] File 33:2, NRA Records; NRA, "Open Price Filing in the Electrical Manufacturing Industry," Work Materials #45 (Washington, 1938); Lyon, *NRA,* 98; CIA, "Report on the NRA," 30–31; NRA, "Problems of Administration in the Overlapping of Code Definitions," Work Materials #39 (Washington, 1937); "Notes on Composite Views of the American Metal Co." and "Material Bearing on the Copper Industry," File 125, Sachs Papers; "Provisions in Proposed Copper Code," File 3, Leon Henderson Papers, FDRPL; "Code Authority Minutes . . . Copper Industry," CD File 172:8; "History of the Code of Fair Competition for Copper," DR File 267:401; "Brass Products," CD File 172:5 (Industry Reports), NRA Records.

16 Ruth Mack, *Controlling Retailers: A Study of Cooperation and Control in the Retail Trade* (New York, 1936), 150–71; CIA, "Report on the NRA," 161, 188–93; "Customer Classification," TPSS File 287:1, NRA Records. The question of resale price maintenance was revived in 1935, in large part due to the combination of continued pressures from beleaguered manufacturers and the price inflation of the NRA era (which undermined the retailers' position). See Hawley, *New Deal and the Problem of Monopoly,* 247–63; Earl Kwinter, *The Robinson-Patman Primer* (New York, 1970), 6–16; Paul Haywood, "The Legislative Attack on Retailing," *Nation's Business 23* (August 1935): 29–31, 63; "Capper-Kelly" file, File 180:34, Robert Wagner Papers,

industry, the NRA ignored the destructive competition among tire firms for large auto industry and retail contracts. As a result, the manufactioners' code raised costs without any meaningful agreement on prices and sparked an unprecedented price war.[17]

Across the economy, the disjointed and drawn-out drafting process ignored the interindustry flow of goods and the competitive dynamics of closely related industries. The NRA focused almost exclusively on production and prices and gave little thought to the importance of enacting complementary codes in industries that consumed each other's products. And many industries were frustrated by its inability to draw all the elements of competition, including those arising from the international market as well as from other New Deal legislation, under the authority of the codes. The major steel firms demanded some assurance that inflated, NRA-dictated prices would not be threatened by imports and that production would be underwritten by public works contracts. Although quick to offer such guarantees, the agency was hard-pressed to deliver them. In food industries, the codes were complicated and confused by the dual impact of the NRA and the Agricultural Adjustment Administration (which raised raw agricultural costs), although this combination often worked to the advantage of larger integrated packers, canners, mills, and dairies who were able to exploit the regulatory turmoil.[18]

The NRA's most serious administrative defect was the delegation of power to industry-dominated code authorities, most of which were simply

Littauer Library, Georgetown University, Washington, D.C. The motion picture industry was the only one in which manufacturers and sellers were covered by a single code. See Louis Nizer, *New Courts of Industry: Self-Regulation under the Motion Picture Code* (New York, 1936), 134–35.

17 "Preliminary Report on Rubber Manufacturing" (March 1935), File 11, Henderson Papers; Alfred Kress, "The Rubber Industry," in Galloway, *Industrial Planning under the Codes*, 260; Michael French, "Structural Change and Competition in the United States Tire Industry, 1920–1937," *BHR* 60 (1986): 47–51; History of the Code of Fair Competition for Rubber Tires, DR File 267:174 (13–23), NRA Records; Fisk Rubber to James Roosevelt (27 November 1939), OF 510; M.H. Horowitz [Serber Rubber] to FDR (27 September 1935), OF 510, FDR Papers.

18 "FTC Report to Senate (20 March 1934), "Preliminary Report on Iron and Steel" (n.d.), file 12; J.F. Dewhurst to Henderson (24 Apr. 1934), File 12, Henderson Papers; "Extracts from [Sachs] Memo" (22 January 1934), File 1983; "Effect of Building Program . . . on Earnings of U.S. Steel" (May 1933), File 147, Sachs Papers; "Memorandum of Information: Iron and Steel," DR File 267:11, NRA Records; TNEC, *Large Scale Organization in the Food Industries*, 38–45; History of the Code of Fair Competition for Baking, DR File 267:445, NRA Records; NRA Division of Review, "The Baking Industry," Evidence Study 26 (Washington, 1935).

trade associations in public garb that made no effort to separate public matters from their private business. As a result, the enforcement of most codes was left in the hands of politically aggressive industry factions. Independent oil firms saw their code as a "clever 'steamroller' agreement which has been connived by these large major oil companies . . . [who] have been trying to oppress the small merchant but found it hard to do so, now they are trying to get the government to do it for them." The aluminum industry's code authority was staffed by ALCOA, which willfully confused industry goals with its own predatory pricing. Yet while these regulatory cabals exceeded their authority (often leaving the NRA unsure whether they or code violators were the greater threat), dominant firms were having no more success at disciplining their industries than they had had before 1933. "Rarely did a code authority have the whole-hearted support of its entire constituency," understated one contemporary report; "divergent interests of pre-code days continue to exist." Another observer noted that code authorities were "somewhat fragile combinations of intra-industrial factions" with "astonishingly little quantitative knowledge concerning their own industries."[19]

The NRA never distinguished between creating and administering the codes, at least in part because the two tasks overlapped well into 1934. Industries sought exemptions and special consideration on virtually every detail of regulation and scrambled for equal treatment whenever another industry browbeat the NRA into accepting an unusually lenient clause. As a 1935 report noted, "No other agency . . . was compelled to approach the trade practice problem in such a milieu of varied counsel, conflicting pur-

19 CIA, "Report on NRA," 21–22, 79–82, (quote) 104; Lyon, *NRA,* (quote) 111, (quote) 118, 222–23; Bobrick, "Voting for Code Authority" (May 1935), CD File 112; "Code Authorities," CD File 173:1; "Handling of Complaints by Code Authorities," CD File 112:1, NRA Records; Senate, *Investigation of the NRA,* 2329–31. On the oil code, see "Transcript of Code Hearing," File 53; Hearings on Oil Code (1933–1934), Files 54–60; "Submission and Adoption of the Code of Fair Competition for the Petroleum Industry," File 53; E.E. Johnson [Columbia Oil] to FDR (18 August 1933), G. Gringer telegram to FDR (21 July 1933); Frank Craven to Johnson (4 August 1933), File 40, Petroleum Administration for War [PAW] Records (RG 232), Federal Records Center, Suitland, MD; J.B. McCracken to Gerard Swope (26 January 1934), File 1173–6, Pierre S. DuPont Papers, Hagley Museum; "Comments of Leading Oil Executives" (n.d.), File 75, Sachs Papers; Planning and Coordination Committee for the Petroleum Industry meeting (6 January 1934), File 419:1, NRA Records; J.S. Codsden to Raskob (31 December 1934), File 494, Raskob Papers; J.E. Pew to G. Pepper (8 February 1934), File 3:73, Sun Oil Papers, Hagley Museum. On aluminum, see "Aluminum," CD File 172:5 (Industry Reports); "History of the Code of Fair Competition for Aluminum," DR File 267:470, NRA Records.

poses, and atmosphere of desperation." Johnson thought it "important to the concept of industrial self-government not to have general rules of what should and what should not be done in the codes" – a sentiment that accurately reflected the NRA's day-to-day operation but completely undermined any hope that it might make some larger political sense out of an otherwise futile and chaotic pattern of industrial self-government. The most damaging concessions made by the NRA (in terms of both consistency and credibility) were on the labor provisions, which were subject to endless qualifications, exemptions, and disclaimers. At one point Johnson even recommended exempting "whole industries and small enterprises in this country which depend for existence on the exploitation of labor."[20]

Finally, the NRA's administrative defects were compounded by the behavior of its principal officials. General Johnson provided an element of bluster and color to the act's early days, but as Hoover noted, his "great powers of vituperation" were backed by a "minimum knowledge of economics." Ickes concurred that Johnson "never appeared to get it out of his head that it wasn't all to be ballyhoo." Johnson was also so fearful of a test case that might strike down the NRA and cost him his job that he caved in repeatedly to business demands. Piqued from the start by Roosevelt's unwillingness to trust him with the NRA's public works program as well, Johnson jealously guarded the industrial program and threatened resignation repeatedly at the slightest inroad of other departments. His propensity for bureaucratic brawling paled beside his personal conduct, which included a serious drinking problem and a scarcely secret affair with his secretary, and by the late summer of 1934, he was considered "dangerous and unstable." Rexford Tugwell confided to Roosevelt that "the opinion is unanimous that Johnson can no longer be useful."[21]

The situation scarcely improved with Johnson's departure. Control was passed to Richberg, banker Averill Harriman (administrative officer), Donald Nelson of Sears (code administration director), and a National Industrial Recovery Board led by Arthur Whiteside of Dun and Bradstreet and Clay Williams of R.J. Reynolds (a rigidly antilabor voice on the cigarette code

20 Lyon, *NRA*, 24–25, 365–66, (quote) 561; Johnson quoted in Hawley, *New Deal and the Problem of Monopoly*, 63, and Johnson Memorandum for FDR (13 December 1933), File 6, Hugh Johnson Papers, FDRPL.
21 Hoover, *Memoirs*, 3:422; (quote) Ickes, *The First Thousand Days*, 71–72, 101, 197–98; Johnson to FDR (30 August 1933), File 6, Johnson Papers; John M. Blum, ed., *From the Morgenthau Diaries* (Boston, 1958) 3:11–17; (quote) Irons, *New Deal Lawyers*, 27–30; (quote) Tugwell to FDR (7 September 1934); Richberg to McIntyre (5 September 1934), OF 466:2, FDR Papers.

authority who would go on to become a director of the Chamber of Commerce and vice-president of NAM). The new setup tilted candidly towards a conservative business viewpoint, and even Richberg (a noted labor lawyer who had been hired as a nod toward the unions) proved his self-promotional abilities and ingratiated himself with the business crowd. As Swope of General Electric noted favorably, Richberg was "coming more and more into favor with business interests. . . . [he] was swinging further to the right all the time and business was strongly for him." For his part, Richberg also dug in to protect his bureaucratic flanks and complained immediately that the NRA divisions were "hot beds of petty politics, jealousies, and fears, which are destructive of any real efficiency."[22]

To be fair, such jealousies and anxieties were hardly unique to the NRA. But they became particularly destructive in a bureaucracy that was unable to define its priorities, powers, or basic administrative rules. The NRA never distinguished between the concessions justified by the goal of bringing industries under the codes and their administration. As a result, NRA officials made a series of debilitating early decisions regarding the codes, separat-ing those for retail from those for manufacturing, willfully allowing the multiplication of codes and code authorities, and delegating responsibility within and without the administration in a piecemeal and inattentive fashion. And all of this occurred in a context of universal uncertainty. Everyone knew the act had only two years to run (a fact that scrambled its organizational logic from the outset), and NRA officials and industrial competitors ap-preciated (and worried) that the Supreme Court might cut its life even shorter.

Wage, Price, and Production Standards

The NRA was unable and unwilling to overcome either the logical dilemmas it inherited from its business patrons or those it created itself by failing to consider the different stake each firm or industry held in federal intervention. "Compromising principles," complained an NRA economist, "won't work when the compromises are different with different industries." Some industries sought permanent regulation. Some welcomed the opportunity to

22 Schlesinger, *Coming of the New Deal*, 157; Senate, *Investigation of the NRA*, 284; William Green to FDR [protesting Williams's appointment] (13 December 1934), OF 142; (quote) Richberg to McIntyre (5 September 1934), OF 466:2, FDR Papers; Ickes, *First Thousand Days*, 219–20, (Swope quote, 212), 375. Johnson complained to Roosevelt that Richberg was "under a spell so evil that every blossom he touched withered and turned to ashes under his hand" (Johnson to FDR [9 February 1935], File 6, Johnson Papers).

shake out marginal competitors but looked to a quick return to "free" competition. Others viewed the NRA with unbridled cynicism and hoped their competitors followed the letter of the code while determining to ignore it themselves. And there were those that, seeing themselves as the targets of unrealistic regulation, had no intention of cooperating as long as compliance meant bankruptcy and noncompliance went unpunished. These divergent interests and expectations were never satisfied or resolved. "Each industry had its own characteristics and problems," a noted antitrust lawyer reminded the Chamber of Commerce; "each industry had its pet panaceas, which it had been theorizing for thirty years. Here was a chance to try them out free from the threat of indictment. . . . Result: complexity and widely varying provisions in codes and often interminable conflict with supervising officers of [the] NRA."[23] The uneasy relationship between particular industrial goals and generic federal law emerged most sharply in attempts to regulate prices, wages, and production.

For business, *price* was the focal point of the NRA. Although they often expressed their goals in terms of fair trade practices, wage regulation, or industrial planning, firms understood and appreciated only how these abstractions were reflected on ledgers and in directly quantifiable comparisons with competitors. As a painstaking Brookings Institution study of the NRA concluded: "It must be recognized that every degree of public spirit and avarice, and of naivete and sophistication went into the code making process. No close observer of the process can, however, avoid the conclusion that the expectation of 'improving' prices by collective action among competitors was the central motivating force." After two decades of restraining industrial price agreements, the FTC took one look at the steel code and agreed that the NRA seemed to simply throw "the authority of the government . . . behind the efforts of the industry to raise and stabilize prices."[24]

Most of what the NRA attempted along these lines were variations on "open pricing" plans, under which each firm made its selling prices available in advance to code authorities. Although seen as a cure for cutthroat competition, open pricing only compounded the problem and its symptoms. Filing the required information with code authorities provided leading com-

23 Teagle Memo (13 June 1934), File 310, Raskob Papers; (quote) DuBrul [GM] to
    Means (30 November 1934), File 2, Gardiner Means Papers, FDRPL; (quote)
    Goldthwait Dorr in "Round Table Conference: New Aspects of the NIRA," CoC
    Proceedings 23/30 (1935), Chamber Papers.
24 Lyon, *NRA*, 94; CIA, "Report on the NRA," 160; (quote) "FTC Report to Senate"
    (20 March 1934), File 12, Henderson Papers.

petitors with prices *and* detailed production costs. Most firms proved unwilling to share these figures honestly, and code authorities were unable to separate public functions from private advantage. Industries and the NRA also fought over whether prices would be provided to consumers as well as competitors and the timing and duration of filed prices. Open pricing, without uniform cost-accounting rules and penalties for noncompliance, left firms free to set prices by manipulating costs or simply lying to code authorities. And NRA pricing standards (minimum prices, prohibitions against sales below cost, discounts, and rebates) were undermined by noncompliance and the inflationary impact of the entire recovery program – which made it increasingly impolitic to enforce pricing provisions.[25]

Although the inconsistencies of NRA price policy were as numerous as the industries covered, a few problems were distressingly common. Foremost was the NRA's indifference to contradictory pricing provisions or rulings. In the bolt-and-nut industry, the NRA disallowed pricing provisions that ran against the grain of an antitrust consent decree among constituent firms; in the cement and steel industries, the NRA revived basing-point systems that had been forbidden by consent decree; and in the aluminum industry, the NRA ignored prevailing FTC rulings altogether. Pricing provisions were also impossible to enforce. The party most likely to stumble across illegal pricing practices was the buyer, who was inclined to exploit rather than report a competitive scramble below code prices. And competitors viewed pricing provisions with unbridled cynicism; as one coal operator reasoned: "It will take from four to six months to assemble the necessary data on which to figure a weighted average cost. . . . there will be nothing done about prices for at least four months and probably longer. . . . those inside the code will have just as much chance in the open market as those outside. No one will be bound by any price."[26]

In this atmosphere of inconsistency and intransigence, the impact of pricing provisions was disastrous. Price filing "worked" in industries that had their own means of enforcing agreements (such as labelling provisions) and failed miserably everywhere else. The NRA estimated that less than one-

25 See NRA, Research and Planning Division, "Tables on the Operation of the NRA" (1935; typescript in imprints collection, Hagley Museum); "NRA Code Provisions Relating to Open Price and Bid Filing Systems," in Lyon, *NRA*, 154–59.

26 Statement of Ruth Ayres and Enid Baird, in Senate, *Investigation of the NRA*, 876–77; CIA, "Report on the NRA," 186; "Report on Code Revision" (n.d.), File 3:7, NRA Records; (quote) Westmoreland to B.F. Gross (1 November 1935), File 399: Virginia File 101, Westmoreland Coal Papers.

third of industries with pricing provisions could count on honest reporting from a satisfactory number of competitors. Some integrated producers (who were able to shuffle costs internally) reaped huge returns from pricing provisions that gave them access to competitors' prices. In most cases, price filing was a spur to greater competition, an opportunity for predatory pricing, or an unenforceable "burden of petty regulation." As long as code authorities controlled cost accounting within industries, prohibitions against selling below cost became invitations to fix prices, and minimum prices became maximums. The NRA and the code authorities toyed with the dilemmas of price policy throughout 1933–35, the only result being that "changes in regulation took the places of changes in demand and supply as the basis for unpredictable price movements."[27]

Wage and hour policies were equally confused, in part because their purpose within the broader NRA framework was never defined. Many industries saw these provisions as a *quid pro quo* for antitrust reform. This was curious reasoning, given the fact that, as Alexander Sachs noted, the share-the-work reasoning of the codes meant merely a "further subdivision of inadequate activity" and a "sharing [of] the poverty among the poor." By contrast, those industries with high labor costs and regional competitors saw the wage and hour provisions as integral to the recovery program, either as part of "a general effort to attain a degree of competitive equality within each industry" or as a means of supporting mass-purchasing power. GM executives complained that the NRA's share-the-work sentiment threatened disposable income and argued privately that the country might be better off with austerity and massive unemployment if it meant that at least those working had enough cash to buy cars. Many firms and industries tried to ensure that wage and hour provisions were uniform and conscientiously enforced, while the remainder tried to avoid shouldering increases or paying industry-wide rates.[28]

27 CIA, "Report on the NRA," 166–67, (quote) 171–73, 181, 184; "Fair Trade Practice Provisions of Codes . . ." (n.d.), File 3:7, NRA Records; Memorandum Report on the NRA [1935?], File 19, Berle Papers; Lyon, *NRA,* 578–79.

28 (Quote) "Extracts from Sachs memo" (22 January 1934), OF 1983, FDR Papers, (quote) CIA, "Report on the NRA," 127; J. H. Pew to Manny Strauss (15 November 1929), PF 88, Hoover Papers; H. Bromley to Emery (9 May 1933); Bromley to Lund (3 May 1933), File 851.2, NAM Papers, Sloan to Raskob (23 October 1934), File 310; Donaldson Brown to Raskob (21 September 1934), File 278, Raskob Papers; Alexander Sachs to Hugh Johnson (27 April 1933), File 176; "The automobile situation . . . as seen by Donaldson Brown" (25 January 1932), File 92; Steven DuBrul Memo (n.d.), File 28, Sachs Papers.

The NRA was also unwilling to confront southern Democrats over the South's systematic low-wage industrial economy and only partially closed regional wage differentials. This concession undermined the goals of industries that identified low-wage southern firms as their principal competitive and organizational liability. At the same time, differentials were closed enough that southern firms saw the NRA as inherently biased against the South, designed to place them "at the complete mercy of [their] competitors in other sections." Southern lumber mills reasoned that the NRA was meant to eliminate "a considerable number of southern enterprises," and barely 2 percent cooperated. This pervasive distrust was complicated by the inability of either industries or the NRA to agree on regional boundaries: eleven of forty-six miscellaneous manufacturing codes set southern wage differentials, but only two of those eleven came even close to agreeing on the geographical limits of "the South." In turn, while codes were organized by industry, NRA compliance boards were organized by region. As a result, code provisions *and* their enforcement varied from state to state. State Recovery Acts, designed to supplement the NRA within safer legal boundaries, only papered over gaps in its authority.[29]

Given the NRA's predisposition to compromise and cut the codes to satisfy as many as possible, regional and industrial anxieties routinely eroded wage provisions. The PRA Policy Board received 566 petitions for exemption from wage and hour standards, and granted almost 400 of them; in only 9 of the first 100 codes were hours set at a level lower than that proposed by employers. Even in industries in which uniform wages were sought by a majority (or powerful minority) of employers, few trusted their competitors to respect standards or the NRA to enforce them. Sachs observed that "in order to accept increases, [employers] insisted on having everybody similarly handicapped. . . . as there would be no first to take up greater burdens, unless, pending the working out of detailed codes, the labor burden was imposed by a sort of fiat." This was the goal of the PRA, but so many ignored or were exempted from its provisions that it had little effect. Acceptance of

29 DuBrul to Raskob (26 July 1934), File 1644, Raskob Papers; Johnson to FDR (20 August 1934), File 6, Johnson Papers; (quote) J.F. Ames to J.D. Rogers (7 May 1934), File II:419, Westmoreland Coal Papers; Lyon, *NRA*, 329; "Memorandum for Chief Counsel," File 7, Henderson Papers; (quote) testimony of David Mason in Senate, *Investigation of the NRA*, 2136–37; "State Recovery Acts," CD File 132:3 (Galvin Office Files), NRA Records. On the South and the NRA, see Gavin Wright, *New South, Old South: Revolutions in the Southern Economy Since the Civil War* (New York, 1986), 213–25.

wage differentials between and within industries further undermined any wage-driven competitive stability.[30]

Attempts to restrict production also failed miserably or, to the horror of the industries concerned, had the opposite effect. Many firms tried to "beat the gun" of NRA cost increases by stepping up production in the weeks before their codes went into effect. In some instances, firms built up sufficiently large precode inventories to upset the market for months. Once codes were in place, the promise of higher prices encouraged new entrants or the reentry of idle plants. In the lumber industry, production quotas applied only to established mills, so anyone who could afford to build new mills did so, and "mills long idle started to get into production again on the theory that the government was going to guarantee them a profit." The prevailing attitude was captured by Weyerhauser, who had always sought to "fix prices and to control unruly competition" but argued privately that "from a strictly company consideration, it seemed desirable to produce as much lumber as possible before any production controls took effect." Production controls were, as the NRA concluded, "used by some branches of the industry to embarrass other branches" and to shift production within industries according to the political and economic clout of leading firms. Production provisions turned legally defined "excess" into speculative channels and only contributed to industry stability in rare instances "where its advantages were universally recognized."[31]

Finally, in an endless chicken-or-the-egg debate, the NRA never understood (or decided) whether high wages would *follow* higher prices or *force* higher prices, let alone the connection between wages, prices, and output. Many saw wage regulation as the foundation of price regulation; the furniture code authority, for one, considered legislated wages "the most important price stabilization scheme from the standpoint of a combination of effect-

---

30 CIA, "Report on the NRA," 113, 127; Barkin, "NRA Policies, Standards, and Code Provisions," 2–3; (quote) "Extracts from Sachs memo" (22 January 1934), OF 1983, FDR Papers; J. H. Pew to Manny Strauss (15 November 1929), PF 88, Hoover Papers; H. Bromley to Emery (9 May 1933); Bromley to Lund (3 May 1933), File 851.2, NAM Papers; Lyon, *NRA*, 317–42; NRA memo "Wage Differentials", File 1173–6, P. S. DuPont Papers.

31 "Extracts from Sachs Memo" (22 January 1934), OF 1983, FDR Papers; CIA, "Report on the NRA," 168, 174–78; Weyerhauser quoted in Twining, *Weyerhauser*, 104; History of the Code of Fair Competition for Lumber and Timber, DR File 267:9 (3, 69–73, (quote) 78, 294–95, 326, 336–40), NRA Records; (quote) "Summary of Findings to Date on Production and Capacity Control" (26 October 1935), File 13:3; (quote) "Fair Trade Practice Provisions of Codes . . ." (n.d.), File 3:7, NRA Records.

iveness and practical workability." Many took the approach of the Chemical Alliance and privately conceded that if their code entailed higher costs, they would then simply "take it out of the hide of Kid Consumer." And many others echoed the dubious reasoning of the leading lumber firms, which hoped that *they* would be able to meet higher costs with higher prices while their marginal competitors would not (the subsequent confusion was blamed on the NRA). For its part, the NRA was horrified when one industry concluded "that it was the policy of the NRA to permit industries to reflect in their selling prices the increased costs arising through [NRA] compliance." But the alternative, holding prices down as wages increased so that consumers did not pay for workers's gains, was even less consistently put forward as official policy. By 1935, most would agree with General Johnson that NRA wage and price policies betrayed "a shivering inconsistency." Because it was never decided whether such policies were supposed to redistribute income or merely expand economic activity, the NRA soon reached an inflationary impasse that not only wiped out higher wages but also catalyzed the "consumer revolt" embodied in 1935 by Clarence Darrow's National Recovery Review Board.[32]

These logical and economic dilemmas infused each code and scrambled the motives, energies, and effects of the recovery program. Failure to coordinate and synthesize strategies resulted in what Steven DuBrul bitterly dismissed as two years of "loose thinking" and "racketeering on the part of trade association promoters."[33] From 1933 to 1935, the NRA walked a constitutional tightrope between its political and economic objectives. Too politically sensitive and legally anxious to make any of the difficult choices necessary to satisfy original arguments for its institution, the NRA satisfied few of its business patrons and lost popular credibility as prices rose. These practical, logical, and administrative problems, however, were merely symptoms of the fundamental defect of the NRA: its inability to effect collective action by enforcing compliance with the codes.

32 Hawley, *New Deal and the Problem of Monopoly*, 26–27, 57–61; Schlesinger, *Coming of the New Deal*, 123–25; furniture code authority quoted in Senate, *Investigation of NRA*, 1240–44; (quote) "Suggested letter . . . to members of the Chemical Manufacturing Industry, giving them the low-down on the chemical manufacturing industry code," File 19, Harrington Papers; *American Lumberman* (20 January 1934): 17, 47; (quote) "Proposed Code . . . Natural Gas," DR File 268:93 Code Histories (never approved), NRA Records; Szelski to Henderson (2 October 1934), File 6, Henderson Papers; (quote) Johnson, *Blue Eagle from Egg to Earth*, 182; Memorandum for FDR (13 December 1933), File 6, Johnson Papers; Memorandum Report on NRA, File 19, Berle Papers; Hacker, "The New Deal is No Revolution."
33 DuBrul to Raskob (26 July 1934), File 1644, Raskob Papers.

Compliance, Coercion, and the Codes

All that distinguished the NRA's brand of industrial self-government from the voluntarism of the 1920s was the promise that competitive standards would be uniform and uniformly enforced. "It was felt that government should be minimized and limited to the acceptance or rejection of the proposals of business groups," reported an NRA study group, "but the Government was expected to enforce accepted rules with rigor."[34] Business expected the NRA to provide a firm and impartial means of regulation that was not motivated or distracted by short-term market goals, ideally supplying a legal footing for trade association platforms and penalizing marginal or regional competitors. In practice, the NRA was unable to perform the only task that business demanded of it. The result, as a handful of laissez-faire cynics had warned in 1933, was the continuation of chaotic and unbridled competition, accompanied by unprecedented, haphazard, and ineffective government "regimentation."

Compliance was a riddle that the NRA was unable and, in many respects, afraid to solve. For business interests *nearly* complete compliance with code provisions was not enough; one chiseler could bring down price, wage, or trade practice standards like a house of cards. Economically, politically, and bureaucratically incapable of enforcing cooperation, the NRA based its policy on willfully optimistic assumptions about business conduct.[35] Its failure to enforce the codes not only undermined its effectiveness and credibility but also pressed firms (or at least those not irretrievably discouraged by the NRA experience) to search for some other means of taming short-term motives for long-term stability and disciplining or destroying marginal competitors.

The NRA demanded the allegiance of all competitors but did not treat them all equally, and it expected cooperation from all competitors even as it drove some of them from the market. "Nothing can alter the fact that code authority members are also competitors," noted one contemporary; "the fact that they have access to intimate business information is sufficient to strike terror, resentment, and suspicion." Most codes, by accident or design, gave a competitive edge to large firms. "In virtually all the codes we have examined," the Darrow Board reported, "one condition has been persistent . . . the code has offered an opportunity for the more powerful . . . interests to seize control of an industry or to augment and extend a control

---

34 CIA, "Report on the NRA," 162.
35 Mack, *Controlling Retailers*, 500–508.

already obtained." Or, as one struggling lumber mill complained, the big mills "saw a chance to break the men that owned the little mills . . . and believe me they surely have made a good job of it."[36] Whether the ability of leading firms or code authorities to reap advantages under the NRA was real or imagined, it sharpened competitive jealousies and undermined the NRA's often facile cooperative spirit.

The irony of the Darrow report and the accompanying public outcry was that the NRA clearly and candidly intended to eliminate marginal firms and cutthroat competition. The fact that the former were now considered "oppressed small business" and the latter, "the free market," reflected more a cynical dissatisfaction with the NRA than any sudden discovery of its true colors. "The NRA has got itself up a tree with another one of those problems that represent an irreconcilable conflict between politics and economics," observed Steven DuBrul; "if [Darrow] tells the truth, it will sound like he is double-crossing the very businesses his Board is supposed to aid."[37] Leading firms and the NRA underestimated the ability of targeted marginal firms to duck and challenge NRA provisions and to make themselves heard in local and congressional politics. And the NRA never confronted the fundamental contradiction between its grand cooperative vision and the fact that organized competition came at the unhappy and uncooperative expense of some competitors. For their part, code authorities tried to maintain the allegiance of marginal firms by publicly blaming the NRA for the troubles of small firms even as they privately applauded its ability to "shake out" competition.

Given the uneasy combination of cooperation, rationalization, and organization, the codes failed where they were needed most and succeeded where they were not needed at all. Monopolistic institutions and practices were strengthened in many industries that had historically "skirted the bounds of the antitrust laws." Many traditionally fragmented industries suffered continued murderous competition and often saw conditions deteriorate with the introduction of a code. "Without a general willingness in an industry to observe its own laws," antitrust lawyer Goldthwait Dorr cautioned, "a code

36 Lyon, *NRA*, 111–12, (quote) 250–51; Darrow Board quoted in Michael Bernstein, *The Great Depression: Delayed Recovery and Economic Change in America, 1929–1939* (New York, 1987), 196; (quote) Copalis Manuf. to M. Smith (1 December 1934), Advisory Council [AC] File 350:3, NRA Records. See also TNEC, *Trade Association Survey,* Monograph 18 (Washington, 1941), 14.

37 Irons, *New Deal Lawyers,* 39; DuBrul to Eaton (9 March 1934), File 28, Sachs Papers.

becomes a Volstead Act. It penalizes the observers, [and] becomes an instrument of unfair competition." And because the NRA's tenure was limited to two years (actually much less, given the time it took to draft the codes), firms stalled implementation, abandoned codes early, or resisted the brief experiment altogether. "So short was the period of trade practice control," noted a 1937 Committee of Industrial Analysis report, ". . . [that] in many cases the speculation which accompanied the beginning, change, and end of a system of control obscured the effect of that control."[38]

In the end, most business interests refused to commit themselves to a program whose *raison d'etre* was complete commitment. Many were so leery of the entire experiment that they undermined their own codes by ensuring, somewhat illogically, that their cooperation was voluntary. When Ford snubbed the NRA, the other major automobile firms would only sign the code on the understanding that they were not committing themselves to anything. "After months of battling with the NRA, " the Chemical Alliance announced smugly,

> . . . we have succeeded beyond all expectations. . . . Most all of the Sap industries have got themselves in a hole right to start with in their codes by using the following words at the end of their preamble, "and be binding upon every member thereof." We were too smart for that however, as it was not our purpose to be bound by anything.

Although leading chemical firms never expected much from the NRA, this logic prevailed in even the most desperately fragmented and competitive industries. Eager to bind their competitors, firms were loath to bind themselves. This Catch–22 of collective action pervaded the NRA experience. "We will endeavor to cooperate as we have always done," as one rubber executive noted ruefully, "minus any binding agreement to do so."[39]

The question of compliance posed an immediate administrative problem as well. For most business advocates, the NRA was a collage of trade associations backed by federal legal authority. The Roosevelt administration,

---

38 (Quote) Typescript of staff study, Division of Industrial Economics [DIE] file 346:3, NRA Records; Hawley, *New Deal and the Problem of Monopoly*, 114; Dorr quoted in "Round Table Conference: New Aspects of the NIRA," CoC Proceedings 23/ 30 (1935), Chamber Papers; (quote) CIA, "Report on the NRA," 202.

39 Fine, *The Automobile and the Blue Eagle*, 44–74; "Voluntary Agreements," Industrial Advisory Board [IAB] File 358 (General Correspondence); "History of the Code of Fair Competition for the Automobile Industry," DR File 267:17, NRA Records; (quote) Suggested letter . . . to members of the Chemical Manufacturing Industry," File 19, Harrington Papers; (quote) R.S. Burke [Kelly-Springfield] to Leon Henderson (23 August 1934), in "History of Code of Fair Competition For Rubber Tires," DR File 267:174, NRA Records.

however, clung to its "something-for-everyone" view of the NRA and was reluctant to admit the need for formal enforcement. During the code-drafting process, the NRA relied almost exclusively on the "social compulsion" that it hoped would follow the "Blue Eagle" campaign of mid-1933; it promoted display of its symbol, a blue eagle, as a sign of patriotism and civic-mindedness and hoped that parades and press releases would encourage cooperation. In a typically hollow exhortation, General Johnson warned that if the NRA caught a violator, it would "remove from him his badge of public faith and business honor and . . . break the bright sword of his commercial honor in the eyes of his neighbors—and throw the fragments – in scorn – in the dust at his feet. . . . The threat of it transcends any puny penal provision in this law." With bad publicity the only penalty and complaints from competitors the only means of flushing out violators, the early record of the NRA was dismal. Even the "We Do Our Part" Blue Eagle placards quickly lost their meaning as competitors and consumers found their display was rarely an indication of code compliance.[40]

The Blue Eagle had some impact in industries where its display went beyond the obligatory office window or corner of company letterhead. Some consumer goods, such as tobacco products or clothing, used Blue Eagle product labels as a token of compliance. In the garment trades, large retailers effectively enforced the manufacturers labelling provision, and the code authority used label sales to finance enforcement. But even this system was threatened by the cynicism that marked display of the Blue Eagle elsewhere, as clothiers began using NRA labels as a mock grading system to push cheaper styles.[41] The NRA also expected some respect for the Blue Eagle from other branches of government. Reconstruction Finance Corporation loans were often conditional on proof of NRA compliance, and standards in the aircraft industry were enforced by government contracts (which accounted for 60 percent of aircraft sales). Aside from these examples, however, the record of intergovernmental cooperation was not impressive. Federal agencies awarded numerous contracts and loans to firms whose

---

40 "Extracts from Sachs Memo" (22 January 1934), OF 1983, FDR Papers; Johnson quoted in Leuchtenberg, *Roosevelt and the New Deal*, 67; Mack, *Controlling Retailers*, 234, 239–241.

41 Senate, *Investigation of the NRA*, 350–52, 1538; "Mens' Clothing Industry," Work Materials #58 (Washington, 1937), 7; "Cigarette, Snuff . . . ," CD File 112:4; "History of the Code of Fair Competition for Cigar Manufacturing," DR File 267:47; C. Baer, "Cigar Industry," CD File 172:1 (Industry Reports); CIA, "Report on NRA," 70; typescript of staff study (459–60), DIE File 346:1; Kansas Office to Compliance Division (13 May 1935), CD File 112:11, NRA Records.

commitment to the NRA was superficial at best. Ford, for example, embarrassed the NRA by ignoring the auto code while continuing to win contracts from a sympathetic War Department.[42]

Once the platitudes of its Blue Eagle campaign had subsided, the NRA expected industries to put their own houses in order and relied on industry complaints to identify violators. While granting that code authorities were scarcely impartial umpires, the NRA argued that they "constitute the only existing organizational tools with which industries under codes now have to work" and that leaving the question of obeying it dictates to the industry at least avoided "sheer dumping of the problem of code compliance upon the Federal Government." If code authorities (as industry representatives) were the most logical and knowledgeable source of compliance, they were also (as competitors) the most likely to distort the process.[43] The complaints system dumped arcane trade disputes into the government's lap and turned the NRA's attention not to those industries with genuine competitive or organizational problems but to those who complained the loudest. With the NRA's energies spent tracking down competitive jealousies, cooperation foundered. Most industries reported little cooperation from southern firms. In some industries (such as oil), significant factions dissented from the code authority position; in others (such as lumber), many firms had little knowledge that code authorities even existed. Some regional offices reported a state of regulatory anarchy, with 90 or 95 percent of firms in open defiance of the codes.[44]

The NRA had scrambled the competitive stakes but given firms little incentive to cooperate. Business was unable to enforce compliance (a fact that had encouraged it to support the NRA in the first place), and the NRA was unwilling to do so (a task for which it was ill-equipped and that threatened to open a hornet's nest of legal challenges). Reluctantly and belatedly, the NRA moved to revamp the entire process of following its directives. During the fall of 1933, compliance rested with code authorities, NRA dep-

---

42 History of Aircraft Code, DR file 268:84 Code Histories (never approved); Ralph Byers to Hosiery Code Authority (12 February 1935), CD File 112:9; War Dept. to NRA (12 February 1935), CD File 175:2, NRA Records.

43 (Quote) "Trade Associations in Relation to Code Authorities" (22 March 1934), CD File 112:1; "Fair Trade Practice Provisions of Codes," File 3:7; typescript of staff study, DIE file 346:1 (442), NRA Records; Senate, *Investigation of the NRA*, 1664; Bigelow Sanford [carpets] to Wagner, File 326:10, Wagner Papers.

44 Martin memo for Glancy (30 August 1934), CD File 112:13; "Dress Manufacturing [report of Boston office]," CD File 112:5, NRA Records; R.W. Stone and U.B. Stone, *The Baking Industry under NRA* (Chicago, 1935), 59, 99–101.

uties, and regional administrators. In late October, however, the NRA accepted that its early emphasis on "banners and ballyhoo" had worn thin and established a formal Compliance Division, which by the end of 1933, was backlogged with over 10,000 complaints. For the duration of the NRA, the Compliance Division faced the familiar conflict between self-government and coercive regulation that infused the recovery program as well as the constant disappointment of industries that expected rewards for cooperation matched with stiff penalties for recalcitrance.[45]

Even with the creation of the Compliance Division, the NRA's ultimate legal authority was uncertain. Cases that clearly involved interstate commerce could be filed in federal courts, but a preponderance of Republican judges and pervasive fear of a constitutional test case discouraged even selective prosecution. Trade practice violations could also be passed on to the FTC, a process that duplicated paperwork and delayed and distracted enforcement. Labor violations were technically handled by the National Labor Board (NLB) and a few industrial labor boards, but their resolution was often a casualty of jurisdictional disputes between the NRA and NLB. Final authority was usually reserved for the NRA, which allowed firms to define labor violations as trade practice violations and bypass the NLB altogether. In most cases, the only penalty imposed by the NRA (usually for underpaying wages or code authority assessments) was restitution. This allowed employers to reap the rewards of noncompliance if they evaded the NRA and, if caught, only forced them to pay their share. With prosecution and punitive fines a distant threat, there was no compelling reason to cooperate.[46]

While trade and labor violations continued unabated, nothing upset business more than the issue of financing code authorities. Firms obeying the NRA's policies resented free-riding on the part of others; recalcitrant firms resented being forced to pay for an act that was designed to put them out of business. Firms commodified the problem of falling in step with the program in part because the stakes were so large. Seventy-one code authorities had annual budgets over $100,000, twenty had budgets over $500,000, and ten had budgets over $1,000,000. Deep pockets, however, were more

---

45 Rosenblatt, "Report on Compliance Conditions" (27 May 1935), CD File 175:8; typescript of staff study, DIE File 346:1 (414–70); J. Ward to L. Martin (21 July 1934), CD File 132:4 (Galvin Office Files), NRA Records; Irons, *New Deal Lawyers*, 35–41.

46 Typescript of staff study, DIE File 346:1 (414–20, 431, 445), NRA Records; CIA, "Report on the NRA," 59–77; Altmeyer to Royall (19 May 1934), CD File 105:1; Henry Collins to H. Myers (3 January 1934), Labor Advisory Board [LAB] File 357:1, NRA Records.

often a sign of pervasive anxiety than successful regulation; those with the largest budgets (including lumber at $4,000,000, construction at $2,750,000, coal at $1,050,000) often had the worst compliance records. In April 1934, the NRA responded to business complaints by adding a Contributions Branch to the Compliance Division and making code assessments mandatory. In the next eight months, the Compliance Division recorded 43,641 trade practice complaints and almost four times as many complaints of non-payment of code contributions. At the same time, evidence of the oppressive and capricious practices of many code authorities was piling up in Washington. The NRA was at a loss, left "teeter[ing] on the fence," as one official noted, ". . . afraid to let [code authorities] take the money, [and] knowing if they didn't get it the entire venture was doomed."[47]

By late 1934, the NRA had lost all credibility. Although strengthened by the Compliance Division, its "crackdown" was too little and too late. As a midwestern regional office reported, "The general feeling is that it will only be a short time until [employers] can do as they please." The NRA was unlikely to garner much support by changing the rules or raising the stakes. "Without more enforcement," admitted Richberg, "we would lose the support of those willing to comply. With more enforcement we would increase the number and vigor of our opponents." In industry after industry, the discrepancy between code rules and code compliance was identified as the NRA's signal flaw: "The great majorities . . . are, of course, willing as they have been from the beginning to continue compliance with the code," argued one lumber mill owner, "as soon as the Government is prepared and able and willing to enforce it." A tobacco merchant agreed that "the greatest drawback . . . has been a lack of procedure under which a code violator could be punished."[48]

The NRA never served as the external regulatory force it pretended to be. It was unable either to define its objectives or to wield the power necessary to attain them. The codes retained some scattered credibility in those

---

47 Typescript of staff study, DIE File 346:1 (450–53); "Fair Trade Practice Provisions of Codes . . ." (n.d.), File 3:7; Gerry Memo for Galvin (25 May 1935), CD File 132:1, NRA Records. Code authority budgets calculated from Department of Commerce, "Code Sponsoring National Trade Associations" (1935).

48 "List of codes involving most administrative difficulties" (8 March 1935), CD File 173:1; (quote) Omaha Regional Office to Compliance Division (n.d.), CD File 175:1, NRA Records; Richberg quoted in Brand, *Corporatism and the Rule of Law*, 104; (quote) C. Shepherd to Comptom (n.d.), AC File 350:3, NRA Records; tobacco merchant quoted in Senate, *Investigation of NRA*, 1364. See also Robert Collins, *The Business Response to Keynes, 1929–1960* (New York, 1981), 32.

industries with their own means of forcing competitors to accept collective goals and continue to observe them under some tangible threat. But in most cases, NRA officials and code authorities assumed that codes would be self-enforcing because most firms wanted them enacted and were unable to escape the logical cul-de-sac of "self government." The public-spirited voluntarism of the Blue Eagle campaign collapsed as it became apparent that industries needed more than window stickers to put their houses in order. The Compliance Division never sorted out its judicial procedures or penalties. And sporadic or belated attempts to enforce the codes only underlined the perceptual and practical dilemmas of the entire recovery program: many firms wanted the restrictive regulations promised by the codes, but few wanted to shoulder the associated costs, and none were willing to play along if competitors were free to opt out of the game.

Workers Organizing Capitalists: Labor and the Codes

Through 1934 and 1935, industry leaders looked increasingly to labor standards as the most logical focus of regulation and to labor unions as the most effective means of ensuring compliance. "There has been no factor so disturbing in price competition within our industry, noted one lumber executive typically, ". . . as the fact that wages were not maintained at fair level." Although the NRA proved its inability to stand above competitive interests, many industries found their codes effectively policed by labor unions. As one NRA study concluded, "Basic labor terms did much to stabilize competition [and] strong labor organization in an industry was found to assure the most effective codes."[49] Industries that had toyed with regulatory unionism in the 1920s were accustomed to unions playing such a role and welcomed the opportunity to strengthen the organizational bonds between workers, unions, and firms. Others viewed the labor provisions of the NRA more cynically but could not avoid comparing the dismal compliance record of open-shop industries with the relative success of unionized industries. Few firms welcomed the gains made by organized labor after 1933, but fewer still questioned the importance of industrial unionism to the competitive world of the 1930s.

---

49 Lumber executive quoted in Simon Knight, "The Pacific Northwest Lumber Industry and its Response to New Deal Labor Policy" (Master's thesis, University of British Columbia, 1993), 15; (quote) typescript of staff study, DIE File 346:2 (7–8), NRA Records.

For many in business and politics, unions filled an organizational void left by competitive anxiety and administrative disarray. The prospect of union-based enforcement encouraged many industries to frame collective goals as labor standards; restrictions on hours or shifts could ration production or restrain excess capacity, and minimum wages could support prices across an industry. Competitive, labor-intensive industries were well versed in this reasoning. As a lumber representative noted, if wages could be effectively regulated, "prices will ultimately take care of themselves." Industry-wide wage rates would "amount to running a knife through at a certain level," agreed Clay Williams; if "we cut off everything below that . . . we uncover immediately, and in a great many industries, some unit that is living on a take-out from the wage of the worker, and if you mark up the level so that there can't be a take-out it amounts to running a razor around the unit's throat."[50] Wage standards also meshed with the "purchasing power" focus of recovery. Basing higher prices on higher wages (rather than vice versa) commanded greater public and political support. And unions made such standards enforceable without raising the hackles of die-hard progressives, antitrusters, or constitutional literalists.

Unions held a unique position in the battle over industrial regulation and recovery. Workers and unions together had a tremendous stake in the political warfare against depressed markets and cutthroat competition. For employers, after all, these were questions of prices, profits, and the specter of bankruptcy; for workers, these were questions of subsistence. Although closely concerned with the survival of firms in which organized labor thrived, unions had a greater ability and incentive to look beyond the competitive self-interest of many of those firms and strive for industry-wide stability of wages and employment. Unions possessed both an intimate, *internal* knowledge of industry conditions (which the NRA lacked) and an *external* collective rationality (which competing firms lacked). As retailer Edward Filene noted wryly, "Our labor unions have a better understanding of what is good for business today than our chambers of commerce have."[51]

50 "Open Price Filing in the Electrical Manufacturing Industry," 175–92; "Memorandum of Information: Iron and Steel," Elwood Steel to Sen. Pat Harrison (25 March 1935), DR File 267:11; typescript of staff study, DIE File 346:1 (113–21, 469, 476), NRA Records; (quote) J. Farrell to National Lumber Manufacturers' Association (3 June 1935), OF 446, FDR Papers; Williams quoted in "Round Table Conference: New Aspects of the NIRA," CoC Proceedings 23/30 (1935), Chamber Papers; Senate, *Investigation of the NRA,* 2704; Robert Wood, "The [Sears] Company and its Future" (17 April 1934), File 45, Robert E. Wood Papers, HCHPL.
51 Filene quoted in Senate, *Investigation of the NRA,* 1431. For similar sentiments, see

Industry and the NRA sporadically appreciated the regulatory role of unions before 1933, but the code experience opened many eyes. "In industries where labor was well organized . . . ," concluded one report, "enforcement was generally quicker and more satisfactory than that obtained through the complicated compliance machinery established by the NRA. The unions checked code compliance, educated workers in the meaning of the codes . . . and continually insisted upon improvements in compliance machinery." The same report went on to note that "of the three types of pressure used, the pressure of public opinion, pressure from within the industry itself, or pressure of organized groups of employees, the last was found to be most effective." This pattern of union-based compliance was both a reality of code administration and a lesson to be applied to regulatory politics after the NRA. An aide to Senator Wagner suggested "two ways in which code enforcement can be secured: one is by the techniques written into the codes themselves, and the other is through the policing of industry by organized labor." Arguing that NRA-enforced pricing, production, and trade standards were merely "a positive invitation to insincere industrialists to evade the provisions," Wagner's aide concluded that unions were "fighting the decent employer's battle . . . by forcing the undercutters to observe code provisions, or by forcing such employers out of business."[52]

Many unionized, competitive industries used the NRA to nurture long-standing patterns of business unionism. In these industries, unions were the foremost proponents and enforcers of codes, and marginal firms complained repeatedly of strikes and organizing drives initiated by closely allied unions and code authorities. In the needle trades, manufacturers candidly relied on Sidney Hillman's Amalgamated Clothing Workers to discipline code chiselers. Indeed, as NRA officials complained, "Code authorities misdirected their efforts to compel small employers either to keep a closed shop or be driven from business." A report on the coat and suit code added that "the code authority offered all possible assistance to the unions . . . not for the

Means to H. Harriman (27 Oct. 1934), File 2, Means Papers; "Report to General Johnson" (n.d.), File 19, Berle Papers; House of Representatives, Committee on Labor, *Six-Hour Day, Five-Day Week* (Washington, 1933), 3; typescript of staff study, DIE File 346:1 (615–16), NRA Records; A.C. Hill to E. Hughes (31 December 1933), (General Correspondence) File 1, Records of the National Labor Board, RG 25, National Archives; Lyon, *NRA*, 248; Daugherty et al., *Economics of Iron and Steel*, 1:296; Vittoz, *New Deal Labor Policy*, 250–63; Grant Farr, *Origins of Recent Labor Policy* (Boulder, 1959), 59.
52 CIA, "Report on the NRA," (quotes) 111–58; (quote) Elinore Herrick, "Enforcement of Codes Through Organized Labor," Labor File 4:36, Wagner Papers.

purpose of obtaining members for those organizations [but] because the provisions of the code and the provisions of the collective agreement were in
the main identical." Hosiery unionists noted "an exceptional degree of compliance in the hosiery industry . . . attribut[able] mainly to the fact that there
has been an effective union in the industry and the union representatives on
the code authority were able to secure cooperation." And, as leading shoe
firms discovered, labor standards were virtually impossible to enforce *without*
a union.[53]

But business was scarcely united in its admiration of the unions' role
under the NRA. Competitive, nonunion industries appreciated the regulatory potential of organized labor but feared radicalism and loss of managerial
authority. Nonunion, noncompetitive industries saw little reason to qualify
their rigid open-shop views, although many pragmatically courted conservative unions as insurance against shop-floor radicalism. GM, for one, privately hoped to flush radicals out of its plants by "subscrib[ing] to the principle of collective bargaining" with a conservative American Federation of
Labor (AFL) union but could (or would) only do so if the rest of the industry
went along.[54] Capital-intensive industries, such as oil or chemicals, paid little
sincere attention to labor standards before or after the NRA. The Chemical

---

53 Steven Fraser, *Labor Will Rule: Sidney Hillman and the Rise of American Labor* (New
York, 1991), 301; (quote) "Necessity of Supervision of Code Authorities" (31 July
1934), CD File 112:1; (quote) History of the Code of Fair Competition for the Coat
and Suit Industry, DR File 267:3; American Cloak and Suit Manufacturers to NRA
(12 July 1933), DR File 267:3, NRA Records; (quote) Rieve in Senate, *Investigation
of the NRA*, 1548; see also Charles Green, *The Headwear Workers* (New York, 1944),
188; Senate, *Investigation of the NRA*, 362–591; Lyon, *NRA*, 436–39; NRA, "Mens'
Clothing Industry, Work Materials #58 (Washington, 1938); "Blouse and Skirt
Industry," CD File 172:7; "Dress, Coat and Suit Industry," CD File 172:7; "Mens'
Clothing," CAS File 33:3; History of the Code of Fair Competition for Hosiery,
DR File 267:16; History of the Code of Fair Competition for the Boot and Shoe
Industry, DR File 267:44, NRA Records; "Memorandum on Boot and Shoe Code"
(5 December 1934), File 1, Henderson Papers; Minutes of meeting of the American
Leather Belting Association (1933), File 53; "Meeting of the Leather Belting In-
dustry to Consider Codes" (2 August 1933), File 53, National Industrial Leather
Association Papers, Hagley Museum. One trade association even admitted in a na-
tional advertising campaign that "beneath all association activities in the cloak and
suit industry lies a single powerful mainspring – the labor union." (Merchant Ladies
Garment Association in *Women's Wear Daily* [May 1933], clipping in File 219:1312,
Wagner Papers).

54 See statements of Knudsen and Sloan in Fine, *Automobile and the Blue Eagle*, 55–
56; Sloan to Raskob (23 October 1934), File 310; (quote) Donaldson Brown to
Raskob (21 August 1934), File 278, Raskob Papers; "The automobile situation . . .
as seen by Donaldson Brown" (25 January 1932), File 92; Steven DuBrul Memo
(n.d.), File 28, Sachs Papers.

Alliance even advised its members to ignore wage provisions and to take advantage of a six-month "learner" wage by hiring and firing on a biennial basis.[55] And many industries split over the impact or role of unions. Smaller, marginal firms who resented the codes resented the threat of union enforcement even more. And among those who supported the codes, many preferred a return to competitive warfare to union-enforced competitive peace.

Business ambivalence reflected the range of interests and strategies among industries and firms and some doubt that even business unions could capture the cutthroat fringes of an industry. "Industry accepted the Recovery Act ... [and] would stand for substantial [wage] increases and lower hours if they knew that *every* other competitive concern on the same day would be put to the same increases," argued a midwestern quarry operator, noting that "this only can be done by taking in the entire group of industries at one time in a new type of national union." Others echoed this sentiment, adding that business unions might "take some of wind out of the implacable type of organizer's sails" and "hold up the wages of the chiseler." While the prospect of union-enforced codes inspired mixed support for collective bargaining, it did force many to confront labor as a competitive and organizational factor. As Cyrus Ching of U.S. Rubber reasoned:

> If we in this room, representing a number of industries, advocate employee representation [company unions] or relationships built up around individual plants, we must depend on our industry through its code authority or some other agency to take care of the substandard conditions which exist ... within a particular industry and if they are unable to do that, then they must depend on organized labor to keep the substandard units of an industry from tearing down the wage structure. I think that is one of the important things that we have to face in this whole code situation.[56]

The NRA's view of labor's position in the codes closely reflected that of business. NRA officials celebrated union-enforced compliance in some in-

55 "Suggested letter ... to members of the Chemical Manufacturing Industry," File 19, Harrington Papers; "Transcript of Code Hearing, File 53; J.A. Moffett [Standard] to FDR (13 March 1933), File 13; Minutes of Meeting of the Executive Committee of the API (7 March 1933), File 13, PAW Records; "Synopsis of Testimony before Code Committee" (November 1933), File 4:66; J.E. Pew to J.H. Pew, File 4:70, Sun Oil Papers.

56 (Quote) Mississippi Lime and Material to Johnson (12 March 1934), (General Correspondence) File 5, NLB Records, National Labor Relations Board Records (RG 25), National Archives; (quote) E.B. George, "Labor Problems and Policies" (24 August 1934), IAB File 358:9, NRA Records; Ching in NICB Proceedings (14 April 1934), File I:7, NICB Papers, Hagley Museum; J. Hancock to Teagle (8 September 1933), IAB File 350:1; "Discussion of Proposed Labor Representation," AC File 350:1; typescript of staff study, DIE File 346:1 (611–12), NRA Records.

dustries while undercutting similar efforts in others. Despite this inconsistency, NRA officials were always attentive to instances of successful code compliance (which were rare) and broadly appreciated the regulatory power of unions within and beyond the code era. "It seems clear that if the labor provisions of the codes can thus be enforced," remarked William Davis of the Compliance Division, "such enforcement would greatly stabilize competitive conditions; so much so that industry would want to retain its codes for the labor provisions alone." Others agreed that compliance seemed possible only through massive litigation or the entry of industrial unions. In late 1934, Davis argued that unions were "the most effective instrument" of policing the codes and that noncompliance "will decrease in each industry in the same proportion that . . . efficient employee organization increases, thereby affording the conflicting interests in that industry an effective mechanism by which they can move along to a solution of their common problems."[57]

By 1935, the NRA, industry, and organized labor had accepted that business-minded unions were the most logical and effective means of regulating industrial competition. "Compliance with code provisions can be secured," noted the AFL's William Green, "[and] the best means of securing compliance is through self-organization of workers."[58] Conservative unionists and NRA administrators, of course, were inspired partly by other concerns; the former wished to rebuild after a decade of setbacks and knew that stable competition meant stable wages and employment as well, whereas the latter were interested in seeing the NRA succeed in its own right and hoped that unions would both provide the discipline necessary to make the codes work and effect a redistribution of income sufficient to renew mass-consumption.

Employers were less easily sold on union-driven regulation, but the NRA experience strengthened long-standing patterns of regulatory unionism in some industries and educated many others in the organizational potential of unionized labor markets. In the summer of 1935, Howell Cheney (a silk manufacturer and NICB director) wrote Roosevelt that "industry as a whole is coming to have a matured faith that the best part of the NRA cooperative scheme can be preserved under voluntary codes . . . and by labor agree-

---

57 (Quote) Davis Memo (19 November 1934), CD File 181:1; Larner to Houston (3 October 1934), DR File 265:3; (quote) Davis to National Industrial Recovery Board (19 November 1934), CD File 181:1; Barkin Memo (11 April 1935), LAB File 357:2; S. Posner, "Labor Complaints" (5 July 1934), DR (Marshall Office Files) File 265:1, NRA Records; CIA, "Report on the NRA," 58, 73.
58 Green in Senate, *Investigation of the NRA*, 626.

ments." Other employers noted that, with conservative unions keeping watch over competitive standards, "the worker [would] now share in the responsibility of a responsible industry." And as congressional hearings on a new collective bargaining law opened in 1935, Harry Millis of the NLB concluded simply that "many employers have found that they can conduct their business more satisfactorily on a union than a nonunion basis."[59]

Industry and the End of the NRA

By 1935, a legal challenge begun by Schecter Bros., a small New York poultry firm, had wound its way to the Supreme Court. In May, the court struck down the NRA as an unconstitutional exercise of federal power. Ongoing congressional hearings on the NRA's future were suddenly faced not only with well-documented failure but also with its dissolution. Days before the *Schecter* decision, Richberg had favored "killing the NRA while it is still respectable" rather than pushing through a qualified extension under which "trade and industry will have no confidence in enforcement and no fear of resisting government pressure." NRA stalwarts seemed, as the *New York Times* sneered, "like people who have a tired bear by the tail and are not sure whether it is safe to let go or not." Business interests and New Dealers scrambled to salvage politically, economically, and legally defensible remnants of the NRA. Some industries tried to maintain code standards but, shorn of federal enforcement, such warmed-over associationalism offered little but further legal troubles. As an alternative, many saw federal labor law, enforced by unions, as an end run around constitutional restrictions. In the wake of the *Schecter* ruling, Compliance Director Davis predicted "an immediate country-wide swing in support of minimum labor standards."[60] Slowly and haphazardly, the Roosevelt administration moved in this direction.

Business scattered in the debate over NRA extension. A large disillusioned minority (ably represented by NAM and the Southern States Industrial

59 Cheney to FDR (10 July 1935), OF 466:3, FDR Papers; Senate, *Investigation of the NRA*, 570; Millis in Senate, Committee on Education and Labor, *National Labor Relations Board* (Washington, 1935), 176.

60 (Quote) Richberg to FDR (1 May 1935), OF 466:3, FDR Papers; *New York Times* cited in Schlesinger, *Coming of the New Deal*, 166; Hawley, *New Deal and the Problem of Monopoly*, 130–31; miscellaneous drafts of NRA extension, OF 466:3, FDR Papers; (quote) Davis Memo: "Compliance," AC File 350:2; Davis telegram to Richberg (28 May 1935), CD File 181:1, NRA Records; clipping, "Without Benefit of NRA," *Wall Street Journal* (10 June 1935), OF 466:12, FDR Papers; "NRA and Administration Policy," (5 June 1935), File 147, Sachs Papers.

Council) wanted to call off the partnership with government and, having attended what amounted to a two–year course in cartelization and collusion, go it alone. The leaders of most code industries, however, favored a system of voluntary trade practice codes confined to major industries. These approaches were sometimes compatible and sometimes contradictory, reflecting each firm's competitive position and NRA experience. With the *Schecter* decision, however, opposition to federal regulation was suddenly muted. For many, the threat of the NRA paled beside the threat of no regulation at all. "The most hostile opponents of the NRA codes during their effective life," observed one code administrator, "were the first to mourn [their] loss." With few illusions about the NRA, a wide array of business interests – including the Chamber of Commerce, the Business Advisory Council, the auto industry (*sans* Ford), the steel industry, and numerous "sick" industries (lumber, coal, textiles, clothing, and trucking) – pressed for an active response to the court's decision.[61]

If few were willing to tolerate the inconsistencies and futility of the NRA, fewer still were ready to return to the competitive evils of (as one steel executive put it) "the years B.C. [Before Codes]." Many industries proposed voluntary codes in the fall and winter of 1935–36. For some troubled industries, Congress and the Roosevelt administration drafted "little NRAs" that replicated the federal codes but were so specialized and so desperately sought by the industries concerned that legal threats were minimal. While voluntary agreements satisfied a constitutionally gun-shy administration, the absence of any means of binding firms to the agreements remained a serious problem. "In industries which have had a high development of the cooperative spirit, the agreements will work fairly well," *Nation's Business* noted wryly; "these are the industries which did not need the NRA. In industries which have had poor internal cooperation, the voluntary agreements will not

61 "Platform of Congress of American Industries and NAM" (Dec 1934), in U.S. Senate, Subcommittee of the Committee on Education and Labor, *Violations of Free Speech and the Rights of Labor*, Part 17, *Employers' Associations and Citizen's Committees: The National Association of Manufacturers* (Washington, 1938), 7718; J. Bancroft to Noel Sargent (17 April 1935); G. Chisholm to Sargent (17 April 1935), file V:1, NAM Papers; Edgerton testimony in Senate, *Investigation of the NRA*, 1591–1617; (quote) Boal to Rose (14 May 1935), CD File 173:1; Graphic Arts Industry Report, CD File 172:4; "Memorandum of Information: Iron and Steel," DR File 267:11, NRA Records; Business Advisory Council to FDR (2 May 1935), OF 466:10; "Richberg Report," OF 466:12; National Auto Dealers Association to FDR (25 June 1935), OF 102:2, FDR Papers; "Round Table Conference: New Aspects of the NIRA," CoC Proceedings 23/30 (1935), Chamber Papers; Hawley, *New Deal and the Problem of Monopoly*, 129, 143–44.

work. These needed the NRA but never succeeded in enforcing their codes anyway." Responsibility for voluntary agreements fell to the FTC and individual industries, both of which had proven their inability to forge any constructive cooperation among firms. "Voluntary cooperative action to continue the maintenance of code standards," noted Secretary of Commerce Roper glumly, "is almost certain to break down immediately."[62]

For firms continuing to search for some means of compelling their market rivals (and themselves) to observe standards of competition, federal labor law was the logical course. Many industries objected to "the continuation of the NRA, *other than the part which applies to labor.*" Howell Cheney observed that "a majority of industrial employers have faith in the validity of establishing maximum hours and minimum wages and have experienced some of the very practical benefits of stabilized costs." The Roosevelt administration, corporate proponents of "business planning," and employers in competitive, labor-intensive code industries all traced the failure of the NRA to the weakness of a potentially regulatory labor movement. Reeling from a decade-long open-shop offensive in much of the industrial economy, organized labor spent the NRA era fighting for basic legal and political recognition. Only where these battles had been previously won were unions able and willing to police codes of fair competition. During the tenure of the NRA and its demise in 1935, industry and the New Deal turned the prevailing approach to anticompetitive and recovery policies inside out. Industrial regulation became less a matter of establishing competitive standards than of empowering those who were expected to enforce those standards: industrial unions.[63]

62 (Quote) V. Iden [American Institute of Steel Construction] to Raskob, File 1644:2, Raskob Papers; Roper, "Memorandum on Course to Be Followed" (8 June 1935), President's Secretary's File 73; J. O'Neill [FTC] to FDR (? June 1934), OF 100:1; "Voluntary Trade Practice Agreements, 1935–1936," OF 466:6, FDR Papers; "Voluntary Agreements," File 358; G. McCorkle [FTC] to H. Cheney (1 August 1935), File 358, NRA Records; "Platform of Congress of American Industries and NAM" (December 1934) in Senate, *Violations of Free Speech and the Rights of Labor*, 17:7718; CIA, "Report on the NRA," 11; *Nation's Business* cited in Brand, *Corporatism and the Rule of Law*, 156; Roper quoted in "Confidential Report of the Industrial Recovery Committee" (28 June 1935), File 1:11, Business Advisory Council [BAC] Papers, Records of the Department of Commerce (RG 40), National Archives.

63 (Quote) R. Appel [handbag] to Wagner (25 March 1935); Oxzyn Company [handbag] to Wagner (25 March 1935); Adset Typography to Wagner (26 March 1935), File 239:2501–2, Wagner Papers; (quote) H. Cheney to FDR (10 July 1935), OF 466:3, FDR Papers; Senate, *Investigation of the NRA*, 16–17, 1372; "Meeting of the Leather Belting Industry to Consider Codes," (2 August 1933), file 53, National Industrial Leather Association Papers; "Round Table Conference: New Aspects of

If the implications and application of labor-centered regulation were contentious and complicated, its reasoning was deceptively simple: In a protected economy, labor standards served the same regulatory purpose as uniform prices or production quotas. The NRA experience had underlined the potential and (not incidentally) the constitutionality of union-driven regulation. And quite aside from its regulatory promise, the labor strategy supported consumption by supporting wages and protected the administration's left flank by extending federal bargaining rights. This was the culmination of the NRA experience, although it was a logical leap that many employers were unprepared to make. As the "First New Deal" drew to a close, the prospects for competitive organization were less ambitious, and the stakes much higher. Industries and the NRA moved cautiously to adapt to the legal strictures of the post-*Schecter* era. Many pursued anew the phantom of "self-regulation." Some reformed their regulatory ties with the government along more limited and discretionary lines. And others, facing not only persistent and severe competition but also internal threats from an invigorated labor movement, turned to federal labor law as a last-bet reprieve from the tortures of the market.

the NIRA" CoC Proceedings 23/30 (1935), Chamber Papers; CIA, "Report on the NRA," 107–9; Barkin, "NRA Policies, Standards, and Code Provisions," 55; DuBrul to H. Eaton (9 March 1934), File 28, Sachs Papers; Hinrichs to Perkins (15 June 1935), OF 466:12, FDR Papers.

6. The Wagner Act
The Political Economy of Labor Relations, 1933–1937

In July of 1935, Franklin Roosevelt signed the National Labor Relations Act, otherwise known as the Wagner Act, into law. It embodied the legal issues hammered out under Section 7a of the National Recovery Act (NRA); granting organized labor basic representation and bargaining rights but tying those rights to federal law rather than the vagaries and inconsistencies of industrial codes. For both contemporary observers and subsequent scholars, the New Deal took a turn in 1935 that seemed both a pointed disavowal of "business" plans for economic recovery and a radical departure from the cozy business-government relations of the NRA era. With few exceptions, business interests opposed the Wagner Act and repeatedly challenged its authority after 1935.

However it may have been perceived, the reality behind this shift in policy was more complex. By 1935, many employers saw federal labor law as a partial and necessary solution to market instability, the persistence of the Depression, and the failure of earlier organizational experiments. Throughout the NRA era, only unions had been able to enforce trade practices and penalize marginal competitors; this experience reinforced regulatory unionism in some industries and introduced it to others. With the end of the NRA, federal legislators also saw union-enforced regulation of hours and wages as the key to economic stability and industrial unions as the only effective (and constitutional) means of establishing or maintaining that stability.[1] In turn, the Wagner Act touched on problems that the NRA had not

---

1 For the debate over the relative influence of business, labor, political, and legal interests in the origins and administration of the Wagner Act, see Stanley Vittoz, *New Deal Labor Policy and the American Industrial Economy* (Chapel Hill, 1987); Thomas Ferguson, "From Normalcy to New Deal: Industrial Structure, Party Competition, and American Public Policy in the Great Depression," *International Organization* 38 (1984): 41–94; Christopher Tomlins, *The State and the Unions* (New York, 1985); Peter Irons, *New Deal Lawyers* (Princeton, 1982); Howell Harris, *The Right to Manage: Industrial Relations Policies of American Business in the 1940s* (Madison, 1982), 15–37; Harris, "The Snares of Liberalism? Politicians, Bureaucrats, and

addressed. The Depression had exacerbated industrial conflict and undermined employers' efforts to contain it through "welfare capitalism" or private cooperation. Federal labor law promised to contain social instability, radical demands, and irresponsible employers. And while chronically confused by the distributive and inflationary implications of such legislation, most hoped it would put cash in the pockets of consumers.

The logic of the Wagner Act, on its own merits or as a strategic residue of the NRA, did not occur to all employers and escaped many others entirely. The "extension of collective bargaining has not up to now taken place as a result of the employer calculating by a cool logic its advantages," as one contemporary noted, " . . . [yet] it remains a fact that this type of agreement would not have been extended . . . if certain definite business and social advantages had not clearly accrued."[2] Clearly, for most employers the prospect of federal legislation guaranteeing workers new organizational rights was not a happy one. Yet had business opposition been as heartfelt and uniform as some of the act's more vocal detractors claimed, there is little likelihood that it would have passed. The persistence of the Depression, the aftermath of the NRA, and the unprecedented prominence of the Left (in the workplace and in politics) narrowed the range of feasible options and blunted resistance. Only a few business interests fully perceived the utility and logic of federal labor law, but fewer still were able to credibly question its premises.

I begin with the central theme of the previous chapter – the emergence of industrial unionism as the most promising form of *business* collective action under the NRA – and look more closely at the legal and administrative history of the NRA's Section 7a. I then trace the Wagner Act's intellectual and legislative background, stressing the influence of the NRA experience and sketching the range of business options and opinions. The latter half of the chapter carries the story beyond 1935, focusing on the logic of labor

the Shaping of Federal Labor Relations Policy in the United States, ca. 1915–1947," in *Shop Floor Bargaining and the State: Historical and Comparative Perspectives*, ed. Jonathan Zeitlin and Stephen Tolliday (New York, 1985), 168–71; David Plotke, "The Wagner Act, Again: Politics and Labor, 1935–1937," *Studies in American Political Development* 3 (1989): 105–56; Michael Goldfield, "Worker Insurgency, Radical Organization, and New Deal Labor Legislation," *American Political Science Review* 83 (1989): 298–315.

2 (Quote) Ordway Tead and Henry Metcalf, *Labor Relations under the Recovery Act* (New York, 1933), 120–21. See also Lloyd Ulman, "Who Wanted Collective Bargaining in the First Place?" *Proceedings of the Annual Meeting of the Industrial Relations Research Association* 39 (1986): 1–13.

relations in previously unorganized industries and on the pragmatic and anxious pattern of business response to the revival of organized labor.

NRA Labor Policy: The Seven Veils of 7a

The NRA's Section 7a granted workers, in pointedly ambiguous terms, "the right to organize and bargain collectively through representatives of their own choosing," free "from the interference, restraint, or coercion of employers." This was less a charter of labor rights than an attempt to mandate the conduct of employers as a condition of their participation in the NRA. Section 7a did not force employers to retreat from long-standing "divide and conquer" labor policies; neither did it require those who bargained with their workers to actually reach an agreement. Firms and industries made Section 7a what they wanted it to be. This flexibility, which was a political necessity, proved to be an economic, legal, and administrative disaster. Marginal firms in competitive industries wanted the same freedom from collective bargaining granted those industries whose codes stripped Section 7a of all meaning. Firms facing the threat of unionization wanted Section 7a enforced sincerely and quickly on all competitors. And organized labor saw little reason to distinguish among industries or firms – a practice that not only discriminated against many workers directly but also pressed the burden of organization (higher prices) on those who remained unorganized.

Although business saw labor provisions as central to the unfolding NRA debate, they disagreed sharply over their meaning and importance. Leading coal, textile, and clothing interests had supported such measures all along, while wage standards and labor rights also appealed to those who viewed the Depression as a crisis of underconsumption. Antiunion stalwarts, led by the National Association of Manufacturers (NAM), dug in against any disruption of "existing satisfactory relationships" and were assured by "the highest authorities in the National Recovery Administration," as one oil executive recalled, "that 'the closed shop' was supposed to have no agreed meaning and no place in the dictionary of the NRA." For many, the NRA vindicated a long-standing campaign for company unions, which had "sprung up like weeds" in cynical compliance with Section 7a. "Big units in the basic industries, such as coal, oil, textiles, automobiles, lumber and steel," as Chamber of Commerce Director Silas Strawn noted, "are fairly well satisfied."[3]

3 Grant Farr, *Origins of Recent Labor Policy* (Boulder, 1959), 69–93; American Iron and Steel Institute to Senator Pat Harrison (1 June 1933), File 15 (accession 7/29/82), Lukens Steels Papers, Hagley Museum and Library, Wilmington, DE; "Section

But they were clearly satisfied for different reasons: some felt the NRA's labor provisions would solve problems caused by cutthroat market competition, while others saw them as a rhetorical concession that made the rest of the NRA's agenda possible and credible.[4]

As industrial codes were drafted through 1933, the NRA echoed business demands and anxieties and ignored their contradictions. Labor participated in the code-drafting process only in those industries in which unions were already well established (only 23 of over 500 code authorities gave labor a vote). The question of how to define the precise legal meaning of Section 7a was raised in numerous code negotiations but General Johnson, who preferred the pomp of "signing on" an industry to any scrutiny of regulatory provisions, balked at the use of the terms "open shop" or "closed shop." After granting the steel industry an open-shop allowance "in an unguarded moment," Johnson pressed the auto industry to couch its championship of the open shop in terms of "the selection, retention and advancement of employees on the basis of individual merit." This language was largely the work of the Special Conference Committee (SCC), which watched labor provisions closely and, through Donaldson Brown of GM, worked on numerous drafts of the auto code. As SCC Secretary Cowdrick observed, the resulting interpretation of Section 7a was "about as favorable as could be

7(a)," NRA Work Materials #45 (Washington, 1939), E:19–27; (quote) E. Lederer [Texas Pacific Coal and Oil], Chamber of Commerce [CoC] Proceedings 23/30 (1935), Chamber of Commerce Papers, Hagley Museum; (quote) Silas Strawn to Hoover (22 December 1933), Post-Presidential Individual [PPI] File 3848, Herbert C. Hoover Papers, Herbert C. Hoover Presidential Library [HCHPL], West Branch, IA; Sensenbrenner [Kimberly-Clark] to Teagle (28 October 1933), Advisory Council [AC] File 350:1; "Collective Bargaining" (n.d.), AC File 350:1, National Recovery Administration [NRA] Records (RG 9) National Archives, Washington, D.C.; E.S. Cowdrick memo for SCC companies (16 August 1933), File 17, Willis Harrington Papers, Hagley Museum; Solomon Barkin, "NRA Policies, Standards and Code Provisions . . ." Work Materials #45 (Washington, 1936), B:1, 13–16, 19.

4 On company unionism during the NRA, see William Hogan, *Economic History of the Iron and Steel Industry* (Lexington, 1971) 3:863–65; Daniel Nelson, "The Company Union Movement, 1900–1937: A Reexamination," *Business History Review* [*BHR*] 56 (1982): 335–57; Robert Dunn, *The Americanization of Labor* (New York, 1927), 127–46; National Labor Relations Board [NLRB], "Characteristics of 60 Company-Dominated Unions," and National Industrial Conference Board [NICB], "Individual and Collective Bargaining under the N.I.R.A." (1933), File 255, National Association of Manufacturers [NAM] Papers, Hagley Museum; National Industrial Conference Board Proceedings (21 December 1933), File I:6, NICB Papers, Hagley Museum; Carroll R. Daugherty et al., *The Economics of the Iron and Steel Industry* (New York, 1937) 1:261–64; Special Conference Committee [SCC], "Report to Clients, 1937," Box 28, Harrington Papers.

expected," as it sanctioned company unions and "definitely approved the principle of the open shop."[5]

But any hope on the part of industry or the NRA of ignoring or finessing the labor problem was frustrated almost immediately by the workers themselves. After a decade of organizational losses and more than three years of the Depression, labor had little to lose and much to gain. Section 7a seemed to offer at least some recourse from the tyranny of the open shop, and unions moved quickly to test the NRA's sincerity. The industrial economy had lost an average of 603,000 worker-days to strike action through the first six months of 1933; in July this figure doubled to 1,375,000 and in August nearly doubled again, to 2,378,000. And many of these strikes (30 percent of all job actions in 1933) were fundamental and contentious battles over union organization or recognition.[6] To the consternation of employers and the Roosevelt administration, the first blush of NRA labor policy encouraged rather than constrained union activists. Suddenly the NRA was not simply juggling business demands but was faced with the political and legal demands of organized labor and incessant threats to public order as well.

As the labor problem spilled beyond the carefully drawn boundaries of code industries, the enforcement of Section 7a's guarantees was further scrambled by contradictions between legal consistency and business expectations. At the insistence of the NRA Labor and Industrial Advisory Boards, an independent National Labor Board (NLB) was formed in August 1933 to "further industrial peace through the adjudication of disputes." The NLB was dominated by those who had been at the forefront of regulatory unionism in the 1920s – including William Green of the American Federation of Labor (AFL), John Lewis of the United Mine Workers (UMW), Leo Wolman of the Amalgamated Clothing Workers (ACW), Gerard Swope of GE, Walter Teagle of Standard, Louis Kirstein of Filene's, and Senator Wagner – and their collective labor relations experience animated its efforts to salvage the NRA's labor provisions. Through the remainder of 1933, the NLB ap-

---

5 Cowdrick memo: Section 7a (24 August 1933); Cowdrick memo: auto code (24 August 1933); Cowdrick memo (21 August 1933); Cowdrick memo: labor provisions (23 August 1933); Cowdrick memo: code provisions (29 August 1933), File 17, Harrington Papers; "Section 7a," NRA Work Materials #45, E:581–64; Department of Commerce, *Report on the Results and Accomplishments of the National Recovery Act* (Washington, 1937), 48, 108–11; Roosevelt to Johnson (19 October 1933), Official File (OF) 407, Franklin D. Roosevelt Papers, Franklin D. Roosevelt Presidential Library [FDRPL], Hyde Park, NY.
6 Irving Bernstein, *The New Deal Collective Bargaining Policy* (Berkeley, 1950), 58, 144; Lizabeth Cohen, *Making a New Deal: Industrial Workers in Chicago, 1919–1939* (New York, 1991), 278, 303–4.

plied a hastily devised set of guidelines – strike termination, reinstatement of striking employees, and a secret ballot "majority rule" election – to disputes in the coal, laundry, shoe, and streetcar industries. This "Reading formula" (named after a benchmark ruling in the hosiery industry) set the stage for a series of major battles over the meaning of New Deal labor policy and, more particularly, the implications of majority rule.[7]

For the duration of the NRA, New Deal labor policy would be a legal and political tug-of-war between consistently diverse business expectations and an inertial, ad hoc "common law" of labor relations. Johnson, NRA Counsel Donald Richberg, and the NLB interpreted Section 7a and the corollary of majority rule in every conceivable light. For a while, the Roosevelt administration calmed business anxieties (and a potential stampede of business opposition) by constantly refining, retreating from, and reversing its public positions. In turn, the NLB's quasi-legal status (derived from the NRA) made it possible for employers to ignore its rulings and put off any final showdown over federal labor policy. As they challenged NLB authority and the meaning of Section 7a through the winter of 1933–34, however, legal consistency and the vigilance of organized labor forced the NLB to support the spirit of the NRA's bargaining provisions. By mid-1934, the NLB had refined its notion of "majority rule," acknowledging that majority agreements applied to all employees and accepting the selection of the majority as the *exclusive* bargaining agent for employees.[8]

Legal refinements, of course, meant little to employers who were free and able to ignore the law when it did not serve their purposes. Although the NLB was created in part because separate labor boards for each industry were "not feasible," many employers objected to the prospect of settling labor disputes according to federal standards rather than industry needs. After late 1933, the idea of industrial labor boards resurfaced, not as a means of rationalizing labor policy on an industry-by-industry basis but as a means of insulating certain industries (notably oil, steel, and autos) from the NLB's increasingly controversial decisions. The industry labor boards ruled primarily on cases of individual grievance and discrimination, but they were

7 Vittoz, *New Deal Labor Policy*, 138–40; Arthur Schlesinger, *The Coming of the New Deal* (Boston, 1958), 146–49; James Gross, *The Making of the National Labor Relations Board* (Albany, 1974), 22–23.

8 Vittoz, *New Deal Labor Policy*, 139–42; Steven DuBrul to Sachs, File 28, Alexander Sachs Papers, FDRPL; Leverett Lyon et al., *The National Recovery Administration* (Washington, 1935), 462–64; "Section 7a," NRA Work Materials #45, E:50–51; Louis Mahrt, "Chronological Development of 'Collective Bargaining' under Executive and Administration Orders . . ." (12 October 1934), File 358, NRA Records.

technically extensions of the NRA and the code authorities and so not an-
swerable to the NLB. The Automobile Labor Board, for example, grew out
of a March 1934 settlement by which the NRA released the industry from
the strictures of recent NLB rulings on majority rule and sanctioned proportional representation.[9]

The NLB shared the legal and political uncertainty of its parent, the NRA,
and lacked any real powers of enforcement. Like the NRA's Compliance
Division, it fielded and catalogued complaints but could only encourage
voluntary compliance. This administrative lacuna made it possible for business to play a constant game of "battledore and shuttlecock" with labor
rulings, allowing the NLB latitude when its decisions seemed harmless or
unenforceable and asserting the primacy of the NRA or code authorities
whenever their interests were threatened. When key NLB rulings against
Budd Manufacturing and Weirton Steel were ignored by the employers in
question *and* by the NRA, the Roosevelt administration admitted that the
NLB was a "helpless body unable to enforce its opinions or rulings" and
that enforcement of Section 7a had "failed almost completely." Through
early 1934, NRA administrators increasingly distanced themselves from
NLB labor policy in a last-ditch effort to maintain business support (culminating in the auto settlement, which plowed under NLB authority and
six months of majority rule decisions). As Senator Wagner complained,
"Control of the NRA is definitely in the hands of the industrialists," adding
that the current NLB could "fold up its tents and slink away; . . . try to find
some way to drag on a miserable existence without any very clearcut mission;
[or] . . . seek definitely to develop an industrial relations policy."[10]

9 Lyon, *NRA*, 446–48, 467–68; Johnson to FDR (20 August 1934), File 6, Hugh
  Johnson Papers, FDRPL; "Confidential: Industrial Relations Boards" (9 May 1934),
  File 358; Staff Study, Division of Industrial Economics [DIE], File 346:2, NRA
  Records; "List of Approved Codes [with] . . . Labor Participation" (n.d.), General
  Correspondence File 1, National Labor Relations Board [NLRB] Records (RG 25),
  National Archives; "Report on an Inquiry into Industrial Relations Boards" (9 May
  1935), OF 716:2, FDR Papers; Donald Brand, *Corporatism and the Rule of Law: A
  Study of the National Recovery Administration* (Ithaca, 1988), 246–47; Daugherty,
  Economics of Iron and Steel, 1:297–30; Committee on Industrial Analysis [CIA],
  "Report on the Results and Accomplishments of the National Recovery Act" (Wash-
  ington, 1937), 154–56.
10 (Quote) "Confidential Joint Statement of the Labor and Industrial Advisory Boards"
  (12 September 1934), Marshall Office File 265:1; typescript of staff study, DIE Files
  346:1 (613–16), 346:2, NRA Records; "Section 7(a)," NRA Work Materials #45,
  E:67–76; Schlesinger, *Coming of the New Deal*, 149–51; (quote) "Memorandum of
  Conversation with Senator Wagner" (3 April 1934), Marshall Office File 265:1,
  NRA Records.

Business was torn over the importance and intent of NLB rulings. For many leading firms, majority rule was a logical extension of the anticompetitive spirit of the NRA. "Industry was to be stabilized by permitting employers to combine together," as an early draft of the NLB's landmark *Houde* decision reasoned, "[and] collective bargaining and the collective agreements resulting therefrom would be an essential part of this process." The NLB went on to argue that "wages, hours, and working conditions should also be stabilized as far as possible, and should be reasonably uniform within each particular industry. In achieving these objectives, collective agreements would play an important, if not indispensable part." This not only struck a chord with "labor capitalists" in coal, clothing, textile, glass, pottery, trucking, and construction, but many mass-production employers admitted that majority rule might be a prerequisite for industrial peace and manageable bargaining. For the latter, federal labor policy was but one variable in a complex and chronically uncertain situation. Employers, after all, had to balance their ideal world (which did not include unions) with the realities of the 1930s; for those facing the prospect of unionization, a federal framework for collective bargaining was clearly preferable to craft or radical unionism.[11]

Publicly, mass-production, small, and southern employers decried the drift towards majority rule and representation (although "the employers' concern over the rights of minorities," as GM's Steven DuBrul conceded privately, ". . . is simply virtuous camouflage [for] the principle of 'divide and rule' "). But this familiar belligerence was increasingly difficult to maintain. Most initiated or expanded upon company unions as a means of satisfying the requirements of the NRA. As I suggested in the context of the 1920s, the establishment of company unions, although designed to stall real organization, also acknowledged the importance of collective representation and introduced the idea to a new generation of workers. As the NLB stepped up its scrutiny of management-dominated unions, employers loosened their grip and, in some cases, granted company unions so much autonomy that they resembled the very threat they were designed to meet. And as organized labor stepped up its efforts throughout the industrial economy, even those firms that opposed NLB rulings recognized the NLB's utility in mediating and tempering industrial disputes. "Decisions which are quickly rendered

11 (Quote) Draft of "In the Matter of Houde Engineering" (30 August 1934) in NLB file 1173-5, Pierre S. DuPont Papers, Hagley Museum; (quote) John Edgerton [NAM] telegram (21 June 1935), II:419, Virginia File 249, Westmoreland Coal Papers, Hagley Museum.

on part of the National Labor Board," admitted Pierre DuPont, "will have more effect in preventing strikes than any other factor."[12]

The course of federal labor policy was influenced by more than business anxieties and administrative chaos. During 1934, while employers fought the NLB (and the NRA and NLB fought over bureaucratic turf), workers took matters into their own hands. Organized labor, caustically dismissing the NRA as the "National Run Around," directed job actions not only at employers but also at the government itself for its failure to sincerely enforce the codes. Although Section 7a provided a yardstick against which to challenge employers, NRA labor policy remained a broken promise. The NLB simply deprived workers of their right to strike in exchange for a protracted and often dubious election procedure, a pattern maverick labor activist A. J. Muste condemned as "wrong, vicious and misleading." Through the middle months of 1934, major strikes (reflecting the collapse of even nominally paternalist labor relations, the pervasive threat of unemployment, and the impact of NRA-spurred inflation) erupted in San Francisco, Minneapolis, Toledo, and throughout the textile industry and seemed imminent in other corners of the nation and the economy. In all, nearly 2,000 disputes involved 1.5 million workers at a cost of 20 million worker-days, half of which were lost between June and September alone.[13]

Union rhetoric and employer anxieties aside, this was scarcely class warfare. The labor threat was scattered by industrial, regional, and jurisdictional divisions and blunted by the absence of any meaningful ties to national politics or political parties. The 1934 strike wave marked only a slight increase over 1933, and by any measure (number of disputes, length of disputes, workers involved, or days lost) it paled beside that of 1919–20. And industrial disputes remained concentrated in a few traditionally contentious industries (coal, textiles, and construction) and regions (in 1932–34 fully 60 percent took place in Massachusetts, New York, Pennsylvania, and New

12 (Quote) DuBrul Memo (n.d.), File 28. Sachs Papers; (quote) P. DuPont to Swope (22 January 1934), NLB File 1173-5, Pierre DuPont Papers; Lammot DuPont to Raskob (21 August 1934), File 15, DuPont Company Administrative Papers, Hagley Museum; CIA, "Report on the NRA," 152–54.

13 Ellis Hawley, *The New Deal and the Problem of Monopoly* (Princeton, 1966), 104; Sachs memos, "Labor Situation and its Implications" (5 September 1934), and "Approaching Labor Cloud, (8 April 1935)," File 123, Sachs Papers; memo, "Cotton Textile Strike" (15 September 1934), OF 407b, FDR Papers; (quote) A.J. Muste to Wagner (27 December 1933), General Corr. File 1, NLRB Records; Tomlins, *The State and the Unions*, 111; David Brody, "The Emergence of Mass-Production Unionism," in *Workers in Industrial America* (Oxford, 1980), 82–119; Vittoz, *New Deal Labor Policy*, 142; *Monthly Labor Review* 42:1 (January 1936): 154–63.

Jersey).[14] If the degree and tenor of industrial conflict were not new, the nature of federal responsibility for private labor relations certainly was. Because these disputes were direct products of the promise and performance of the NRA, industrial unrest forced the administration's hand.

In June of 1934, the NLB was reconstituted by executive order into a new National Labor Relations Board (NLRB), which had more autonomy from the now-moribund NRA and a narrower focus on dispute resolution. This administrative shuffle still left the central question of the board's legal and punitive powers unanswered. And while the NLRB's independence gave it the freedom to further refine the concept of majority rule, it also invited stiff opposition from business and the remnants of the NRA. By August, the Roosevelt administration was in a state of perpetual confusion. NRA officials openly derided the NLRB; when NLRB chair Lloyd Garrison suggested an intra-agency rapprochement, Johnson responded testily that Garrison had not been in the job or "on this planet long enough to advise [him]." In a report to Roosevelt in January, Francis Biddle (who had succeeded Garrison) admitted that the NLRB was "powerless to enforce its own decisions" and that, without new legislation reaffirming NLRB authority (now threatened by the death of the NRA), the administration was condemning itself to chronic infighting and industrial strife.[15]

It is easy to make too much of the subtleties of Section 7a or the emerging legal culture of federal labor policy. The NRA simply underlined a critical tension between the discretionary, industrial focus of the codes and the nationwide application of federal labor standards. Labor relations and labor policy under the NRA was an ongoing scramble between and among employers, legislators, and administrators over what was desirable, possible, and necessary in an ongoing effort to accomplish industrial and overall economic recovery. Employers were largely able to interpret or disregard Section 7a along narrowly self-interested lines, a fact that at least gave the NRA and NLB the freedom to tinker with labor policy in the hope of finding something that would work. In all, labor activism and scattered business expectations and demands gave a sort of accidental momentum to the NRA's

14 Goldfield, "Worker Insurgency, Radical Organization, and New Deal Labor Legislation," 1264; Melvyn Dubofsky, "Not So 'Turbulent Years': A New Look at the 1930s," in *Life and Labor: Dimensions of American Working Class History*, ed. Charles Stephenson and Robert Asher (Albany, 1986), 213–14; *Monthly Labor Review* 42 (January 1936): 154–63; *Monthly Labor Review* 43 (July 1936): 68–97.

15 Vittoz, *New Deal Labor Policy*, 145–46; Garrison to Johnson (17 August 1934), and (quote) Johnson to Garrison (18 August 1934), OF 466:2; (quote) NLRB Report to the President (January 1935), OF 716:2, FDR Papers.

agenda. Through consecutive crises of policy or authority, including the strike-ridden summers of 1933 and 1934 and the *Schecter* decision of 1935, industry and the New Deal moved to refine rather than abandon the basic premises of federal labor law.

Whatever their view of New Deal legislation, employers keenly resented its inconsistent enforcement and the fact that its costs were borne by the very firms it might benefit. Many labor-intensive firms supported a stricter and more honestly enforced labor law but, after the NRA debacle, doubted that such was possible. Small and southern firms, of course, opposed any policies that effectively muted wage competition. The Roosevelt administration, faced with the failure of the NRA and the splintering of business support, preferred to ignore contradictions that might force it to choose between political consistency and the goodwill of industry leaders.

At the same time, New Dealers both in and out of government (including Wagner and a cadre of NRA economists and compliance directors) simply followed the original business view of the NRA – industrial organization enforced by political coercion – to its logical conclusion. They argued that federal labor law might unify standards within industries, supplement or replace inconsistent (and legally suspect) federal enforcement with industrial unions, entrench the political support of organized labor, and ensure that effective regulation was buttressed by the inflation of mass-purchasing power.[16] By 1935, federal policy had come full circle. After a long and disastrous detour around the intent and implications of the original Black Bill, uniform labor standards were again being considered. The NRA experience had underlined a nagging dilemma – the concessions to industrial and regional autonomy that made the NRA politically safe also made it an economic disaster. In 1935, however, the issue of federal labor standards was raised not as a precursor to a more flexible "business-minded" alternative but as a response to the utter failure of that alternative and the need for a feasible means of addressing the chaos of industrial and regional competition.

The Employers' Frankenstein: Passing the Wagner Act

The Wagner Act reflected both disgust with the NRA experience and scattered business backing for certain promises and provisions of federal labor

16 Sloan [GM] to Raskob (21 August 1934), File 278, John J. Raskob Papers, Hagley Museum; Lyon, *NRA*, 403–9; Tomlins, *State and the Unions*, 119–27; "Confidential Conference with Senators" (14 April 1934), President's Secretary's File [PSF] 188, FDR Papers; Miller memo for Wagner (7 May 1934), Marshall Office File 256:1, NRA Records; Millis to FDR (21 June 1936), OF 316, FDR Papers.

law. Some labor-intensive industries and firms hoped the act would give teeth to the NRA's policies, which had placed the onus of organization on a weak labor movement and done little to coerce chiselers. Some mass-production firms hoped the act might encourage industrial rather than craft unionism, arguing that the former made it possible to regulate labor costs across an industry with little managerial sacrifice. And some consumer-goods firms and retailers, again pointing to the failure of the NRA, continued to hope that the act might revitalize or redistribute mass-purchasing power. Although many saw the Wagner Act as the logical culmination of two decades of competitive and organizational strategy, few supported it without serious reservations. Vague hopes that unionization might be exploited to accomplish business goals rarely outweighed anxieties over managerial rights. Federal law was shaped largely by New Dealers in Congress and the Roosevelt administration, who moved frantically to balance a cacophony of demands from industrial interests with not only those of workers and voters but also with the administrative and legal requisites for recovery. While business pilfered the corpses of private and NRA strategies in a search for competitive stability, it fell to the administration to assemble the remains into a political form. The result surprised and haunted its creators.

Business viewed the prospect of federal labor law with confusion and uncertainty. Firms that actually favored politically regulated collective bargaining were scattered and, at least at the federal level, not politically powerful. And those rhetorically committed to "social peace" or "industrial democracy" had neither the prescience nor the predisposition to surrender managerial prerogatives for the greater good; indeed, the putatively liberal or corporatist management of firms such as GE were among the firmest opponents of the act and the first to challenge its authority after 1935. But the basic premises and parameters of the Wagner Act were nothing new to U.S. business. Since at least 1929, many firms had demanded some "exercise of government authority" to compel marginal competitors to respect standard labor costs and trade practices. With the NRA in tatters, business sought something in its place. Competitive stability and economic recovery were doomed, warned one textile executive in mid-1935, "unless further legislation lays a firm foundation for trade practices and labor agreements rather promptly."[17]

17 T.W. Lamont to N. Davis (1 October 1934), PSF 156, FDR Papers; (quote) "From the Report of the Committee on Working Periods in Industry of the Chamber of Commerce" (1933), File 17, Harrington Papers; (quote) Howell Cheney to FDR (10 July 1935), OF 466:3, FDR Papers; Sloan to Raskob (21 August 1934), File 278, Raskob Papers.

The strongest business argument for the Wagner Act rested on the same reasoning that had shaped two decades of regulatory unionism in some competitive industries and, less consistently or successfully, shaped the interpretation of Section 7a. There remained, as Harry Millis of the NLRB argued, "the need for standardization and control, . . . placing all firms in a market on pretty much the same plane of labor costs." Or as a midwestern quarry owner wrote the NRA, "Industry is perfectly willing to pay considerably higher wages on shorter hours, . . . if we can be quite positive that all our competitors will likewise do the same." Competitive, fragmented, labor-intensive industries "whose managements could not look after themselves" were the leading proponents of this reasoning.[18] Wagner's Senate Committee on Education and Labor pointedly solicited the testimony of coal and clothing executives, unionized tobacco manufacturers (Axton-Fisher and Brown & Williamson) who wanted to see their larger competitors unionized, and other core firms in competitive industries. As a Wagner aide noted of one proposed witness (a cannery owner), "He wants to have his men organize, in the hope that this will force organization (and [code] compliance) among his competitors."[19]

Many others, while leery of federal intrusion and any loss of managerial prerogative, appreciated certain aspects of the Wagner Act or showed a willingness to live with it. Some mass-production firms reasoned that *if* unionization were imminent, then "bread and butter" industrial unionism was preferable to the administrative chaos of craft unionism. After a meeting with Arthur Young, NRA officials noted that while unionization would "nullify everything that he regards as decent in personnel administration," the U.S. Steel executive had also suggested that he wanted "an industrial union and not a congerie of craft unions." *Fortune* noted that "most employers of labor who have considered the matter would prefer the industrial union to the craft union as the lesser of two evils and there are even a few who would accept it as no evil at all." Leading auto and steel firms feared "the kind of sprawling, uncoordinated, political thing" that they saw in the AFL and its

18 (Quote) Millis in U.S. Senate, Committee on Education and Labor, *National Labor Relations Board* (Washington, 1935), 173; (quote) Mississippi Lime and Material to Johnson (12 March 1934), General Corr. File 5, NLRB Records; Harris, "The Snares of Liberalism," 171.

19 See "Suggestions for Appearances," especially (quote) E. Smith to Keyserling (13 March 1935), File 36, Robert F. Wagner Papers, Littauer Library, Georgetown University, Washington, D.C. On the situation in tobacco, see testimony in Senate, *National Labor Relations Board*, 212–18; *Wall Street Journal*, 12 March 1936, clipping in File 1139:2, Pennsylvania Railroad [PRR] Papers, Hagley Museum.

affiliates. And unionized cigarette firms, as the *Wall Street Journal* noted, "vastly prefer to deal with the industrial union than with a multiplicity of craft unions." Others lumped their endemic fear of craft unions with competitive concerns and favored "a vertical union along the lines of the coal mines . . . thereby eliminating the possibility of individual companies being harassed to join the present trade unions with tremendous increases in wage scales while their competitors . . . are not subject to the same."[20]

Business support for federal labor law also came from those who saw underconsumption as the root of the economic crisis. "We cannot operate this American machine . . . unless the masses can buy on a scale which was never before heard of," urged retailer Edward Filene, adding that "the masses cannot buy on such a scale unless wages are removed from competition and organized business and organized labor cooperate on seeing how high those wages can be made" (and, as an aside, that "the best thing for my business . . . would be to largely increase wages and salaries"). Morris Leeds (Leeds & Northrup) agreed that NRA-style regulation should be supplemented or supplanted by the "sufficient organization of labor to give it the necessary bargaining power" to provide workers with substantial disposable incomes. While many agreed that consumers should have more cash in their pockets, few were willing to extend this reasoning to bargaining with their own workers. Producer-goods manufacturers, such as steel or rubber, rarely made the connection between the wages they offered and the demand for their products. Many consumer-goods manufacturers, such as the major auto firms, saw the connection more clearly but were in no position to gird aggregate demand with local wage increases.[21]

Finally, business support for (and response to) New Deal labor policy reflected the unusual social and political circumstances of the ongoing economic crisis. Industries and firms found themselves constantly adjusting their goals and priorities to the implementation and administration of federal

20 "Memorandum of Conversation with Arthur Young [US Steel]" (3 April 1934), Marshall Office File 265:1, NRA Records; *Fortune* cited in Vittoz, *New Deal Labor Policy*, 150; "Steel, Automobile, and Labor Situations based on a Conference with E. S[tettinius] and a GM Executive [Steven DuBrul?]" (20 September 1934), File 101, Sachs Papers; *Wall Street Journal* clipping, 12 March 1936, File 1139:2, PRR Papers; Mississippi Lime and Material to Johnson (12 March 1934), General Corr. File 5, NLRB Records.

21 (Quote) Filene in U.S. Senate, Committee on Finance, *Investigation of the National Recovery Administration* (Washington, 1935), 1434; (quote) Leeds to Cooke (3 June 1932), File 79, Morris Cooke Papers, FDRPL; "GMAC Unemployment Refund Plan," File 28; "Stimulation of Auto Sales . . ." (May 1933), File 92, Sachs Papers.

law, to the social and political threat posed by the Depression-era labor movement, and finally to the range of what seemed reasonable and possible at any point in time. Passage of an equivalent to the Wagner Act, of course, would have been unthinkable before 1929 (when concessions to workers were unnecessary) or immediately after 1929 (when other approaches to recovery and regulation had not been exhausted). Faced with a choice between an unfettered open shop and federal labor law, U.S. employers invariably chose the former. But in 1934–35, employers faced a more complex choice – bounded by the legacy of NRA, by the persistence of the Depression, and by the unprecedented managerial and political threat of organized labor – between the risks of ignoring the labor problem and the benefits of accommodating it on the most conservative terms possible. That some saw this as no choice at all should not confuse the fact that, for most, the Wagner Act was a necessary concession under unhappy circumstances.

Although arguments from the business community shaped federal legislation, they scarcely constituted support for the Wagner Act. Scrambled by both the persistence of the Depression and the demise of the NRA, business strategies ranged from the determination of a few "labor capitalists" to regulate industry through federal labor law to a disparate range of hopes and fears that such law might at least be tolerable or useful. For most, however, the Wagner Act broke open a nest of contradictions that Hoover's Department of Commerce and the NRA had scrupulously avoided. Business interests demanded regulation of competitors and freedom for themselves. Those who sought the stability and certainty of coercive agreements also demanded the freedom to bail out of such agreements at a moment's notice. All sought the benefits of a regulated market without any of its political or pecuniary costs. Limited economic horizons and chronic political anxiety left individual industries and firms without a firm grasp on their own best interests or the course of public policy. Even those who argued that the Wagner Act might regulate competition, divert radical unionism, or increase aggregate purchasing power realized the risks and dilemmas attached to any federal legal solution to such profound problems of collective action.

While support from business was sporadic and uncertain, its opposition to the Wagner Act was often superficial and cynical. Vocal opponents owed their competitive status to low wages, feared the loss of the "right to manage," or were unable (for various reasons) to pass on the costs of unionization in the form of higher prices.[22] All the major business organizations, pressed

22 The congressional testimony of "company unionists" did little to gird the conser-

by such interests, closed ranks against the Wagner Act, but its opponents were hard-pressed to defend their position, offer alternatives, or ignore the compelling links between business strategy, the NRA experience, and the Wagner Act. And in some respects, employers found their deeply rooted anxieties over the "right to manage" turned against them; in exaggerating the independence and importance of company unions, most found it difficult to sell the managerial threat of real unions. As an SCC lobbyist reported:

> Testimony of opponents has been made less effective because many of them don't know – or at any rate can't explain – what it is they don't like in the Wagner Bill. What frequently happens is something like this: An employer or an employee representative describes a successful representation plan and urges the committee not to recommend the Wagner Bill because he wants to continue the plan that has been satisfactory in his company. Then Wagner or [Senator] Walsh ask him just what provisions of the bill are contrary to the kind of "company unionism" he has described. The witness hesitates, stammers, and finally withdraws in confusion, leaving Wagner's assertion that his bill will do no harm.

In May 1935, Alexander Sachs noted that "the position of business, represented by the former chief opponents of the bill – the General Motors–DuPont interests – has itself become confused and compromising." In the context of the persistent Depression, pining for a return to the labor relations of the precrash era scored few political points.[23]

Most employers shared a peculiarly short-sighted view of emerging federal labor policy. They liked the industrial autonomy of the NRA but recognized the futility of supporting it precisely because it was poorly and inconsistently enforced. They reacted anxiously to the development of the majority rule doctrine, embraced the basic tenets of the March 1934 auto industry settlement, and argued strenuously that the Wagner Act went "too far." Yet while many wanted to use the template cut in the auto industry as

vative position. When a Senate committee asked members of Jones & Laughlin's company union about further testimony, the workers walked over to the Jones & Laughlin executive a few seats away to see how they should reply. As one observer noted, "The Jones & Laughlin officer frantically waved them away and groaned to his neighbor, 'This is embarrassing.' " See Blankenhorn to Wagner (28 May 1935), File 36, Wagner Papers.

23 (Quote) E.S. Cowdrick Memo (27 March 1935), in U.S. Senate, Subcommittee of the Committee on Education and Labor, *Violations of Free Speech and the Rights of Labor*, Part 45, *Memorandum Concerning The Special Conference Committee* (Washington, 1939), 17016–17; Minutes of the Employment Relations Committee (1 November 1934), File V:1, NAM Papers; Roper to FDR (22 May 1935), OF 3:1; Business Advisory Council [BAC], "Report of the Committee on the Wagner National Labor Relations Bill" (10 April 1935), OF 3q, FDR Papers; (quote) "Labor Situation" (17 May 1935), File 123, Sachs Papers.

a defense against the further encroachment of unions and bureaucrats, most also appreciated its time-worn contradictions. In late 1934, a GM consultant complained that the Roosevelt administration seemed "constitutionally reluctant to make clear decisions" and feared that "contradictions in basic policies can no longer be resolved by verbal coordination and twitting of opponents."[24] Most appreciated that the experimental enthusiasm of the NRA would not simply melt away and that recovery depended on something different rather than something less.

Through 1935, many stumbled along with the reasoning of the Wagner Act, hoping to avoid or salvage or exploit its provisions. Industrial unionism under federal jurisdiction was not, for business, an ideal state of affairs in an ideal world. But faced with persistent economic depression and industrial conflict, it was certainly the best of the available options and probably the only means of reaching the organizational and consumerist goals mishandled so badly by the NRA. The Wagner Act, as a business consultant to Secretary of the Treasury Morgenthau reasoned, provided a "working basis for developing the increased jobs and purchasing power on which prosperity for the nation as a whole depends." In turn, while many employers candidly feared the impact of the Wagner Act, they seemed ready to play by the new rules once they were in place. "The question," noted Sachs, was not whether business would be penalized by the law, but "whether business [was] sufficiently willing to experiment with a governmental labor conciliation mechanism to adopt the Wagner Bill to its own needs."[25]

In the end, the vagaries of the business position were less important than the administration's spin on it. With business hopelessly divided and pressures for recovery and economic justice increasing from other quarters, New Dealers moved to protect their flanks and extend the strategies embodied by the NRA according to their own view of the legal, political, and regulatory requisites for recovery. The administrative and economic embarrassment of the NRA precluded another political attempt to please all by allowing them to interpret (or ignore) the law according to their own interests. New Dealers did not see the Wagner Act as a radical departure from the NRA. "The

24 Roper to FDR (20 June 1935), OF 407; Teagle to FDR (27 March 1934), OF 716:1; Roper to McIntyre (11 June 1934), OF 716:1; Alfred Reeves [American Management Association] to FDR (5 April 1935), OF 102:2, FDR Papers; miscellaneous business responses to labor legislation (1934), File 228:1698, Wagner Papers; "Thirty Hour Week," Industrial Advisory Board [IAB] File 358, NRA Records; (quote) "Labor Situation and its Implications" (5 September 1934), File 123, Sachs Papers.
25 J. Roche memo for Morgenthau (4 January 1936), 51:19–20, Morgenthau Diaries, FDRPL; "Labor Situation" (17 May 1935), File 123, Sachs Papers.

underlying principle of the Wagner Bill," noted one New Deal economist, was simply to "eliminate (from the standpoint of employer-employee rela- tions) the necessity of codes in every industry." The NLRB's Millis agreed that "the Wagner Bill, in the limitations and responsibilities placed upon employers, does nothing more than confirm the interpretations of 7(a) made by our Board." Indeed, many saw the act as not only a step beyond the "intellectual dishonesty" of NRA labor policy but also as a sincerely pro- business alternative. "Efficient industry depends for stability upon arrange- ments with organized labor," argued Leon Henderson; "industry has failed to appreciate the protection these [Section 7a] decisions afford against the irresponsible demands of minority unions."[26]

The Roosevelt administration also found compelling legal and adminis- trative reasons to proceed with the Wagner Act. For the remnants of the NRA and NLRB bureaucracies, the act promised a foundation of "profes- sional lawyerly standards and procedural precision" upon which to base federal policy. Through the Wagner Act, the administration also avoided flirting with further revision of the antitrust laws and exceeding its authority in intrastate commerce. Federally protected unions (which were exempt from antitrust prosecution and unconstrained by the commerce clause) could provide the regulatory force that had been historically frustrated by feder- alism and competitive self-interest. These ideas were familiar to some in- dustries and well rehearsed at the federal level in the Transportation and Railroad Labor Acts of 1920, 1926, and 1934. In the aftermath of the NRA, such concerns with bureaucratic procedure and precision overwhelmed any more substantive defense of workers' rights. "We are part of a competitive economy in which . . . various groups are struggling for immediate economic advantage," argued a Twentieth Century Fund report, adding that "the organization of workers and their choice of representatives are, after all, only means to an end – the establishment and observance of written agree- ments."[27]

26 J. Miller to Wagner (7 May 1934), File 11:1; Miller memo for Wagner (7 May 1934), Marshall Office File 265:1, NRA Records; (quote) Millis to FDR (21 June 1936), OF 716, FDR Papers; Biddle in Senate, *Investigation of the NRA*, 1538–41; (quote) "Suggestions for Revision of NRA" (n.d.), File 6, Leon Henderson Papers, FDRPL; NLRB official (E. Smith) quoted in Tomlins, *State and the Unions*, 143–44; Milton Derber, "Growth and Expansion," *Labor and the New Deal*, ed. Milton Derber and Edwin Young (Madison, 1957), 8–9; Harris, "The Snares of Liberalism," 169.
27 Tomlins, *State and the Unions*, 132–40 (quote, 133); Lyon, *NRA*, 263–64; on par- allels between the NLRA and Railway Labor Act, see "Railroad Labor Act of 1926," File 952:13; File 494:10–14, PRR Papers; Twentieth Century Fund report (coau-

Aside from the organizational promise of federal labor policy, the administration also hoped that it would address the debilitating imbalance between production and consumption. Many of the strongest proponents of the act were inspired by a loosely Keynesian attachment to income redistribution. "The machinery of the codes, though establishing certain minimum-wage requirements and largely eliminating child labor, has not yet effected any real distribution of income," as Francis Biddle argued; "if collective bargaining may be effective for such a purpose, by all means let us attempt it." Indeed, Wagner and his advisors were as attentive to the collapse of purchasing power as they were to more abstract questions of workers' rights. While at times blithely accepting the advertised virtues of company unions, Wagner consistently argued that they had "failed dismally to standardize or improve wage levels, . . . a general [question] whose sweep embraces whole industries, or even the Nation." An early draft of the Wagner Act noted that "the failure of the total volume of wage payments to advance as fast as production . . . has resulted in inadequate purchasing power."[28]

Although the consumption issue was, for many, the most compelling aspect of the act, not all members of the Roosevelt administration were captivated by its reasoning. "In any given industry or group of industries," argued Adolph Berle, "the result of an agreement between labor and employing groups may very well be the same as the result of an agreement among employing groups, namely, to raise the price." Others agreed that union agreements in coal or construction amounted to little more than bilateral monopolies that thrived on the disorganization of workers in other industries and that the extension of this pattern of bargaining throughout the industrial economy would be merely inflationary. Clearly the redistributive implications of federal labor law were problematic and ill-conceived. Between 1933 and 1937, nonunion wages outstripped union wages as em-

thored by retailer Edward Filene, NRA compliance director William Davis, labor economists William Leiserson and Sumner Slichter, and paper manufacturer Henry Dennison) cited in Christopher Tomlins, "The New Deal, Collective Bargaining, and the Triumph of Industrial Pluralism," *Industrial and Labor Relations Review* 39 (1985): 27–28.

28 Senate, *National Labor Relations Board*, 34–35, 47–48, 75–77 (Biddle quote, 77), 95–99, 125; Szelski to Henderson (2 October 1934), File 6, Henderson Papers; R.W. Fleming, "The Significance of the Wagner Act," in *Labor and the New Deal*, 130–36; Millis to FDR (21 June 1936), OF 716, FDR Papers; Steven Fraser, *Labor Will Rule: Sidney Hillman and the Rise of American Labor* (New York: Free Press, 1991), 261–70; Wagner quoted in Tomlins, *State and the Unions*, 123, n.64; Leon Keyserling drafts of the NLRA (n.d.), File 28, William Leiserson Papers, State Historical Society of Wisconsin, Madison.

ployers tried to stem organization with preemptive wage hikes. Industrial unionism simply skewed the distribution of incomes between the organized and the unorganized. Across the economy, the share of national income counted as wages was unaffected by the organizational turmoil of the 1930s, and within most unionized industries, the value-added going to wages remained unchanged or actually fell.[29]

Finally, of course, these were all intensely political decisions. A routinely chaotic pattern of expediency, constituency service, and institutional horse-trading at the best of times, American politics in the 1930s was scrambling through a protracted crisis of legitimacy, credibility, and social disorder. New Dealers were not merely counting votes during the development of federal labor policy, but legislative debate and executive initiatives heated up noticeably as November of 1934 and 1936 approached. At least one employer dismissed early drafts of the Wagner Act as products of the "political nature of the present election year." The Roosevelt administration was also forced to acknowledge the progressive leanings of many local and state politicians, many of whom not only recognized the numerical power of workers but also proved less willing than they had in the past to provide tacit or direct assistance to union-busting employers. And many felt that intransigent employers undercut both the efforts of more progressive firms and the political and economic stability of the nation itself. "America is now sitting on a political volcano," warned an NRA official; ". . . [the Wagner Act is] inducing industry to take those steps that will protect us from disorder, violence, and bloodshed."[30]

The Wagner Act passed without a clear purpose or constituency. Although many in business and government saw it as a logical legacy of the NRA, few (especially in business) saw it as a necessary or attractive inheritance. Certainly the act embodied much more than business objectives.

29 (Quote) "Memorandum Report on the NRA" (n.d.), File 19, Adolph Berle Papers, FDRPL; DuBrul to Means (11 October 1934), File 2, Gardiner Means Papers, FDRPL; Harold M. Levinson, *Unionism, Wage Trends, and Income Distribution, 1914–1947* (Ann Arbor, 1951), 47–79, 82–92, 112–13. Union members hoped that the Wagner Act would support wages, in part because they expected the passage of the Social Security Act to cut into their pay (see "Approaching Labor Cloud" [8 April 1935], File 123, Sachs Papers).

30 (Quote) "Labor Situation: Notes of Conference with Leading Members of the Automobile Labor Board" (25 May 1934), File 123, Sachs Papers; on local politics, see Vittoz, *New Deal Labor Policy*, 157; Perkins to Mayor Entremount [Reading, PA] (10 August 1933); J.M. Wright to Louis Howe (16 October 1933), OF 407b:5, FDR Papers; (quote) Rastall Memo on Wagner Act (14 March 1935), IAB General Corr. File 358:30, NRA Records.

Chronic industrial conflict, electoral politics, the legal and administrative chaos of the NRA, and political perceptions of business objectives all shaped federal policy and narrowed business's options. In reasoning that was part desperate (hoping to salvage the recovery program), part cynical (hoping to attract business support), and part sincere (hoping to rescue business from itself), New Dealers stressed the continuities between the NRA and the Wagner Act and seemed convinced that the latter would accomplish what the former could not: politically defensible competitive stability coupled with a renewal of mass-purchasing power.

Realists and Reactionaries: Industry Under the Wagner Act

The short-sighted confusion that characterized the debate over the Wagner Act was even more pronounced once the act had passed. Business response was tempered by the widespread belief (or wish) that the law shared the shaky legal legs of the NRA. Employers, unions, and legislators braced for a battery of constitutional tests but were unwilling or unable to ignore the law in the time required for a legal challenge and were not at all certain that such a challenge would be successful. In the months to follow, the administrative and legal premises of the new law were, as one student notes, pieced together "on a crisis by crisis basis."[31] In many industries and firms, the Wagner Act twisted and distorted business strategies by curtailing the option of the open shop and establishing a new set of constraints under which employers would have to deal with the organizational and material liability of labor. In late 1935, employers entered an uncertain era of labor relations. If unions maintained their militancy and their gains were legally protected, it was unclear how long open-shop stalwarts could hold out. Business's routine defense of the right to manage became more urgent and anxious as workers took advantage of the new law. And even those who had toyed with notions of regulatory unionism before and after the NRA began to fear that enforceable labor standards were coming at too great a price.[32]

31 (Quote) Gross, *Making of the National Labor Relations Board*, 15. On the legal refinement and definition of the Wagner Act, see also Karl Klare, "Judicial Deradicalization of the Wagner Act and the Origins of Modern Legal Consciousness, 1937–1941," *Minnesota Law Review* 62 (1978): 265–339; Tomlins, *The State and the Unions*, 99–243; James Atelson, *Values and Assumptions in American Labor Law* (Amherst, 1983), passim; Joel Rogers, "Divide and Conquer: Further 'Reflections on the Distinctive Character of American Labor Laws,' " *Wisconsin Law Review* 1 (1990):1–148.

32 My discussion of business response to the Wagner Act draws deeply from Vittoz, *New Deal Labor Policy*, 153–73; and Harris, *Right to Manage*, 15–40.

Perhaps more importantly, uncertainty about the new law and markedly different patterns of militancy and organization immediately scrambled business strategies. Leading mass-production firms feared unionization but feared its haphazard progress within industries and regions even more. Many employers were concerned less with the advance of organized labor per se than with the potential for uneven gains within industries and the prospect that leading firms would be the first and only targets of an emboldened union movement. Their ability and willingness to fight labor constrained, such firms were more likely to ensure that industrial unionism took reasonably conservative forms and left no competitors untouched. "As long as we have this [Wagner] Act with us," reasoned Walter Drew of NAM and the anti-union Metal Trades Association, "it ought to be made to apply *in as wide a scope as possible* in order to stop chiseling." Others concurred that collective bargaining seemed to hold some organizational promise for "collective" groups of employers. Delegates to a 1937 meeting of NAM's National Industrial Council noted approvingly the experience of the Window Glass industry, which had emerged unscathed from an antitrust suit because its "combination in restraint of trade" had simply been a collective bargaining agreement between the Glass Manufacturers' Association and the union.[33]

The Wagner Act had its greatest impact in mass-production industries. Yet even in these bastions of managerial conservatism, labor relations would be less a revival of old anxieties than a practical response to new circumstances. In steel, rubber, auto, pulp and paper, lumber, chemicals, and the like, organized labor was historically weak, and employers were wary of the strategic utility of unions or uniform labor standards. But the initiative of workers after 1933 and the political logic of regulatory unionism quickly thrust the issue of unionization into the boardrooms of even these traditionally open-shop concerns. Most mass-production firms responded with bitter, even violent, opposition. At the same time, however, leading firms practically and haphazardly began to include the prospect or reality of unionization in their competitive calculations. In 1935, as Sachs observed, conservative employers "frankly relied upon the Courts to compel modification of such elements as business considers vicious in the Wagner Bill, [but felt] that the Wagner Bill will be annoying but not dangerous." Sachs went on to note a "change in the industrial attitude towards the Wagner Bill" among many employers who "wonder[ed] whether something [could not] be made out of

33 "Proceedings of the National Industrial Council" (April 22, 1937), 13 (Drew quote), 14–16, 41–42, (in imprints collection, Hagley Museum).

the Wagner Bill in the direction of substituting governmental avenues of conciliation for the threatened detours of labor into disorder."[34]

Mass-production firms sat at a strategic watershed. Most clung to the managerial freedom of the open shop. But for many, competitive conditions, market stagnation, and the threat of unionization rendered such recalcitrance impractical, dangerous, and unrealistic. By the late 1930s, many were resigned to the new state of affairs, hoping at least to ensure orderly and complete unionization and to avoid the ultimate nightmare of radical unionism. As one executive confided of his first contact with the newly formed Congress of Industrial Organizations (CIO):

> We signed up for two reasons. First, we believe the union has come to stay in our industry; and second, we knew we were the next citadel for assault by the CIO, and, in point of fact, we *had* to sign. Financially, we were in no position to stand a two to three month shutdown of production or to carry the ball for the rest of the industry. Since signing the contract we have had little trouble; in fact we dumped into the lap of the union a lot of routine grievances we used to worry about.

Labor relations under the act quickly reflected its business-minded premises. In the end, many found that the costs of complying with the Wagner Act and encouraging "business unionism" paled beside the costs, actual or potential, of persistent conflict.[35]

Consider the post-Wagner steel industry. Although united in its opposition to both Section 7a and the Wagner Act, the industry's experience before and after the NRA increasingly pointed to the regulatory potential of industrial unionism. Decades of complex shop-floor management, the erosion of U.S. Steel's price leadership, a dismal NRA experience, and the status of leading U.S. mills in a recovering world industry all pushed steel executives to go "so far as to say that, given a progressive, cooperative union such as those which they understood existed in the apparel industries, [they] might not be averse to trying out a collective bargaining relationship." Given chronic excess capacity and the decline of U.S. Steel, success of the Steel Workers' Organizing Committee (SWOC) seemed "a means of achieving the objectives of price stability during a period when conventional methods had apparently failed." As industry leaders reasoned, "If [CIO and SWOC leader] John L. Lewis could furnish the industry with a floor under wages,

---

34 "Labor Situation" (17 May 1935), File 123, Sachs Papers.
35 Employer quoted anonymously in "The Industrial War," *Fortune* 16 (November 1937), 180; the circumstances and sentiments suggest he was an executive of U.S. Steel.

could one be certain that his demand for recognition was the knock of doom and not of opportunity?"[36]

For calculated business reasons, U.S. Steel executives signed a contract with SWOC in late February 1937; the firm's decision was primarily a means of reasserting its price leadership. As early as 1934, Myron Taylor of U.S. Steel had confided to Roosevelt that "we know of no way of meeting this [competitive] situation and insuring peace in the industry other than to grant [a] wage increase of 10 percent and make the necessary increase in prices." For U.S. Steel, SWOC made such wage increases palatable by making them binding on rival mills. Historically, competitors had either mimicked U.S. Steel's wages as part of the price agreement or used them as a benchmark for wage and price chiseling. The presence of an industrial union closed this avenue of competition and ensured that the costs of unionization would eventually be borne by the industry as a whole. As the *Wall Street Journal* noted, steel had "decided to trust a combination of agreed wage standards and employer self-interest to prevent renewal of predatory competition." Uniform labor costs, enforced by organized labor, became the foundation of a new price front. As Thomas Lamont (representing U.S. Steel's principal creditor, J.P. Morgan) noted in 1938, the maintenance of the SWOC agreement would keep U.S. Steel on top by preventing "the spectacle of 'the independents' jumping in and slashing wages roughshod."[37]

36 Daugherty et al., *The Economics of the Iron Steel Industry*, 2:982; Senate, *National Labor Relations Board*, 359–404 (for steel's opposition to Wagner); Lloyd Ulman, "Influences of Economic Environment on the Structure of the Steel Workers Union," *Proceedings of the Industrial Relations Research Association* 14 (1961): 228 (quote), 231–32. Frederick Harbison, "Collective Bargaining in the Steel Industry," manuscript in File 256, NAM Papers, echoes this point: "Some executives went so far as to admit that national collective bargaining might be beneficial in stabilizing labor conditions . . . if only they could be carried on with a conservative and responsible organization." See Vittoz, *New Deal Labor Policy*, 158–64; David Brody, "The Origins of Modern Steel Unionism: The SWOC Era," in *Forging a Union of Steel*, ed. Paul Clark (Ithaca, 1987), 17–23.

37 Transcript of telephone conversation, Taylor to FDR (27 March 1934), OF 342; "Without Benefit of NRA," *Wall Street Journal*, 10 June 1935, in OF 466:12; "Facts About Republic Steel," OF 4–7b:11; (quote) Lamont to FDR (30 June 1938), PSF 156, FDR Papers. See also Follansbee Brothers [Steel] to Manny Strauss (18 November 1929), Presidential File 88, Hoover Papers; Vittoz, *New Deal Labor Policy*, 163; "It Happened In Steel," *Fortune* 15 (May 1937), 179; U.S. Congress, Temporary National Economic Committee, *Hearings: Investigation of the Concentration of Economic Power*, vol. 26, *Iron and Steel Industry* (Washington, 1940), 10496–97, 10527–28, 10710; Robert Tilove, *Collective Bargaining in the Steel Industry* (Philadelphia, 1948), 27, 29–30.

Coming just four days after U. S. Steel and Bethlehem had joined the International Steel Cartel (ISC), the SWOC agreement also marked an attempt by the industry leader to gain a leg up in international markets. U.S. Steel looked to international markets not only as a means of breaking the spiral of domestic competition (and barring European mills from exacerbating it) but also as a means of participating in the European-led recovery of the world steel industry. In the year before the SWOC–U.S. Steel agreement, U.S. mills had increased their utilized capacity from 70 to almost 90 percent. Much of this activity was spurred by U.S. naval contracts and European armaments orders. The provisions of the SWOC agreement echoed the recently passed Walsh-Healy Act, which set basic hour and wage conditions on government contracts. And foreign orders, while not conditional on standards in U.S. plants, were conditional on peaceful and constant production. "Taylor signed up with Lewis," noted one observer, "because of heavy orders from England offered only on the basis of uninterrupted delivery."[38]

U.S. Steel also saw SWOC, and later the United Steel Workers of America (USWA), as a means of sorting out the industry's chaotic organization of jobs and work. Although initially perceived as a means of segmenting the interests of a homogeneous workforce, elaborate job designations and promotional ladders had backfired and made any intelligent analysis of production impossible. "A reliable contract with a vertical, industrial union such as that being organized by the SWOC," concluded the editors of *Fortune*, "would constitute a first necessary step toward a new and simplified industrial technique." Throughout the 1920s and under the NRA, the industry had installed company unions to forestall real unionization and in recognition of compelling problems of organization, authority, and representation on the shop floor. When push came to shove, both SWOC and U.S. Steel found company unions (which, as *Fortune* admitted, "had a boomerang action in many mills, serving to educate the workers in organization practices") a useful vehicle for genuine organization. For its part, the USWA welcomed its managerial role and in 1940 published a lengthy and sympathetic analysis of the industry's organizational woes.[39]

38 See Richard Lauderbaugh, *American Steelmakers and the Coming of the Second World War* (Ann Arbor, 1976); Ervin Hexner, "American Participation in the International Steel Cartel," *Southern Economic Journal* 8 (1941): 54–79; William Hogan, *Economic History of the Iron and Steel Industry* (Lexington, 1971), 3:1170; Daniel Roper, "Economic Effects of the Rearmament Program," (n.d.), PSF 73, FDR Papers; Vittoz, *New Deal Labor Policy*, 162; (quote) "Strike News" (n.d.), File 123, Sachs Papers.
39 "It Happened in Steel," 179–80; "Supplementary Report on Steel" (n.d.), and

Finally, U.S. Steel had to consider the timing of SWOC's threat. The industry was recovering rapidly in 1936–37. With the specter of the GM sit-down strike, the prospect of foreign munitions orders, and restrictions on federal contracts fresh in their minds, U.S. Steel executives fully realized that "to become tied up in a labor war would be to forfeit net profits the like of which had not been seen since before the depression." A full year before the U.S Steel–SWOC pact, the *Wall Street Journal* noted that "the [SWOC] drive comes at a time when the industry is just emerging from the red, and may therefore be expected to prove reluctant to accept a period of expensive strikes." *Business Week* agreed that U.S. Steel "realized that it was picked by the CIO as a 'fall guy' for the industry . . . and saw no good purpose in being tied up as General Motors was, while its competitors got the business." U.S. Steel's decision may have been constrained by its position in the industry and by the competitive problems and prospects of the late 1930s, but it was a prudent and rational decision under the circumstances.[40]

U.S. Steel clearly hoped to ensure unfettered production and reverse its competitive decline by dragging other members of the industry into the agreement with SWOC. Meanwhile, SWOC's hope had always been to organize U.S. Steel as an entering wedge into the industry. These strategies converged in the secretive bargaining between Lewis and Taylor in early 1937. That unionization in steel came in 1937 and not earlier reflected both market recovery and the influence of the Wagner Act – which guaranteed SWOC *and the management of U.S. Steel* that a union-centered organizational strategy would last. Of course, U.S. Steel's strategy didn't work very well. "Little Steel" grabbed an immediate competitive advantage by holding out through the recession of 1937 and resisting SWOC until 1941. Even at this point, executives of the smaller mills pressed for plant bargaining so that their competitive gains of the last decade would not be wiped out by U.S. Steel's puppeteering of the SWOC agreement. Ironically, the union

"Statement by P. Murray" (8 November 1936), Reel 1, Katherine Ellickson [CIO] Papers, FDRPL; Harbison, "Collective Bargaining in the Steel Industry," 1–8; Robert Brooks, *As Steel Goes: Unionism in a Basic Industry* (New Haven, 1940), 1–8, 75–109; Lauderbaugh, *American Steel Makers*, 93; Harold Ruttenburg, "The Strategy of Industrial Peace," *Harvard Business Review* 17 (1938): 159–76; Philip Nyden, *Steelworkers Rank-and-File: The Political Economy of a Union Reform Movement* (New York, 1984), 25; Morris Cooke and Philip Murray, *Production Problems* (New York, 1940).

40 "It Happened in Steel," 91, 179; "Steel and Labor," *Wall Street Journal*, 6 June 1936, in File 1139:2, PRR Papers; Vittoz, *New Deal Labor Policy*, 162 (*Business Week* quote).

soon found itself protecting (through direct concessions) jobs in the smaller, marginal firms that were the targets of pattern bargaining.[41]

In the auto industry, the experience of GM echoed these patterns of compromise and strategic self-interest. While the revelations of the La-Follette Committee and the introduction of the sit-down strike strategy testified to the stubborn antiunionism of auto employers, business conditions and competitive strategies quickly eroded any united front. For the major auto firms, the principal threat posed by the auto workers after 1933 was not simply unionism, but factional, radical, or inconsistent varieties thereof. At a meeting with NRA officials in July 1933, Walter Chrysler (with an eye on the absent and uncooperative Ford) emphasized only that they wanted "every advantage and disadvantage equal." William Knudsen of GM went considerably further, musing that he and his colleagues would have no objection to a single industrial union of auto workers. During code negotiations, GM's Sloan maintained he "would rather be in the hands of the labor unions than in the hands of the politicians." And a year later, GM's Donaldson Brown would add, "I think there are very few in the automobile industry who are not ready to subscribe to the principle of collective bargaining provided that principle can be applied soundly."[42]

The Big Three, unlike the management of U.S. Steel, saw little regulatory utility in the prospect of a single industrial union. But the threat of radical unionism, in auto plants and in "bottleneck" tool-and-die, glass, rubber, and parts plants, was a constant and serious threat, and during the NRA years, this inspired a great deal of confusion. Employers objected to the doctrine of majority rule and clung to the divide-and-conquer reasoning of "proportional representation" of the March 1934 auto settlement. At the same time, GM executives expressed grave doubts about the implications of multiple bargaining and saw proportional representation as a stopgap measure founded on union weakness. With sufficient strength, the claims of minority unions could pose real problems. Majority rule, as DuBrul argued, could "frequently aid the management in cleaning radicals out of both the union and the plant" and seemed "much better than being caught in the jurisdictional nutcracker of the craft unions." Employers were torn between con-

---

41 See Address by Ernest Weir before Economic Club of Chicago (1 December 1937), File 125-2, American Iron and Steel Institute Papers, Hagley Museum; Tilove, *Collective Bargaining*, 34; Harbison, "Collective Bargaining."

42 Sidney Fine, *The Automobile under the Blue Eagle* (Ann Arbor, 1963), 55–56; Donaldson Brown to John Raskob (21 September 1934), File 278, Raskob Papers; W.H. McPherson, "Automobiles," in *How Collective Bargaining Works*, ed. Harry Millis (New York, 1942), 571–630.

tinuing to fight (and thereby radicalize) workers and directing organization along a conservative path. "The bigger the plant is that is unionized," added DuBrul, "the harder the problem of control is *unless the employer assists the union in controlling the men.*"[43]

The March 1934 settlement had struck a precarious balance. Industry leaders were "tremendously happy" to be released from the strictures of NLB labor policy but less than sure of the long-term viability of multiple bargaining through the Automobile Labor Board. For labor, the settlement was disappointing but necessary. Employers used spring "model year" lay-offs as a pretext for winnowing out radicals and troublemakers; an immediate deal was needed to grant some antidiscrimination and grievance machinery, but the AFL also had little faith in the March agreement. Through the fall of 1934, employers became increasingly anxious about the abrogation of the settlement by either side and the threat of labor militancy. GM even minimized model changes in order to sidestep the tool-and-die unions. By the new year, industry advisers to the NRA noted a "sizeable percentage of workers obviously tending towards communistic points of view . . . a real danger for the government, for the automobile manufacturers, and for the American Federation of Labor." Their recommendation, seconded by executives at GM and Chrysler (Ford was still shunning Washington), was constructive cooperation with conservative unionists.[44]

In 1935, the uneasy truce in the auto industry began to erode. GM executives feared strikes not only in their own plants but also in the vulnerable rubber and glass plants upon which they depended. GM and the other major firms were also in the midst of a relative boom in auto sales. Sachs noted the promise of steady profits in the spring season, but warned that the "labor situation still looms." As the Wagner Act passed, auto firms seemed determined to continue labor relations in the spirit of the 1934 settlement, hoping,

43 DuBrul Memo (n.d.), File 28, Sachs Papers (emphasis added). Concerning the conservative unionists DuBrul was courting, see Report of F.J. Dillon, *Proceedings of the First Constitutional Convention of the United Automobile Workers* (August, 1935), which castigates union radicals and promises a "mutually satisfactory employer-employee relationship" (31).

44 (Quote) Roger Keeran, *The Communist Party and the Auto Workers Union* (New York, 1980), 109; "Final Report of the Automobile Labor Board," (n.d.), OF 102b; E. Herrick to FDR (21 March 1934), OF 407b:8; W. Green to FDR (11 September 1934), OF 407b:8; Green to FDR (6 November 1934), OF 466:4; Automobile Manufacturers' Association to FDR (14 January 1935), OF 466:4; George Berry to FDR (29 January 1935), OF 466:4, FDR Papers; "Steel, Automobile, and Labor Situations based on a conference with E. S[tettinius] and [Steven DuBrul]" (20 September 1934), File 101, Sachs Papers.

as Knudsen argued, that collective bargaining could still mean "bargaining without letting the other side do the collecting." By late 1936, GM's investment in the upcoming model year was considerable. According to Sachs, auto markets were "extremely bullish" and "strikes [were] the only adverse possibility." Despite the extremely vulnerable position in which GM found itself, the corporation did little about the labor problem except wishing it would go away. The threat of radical unionism and the recalcitrance of Ford distracted any functional solution. By December, GM even considered engineering a general strike in order to "inconvenience the public" and turn popular opinion against labor.[45]

By this time, however, GM had lost the upper hand. Militant unionists had continued their efforts with little regard for the NRA, the 1934 settlement, or the Wagner Act (although the latter allowed organizers to overcome some of the factionalism that had plagued auto workers). In the last hours of 1936, "guerilla forces of wrench-wielding unionists" began a series of sit-down strikes in GM plants. The United Auto Workers (UAW) chose GM in part because Ford was too formidable and in part because Chrysler, Hudson, and Studebaker depended on GM components. GM's alternatives were limited. Although the strikers won little sympathy in Washington, an effective federal settlement (after the debacle of 1934) was unlikely. And Governor Murphy of Michigan not only denied GM the courtesy of strike-breaking state officers but shocked the firm with an "equivocal attitude" toward the strikers and a public call for the company to allow the UAW exclusive bargaining. As the strike wore on, GM lost spring orders to Ford and Chrysler, and DuBrul noted gloomily that "unless [GM] made satisfactory concessions it would be losing the greater part of this year's market."[46]

45 Vittoz, *New Deal Labor Policy*, 154–58; (quote) "Approaching Labor Cloud" (8 April 1935), File 123; (quote) "Notes on Automobile Show" (10 June 1935), (Knudsen quote) "Automobile Notes" (22 July 1935), (quote) "Automobile Industry" (9 July 1936), "Automobile Industry" (4 November 1936), and "Impressions of Labor Situation" (31 December 1936), File 92, Sachs Papers.

46 Keeran, *Communist Party and the Auto Workers*, 77–99; William McPherson, *Labor Relations in the Automobile Industry* (Washington, 1940), 16–33, 38–39; Vittoz, *New Deal Labor Policy*, 156; Seltzer Memo: Automobile Labor (5 January 1937), 51:48–49; (quote) "Developments in GM Situation" (8 January 1937), 51:144, Morgenthau Diaries; "Motor Industry" (24 February 1937), and "Notes on Automobile Industry" (6 May 1938), File 92; DuBrul quoted in "Labor" (n.d.), File 123, Sachs Papers; "Memorandum for the President" (8 February 1937), OF 407b; "Auto Workers Strike 1937," OF 407b, FDR Papers.

Compelling business considerations pressed GM to settle quickly. GM certainly did not welcome being singled out for special attention by the CIO, but its response was a product of short-term self-interest in a recovering economy and a less-than-certain long-term calculation of the union's ability to govern industrial competition and internal labor problems. "The policies of such managements as General Motors and U.S. Steel point towards workable cooperation with the Lewis-CIO regime," reasoned Sachs, "in the conviction that that regime is not going to interfere but may rather promote efficiency and quiet." A contemporary student of industry labor relations agreed that "a small but gradually increasing minority [of automobile executives] granted almost complete acceptance to the union in the hope of gaining its cooperation in the handling of basic problems of labor management."[47]

Other mass-production industries echoed this realistic response to the Wagner Act and the CIO. In the rubber industry, excess capacity, chiseling by small firms, and pressure from bankers and auto makers to fight the union forestalled any easy rapprochement. Goodyear, Goodrich, Firestone, and U.S. Rubber held off unions with welfare capitalism and no less than six preemptive wage increases between 1933 and 1937. But, as Howell Harris notes, "constructive accommodation to the new circumstances" made better business sense than belligerency or violence, especially in the single-consumer rubber industry. U.S. Rubber (the only major tire manufacturer not located in Akron) embarked on a gradual and peaceful recognition of the United Rubber Workers (URW). The other "rubber barons" fought the URW at every turn and waited until the Wagner Act had passed its last constitutional test in 1937 before entering into collective agreements. And labor relations remained complicated by regional competition. URW agreements were confined to Akron and Detroit while, by the late 1920s, most rubber production had drifted to the South and West. Because low-wage competition came not from independents but from Sunbelt branches of the

---

47 William Leuchtenberg, *Franklin D. Roosevelt and the New Deal* (New York, 1963), 240; Steve Jeffreys, *Management and Managed: Fifty Years of Crisis at Chrysler* (New York, 1986), 18–23; Memorandum on Auto Situation (5 February 1937), PSF 77, FDR Papers; (quote) "General Motors Favorable Attitude . . ." (5 May 1937), File 104, Sachs Papers; (quote) McPherson, *Labor Relations in the Automobile Industry*, 4. In the late 1930s (but even more so after 1945), the large firms also embraced an integrated, stable, and conservative UAW as an effective weapon against smaller competitors who suffered disproportionately the effects of high union wages (Robert MacDonald, *Collective Bargaining in the Automobile Industry* [New Haven, 1963], 307).

four biggest producers, employers never considered the union as a means of stemming wage competition. At the same time, however, opposition was qualified by a genuine admiration of the AFL's conservatism.[48]

In the pulp and paper industry, union strength (historically centered in northern newsprint firms) had slowly collapsed with the rise of southern newsprint and the free entry of Canadian paper after 1913. By 1932, the Pulp, Sulphite and Paper Mill Workers counted barely 4,000 members. Yet the increasing isolation of labor markets in the Northwest, the market power of the northwestern giants Weyerhauser and Crown-Zellerbach, and the specter of radical unionism encouraged employers – despite union weakness – to pursue a preemptive accord. Philip Weyerhauser saw the potential of union-regulated wages as early as 1932 and pressed for the stabilization of wages, "the higher the better." For Weyerhauser and Crown-Zellerbach, rubbing shoulders with union officials at NRA code meetings had been an instructive experience that would not be forgotten after 1935. When the union suggested the formation of the Pacific Coast Association of Pulp and Paper Manufacturers for the purpose of regionally organized collective bargaining, Zellerbach and others leapt at the opportunity. The union exchanged a no-strike pledge for a maintenance-of-membership agreement in 1936, although the latter was as much management's way of holding association members in line and preventing inroads by rival unions. Labor also made sporadic gains in the South, where International Paper declined to risk a strike at its highly profitable Southern Kraft plant.[49]

Although the full history of industrial relations in these and other industries in the years after 1935 is beyond the scope of this study, certain patterns of post-Wagner unionism were clearly emerging. The foremost competitive and strategic consideration for employers after 1935 was an assessment of

48 Harris, *The Right to Manage*, 32–34; Cyrus Ching memo for C. Seger, "Activities of the AF of L," (15 October 1926), File 8, DuPont Company Administrative Papers; Daniel Nelson, *American Rubber Workers and Organized Labor, 1900–1941* (Princeton, 1988), passim; Donald Anthony, "Rubber Products," in *How Collective Bargaining Works*, 631–81; "Notes on the Akron Rubber Situation" (17 January 1936), Reel 1, Katherine Ellickson Papers [CIO].

49 See Robert Zieger, *Rebuilding the Pulp and Paper Workers Union, 1933–1941* (Knoxville, 1984), 66–167; James Gross, "The Making and Shaping of Unionism in the Pulp and Paper Industry," *Labor History* 4 (1963): 190–97; "The Crown Zellerbach Corporation and the Pacific Coast Pulp and Paper Industry," *The Causes of Industrial Peace*, vol. 1 (Washington, 1948), 34; Charles Twining, *Phil Weyerhauser: Lumberman* (Seattle, 1985), 96. As early as 1928, George Mead of Mead Paper lauded "the foresightedness of the union leaders . . . in their attention to business conditions," noting with particular appreciation a union-initiated cut in production the previous year (Mead, "Why I Unionized My Plant," 1928 clipping, File 50, Raskob Papers).

how the Wagner Act (or the militancy of workers protected by the act) might affect current labor relations and future alternatives. Constitutional challenges aside, the Wagner Act suddenly rendered labor relations less a battle over open-shop principles than a battle over what form closed, or union, shops might take. Constructive accommodation to labor's new power and legal rights often involved some preemptive strategy of encouraging or sponsoring conservative unionists. Key rubber and paper firms preferred the AFL to the new CIO unions; auto firms preferred the CIO-affiliated UAW to factional radicalism (although all the radicals ended up in the UAW); and rigidly traditionalist DuPont pressed its company unions to apply for CIO charters "in hopes that the conservative employees composing the Association would be able to take charge of [the] union."[50]

Once organized, employers also trumpeted conservative unionism as a solution to the organizational problems of modern management. Although employers (always anxious on issues of managerial control) were less than certain on this point, their strategies certainly bore fruit in the subsequent bureaucratic, business-minded growth of unions such as the UAW and USWA. The Wagner Act strengthened regulatory unionism in those industries in which it had always played an important role by giving the union and union firms recourse to the law in their effort to force recalcitrant and marginal competitors into collective agreements. In industries that had never perceived or pursued the anticompetitive possibilities of unionism, employers quickly learned to turn unions to their advantage (or at least to minimize disadvantage) by encouraging the organization of competing firms. CIO-era contracts in many industries made wage rates or representation conditional upon the union's ability to exact the same concessions from all competing firms. The experience at Hormel in Austin, Minnesota, was typical; George Hormel reasoned that his plant could not weather a protracted strike, so after settling quickly with striking workers, as one unionist recalled, "he suggested that we go out and organize the other packing plants" before actually sitting down to hammer out contract details.[51]

Of course, many employers were not nearly so sanguine at the prospect of unionization or federal labor legislation. For many, labor relations remained an article of faith, especially when the regulatory perks of collective

---

50 (Quote) Callahan memo, "Flint Labor Situation" (10 June 1937), File 24; W. Foster to Harrington (19 September 1934), File 15, Harrington Papers; see also "Talk with John Lewis on the Telephone" (6 January 1937), File 123, Sachs Papers.

51 Roger Horowitz, *Organizing the Makers of Meat: Shop-Floor Bargaining and Industrial Unionism in Meatpacking, 1930–1990* (Urbana, forthcoming), chapter 1.

agreements were slight or eclipsed by the threat to managerial prerogative. The Wagner Act often set such conflicts in sharp relief, but it did not transform the face of U.S. labor relations. The share of strikes over recognition continued to increase between 1935 and 1939, a pattern that had begun in 1933. But the percentage of workers involved in work stoppages hovered around 5 percent (as it would throughout the 1930s), paling against the experience of 1919 or 1946. And while these industrial battlegrounds were staked out by workers and employers, the war was largely being fought among competing business interests, some of whom had recognized unions of their workers as a logical or necessary concession to industrial peace, stability, and organization and some of whom were the targets of such agreements. The UAW struck constantly in an attempt to capture Ford plants and as a rearguard defense against GM (whose prudent deal with the UAW was eroded by Ford's recalcitrance). Southern textiles, "Little Steel," and the Akron rubber firms all continued to fight organized labor, in part as a direct battle over control of the workplace and in part as an indirect battle against unionized competitors.

Business, Labor, Politics, and the "Right to Manage"

Business influence in the origins and administration of the Wagner Act was more pervasive and more diverse than most scholars have allowed. Indeed, it is important to neither underestimate nor exaggerate the role of business interests in this context. To suggest that the act was something that business uniformly opposed would be to ignore the immense (if disorganized) influence of business in U.S. politics. And to suggest that the Wagner Act, by some loose poll of business opinion, was "anti-business" also misses the point. Economic legislation almost always involves an attempt by some producers to pass the costs of regulation on to others or to spread those costs among as many as possible. In short, while the Depression and the failure of the NRA did not suspend the indirect and direct influence of business in U.S. politics, they did highlight competitive and structural divisions, magnify the organizational weakness of industries and firms, exacerbate the crisis of underconsumption, and raise the stakes of private industrial relations and public labor law in such a way that employers and legislators could no longer ignore workers' demands and workers' rights.

Yet to suggest that the Wagner Act was something that even an influential minority of business interests wanted would be to ignore deeply rooted anxieties over managerial rights and prerogatives. Indeed, the key to understanding the passage of the act lies in both the wider logic of the New Deal (the way in which private strategies and the NRA experience increasingly pointed to collective bargaining law as the key to competitive organization) and the exceptional circumstances under which the act was passed. Put another way, our understanding of the Wagner Act must reconcile two seemingly incompatible realities: the privileged position of business in U.S. politics and the unique and persistent antipathy of U.S. employers toward collective bargaining of any sort. How and why, in a notoriously business-dominated polity, did the Wagner Act become law? Most have answered this question by pointing to the interplay of worker insurgency and state intervention, although there is substantial debate over the relative importance of state actors and their radicalized constituents.[52] Given business's political prominence (as I have argued above), the ways in which business adjusted to the cumulative effect of worker insurgency, the NRA experience, and the prospect of further political experimentation are even more important.

The right to manage is, of course, a central premise of U.S. business culture, at once an elaboration of the moral and political virtues of private enterprise, a defense of the class skew in U.S. politics and political culture, and an anxiety over managerial prerogative in the seedbed of mass-production. Yet the right to manage was not an immutable ideological construct and, in its most belligerent forms, was simply a symptom of a culture in which radical threats to political and economic organization were virtually nonexistent. For Western European employers, relatively conservative and bureaucratic forms of collective bargaining were a middle ground between unfettered capitalism and electoral socialism. For U.S. employers, both their own political prominence and the institutional conservatism of the labor movement made such concessions if not materially dangerous, at least politically unnecessary.[53] Indeed, rhetorical antiunionism rang through the debate over the Wagner Act. Many who hoped the act would sort out their competitive troubles soon realized that the costs in terms of managerial rights was too great, and many clung tenaciously to the right to manage *despite* the fact that the long-term interests of their firms would have been better served by accommodation or compromise.

Perhaps more importantly, the Depression shook the foundations upon which the peculiarly strident U.S. defense of the right to manage was based.

52 See Michael Goldfield, Theda Skocpol, and Kenneth Finegold, "Explaining New Deal Labor Policy," *American Political Science Review* 84 (1990): 1297–1315.
53 Harris, *The Right to Manage*, 15–40; Lloyd Ulman, "Who Wanted Collective Bargaining in the First Place?" *Contemporary Policy Issues* 5:4 (1987), 2–8.

Worker insurgency and political radicalism stretched the boundaries of the nation's politics. The persistence of both competitive disorganization and the depression eroded the willingness and ability of employers to resist unionization. And the growth in federal power through the early New Deal displaced judicial and local sanction of antiunion repression.[54] In this atmosphere, accommodation of conservative elements of the labor movement and at least tacit support of the Wagner Act – for all of the reasons outlined above – were at best an attempt to salvage and perpetuate the spirit of the NRA and at worst the lesser of many potential evils. For some, the Wagner Act was the logical culmination of organizational experimentation (and failure) before and after the NRA; for others, it was a tactical and temporary concession that was unlikely to last if they could not use it to their advantage or if the circumstances surrounding its passage changed.

In this respect, business interests battled over the passage and administration of the Wagner Act not because they objected to the premises of industrial unionism and collective bargaining but because they could not agree among themselves over the utility and costs of unionization. In an economy substantially protected from international competition, few doubted their ability to absorb higher union wages. The real question was whether or not the managerial threat of unionism outweighed the regulatory benefits of union wages. Some firms supported the Wagner Act as a necessary and logical extension of the NRA and, with less certainty, as a legal blessing of conservative industrial unionism. Others recoiled at the prospect of empowering their employees and continued to resist organized labor. The majority of employers fell somewhere in between; similarly motivated and with equally limited horizons, they found themselves haphazardly directing, accommodating, resisting, and exploiting a union movement over which they had little control.

Politics haphazardly filled the breach left by business disunity. New Dealers clearly felt they were pursuing a program that business interests themselves had lost the ability to articulate or direct. Persistent dilemmas of collective action – the regulatory inertia of the NRA, the political and social threat of labor, the ongoing crisis of consumption – demanded political solutions. The Wagner Act shared the organizational premises of the NRA but sharply raised the stakes of stability and collective action. The persistence of regional and competitive pressures and the determination of employers

---

54 Sanford Jacoby, "American Exceptionalism Revisited: The Importance of Management," in *Masters to Managers: Historical and Comparative Perspectives on American Employers*, ed. Sanford Jacoby (New York, 1991), 174–200.

to pass on the costs of unionization in the form of higher prices undermined the business premises of the act almost immediately. In the scramble to accomplish immediate regulatory and recovery goals, federal labor policy confused both basic distributive issues within and among industries and the larger relationship between income distribution and consumption and inflation. A decade later, labor's share of national income remained essentially unchanged, and the state-by-state deconstruction of federal standards (culminating in the Taft–Hartley Act of 1947) was in full swing.[55]

The Wagner Act was a logical synthesis of private experiments with regulatory unionism in the 1920s, the search for a means of enforcing trade agreements under the NRA, and scattered concern about underconsumption. Labor hoped the act would deliver the basic bargaining rights it promised. New Dealers hoped the act would make it possible to salvage some administrative debris from the wreck of the NRA. A widely varied range of firms hoped that political regulation would provide them with the coercive powers needed to mitigate competition while compelling them to do nothing that harmed or interfered with their particular competitive concerns. Business interests approached the Wagner Act in much the same way they had approached the NRA; each firm hoped to write its own ticket, drawing selectively on the opportunity of union-enforced labor standards while assiduously avoiding its costs. The Wagner Act, however, was a different beast. Its standards and expectations were much less malleable than business hoped or expected. And labor activism in a more encouraging legal environment forced firms to constantly readjust their bargaining goals and options and to confront the contradictions and costs of voluntarism, regulation, and collective action.

55 Darryl Holter, "Labor Law and the Road to Taft–Hartley: Wisconsin's 'Little Wagner Act,' 1935–1945," *Labor Studies Journal* 15 (1990): 20–47; Sanford Cohen, *State Labor Legislation, 1937–1947* (Columbus, 1948), 3–34.

7. The Social Security Act
The Political Economy of Welfare Capitalism, 1920–1935

Although the ongoing debate over federal labor law dominated politics after the demise of the National Recovery Administration, business was also deeply involved in the progress of federal welfare law. The Social Security Act (SSA) of 1935 was imbued with the same concerns as the NRA and the Wagner Act. A disparate range of welfare capitalists, leading northern firms, and larger firms in competitive industries hoped that it would remove the inequalities among regions and within industries created by a complex system of private and state-mandated employment benefits. Clearly, most employers saw social security as a sideshow to the more fundamental debates over federal fiscal, regulatory, and labor policy; however, the SSA is perhaps the most important legacy of the New Deal. Its passage laid the cornerstone for the modern welfare state, and the debate behind its passage neatly captured the patterns of economic competition and competitive federalism that underlay the entire New Deal.

Scholars have routinely portrayed the SSA, perhaps more than any other aspect of the New Deal, as evidence of the state's ability to countervail the power of business; as proof of the predominance of a technocratic, corporatist political synthesis; or as an expression of the state's unique ability to save capitalism from itself.[1] The debate over whether or not capitalists "shaped" social security, however, fails to appreciate business's unique influence in

---

1 See Theda Skocpol and John Ikenberry, "The Political Formation of the American Welfare State," *Comparative Social Research* 6 (1983): 87–120; Skocpol and Ann Orloff, "Why Not Equal Protection? Explaining the Politics of Public Social Spending in Britain, 1900–1911, and the United States, 1880–1920," *American Sociological Review* [*ASR*] 49 (1984): 726–50; Orloff, "The Political Origins of America's Belated Welfare State," in *The Politics of Social Policy in the United States*, ed. Margaret Weir et al. (Princeton, 1988), 38–80; Claus Offe, *Contradictions of the Welfare State* (Cambridge, 1984), 130–46; Ian Gough, *Political Economy of the Welfare State* (New York, 1979), 8–11, 55–74; James O'Connor, *Fiscal Crisis of the State* (New York, 1973), 162–69; Frances Fox Piven and Richard Cloward, *Regulating the Poor: The Functions of Public Welfare* (New York, 1971), 3–79.

240

the U.S. polity, the pressures of industrial and regional competition, or the sheer breadth and variety of business interest in federal welfare law. In this respect, the question is not whether or not capitalists shaped social security but *which* capitalists shaped social security and under what circumstances.[2] Federal welfare law, although a long-standing goal of academic and social reformers, was largely the product of business anxieties and demands. The SSA, of course, also counted many business opponents; some felt targeted by welfare-based regulation at the time; and others were soured by the administration of the act or by changes in the competitive conditions under which it was first drafted. By and large, however, the passage of the SSA reflected a scramble for competitive or political advantage among business and regional interests.[3]

Federal welfare law was the logical culmination of a quarter-century battle over the scope and costs of industrial welfare plans and a direct descendant of the anticompetitive business strategies of the 1920s. For employers strapped by struggles for market dominance and sharply federated and inconsistent business regulation, the standardization of welfare costs became an important goal. In the aftermath of World War I, many employers instituted welfare programs as a means of retaining skilled workers, moderating turnover, encouraging employee loyalty, and discouraging unionization. Through the 1920s, efforts by employers to escape the costs of these private plans merged with broader social concerns (expressed through unions and ballot boxes), which ensured that any attempt to remove welfare costs from competition would require spreading those costs to other firms (by political

2 See Sanford Jacoby, "From Welfare Capitalism to Welfare State: Marion B. Folsom and the Social Security Act of 1935" (unpublished, 1991), 1–3; Barbara Brents and J. Craig Jenkins, "Capitalists and Social Security: What Did They Really Want?" *ASR* (1991): 129–32; Edwin Amenta and Sunita Parikh, "Capitalists Did Not Want the Social Security Act," *ASR* (1991): 124–28. I have examined these theoretical questions more thoroughly in Colin Gordon, "New Deal, Old Deck: Business and the Origins of Social Security, 1920–1935," *Politics and Society* 19 (1991): 166–67.

3 I focus narrowly on the economic dimensions of the social security debate. More broadly, of course, federal welfare law also reflected and reinforced the racial and gendered underpinnings of the modern political economy. Race and gender shaped the formation of the welfare state in the sense that white, male, and often organized workers would receive the greatest political attention and that the adminstration of benefit and entitlement programs would challenge neither the racial premises of the southern economy nor the patriarchal premises of familial organization. The simple fact that long-standing debates over public welfare (which cut to the core of the regulation of public and private life) were, by the 1920s, dominated by business was itself a matter of no small importance. See Barbara Nelson, "The Origins of the Two-Channel Welfare State," in *Women, the State, and Welfare*, ed. Linda Gordon (Madison, 1990), 123–25.

means if necessary) rather than abandoning existing commitments. In the states, employers hoped welfare law would discipline marginal firms in locally competitive industries and alleviate the burden of privately initiated but badly orchestrated welfare plans. With state welfare concentrated in the Northeast and Midwest, employers in these regions – whether or not they had supported the laws – lobbied for federal regulation as a means of forcing their competitors to share the costs of a regulated market.

Unlike the Wagner Act, the SSA was deeply rooted in private and state-level policies of the 1920s and less directly tied to the failure of the NRA. For these reasons (and because the progress of social security is so emblematic of the New Deal's approach to problems of economic and political competition), any exploration of the origins of the U.S. welfare state rests on both the exceptional circumstances of 1933–35 and the experience of the 1920s. I begin by tracing the ways in which employers saw welfare capitalism as a palliative to the open shop and as a relatively inexpensive means of cementing the material consent of workers. I then suggest that employers, pressed by the costs and inconsistencies of private welfare, looked to the states to socialize the resultant financial burden; in turn, inconsistent state legislation compounded the inequities of that burden and encouraged welfare capitalists to look to the federal government. As I argue in the final section, the impact of the Depression on private and state welfare and the renewed attention to labor standards that colored the end of the NRA era magnified the importance of federal welfare law, both as a means of sorting out a patchwork of private and state-level initiatives and as a complement to the regulatory premises of the Wagner Act.

The Business of Welfare: Welfare Capitalism

Welfare capitalism was an integral thread in the wide-ranging and frantic response to the complex problems of early twentieth-century labor relations. Employers saw welfare policies as a pragmatic means of preventing labor organization; accompanying a rash of strike breaking after 1919, benefits were offered that encouraged identification with the firm rather than with fellow employees and served as both a superficial response to workers' needs and a contract against further confrontation. "Welfarism," as an historian of International Harvester concluded, was "no more than a veil spread over the unmet needs of Harvester workers."[4]

4 David Gordon et al., *Segmented Work, Divided Workers* (New York, 1982), 14–15;

As the Special Conference Committee (SCC) noted in 1920, private welfare held the promise of "reducing labor turnover and increasing the interest of the employees in the success of the company as a whole." Employment benefits and wages deferred to pensions, savings, or company stock encouraged workers to equate their own economic future with the prosperity and good favor of their employers. "Many of you are now real 'partners' . . . because you have your share of the 'surplus profits,' " a 1920 circular of the Endicott-Johnson Shoe Company reminded employees; "your own selfish interest, now, demands that you protect this business." Employers designed welfare programs with their own needs almost exclusively in mind and dismissed their costs as "efficiency expenses." Even housing and recreation programs were undertaken either to bind employees or in response to the inability of municipalities to provide services during periods of rapid industrial expansion. Not surprisingly, welfare capitalism and scientific management, both focused on efficient and productive employment, were often pursued simultaneously by the same firms.[5]

Welfare programs were adopted by mass-production industries seeking to forestall unionization and regulate unwieldy workforces as well as by specialized manufacturers attempting to retain or attract skilled workers. Industries and firms cut plans to fit their particular needs. The automobile industry experimented with welfare benefits as a means of stemming turnover before 1920 but abandoned its efforts as labor markets in Detroit soft-

Katherine Stone, "The Origins of Job Structures in the Steel Industry," *Review of Radical Political Economics* 6 (1974): 61–97; Irving Bernstein, *The Lean Years: A History of the American Worker, 1920–1933* (Boston, 1960), 149–57; (quote) Robert Ozanne, *A Century of Labor-Management Relations at International Harvester* (Madison, 1967), 104. On welfare capitalism generally, see Stuart Brandes, *American Welfare Capitalism, 1880–1940* (Chicago, 1970); Bernstein, *The Lean Years*, 157–89; David Brody, "The Rise and Decline of Welfare Capitalism," in *Workers in Industrial America* (New York, 1980), 48–81.

5   "Report of the Special Conference Committee [SCC], 1920," Pennsylvania Railroad [PRR] Papers 825:7, Hagley Museum and Library, Wilmington, DE; (quote) Gerard Zahavi, *Workers, Managers, and Welfare Capitalism: The Shoeworkers and Tanners of Endicott Johnson, 1890–1950* (Urbana, 1988), 38, 41; Daniel Nelson, *Managers and Workers: Origins of the New Factory System in the United States* (Madison, 1975), 117; Nelson and Stuart Campbell, "Taylorism versus Welfare Work in American Industry: H.L. Gantt and the Bancrofts," *Business History Review [BHR]* 46 (1972): 3–10; Nelson, "The New Factory System and the Unions: The National Cash Register Company Dispute of 1901," *Labor History [LH]* 15 (1974); 89–97; E.S. Cowdrick, "Financial Incentive Plans," File II:17, Archibald Johnson Papers, Hagley Museum. As calculated by *Business Week*, 28 September 1929, p. 5, the turnover of industrial labor stood at 123 percent in 1920, 90 percent in 1923, and 37 percent in 1928.

ened after the war. At Norton Abrasives, management hoped welfare programs would promote the health and loyalty of skilled workers. At photographic giant Eastman-Kodak, welfarism was inspired by fears of industrial sabotage and espionage, antitrust pressures, and the importance of skilled labor.[6]

Other firms and industries saw welfare capitalism less as a labor relations ploy than as a partial solution to broader social and economic problems. Retailers and consumer-goods producers hoped that private pensions and unemployment insurance might stem the collapse of purchasing power. As Ernest Draper (vice-president of Hills Brothers and later U.S. secretary of commerce) argued, income support and employment stabilization were essential to "the continued success of large scale production, of quick turnover and of installment buying" and as a means of keeping enough workers "working and therefore able to buy in normal volume." Banking and high-technology firms also supported welfare capitalism; their advocacy arose in part out of concerns with aggregate demand and the economic and political potential of organized labor but primarily because (whatever the putative benefits of welfare) as capital-intensive firms they stood to bear few if any of the costs.[7] This broad profile of "welfare" firms and industries shifted constantly through the 1920s and 1930s. While some employers would try to place industrial welfare in a larger ideological framework, they continued to view it in sharply material terms and capriciously abandoned or adopted benefit programs according to short-term calculations of their costs and benefits.[8]

6 See Thomas Klug, "Employer's Strategies in the Detroit Labor Market, 1900–1929," in *On the Line: Essays in the History of Auto Work*, ed. Nelson Lichtenstein and Stephen Meyer (Urbana, 1989), 54–63; David Gartman, *Auto Slavery: The Labor Process in the American Automobile Industry, 1897–1950* (New Brunswick, 1986), 227–29; Stephen Meyer, *The Five-Dollar Day: Labor, Management and Social Control at the Ford Motor Company, 1908–1921* (Albany, 1981), 196–97; Charles Cheape, *Family Firm to Modern Multinational: Norton Company, A New England Enterprise* (Cambridge, 1985), 130–33; Jacoby, "Welfare Capitalism to Welfare State," 7–9. See also Bryce Stewart, *Unemployment Benefits in the United States* (New York, 1930), 8, 13; Brandes, *American Welfare Capitalism*, 19; Norman Wood, "Industrial Relations Policies of American Management, 1900–1933," *BHR* 34 (1960): 408; Executive Committee Meeting (6 December 1927), Reel 1, Leeds & Northrup Papers (microfilm), Hagley Museum.

7 Draper, "Memorandum on Unemployment" (1928), File 17-9, Thomas W. Lamont Papers, Baker Library, Cambridge, MA. On capital-intensive industries, see Thomas Ferguson, "From Normalcy to New Deal: Industrial Structure, Party Competition, and American Public Policy in the Great Depression," *International Organization* 38 (1984): 51–66.

8 Cf. Kim McQuaid, "Henry S. Dennison and the 'Science' of Industrial Reform,

For its part, organized labor understood employers' motives and the conditional and limited nature of benefits. During the 1920s, unions consistently opposed the introduction of employer-initiated welfare plans and, when plans were introduced in union firms, fought to ensure that they would be administered equitably. Before 1929, organized labor also opposed the passage of state or federal welfare law. Although the latter position softened after 1929, unions generally regarded employment benefits as bargainable rights and resisted managerial or governmental control over this area.[9] Their view underscored the limits of welfare capitalism and complicated later efforts (by employers) to politicize or socialize welfare costs.

Although much of welfare capitalism (which denoted everything from sponsoring baseball leagues to supplying bathroom tissue) represented little commitment of time or money, those programs that did entail real costs and benefits (stock ownership plans, pensions, workers' compensation, and unemployment insurance) proved difficult to either maintain or abandon. Costs began outstripping benefits, and welfare pledges and liabilities emerged as an element of competition. Many firms found themselves forced to choose between abandoning welfare programs (incurring the wrath of employees and public opinion) or spreading their costs among competitors and consumers through state and federal legislation. With little forethought, employers chose the latter. A closer look at these private programs underlines the key elements of this argument: first, individual plans were justified and appraised in terms of their direct returns to the company; second, these returns were either too small or too short-lived to allow any company to continue making payments its competitors were avoiding.

The motives and biases of industrial welfare were captured by stock ownership plans. Proponents advertised stock plans as guarantees of loyalty and efficiency, but their operation betrayed more mundane concerns. For employers, the oversubscription of World War I Liberty Bonds and the prec-

1900–1950," *American Journal of Economics and Sociology* 36 (1977): 79–98; McQuaid, "Young, Swope and General Electric's 'New Capitalism'," *American Journal of Economics and Sociology* 36 (1977): 323–34; Edward Berkowitz and McQuaid, "Businessman and Bureaucrat: The Evolution of the American Social Welfare System, 1900–1940," *Journal of Economic History [JEH]* 38 (1978): 120–41.

9 "Labor's Appeal for Economic and Legislative Relief" (1930), Presidential File [PF] 59, Herbert C. Hoover Papers, Herbert C. Hoover Presidential Library [HCHPL], West Branch, IA; Jill Quadagno, *The Transformation of Old Age Security* (Chicago, 1988), 51–75, 108–09; Rick Halpern, "The Iron Fist and the Silk Glove: Welfare Capitalism in Chicago's Packinghouses, 1921–1933," *Journal of American Studies* 26 (1992): 159–83; Alexander Keyssar, *Out of Work: The First Century of Unemployment in Massachusetts* (New York, 1986), 291–98.

edent of financing such purchases through payroll deductions suggested an untapped source of capital: workers themselves.[10] As the SCC noted approvingly in 1923, GE had "cleverly devised" its stock plan to facilitate "its large financing of public utilities and other corporations." Plainly intended to raise capital rather than redistribute ownership, only one-third of 496 plans studied in 1929 purchased stocks already on the market. Sale of stocks to employees occurred primarily in expanding, nonunion industries: oil, new technology (Bell, AT&T, and Kodak), utilities, steel products, and chemicals. Retail, financial, and service sectors also participated with more limited plans aimed at upper management.[11]

Most plans forced workers to pay for a block of stocks in installments, limiting both control of stock and its resale. After early plans were rocked by speculation and stock dumping in 1921, employers usually prohibited resale (undermining the rhetorical goal of making every worker a capitalist). Restricted voting also increased the value of voting shares; "Diffusion of ownership," as the National Industrial Conference Board (NICB) noted, "means stability of control in the hands of those small minorities which direct the management policies." Installment payment and wage or service restrictions further bound employees. An early historian of U.S. Steel questioned "whether this is really a stock-owning plan or simply a method of holding employees." GM executives gave "preference to men who are in or are willing to join [the stock plan] when the time comes to hire and fire," and International Harvester introduced its plan, with characteristic audacity, on the same day union leaders were fired. For some, stock plans facilitated expansion or financial reorganization. For others, the importance of stock plans was not the distribution of ownership or dividends but "the exact form

10 This use of payroll deductions was not confined to stock plans. Wages deferred to welfare programs or charitable "mutual benefit" societies trimmed labor costs and served as a source of capital. See "Relief Measures of Special Conference Committee Companies" (October 1931), Box 19, File 5, Records of the President's Organization on Unemployment Relief [POUR] (RG 73) National Archives, Washington, D.C. For an attempt to profit from employee welfare programs in the Hormel Company, see Roger Horowitz, *Organizing the Makers of Meat: Shop-Floor Bargaining and Industrial Unionism in Meatpacking, 1930–1990* (Urbana, forthcoming), chapter 1.

11 Chamber Of Commerce [CoC] Proceedings, 18/25 (1930), 653, Chamber of Commerce Papers, Hagley Museum; (quote) SCC, "Report of Conference with GE Officials" (1923), File II:17, Archibald Johnson Papers, File "GE," Box 64, National Civic Federation [NCF] Papers, New York Public Library, NY; Robert Foerster, *Employee Stock Purchase Plans in the United States* (Princeton, 1926), 1–3, 103–74; National Industrial Conference Board [NICB], *Employee Stock Purchase Plans in the United States* (New York, 1928), 8–15, 41–44, 203–21.

of stock, the way it is paid for, the restriction upon its sale, its relation to union membership and the like."[12]

Industrial pensions, as private experiments and a spur to public policy, were the most important facet of welfare capitalism. Almost half of private pension plans were in nonunion northern manufacturing (steel, paper, chemicals, electrical, and machinery), with the remainder distributed among railroads, public utilities, banking, and insurance. By 1935, 80 percent of workers in these sectors belonged to pension plans (although barely 4 percent of male workers and 3 percent of female workers ever met the underlying service requirements). Pensions were more common in larger firms, as small firms were often unwilling to shoulder the accompanying administrative and financial burden. Pension plans varied widely between and within industries, but most employers understood and justified them on purely economic grounds (although their existence underlined the degree to which labor had become an ethical as well as financial liability). Through the 1920s and 1930s, employers initiated pension plans as a means of averting strikes and moderating labor turnover. With the exception of early attempts in the railroads and scattered craft union initiatives, pensions were confined to unorganized industries and (seen as deferred wages) opposed by organized labor. "Rarely, if ever," concluded an exhaustive 1931 study, ". . . has the inauguration of a pension plan come about as the result of demands from employees."[13]

12 NICB, *Stock Purchase*, 7, 14, 50–66, 116, 120–21, (quote) 138–39; "Stock Purchase Plans by Employees, 1928–1931," File 1029:9, PRR Papers; Foerster, *Stock Purchase*, 12–13, 28; (quote) Charles Gulick, *Labor Policies of the United States Steel Corporation* (New York, 1924), 180; John J. Raskob to Donaldson Brown (28 July 1933), File 278, John J. Raskob Papers, Hagley Museum; Ozanne, *Labor-Management Relations*, 36–44, 94; (quote) Henry Dennison to W.J. Donald (21 October 1922), Box 2, Henry Dennison Papers, Baker Library. Southern textile capitalists, anxious to finance expansion without recourse to northern capital, issued stock on installment plans of as little as $0.50 a week [Gavin Wright, *Old South, New South: Revolutions in the Southern Economy since the Civil War* (New York, 1986), 131]. U.S. Rubber stock dropped so precipitously during the 1919–24 subscription that management thought it "detrimental to [employee] morale and [the] interests of company to compel payment" on outstanding shares [Glenn Babcock, *A History of the United States Rubber Company* (Bloomington, 1966), 160–61].

13 Quadagno, *Old Age Security*, 82–83, 91; NICB, *Industrial Relations Programs in Small Plants* (New York, 1929), 16–17; *American Labor Legislation Review* [*ALLR*] 19 (1929): 55–56; NICB, *Elements of Industrial Pension Plans* (New York, 1931), 1, 8–9; NICB, *Industrial Pension Systems in the United States* (New York, 1925), 101; Charles Dearing, *Industrial Pensions* (Washington, 1954), 38–39; Murray Latimer, *Industrial Pension Systems in the United States and Canada* (New York, 1931) 1:17–18, (quote) 19, 24–28, 40, 44–45, 2:774–79.

As one management consultant noted, one immediate goal of private pensions was to "purge the payroll." Retirement of older employees, at least in the first years of a plan, reduced payrolls because replacement wages were substantially lower or positions were not filled. At Kodak, pensions were introduced as a means of flushing out the "privileged senility" and "deadweight" of older workers, and half of pensioned employees were not replaced. At the Pennsylvania Railroad, redundancy ran at about one-third, "showing a distinct saving to the company." In a detailed survey of 302 workers pensioned at DuPont between 1923 and 1930, 39 positions were scrapped, 89 were divided among existing employees, and 180 were filled by new hires; for those years at least, savings ran at $200 per pensioner.[14] Such economies were far from universal and became difficult to sustain as pension rolls grew. Indeed, the payroll–savings argument was often simply a boardroom rationale for a plan aimed at turnover and the retention of skilled workers (in firms with promotion or seniority ladders, it was difficult to envision any real saving). Nevertheless, such material considerations helped to justify the introduction of pensions and induced many firms to make commitments they would soon regret.

Most saw pensions, or more importantly the conditions placed on pension eligibility, as weapons against turnover and unionization. International Harvester and U.S. Steel maintained pensions except "in case of misconduct on part of beneficiaries," and most firms (95 percent of those examined in an NICB survey) required between 15 and 30 years of service. Such restrictions were often quite effective; painters and trimmers sat out a 1920 strike at Studebaker in order to maintain benefits, and the railroads lured striking shopmen back to work in 1922 when their accrued benefits were threatened. In turn, two-thirds of pensions surveyed in 1925 were noncontributory and discretionary – what one cynic dubbed the "if and maybe" pension. Even contributory plans rarely guaranteed payment; in 1929, only 10 percent of pensions obligated companies to pay. When the Armour and Morris meatpacking firms merged in 1926, Morris employees lost all their pension benefits (save a callous offer that allowed them to buy into the Armour plan at a prohibitive price). Often pensions were little more than discretionary awards requiring a working retirement of light labor or giving firms "first

14 (Quote) E.S. Cowdrick in CoC Proceedings 17/23 (1929), 878, Chamber Papers; NICB Proceedings (18 September 1930), File I:1, NICB Papers, Hagley Museum; (quote) Jacoby, "Welfare Capitalism to Welfare State," 10; "Pensions Granted," File 1029:10, (quote) W.W. Burrell to T.W. Demarest (1 May 1934), File 1030:1, PRR Papers; H. Sedwick memo (30 August 1937), Box 24, Willis Harrington Papers, Hagley Museum.

call upon the services of a retired employee," often as strikebreakers. As Frank Vanderlip of National City Bank noted, a worker "would sacrifice much of his personal liberty, including his right to strike for better wages or shorter hours" for a pension.[15]

Workers' compensation developed as a gradual reaction to legal refinement of the notion of employer liability, and to what President Taft called "undue emotional generosity on the part of the jury." Under a combination of a federal liability law that applied primarily to the railroads and a variety of state laws, compensation was sporadic and inadequate for injured workers. But reform followed the needs of employers, who found legal awards frighteningly unpredictable.[16] As early as 1917, the NICB favored compensation "as a certain and speedy redress . . . against the uncertain and expensive recovery through litigation." Through compensation plans, employers sought to pass costs on to the consumer as a predictable operating expense. "The American compensation system," noted one legal analyst, "at the moment of creating the liability also created the means of relieving the employer of the real burden of that liability." Firms sought refuge from the uncertainty of insurers and courts by establishing private plans. U.S. Steel required

15 NICB Proceedings 18 (September 1930), 109–10, 122–23, 132–33, series I, NICB Papers; "Transcript of Luncheon Conference" (26 April 1928), Box 59, NCF Papers; NICB, "The Cost and Administration of Industrial Pensions" (1925), File V:12, NICB Papers; NICB, *Industrial Pensions*, 3; Jill Quadagno, "Welfare Capitalism and the Social Security Act of 1935," *ASR* 49 (1984): 637; Ozanne, *Labor-Management Relations*, 82–84; (quote) Robert Dunn, *The Americanization of Labor* (New York, 1927), 155; Latimer, *Industrial Pension Systems*, 1:44, 2:719–20, 755–56, 968–73, 996ff.; NICB, *Elements of Industrial Pensions*, 23; Sanford Jacoby, *Employing Bureaucracy: Managers, Unions and the Transformation of Work in American Industry* (New York, 1985), 197; Cheape, *Family Firm to Modern Multinational*, 134; (quote) E.S. Cowdrick (SCC), "Memo on the Morris Pension," Box 8, DuPont Company Administrative Papers, Hagley Museum; *ALLR* 17 (1927): 36–37; Ralph Easley to W.J. Graham (11 November 1924), Box 27, NCF Papers; Vanderlip quoted in William Graebner, *A History of Retirement* (New York, 1980), 131.

16 Taft quoted in R. Robinson to J.C. Rose (15 July 1921), file 1175:10, PRR Papers. Between 1875 and 1905, in one survey of appellate decisions, employers prevailed in 98 of 1,034 cases, and the number of cases rose from 92 to 736 per year. In turn, adjudication by jury increased, and courts slowly closed the "fellow-servant" loophole (which made other workers liable before employers). See Edward Berkowitz and Kim McQuaid, *Creating the Welfare State: The Political Economy of Twentieth Century Reform* (New York, 1980), 34; James Weinstein, *The Corporate Ideal in the Liberal State* (Boston, 1968), 43–44; Samuel Horvitz, "Current Trends in Workmen's Compensation," *The Law Society Journal* 12 (1947): 470; Nuala Drescher, "The Workmen's Compensation and Pension Proposal in the Brewing Industry: A Case Study of Conflicting Self-Interest," *Industrial and Labor Relations Review* 24 (1970): 32–46.

employees to sign a release specifying that "no relief will be paid to any employee or his family if suit is brought against the company." In 1924, Studebaker forced subscription to a company compensation plan over worker protests.[17]

Although workers' compensation had a more complicated legal history than other welfare policies, it betrayed important similarities. Plans were organized along regional and industrial lines. Compensation and safety legislation in the soft coal industry repeatedly broke apart on the rock of West Virginian noncompliance. Textile capitalists in South Carolina strongly favored compensation legislation, but the state's lumber industry opposed the law (feeling individual settlements with its black workforce would be less costly). As state legislation replaced private uncertainty, it was defined so closely by competitive and regulatory concerns that claimants repeatedly challenged the industry-specific nature of compensation law as a violation of "equal protection" as guaranteed by the Fourteenth Amendment. As in other areas of welfare law, casual and agricultural labor were excepted without question.[18]

Unemployment insurance was the most limited of private welfare programs. No more than sixteen plans existed between 1916 and 1934. In 1928, only three companies were contributing in any substantial sense to unemployment plans, and in 1931 only 50,000 workers were covered. Firms crafted unemployment insurance not to relieve the jobless but to regulate employment by compelling continuous employment and curtailing the freedom of fly-by-night competitors. As one employer observed, the point was

17 Skocpol and Ikenberry, "Formation of the American Welfare State," 108–109; Berkowitz and McQuaid, *Creating the Welfare State*, 33–40; Weinstein, *Corporate Ideal*, 40–61; Robert Asher, "Business and Worker's Welfare Relief in the Progressive Era: Workmen's Compensation in Massachusetts, 1880–1911," *BHR* 43 (1969): 452–75; Robert Asher, "Radicalism and Reform: State Insurance of Workmen's Compensation in Minnesota, 1910–1933," *LH* 14 (1973): 19–41; Robert Wesser, "Conflict and Compromise: The Workmen's Compensation Movement in New York, 1890–1913," *LH* 12 (1971): 345–72; Joseph Tripp, "An Instance of Labor and Business Cooperation: Workmen's Compensation in Washington State," *LH* 17 (1976): 530–50; Harry Weiss, "The Development of Workmen's Compensation in the United States," (Ph.D diss., University of Wisconsin, 1933), 20–23; (quote) Second Meeting of the Executive Committee (16 May 1917), Series II (Reel 1), NICB Papers; (quote) Arthur Larson, "The Nature and Origins of Workmen's Compensation," *Cornell Law Quarterly* 37 (1952): 215–20; U.S. Steel cited in Stone, "Job Structures," 76; Robert Dunn, *Labor and Automobiles* (New York, 1925), 153–55.
18 *ALLR* 10 (1920): 155; James Coleman, *State Administration in South Carolina* (New York, 1935), 180–82; Walter Dodd, *Administration of Workmen's Compensation* (New York, 1936), 29–30, 38–39.

"not so much to give workers compensation for lack of employment as to punish the [seasonal] manufacturer." Most plans were noncontributory in order to avoid any implication that employees had a legal right to reserves (although employers and employees alike viewed benefits as deferred wages rather than insurance). Such private guarantees of employment were notoriously undependable, and as one observer noted, tended "to collapse when they [were] most needed." A Leeds & Northrup executive observed with characteristic perception (in the spring of 1929) that their unemployment insurance plan seemed secure "unless a Depression came upon us very suddenly."[19]

The most important industrial unemployment plans of the interwar era were in the New York, Chicago, Rochester, and Cleveland garment industries (in the latter, the insurance plan cut the number of competing firms from thirty-three to fifteen). The Rochester plan reflected the concerns of both the savagely competitive needle trades and employers of skilled labor in the optical (Bausch and Lomb) and photographic industries. Both the Rochester plan (under the tutelage of Louis Kirstein of Filene's and Marion Folsom of Eastman-Kodak) and the Chicago plan (under clothing giant Hart, Schaffner and Marx) allowed employers to draw upon their own contributions to a central fund and reduced those contributions as firms demonstrated their ability to maintain stable payrolls. These plans were undertaken with union cooperation and underlined the distinct biases of U.S. social insurance; while European plans placed the burden of unemployment insurance on large firms through payroll taxes, the burden of the few established U.S. plans fell, quite pointedly, on marginal firms.[20]

Company unemployment plans were scattered among small manufacturers seeking to smooth over seasonal fluctuations in supply and demand and

19 Daniel Nelson, *Unemployment Insurance: The American Experience* (Madison, 1969), 47–50; Stewart, *Unemployment*, 8, 13, 96, 142–45; SCC statement (11 March 1921), File 279, Raskob Papers; Senate Committee on Education and Labor, *Unemployment in the United States* (Washington, 1929); (quote) William Mack address, Re: Unemployment Insurance, acc. 8/2/75, Box 1, Lukens Steel Papers, Hagley Museum; (quote) Bryce Stewart, "American Voluntary Attempts at Unemployment Benefits," *Annals of the American Academy of Political and Social Science* 170 (1933): 55–60; (quote) C. S. Redding to the Executive Committee (26 March 1929), Reel 2, Leeds & Northrup Papers.

20 Senate, *Unemployment*, 214–18, 221–65, 353ff. (this survey also noted plans in the Kingston, New York, and Scranton, Pennsylvania lace industries); Louis Kirstein to Clothiers Exchange (13 November 1911), Box 68, Rochester file C-2, Kirstein Papers, Baker Library; "The Next Labor Offensive," *Fortune* 7 (January 1933), 61, 92–94; "Digest of Plans," File 19:5, POUR Records; Monthly Labor Review [*MLR*] 36:1 (January 1933).

specialized manufacturers (large and small) seeking the loyalty of skilled workers. The former were often producers of essential consumer goods (able to turn stable demand into stable employment) or producers of small non-perishable goods (able to produce for inventory). A 1929 Senate survey identified plans in three northeastern fine paper plants; two New York fabric finishers; two midwestern soap, oil, and wax processors; a midwestern cannery; a New York diamond finisher; and a Pennsylvania laboratory instrument manufacturer. Perhaps the most celebrated (and representative) plan of the interwar era was that of General Electric. In 1924 and 1925, GE workers clearly understood the costs and benefits of unemployment insurance and rejected company plans. And in the early 1930s, as GE President Gerard Swope advertised his company's initiatives during the debate over the SSA, he admitted that the company only offered employment "assurance" at GE's incandescent lamp plant, "where merchandise can be made up for stock, which is not subject to changes in design or fashion."[21]

During the 1920s and early 1930s, many employers considered private unemployment insurance but few followed through with full-fledged plans. Unlike pensions (which could directly benefit individual firms), unemployment insurance was only effective when enacted on an industry-wide basis. As early as 1922, coal firms saw it as an means of shaking out marginal competition but realized that such plans would not work "unless all the mines in the country are brought under one agreement." By 1930, advocates acknowledged that private plans were doomed "unless the officers of the business men's associations will hold themselves responsible for making all their members adopt this voluntary unemployment insurance." Although employers appreciated its regulatory potential, the inauguration of industry-wide unemployment insurance posed serious collective action problems. Firms that stood to benefit from industrial plans were unable to initiate or enforce them; marginal or seasonal firms that stood to bear the costs of such plans were unlikely to do so voluntarily. Finally, private unemployment

21 Nelson, *Unemployment Insurance*, 31, 79–103; Stewart, "Voluntary Attempts at Unemployment Benefits," 53–54; Stewart, *Unemployment*, 151; NICB, "Reducing Fluctuations in Employment: Experience in 31 Industries," *Studies in Personnel Policy* 27 (November 1940): 14–34; Jacoby, *Employing Bureaucracy*, 200–201; Senate, *Unemployment*, 278–352; P. White to Thomas Lamont (5 October 1930), File 72–26, Lamont Papers; Josephine Young Case and Howard Needham Case, *Owen D. Young and American Enterprise* (Boston, 1982), 379; (quote) Swope to Robert Wagner (30 December 1934), File 15, Records of the Committee on Economic Security [CES], Social Security Administration (RG 47), National Archives; Swope Address (21 March 1935), President's Personal File [PPF] 2943, Franklin D. Roosevelt Papers, Franklin D. Roosevelt Presidential Library [FDRPL], Hyde Park, NY.

insurance fell far short of the income support sought by the producers and distributors of consumer products; the "worst feature" of private, voluntary plans, complained one retailer, "is that it does not permit the unemployed to live on a scale which is of any use to business."[22]

The Welfare of Business: State Welfare Policy

Welfare capitalism buttressed the business offensive of the 1920s. As capital displaced workers and unionization fell to prewar levels, manufacturing wages rose only 6 percent, and only a steady decline in farm prices kept nonunion wages near 1914 levels. International Harvester, for one, attributed its ability to suppress wages largely to its welfare policies. Yet despite these tangible benefits, welfare plans were losing their appeal. Pensions reached their height of popularity by 1920, stock plans never recovered from the panic of 1921, unemployment insurance fared badly in 1921 and again in 1924, and private compensation plans began feeling the pinch of high premiums in the early 1920s. Firms found welfare costs, although averaging only 2 percent of payroll, increasingly burdensome. Pension liabilities ballooned with each year's retirement, unanticipated expenses and legal awards continued to rankle, and administrative and benefit costs grew steadily. At DuPont, welfare costs grew from $2 million and 3 percent of payroll in 1930 to nearly $5 million and 5 percent of payroll in 1934.[23] Welfare capitalists had anticipated neither spiraling costs and liabilities nor the advantages reaped by competitors without welfare obligations. To complicate matters, labor and reform interests kept employers from backing off their commitments and steered business discontent toward political solutions.

Pensions highlighted the crisis of private welfare. Despite promises of efficiency and savings, private pensions proved an expensive gamble. "We started this pension system with very little knowledge what it would cost," as one employer admitted, " . . . and the financial side of it was a real embarrassment." The NICB noted that "many companies found themselves

22 Edwin Ludlow letter (23 June 1922), Commerce File [CF] 101; Evanson to Ludlow (27 June 1922); CF 101; E.A. Filene to Hoover, PF 89, Hoover Papers; E .A. Filene, "The Consumer's Dollar" (1934), File 6, John H. Fahey Papers, FDRPL.
23 Frank Stricker, "Affluence For Whom? – Another Look at Prosperity and the Working Classes in the 1920s," *LH* 24 (1983): 5–33; Ozanne, *Labor-Management Relations*, 236; Latimer, *Industrial Pension Systems*, 1:42, 397, 940, 2:634–35; NICB, *Stock Purchase Plans*, 16; Stewart, *Unemployment*, 96–97; *Bulletin of the Bureau of Labor Statistics* [*BBLS*] 544 (November 1931): 13; DuPont plans in Box 24, Harrington Papers (in the capital-intensive and tightly organized chemical industry, DuPont did not find these costs as weighty as would firms in other industries).

seriously embarrassed by their pension obligations," and the SCC thought it "unlikely that the ill-considered liberality of some of the older pension plans will ever be repeated." From 1928 to 1931, aggregate pension costs increased by 50 percent and liabilities swelled to over $2 billion. Firms such as DuPont complained that their pension plans were "financially unsound" and "too elastic and indefinite." At the Pennsylvania Railroad, pension costs grew from 1.5 percent of net operating income in 1916 to almost 5 percent by 1924; for all railroads, pension costs doubled between 1920 and 1924. As one observer noted, private pensions "will ultimately result in a level of payments which no company can bear if it is competing with companies who do not have such charges."[24]

For many employers, emerging legal constraints also took the shine off private pensions. Most early plans had been discretionary. But as workers made a series of legal claims to noncontributory pension funds during the 1920s, the courts gradually accepted private pensions as a contractual right rather than merely discretionary compensation. Without the assurance that workers had no vested right to pension funds, employers moved away from noncontributory plans. And increasingly, as one industrial advisor reasoned, a "large company . . . under any public scrutiny" was morally and legally bound to honor pension agreements however they were financed. After 1923, new pension plans were overwhelmingly contributory and insured, and many employers pared back their programs or simply stopped notifying workers or their dependents of pension eligibility.[25]

24 "Luncheon Conference" (26 April 1928), Box 59, NCF Papers; NICB, "Company Pension Plans and the Social Security Act," *Studies in Personnel Policy* 16 (1939): 21; NICB, *Elements of Industrial Pension Plans*, 4–5; "Annual Report of the Special Conference Committee, 1934," Box 19, Harrington Papers; Latimer, *Industrial Pension Systems*, 1:216–19, 2:894; H.F. Brown to Irenée DuPont (3 October 1919), Box 8, DuPont Administrative Papers; railroad statistics from "Comparative Statement of Railroad Pension Plans, 1920–1924," File 1150:12, PRR Papers; Latimer, "Old Age Pensions in America," 63–65; *Business Week*, 16 November 1929, 37–40.
25 A. Williams to Gertrude Easley (29 April 1927), Box 56, NCF Papers; Latimer, *Industrial Pension Systems*, 1: 45–51, 59–60, 2:688–99, 910; Quadagno, *Old Age Security*, 92; NICB, *Elements of Industrial Pension Plans*, 14–18; Ingalls Kimball, "Industrial Pensions," *Annals* 161 (1932): 33–39; "Annual Report of the Special Conference Committee, 1930," and "Annual Report of the Special Conference Committee, 1932," Boxes 6 and 17, Harrington Papers; Glenn Bowers [Industrial Relations Counselors] in CoC Proceedings 17/23 (1929); address of James Kavanaugh [Metropolitan Life], CoC Proceedings 12/16 (1924), Chamber Papers; J.C. Clark, "Railroad Employees Pension Plans" (17 April 1926), File 1150:12; "Railroad Retirement Board – Legislative History," File 1154:1; "Pension Plans of other Companies," File 1154:7; G.L. Peck to Pension Department (n.d.), File 1150:12; E.B. Hunt to G. L. Peck (15 April 1925), File 1150:12 and Dile 1154:9, PRR Papers.

In 1925, the National Civic Federation (NCF) sponsored a conference on the funding crisis of private pensions. The large insurers that dominated the NCF Welfare Department claimed that employers "had given no more attention [to pensions] than they [had] to the purchase of lead pencils" and urged firms to seek private actuarial backing (largely as a defense against state insurance). To the palpable dismay of insurers, however, the NCF campaign alienated more employers (who resented being reminded of their ill-considered pension commitments) than it attracted. In addition, payroll costs often paled beside private insurance premiums. The NCF debate was revealing if inconclusive; insurers belittled company and state pensions, many employers (notably GE and AT&T) resented the "embarrassing" legal and moral baggage of their plans, and a resigned majority hoped to spread the costs (in the words of John Raskob of GM and DuPont) by "making [pension] plans compulsory throughout industry as rapidly as it was practicable."[26]

Although not as widespread or costly as pensions, other welfare programs felt the crunch of bad planning and competition. Worker's compensation depended on the vagaries of liability law and local enforcement and the occupational risks of given jobs, but for many employers the attempt to limit liability through compensation plans was a bust, in part (as Pennsylvania Railroad executives noted) due to the "disinclination of employes to accept compensation in serious cases of liability and the greater activity of negligence case lawyers . . . making a specialty of actions under the federal law." With premiums climbing steadily, private insurance of compensation did little to alleviate the uncertainty. Stock ownership plans never recovered from the depression of 1921 and, whatever their motives, few could coax employee confidence after 1929. "It will be a long time," observed *Fortune* in 1933, "before wage earners will believe wholeheartedly in stock values again."[27]

26 Ingalls Kimball [Metropolitan Life] to Gertrude Easley (12 August 1924); Ralph Easley to G.C. Sykes (24 January 1925), Box 56; "Memorandum for Mr. Sherman" (25 February 1925); Box 57; Kimball to W.J. Graham [Equitable Life] (30 October 1924), Box 27; (quote) "Abstract of Discussion: Meeting of Committee on Old Age Pensions" (30 May 1924), Box 59, NCF Papers. In the later 1920s, new pension plans owed their existence "to a considerable extent [to] the activities of the insurance companies" ["Confidential Report on NCF Conference Regarding Pensions" (3 March 1925), Box 59, NCF Papers].

27 (Quote) J.C. Rose to F. Gowen (10 February 1921); and F. Gowen to S. Neale (21 January 1914), complaining that lawyers "have got a stronger hold upon the situation than we imagined," File 1175:10, PRR Papers; Virginia File 132, box II:452, Westmoreland Coal Papers, Hagley Museum; (quote) "The Next Labor Offensive," 61.

Finally, while rare as a private initiative, unemployment insurance (especially for employers who had formalized private plans or tried to minimize their share of the unemployment burden after 1929) became the cornerstone of business-sponsored welfare law. Employers borrowed heavily from the logic used by reformers and welfare capitalists arguing for a socialization of pensions. Although "the universal adoption of [unemployment] plans present serious obstacles," argued the SCC, "for the protection of employers in general, and to equalize cost burdens among competitors, there probably will be need for funds built up and administered under the direction of public authorities." In all respects, private welfare initiatives were doomed as long as individual firms bore the costs inequitably. Following "the unsatisfactory experience of private funding," as one observer concluded, "financial expediency may demand that [welfare] rest on the taxing power of the state."[28]

Employers did not suddenly discover the limits of private welfare and considered many alternatives to state law. Many experimented with private insurance as a means of contracting out the financial and administrative headaches of such plans, but their experiences merely strengthened business support of state law as commercial premiums proved unpredictable and onerous.[29] Here too, the logic of the various welfare programs diverged. Insurance of pension plans meant simply that commercial insurers took over pension administration and provided employers predictable costs based on actuarial financing. Unemployment insurance, however, was a newer and far less certain risk. Private insurers were largely unsuccessful (most notably in New York) in revising state insurance law in such a way that would allow them to underwrite unemployment in firms or industries. Overall, employers

---

28 (Quote) "Annual Report of the Special Conference Committee, 1934," Box 19, Harrington Papers; "Stabilization of Employment in Virginia" (1934), Box II:537, Westmoreland Papers; (quote) Latimer, "Old Age Pensions," 55.

29 There was precedence for state responsibility in accident and compensation insurance. Industrial accident insurance premiums rose from under $200,000 in 1887 to over $35 million in 1912. Industries such as steel reduced their premiums through safety campaigns, others (such as coal) found it impossible to even obtain insurance, and most leapt at the opportunity of state insurance. Those familiar with state-operated insurance also noted that its rates were 25 to 30 percent cheaper and that state insurers performed little or no inspection. See Gulick, *Labor Policy of U.S. Steel*, 151; *ALLR* 10 (1920): 137–38; "Missouri Employers Get a Lesson in Commercial Insurance Tactics," *ALLR* 17 (1927): 23–26; "Employers Favor State Accident Insurance," *ALLR* 10 (1920): 155–57; *ALLR* 14 (1924): 234–35; *ALLR* 16 (1926): 126, 194, 205; "Employers Coming to Grips with Compensation Costs under Commercial Insurance," *ALLR* 17 (1927): 124–27; Roy Lubove, *The Struggle for Social Security, 1900–1935* (Cambridge, 1968), 51–55.

sought state plans as an escape from high premiums; insurers opposed only state insurance monopolies and strongly supported state-mandated insurance, which resulted in lower premiums from a vastly increased market. Insurers lobbied eagerly for unemployment insurance unless it became clear that the state would control funding, at which they responded testily that employment was "uninsurable."[30]

Faced with the failure of both private and commercially insured plans, many employers considered abandoning their welfare commitments altogether. But while some did scale back or simply dump their pension and unemployment programs, most preferred to force competitors, consumers, and taxpayers to pick up the tab. Many continued to appreciate the regulatory utility of legislated welfare (especially unemployment insurance). Some realized that, given the efforts of labor and reform interests, legislation posed fewer problems than retrenchment. And many felt bound by the legal and moral obligations implied by existing policies (especially pensions). "If at this time . . . it should become publicly known that a change will be made in the pension plan," reasoned one employer, "a veritable avalanche of criticism will inevitably follow, and undoubtedly will have a most serious effect on the public attitude toward this [company]."[31]

State welfare law, although inspired in part by genuine political concern for working conditions and social stability, reflected three distinctly business-minded concerns: the spiraling costs of private plans, competition in specific industries, and the collapse of purchasing power. By the late 1920s, industry leaders were pressing for legislation that would ease the moral and fiscal burden of private plans and impose higher and less flexible labor costs on competitors. Once such political solutions were raised, the compass of industrial welfare narrowed to exclude stock ownership plans (which had little impact on competition) and workers' compensation (which hinged on liability and risk in given industries) and expanded to include wage and hour legislation.[32] Employers resented the unequal burden of pri-

---

30 Haley Fiske [Metropolitan Life] to Hoover (13 March 1924), CF 672; Frederick Ecker [Metropolitan Life] to Hoover (n.d.), Presidential Personal File [PPF] 80, Hoover Papers; I.M. Rubinow, "Is the Unemployment Risk Insurable?" *Annals* 170 (November 1933): 40–44.

31 C.S.K. to G.L. Peck (7 December 1925), file 1030:3, PRR Papers.

32 Wages were far more important than welfare benefits, but federal wage and hour regulation had quite a different legislative trajectory; it was a major thrust of the NRA codes but was barely mentioned in the debate over social security and not legislated until the Fair Labor and Standards Act of 1938. See U.S. Department of Labor, *The Development of Minimum Wage Laws in the United States, 1912–1927*

vate welfare costs but framed their political demands loosely and raised the possibility of socializing welfare costs in both federal and state legislatures. In the short run, easier access to state politics and constitutional constraints on federal action channelled business discontent towards state capitals. As welfare capitalism collapsed under the weight of its costs and contradictions, states provided the first political support.

Beyond the desperation of welfare capitalists seeking to spread costs among their competitors, business support for state welfare law was uncertain and scattered and closely reflected industrial and political conditions. Leading firms in the canning industry, for example, hoped that such measures would remove labor costs from competition and limit the seasonal entry of small competitors and were "willing to submit to a fair advance [in wages and benefits], provided all in the industry [are] placed on the same basis." Firms facing local *and* interstate competition were less consistent advocates of state welfare, which created as many problems as it purported to solve. Northern textile firms supported state laws but found that their efforts compounded interstate competition and pressed them into campaigns for federal or uniform state standards (usually focused on hours or child labor). Competition in the needle trades sparked numerous municipal unemployment insurance plans and the first state unemployment law (in Wisconsin), all of which merely broadened the scope of regulatory disadvantage. Competition in the soft coal industry encouraged both state and federal action, and state safety law mitigated local competition at the expense of interstate conditions. In all, welfare capitalists suffering local competition "repeatedly emphasize[d] the variation between factories" and pressed for legislated, uniform welfare provisions. As Ernest Draper argued, industrial stability seemed impossible unless such programs were "uniformly required of all business concerns by state legislation."[33]

(Washington, 1928); Walter Boles, "Some Aspects of the Fair Labor Standards Act," *Southern Economic Journal* [*SEJ*] 6 (1940): 498–511.

33 National Consumers' League, *State Minimum Wage Laws in Practice* (New York, 1924), 44, 51, 55, 135–45; Stanley Vittoz, *New Deal Labor Policy and the American Industrial Economy* (Chapel Hill, 1987), 34–69; Nelson, *Unemployment Insurance*, 79–125; Arden Lea, "Cotton Textiles and the Federal Child Labor Act of 1916," *LH* 16 (1975): 485–94; NICB, "Reducing Fluctuations in Employment," 15; Senate Subcommittee of the Committee on Manufacturers, *Establishment of a National Economic Council* (Washington, 1935), 149; Victor Morris, *Oregon's Experience with Minimum Wage Legislation* (New York, 1930), 204–5; Quadagno, "Welfare Capitalism and the SSA," 634–35; Stewart, *Unemployment*, 65; Draper quoted in *ALLR* 22 (1932): 31.

To complicate matters, business viewed pension and unemployment legislation quite differently. State pension laws of some form were widespread, but few actually mandated participation; business interests were concerned primarily with the scope and state-to-state disparity of such laws. Many smaller firms feared they would bear the burden of mandatory state plans, and interstate competitors feared they would lose markets to low-wage states. State business organizations managed to defeat or dilute progressive state pension proposals, usually by ensuring that county options left the coverage of such laws largely undefined. Such provisions, of course, did little to provide the uniform and mandatory coverage that many saw as the *raison d'etre* for state law. And employers in some industries and regions faced reform and labor pension initiatives (most notably by the United Mine Workers in Pennsylvania and UMW–Fraternal Order of Eagles coalitions in Ohio and Illinois) that often made it necessary to draft and support "business-minded" alternatives.[34]

State unemployment insurance attracted more scattered support, usually confined to firms that had successfully stabilized their (usually skilled) workforces or been able to include self-insurance or "merit rating" provisions in prospective legislation. Marion Folsom championed a New York unemployment plan in the hope that it would simply allow Kodak (and other Rochester employers) to maintain their municipal plan while forcing other firms to share its costs. As early as 1924, the Ohio Manufacturers' Association supported state unemployment insurance, primarily because major firms (including National Cash Register and the leaders of the Dayton and Cleveland garment industries) already had plans and could self-insure under the proposed law. Many firms that had tried to stabilize employment, usually far short of insurance, welcomed the opportunity to spread the costs of their plans. As one Wisconsin employer reasoned, influential employers "already had in their establishments a form of unemployment insurance which they introduced voluntarily, and in order to get other manufacturers to get in line, they naturally supported a law which made it compulsory for all manufacturers to adopt some form of unemployment insurance."[35]

34 P. Sherman to Gertrude Easley (12 November 1924), Box 28, NCF Papers; CoC Proceedings 19/26 (1931), 757–65, Chamber Papers; Quadagno, *Old Age Security*, 64–72; *MLR* 37:2 (August 1932): 251.
35 Jacoby, "Welfare Capitalism to Welfare State," 13; Dayton Committee on Stabilization of Unemployment to William Leiserson, File 11; E.S. Cowdrick to Leiserson, File 10, Leiserson Papers, State Historical Society of Wisconsin, Madison; C. Kiehl, "Stabilization of Employment," File 24; "Correspondence on Company Plans," File

The politicization of welfare was not without its pitfalls or its opponents. Support for state law was often shortsighted and fragmented. Many firms, according to prevailing patterns of labor relations and welfare policy, proved willing to support specific programs but objected to political efforts that combined them in omnibus "welfare" law. Others objected on distinctive competitive or regional grounds; Pacific canners, for example, were relatively isolated from market rivalries and found private welfare less burdensome than their eastern counterparts (although large firms in both regions favored state or federal law as a means of driving out seasonal competitors). More concentrated industries, such as cigarmaking, often balked at state legislation that would leave out-of-state competitive fringes untouched. Many simply feared an increase in manufacturing taxes, preferred the flexibility of private control, or felt they were the targets of regulatory welfare law. And even its initial proponents foreswore state welfare when it threatened interstate markets.[36]

In general, a wide range of business interests felt that state welfare law was the best, or at least most practical, alternative to the uncertainty and inequity of private plans. At the same time, of course, reform advocates in many states were also championing public pensions and unemployment insurance. Although these reformers were undoubtedly sincere, business objectives and anxieties circumscribed their political influence. Many "reform" groups – including the American Association for Labor Legislation (AALL), the American Association for Social Security, and Senators LaFollette of Wisconsin or Wagner of New York – had close ties to state business interests and often served as merely an articulate voice for the regulatory programs of local industries and firms. And although some mavericks had advocated state pensions and unemployment insurance since the turn of the century, such laws were not seriously considered until their utility to business interests was well established. Finally, state laws (drafted by business, political,

---

25; (quote) Highway Trailer Company to Edwin Witte (5 April 1935), File 54, CES Records.

36 William Graebner, "Federalism in the Progressive Era: A Structural Interpretation of Reform," *Journal of American History* [*JAH*] 64 (1977): 337–38. At DuPont, which faced little intrastate or interstate competition, welfare was thought better off in private hands. "It seems to me wise for private citizens to do the relief part so as to avoid the opening wedge of a 'dole' which the politician will never shut off," reasoned Irenée DuPont, "[while] private citizens can discontinue their contributions." The DuPonts provided surrogate relief in a number of communities, distributing funds that were in turn solicited from DuPont employees [I. DuPont to H.F. DuPont (27 October 1931); DuPont circular (15 March 1932), File 189, Irenee DuPont Papers, Hagley Museum].

and reform interests whose goals and clout varied from state to state) merely raised the political stakes. The resulting patchwork of state law pressed national political and economic interests to search for a federal solution that might achieve the regulatory benefits of public welfare while avoiding the costs of inconsistent and potentially radical state law.[37]

Competitive Federalism and Welfare Law

State pension and unemployment laws loosely reflected business goals but also created their own political and economic problems. Just as welfare capitalists saw their paternalism evolve into competitive disadvantage, progressive states (and firms in those states) bore the economic burden of scattered and uncoordinated state law. By the late 1920s, the competitive strategies of firms were intertwined with those of states and regions. Widely variant state law joined cutthroat competition as a central concern of employers and state politicians.

State legislation was crowded into northeastern and midwestern industrial states – that is, into those states in which the threat of industrial conflict made private and public welfare necessary. Legislators proposed state pensions in Massachusetts, Pennsylvania, and New Jersey before the war and in Massachusetts, New Jersey, and New York in virtually every legislative session after 1919. Pennsylvania passed the first state pension plan in 1923, three years before any southern state even considered the issue. By 1932, seventeen states (all in the North) had pension laws. More importantly, as counties opted into this patchwork of state pensions, northern states (and the region as a whole) bore the costs; between 1928 and 1934, the number of participating counties rose from 56 to 924, pensioners covered rose from 1,500 to 240,000, and disbursements skyrocketed from $300,000 to $32 million. Only Wisconsin legislated unemployment insurance before 1935, but there was a distinct regional alignment to the agitation for legislation. Be-

37 The connections between "reform" and corporate interests are commonly overblown [see, for example, William Domhoff, *The Higher Circles* (New York: Vintage, 1970), 156–250]. Business interests simply enjoyed the same material and organizational advantages in these forums as they did in politics generally. Moderate reform organizations (such as the American Association for Labor Legislation) depended heavily on corporate patronage. And many state-level reformers simply represented moderately progressive business interests. In Wisconsin, for example, the La-Follettes were extremely close to a number of industry leaders, including Robert Wood of Sears and H.W. Story of Allis-Chalmers (whose brother-in-law was the other Wisconsin Senator, Ryan Duffy). And Wisconsin reformer William Leiserson was strongly influenced by his work as an arbitrator in the needle trades.

tween 1916 and 1930, twenty-four bills were tabled in six northern states, whereas only one made it to the order paper in the South. Of 161 bills proposed in the next three years, 128 were in the Northeast and, in the first eight months of 1933, bills passed at least one house in five northern and two western states.[38] State unemployment insurance was not widespread enough to affect industrial or interstate competition, but the threat of inconsistent legislation was a constant worry for (especially northern) employers.

Legal and practical variations in state law exacerbated regional competition. Newer pension laws were contributory, insured, and placed fewer conditions on eligibility. Legislated and prospective unemployment insurance laws included the Wisconsin law (which reformers dismissed as "a business bill"); an AALL proposal that awarded employers incentives based on their track record under the law; draft bills in Michigan and Ohio that based merit ratings on existing conditions in given industries; and different methods of pooling employer contributions in every state. Federal legislation seemed the only escape from this "maddening diversity of benefits," especially given its sharp regional cast. Few southern states had legislated welfare, and fewer still took the provisions of their laws (mostly wage and hour standards) seriously, excepting key industries and "protecting" only a handful of workers.[39] Employers and reformers (for their own reasons) pressed for compulsory state pension and unemployment laws and, less certainly, a constitutional amendment that might facilitate a federal law. In 1933, industrial

38 Kevin Cox, "The Social Security Act of 1935 and the Geography of the American Welfare State" (unpublished, 1993), 3; on state law, see *ALLR* 15–25 (1915–1935); *MLR* 41 (1935): 303–26; Quadagno, *Old Age Security*, 72; John Andrews, "Prospects for Unemployment Compensation Laws," *Annals* 170 (1933); Industrial Relations Counselors, *An Historical Basis for Unemployment Insurance* (Minneapolis, 1934), 72–73, 177; Stewart, *Unemployment*, 570; Lubove, *Struggle for Social Security*, 53, 135–36; *BBLS* 496 (November 1929): 1–10; Edwin Witte, "Organized Labor and Social Security," in *Labor and the New Deal*, ed. Milton Derber and Edwin Young (Madison, 1957), 247–48. Workers' compensation followed similar regional lines, passing most northern legislatures in 1910 or 1911, while the "backward five" of the deep South were without compensation law as late as 1929.

39 Gender and ideologies of domesticity were crucial to the form and focus of "protective" labor and welfare laws and served as an important ancillary to their purely economic regulatory functions. See Susan Lehrer, *Origins of Protective Labor Legislation, 1905–1925* (Albany, 987); Heidi Hartmann, "Capitalism, Patriarchy and Job Segregation by Sex," *Signs* 1 (1976): 137–69; Patricia Brito, "Protective Legislation in Ohio: The Interwar Years," *Ohio History* 88 (1979): 173–97; Nancy Erickson, "Historical Background of 'Protective' Labor Legislation: Muller v. Oregon," in *Women and the Law*, ed. D. Kelly Weisberg (Cambridge, 1978) 2:155–86.

advisors to the NRA agreed that, given the inequities of state plans, "federal legislation probably is necessary."[40]

The specter of interstate competition not only pressed those who had passed state laws to lobby for federal intervention but also discouraged the passage of further state-level welfare law. As Justice Hugo Black concluded, "Individual states cannot and will not pass protective laws . . . if the manufacturers of other states are free to gain competitive advantage." Here the "all or nothing" strategy of northern employers paralleled the goals of labor and reform interests, all of whom supported federal law, especially as interstate competitive conditions stalled the progress of social legislation in the North. For northern "welfare" states, specific industries remained the basic unit of regulation, and the utility of uniform labor costs made federal legislation preferable to the relaxation of their own laws. The motives of "backward" southern states were, of course, quite the opposite. As welfare capitalism in northern firms became welfare policy in northern states, the absence of such legislation in the South became a cherished political and economic advantage.[41]

Business interests were forced to juggle the legislative conditions of certain states and the competitive conditions of certain industries. Most feared both

40 House Committee on Ways and Means, *Economic Security Act*, 74/1 (Washington, 1935), 56; Senate, *Unemployment*, vii–xv, 257–59; George Wheeler and Eleanor Wheeler, "Individual Employer Reserves in Unemployment Insurance," *Journal of Political Economy* 43 (1935): 250; Carter Goodrich, "An Analysis of American Plans For State Unemployment Insurance," *American Economic Review [AER]* 21 (1931): 399–415; Walter Morton, "The Aims of Unemployment Insurance with Especial Reference to the Wisconsin Act," *AER* 23 (1933): 400–401; E.E. Muntz, "An Analysis of the Wisconsin Unemployment Compensation Act," *AER* 22 (1932): 414–28; Leiserson to Leo Wolman (26 January 32), File 15; Leiserson to John Andrews (9 December 1931), File 1; E.A. Filene to Leiserson, File 14, Leiserson Papers; (quote) R. Williamson to M.G. Murray (15 January 1935), File 14, CES Records; "Report of the Unemployment Insurance Committee" (19 June 1934), File 350:8; Industrial Advisory Board, (quote) "Memorandum On Unemployment Insurance" (April 1934), file 350:8, National Recovery Administration [NRA] Records (RG 9), National Archives. On the South, see Quadagno, *Old Age Security*, 15–18; George Tindall, *The Emergence of the New South, 1913–1945* (Baton Rouge, 1967), 319, 433; Clarence Heer, *Income and Wages in the South* (Chapel Hill, 1930), 23–25; Wright, *Old South, New South*, 65–70, 198–238; "Study of the Workings of the Minimum Wage Laws" (1922), File V:16, NICB Papers; Department of Labor, *Minimum Wage Laws*, 14–17; *BBLS* 285 (July 1921): 16–21; NICB, *Industrial Progress and Regulatory Legislation in New York* (New York, 1927), 56–93; Nelson, *Unemployment Insurance*, 114–28; Dodd, *Administration of Workmens' Compensation*, 30–33.

41 M. Murray to Wagner (n.d.), File 228:1709, Robert F. Wagner Papers, Littauer Library, Georgetown University, Washington, D.C.; Black Address (15 July 1937), File 249, National Association of Manufacturers [NAM] Papers, Hagley Museum.

the prospect of competing on unequal terms in interstate commerce and the potential radicalism and fiscal irresponsibility of state governments. While some exploited inconsistencies in state law (the Pennsylvania Railroad opted in and out of worker's compensation plans according to an ongoing comparison of costs), the burden of multiple reporting and the uncertainty of operating on a "litigious borderland" hammered home the importance of federal, or at least coordinated, welfare law, as a means of avoiding competitive disadvantage. Most employers took a more shortsighted tack, seeking either uniform legislation in those states in which competing firms were located or (focusing on labor markets rather than product markets) uniform legislation in bordering states. The former option raised the dangers of industry-specific law; legislative unity could be pursued in the states that comprised the Central Competitive Coal Field, for example, but manufacturers were more or less able to flee burdensome legal control. The latter option held out the potential of controlling regional labor costs but stopped short of addressing regional competition.[42]

Labor-intensive and regionally competitive industries led the fight against regional disparity in welfare law. In textiles, a steady migration of spindles from the North had made federal welfare standards a long-standing goal of northern mills. In the needle trades, the organizational weakness of the employers themselves forced those paying higher costs (large northern urban firms) to lobby for uniformity where costs diverged most sharply: wages and welfare. Although welfare expenditure was not a major concern for most competitors, mandated unemployment insurance or pensions could destroy the ability of "gypsy" contractors to compete at all. In soft coal, plummeting demand, high fixed costs, and volatile levels of organization among both capital and labor left southern states dragging their heels over industry-wide welfare law. Uniform safety and compensation costs were dominant concerns of northern operators, and early federal discussion of unemployment insurance was inspired in part by the prospect of rationalizing competition by compelling continuous operation. Of course, leading firms in these industries also leaned on unions to enforce uniform labor standards (including adherence by all competitors to state or industry welfare law). Welfare law re-

---

42 Jacoby, "Welfare Capitalism to Welfare State," 16; "Witte memo of Conversation with Raskob" (October 1934), File 21, CES Records; Business Advisory and Planning Council, "Industry's Responsibility to the Unemployed" (1934), File 310, Raskob Papers; Frank Whiting [New York Central] to S.J. Peterson (4 December 1923), File 1175:10; "Report of the Subcommittee to Consider Federal Workmen's Compensation" (22 August 1932), File 1175:11; Duncan Brent memo (25 January 1933), File 1175:12, PRR Papers; NICB, *Legislation in New York State*, 2, 93, 147.

mained an important alternative to regulatory unionism, especially considering union weakness and the attendant risks of unionization.[43]

Competitive labor-intensive industries and those relying upon skilled labor (including many early champions of welfare capitalism) preferred federal standards to the heavy hand of unions or the inconsistent grip of state law. As a congressional advisor argued, "These acts are not health or safety laws but business laws to eliminate unfair competition between states."[44] Federal welfare, however, faced legal and practical obstacles. Constitutional precedent tolerated little federal regulation of interstate commerce and, throughout the 1920s, the courts had pointedly limited federal welfare initiatives. As a result, provisional attempts at interstate cooperation preceded federal action.

States had experimented with interstate regulatory cooperation in the Progressive era and renewed their efforts in response to interwar disparity in welfare law. A lengthy study of welfare law sponsored by the Associated Industries of New York was predicated on cooperation among the top twelve industrial states (which, with the exception of California and Missouri, bordered each other in the Northeast). Roosevelt tried to "stimulate collective action" on this front at a Governor's Conference in 1929 but, for the most part, interstate cooperation focused on limited and discretionary problems

43 Some labor-intensive industries resisted welfare law. The lumber industry, for example, had uniformly dismal labor conditions, virtually no existing unionization, and a competitive "cut and get out" ethos. The industry was also without a northeastern core and leading firms; it was common practice to dissolve a company after logging a given area and take only capital to the next site. And slipping demand made the industry as a whole reluctant to weather a general increase in costs. Ironically, it was southern operators who initiated meager welfare provisions under these conditions, hoping that housing and benefits would stem the migration of workers to the North. See Vernon Jensen, *Lumber and Labor* (New York, 1945), 12–21, 24–34, 154–61; Charlotte Todes, *Labor and Lumber* (New York, 1931), 75–89, 101, 170–80; James Fickle, *The New South and the "New Competition": Trade Association Development in the Southern Pine Industry* (Urbana, 1980), 287–329; William G. Robbins, *Lumberjacks and Legislators: Political Economy of the U. S. Lumber Industry, 1890–1941* (College Station, 1982).

44 *ALLR* 14 (1924): 54–59, 71. Many industries viewed the standardization of welfare costs in the context of federal protection on other fronts. Protectionist producers were willing to tolerate uniform labor costs as long as they were reflected in tariffs and import quotas, and the railroads were open to any industry-wide advances in benefits as long as Interstate Commerce Commission (ICC) rates were adjusted accordingly. It proved difficult, however, to graft welfare onto federal regulation of the railroads, and the existence of the federal ICC actually hampered efforts to include the railroads in New Deal welfare law. See Carman Randolph, "Memorandum on the Federal Workmen's Compensation Commission" (n.d.), File 1175:8; and "Fair Labor Standards Act, 1938," File 909:27–29, PRR Papers.

among small groups of states. State business and political interests pursued interstate compacts through loosely knit industrial and political organizations such as the NCF, the National Conference of Commissioners on Uniform State Laws, the New England Council, the Association for the Coordination of Law and Industry, various state committees on cooperation, and the Rockefeller-financed AALL. From 1910, when eight northern states agreed on uniform compensation laws, to 1934, when a different eight northern states drafted uniform employment standards, regional cooperation was a crucial (if politically impotent) facet of state legislation.[45]

Interstate initiatives tended to cement rather than solve regional competition. Through the 1920s, northern states pursued regional agreement through legislative cooperation, while southern states tacitly agreed to maintain their advantage by shunning any such pacts. Moreover, interstate agreements existed in a constitutional twilight and were rarely binding. Attempts to integrate the Northeast collided with the legislative agendas of specific industries. Although most large firms in Ohio or Pennsylvania favored uniformity with their industrial neighbors, mining interests in these states had to contend with southern operators. In 1919, legislators from Oregon, Washington, California, and British Columbia concluded a futile effort to set standards with no choice left but to "urge federal regulation" of wages and welfare. Agreements among northern states did little for those competing with the South, and international competition in some sectors and border states eroded support for any regional regulation. Inequitable state law and the futility of interstate agreements were so apparent by the early 1930s that most states and industries lobbied directly for federal law.[46]

45 James T. Patterson, *The New Deal and the States: Federalism in Transition* (Princeton, 1969), 17–37; Mass. Dept. of Corporations and Taxation to Delaware State Tax Commission (30 December 1926), File 765:1, Pierre S. DuPont Papers, Hagley Museum; Roosevelt cited in Raymond Munts, "Policy Development in Unemployment Insurance," in *Federal Policies and Worker Status Since the Thirties*, ed. Joseph Goldberg (Madison, 1976), 75; Memo for Conference with Governors (March 1933), President's Secretary's File 74; Joseph Ely [Mass. Governor] to FDR (6 July 1934), Official File [OF] 407, FDR Papers. See also the National Conference of Commissioners Records, Files 17–22, Nathan MacChesney Papers, HCHPL; Jane Perry Clark, "Interstate Compacts and Social Legislation," *Political Science Quarterly* 50 (1935); 502–24; Clark, "Interstate Compacts and Social Legislation II: Interstate Compacts after Negotiation," *Political Science Quarterly* 51 (1936); 36–60; Graebner, "Federalism in the Progressive Era," 341–57.

46 NICB, *Legislation in New York*, 10–11, 28–30, 50–55; *Report of the Commission on Compensation for Industrial Accidents* (Boston, 1912), 17–20, 26–27; Connecticut Unemployment Commission, *Measures to Alleviate Unemployment in Connecticut* (Orange, 1932), 26, 159–64; Senate, *National Economic Council*, 409, 485–86, 547; "Re-

Before 1935, federal welfare initiatives were few and far between. Civil War pensions, federal authority over the District of Columbia, and wage standards for government employees or contracts were all seen as potential seedbeds for national standards. Federal regulation of the railroads also served as a promising constitutional foot-in-the-door; under the Transportation Act of 1920 and the Railway Labor Act of 1926, federal administrators and railway executives had clearly established the benefits of uniform labor standards and encountered few political or constitutional obstacles.[47] But such initiatives had little impact. In peacetime, federal employment and contracts lacked the economic power to drive policy. Regulatory law for the District of Columbia (with its limited industrial base) had little influence. And the operation of the railroads was so historically intertwined with federal rate regulation that pressure for legislation resulted in a run of discretionary laws for the railroads alone.[48]

Beyond these areas, the courts consistently interpreted federal welfare policy as an attempt to regulate state industry under the guise of the interstate commerce clause, an argument set forth in the decision overturning the Federal Child Labor Act of 1916. In the wake of this setback, federal business and political interests began crafting the legal basis for the SSA. As early as 1924, federal enforcement of national standards through uniform state law and conditional grants-in-aid was raised as a possible end-run around constitutional restrictions.[49] Legal precedent effectively collapsed

port of the Committee on Employer's Liability and Workmen's Compensation" (1912), File 1175:8, PRR Papers; "Interstate Compact on Minimum Wages" (1934), File 249, NAM Papers; Minutes of First Executive Committee Meeting (5 May 1916), Reel 1, NICB Papers; NAM Annual Report (1934), File 851.1, NAM Papers; Morris, *Oregon's Experience with Wage Legislation*, 207–8; Quadagno, *Old Age Security*, 101. Ohio manufacturers argued that Canadian competition forced them to fight welfare law at state and federal levels [Senate Committee on Finance, *Economic Security Act* (Washington, 1935), 1102].

47 NRA, Division of Review, "Possibility of Government Contract Provisions as a Means of Establishing Economic Standards," Work Materials #26 (Washington, 1938); Skocpol and Ikenberry, "Political Formation of the Welfare State," 95, 111–12; Latimer, *Industrial Pension Systems*, 1:34–37.

48 G.L. Peck memo, File 1175:6; "Report of the Special Committee on an Unemployment Compensation Plan for Railways" (27 January 1938), File 806:1; "Railroad Unemployment Compensation Act, 1936–1938," File 806:1, PRR Papers; *ALLR* 14 (1924): 326–27; Latimer, *Industrial Pension Systems*, 2:650–55, 675; Quadagno, *Old Age Security*, 72–74; NICB, "Trends in Company Pension Plans," *Studies In Personnel Policy* 61 (1944): 44–48.

49 *ALLR* 14 (1924): 72–80. The federal government did sanction the private welfare system by amending tax laws in 1916, 1919, and 1928 to allow deduction of employer

with the economy in 1929 and, although federal law did not follow quickly or without legal challenge, the Depression allowed the proponents of federal welfare, including many business interests, to steal the constitutional high ground from recalcitrant business and political factions.

The Origins of Social Security

The Depression thrust welfare into the spotlight of state and federal politics. Regulation (even socialization) of private welfare benefits, long an idle wish of welfare capitalists and progressive northern states, took on a new urgency with the economic collapse. Massive unemployment and the bankruptcy of local relief spurred numerous state welfare laws, and organized labor abandoned its traditionally voluntarist and skeptical approach to social insurance.[50] Business demands for some sort of federal welfare law, however, quickly overshadowed or redirected reform and labor initiatives. Employers managing private pensions or in states that had passed pension laws continued pushing for a federal law. Firms or industries managing their own unemployment plans were anxious to be relieved of the costs, and, more importantly, leading employers sought to stem any advance in state-level law. Even amidst the widespread misery of the early 1930s, business was able to keep employment-based welfare within the regulatory channels established in the 1920s.

Although relief from private pensions and inconsistent state pension law had been a goal of welfare capitalists since the early 1920s, unemployment insurance took center stage in welfare debates after 1929. Only five states had unemployment insurance laws by 1935 (and all except Wisconsin's were passed within weeks of the SSA), but the threat of genuinely progressive state law and "radically different requirements" from state to state pressed employers to bypass further state-level experimentation and lobby for a comprehensive federal law. "Partial adoption of unemployment insurance would make cost burdens unequal among competitors," cautioned Roosevelt's advisers; "to meet these difficulties and to supplement voluntary adoption of

welfare contributions and in 1926 to exempt interest earned on pension funds from taxation. The ICC allowed the calculation of welfare liabilities as an operating expense. The connection between welfare benefits and federal tax policy was not driven home until 1942, when the IRS made pension funds fully deductible. See Dearing, *Industrial Pensions*, 35–36, 40; Rainard Robbins, *Impact of Taxes on Industrial Pension Systems* (New York, 1949), 8, 46–47, 71.

50 "Labor's Appeal for Economic and Legislative Relief" (1930), PF 59, Hoover Papers; Keyssar, *Out of Work*, 291–98.

unemployment compensation plans, employers should be required by legislation to make some provision for unemployment reserves."[51]

For their part, employers were of three minds regarding the passage of a federal pension and unemployment insurance law. Welfare capitalists and leading firms in competitive industries continued to lobby for a federal law that would relieve them of the costs of private and state plans and regulate competition by imposing higher labor costs on their rivals. The Depression, after all, had underlined the costs of private welfare and exacerbated the relentless competition that public welfare might help regulate. Small firms and southern political and economic interests resisted efforts to socialize or nationalize the costs of industrial welfare. And a substantial number of northern and southern employers, many of whom had considerable clout in state and local circles but less-certain status in federal politics, reasoned that "if the flood is upon us, then let us seek to direct the channels and save as much destruction as possible."[52] In this respect, the passage of state laws significantly broadened business support for a federal law. Even those for whom pension or unemployment law promised few material or regulatory returns were likely to support a federal initiative once programs were imposed or threatened in the states.

Through 1930–31, business fought to control (or contain) federal welfare policy through Congress and a network of formal and informal advisory committees. Senator Wagner served as a congressional conduit for proposals drafted by the AALL; a House investigation of unemployment flirted with uniform state law compelled by federal taxes (foreshadowing the SSA); and leading corporate interests, in part through the President's Organization on Unemployment Relief, began "a quiet study of the best compulsory insurance laws" in preparation for a federal law. Swope of GE provided the most important public synthesis of the business view in his 1931 testimony before the Senate Committee on Manufacturers. Amidst his wide-ranging plea for

---

51 F. Ecker [Metropolitan Life] to Hoover (24 Febuary 1931), PPF 80, Hoover Papers; (quote) "Preliminary Report on Unemployment Insurance" (April 1934), File 14, Leon Henderson Papers, FDRPL. Although most major employers did not object to universal adoption of the distinctly business-oriented Wisconsin bill (which provided for reserves segregated by employer), laws drafted in other states through the early 1930s were more progressive. Most notable of these was New York's Byrnes-Condon Law (passed in early 1935), which provided for a statewide compensation pool. See "Memorandum for the President: Unemployment Insurance" (11 September 1931), PF 176, Hoover Papers; Francis McConnell to Leiserson (1 May 1935); Abraham Epstein to Leiserson (5 Apr. 1934), File 2, Leiserson Papers.

52 Edwin Michael to H.B. McCormack (16 September 1935), File V:341, Westmoreland Coal Papers.

trade association autonomy and antitrust revision, Swope clearly appreciated the regulatory potential of federal welfare. "If you wait for state legislation," he noted, "you are bound to have different laws enacted in different states, with, therefore, varying burdens upon the industries who have to compete with each other across state lines." The solution was a federal law that would enforce uniform business policy. "I think it is impossible to get 100 percent acceptance on [a] voluntary basis, even in as enlightened an industry as the electrical manufacturing industry," Swope argued; "if, therefore, you want to have some plan of stabilization of industry . . . you must have some form of Federal Legislation."[53] The welfare provisions of the Swope Plan remained at the core of the debate over welfare policy.

The passage of the NRA in 1933 interrupted the federal welfare debate but included (in its collective bargaining provisions) a similarly premised attempt to regulate labor costs. In practice, of course, the NRA accomplished little. While some hoped that the organizational benefits of union wages would outweigh their costs, most resented either the initial intrusion or the ultimate failure of NRA labor policy. The NRA strengthened collective bargaining in some industries, but wages and benefits were still determined by limited bargaining power in a depressed economy. And under the industrial codes, wage differentials between North and South were more often frozen than closed. In the end, the NRA simply strengthened the conviction that business should establish terms of competition "subject to federal government supervision [and] . . . agree on standard minimum labor costs."[54]

Throughout the tenure of the NRA, employers continued to consider federal welfare law on its own merits and as a defense against more radical state and labor proposals. In 1934, the business-led Committee on Economic Security (CES) reworked the Swope Plan, hoping that "standards for all states in such a federal co-operative system would furnish the bottom below which there must be no chiseling or exploitation" and complaining that the plan left marginal firms unchecked (by exempting those who employed less than fifty workers) and perpetuated the nagging contradiction between voluntarism and effective regulation (by focusing on trade associations). Through 1934, most employers were divided between a plan of federal taxes

53 (Quote) CoC Proceedings 19/26 (1931), Chamber Papers; "Mr. Swope's Insurance Plan," *The New Republic* (1 April 1931): 202; "Memorandum on Swope-Young Plan" (1931); Draft: "Swope-Young Plan" (1931), PF 92, Hoover Papers; (Swope quoted in) Senate, *National Economic Council*, 308; Grant Farr, *Origins of Recent Labor Policy* (Boulder, 1959), 20–22.

54 Bryce Stein, "Unemployment Insurance," File 21, CES Records. On NRA wage differentials, see Wright, *New Deal, Old South*, 216–19.

and grants-in-aid designed to establish state-to-state uniformity and a congressional plan (favored by Senator Wagner) that gave more leeway to the states and "secure[d] uniformity where uniformity is essential, namely the equalization of competitive costs." Most agreed, however, that industrial regulation was the central premise of federal welfare. Wagner noted "considerable sentiment for the enactment of a single and uniform national system" that might erase the "competitive advantage" enjoyed by firms or states without welfare costs.[55]

The SSA included provisions for a broad range of aid and relief, but the pension and unemployment insurance programs were central. Both were keyed to industrial labor markets (as a compromise with southern Democrats, domestic and agricultural labor were excluded) and provided relief only incidentally to their regulatory functions.[56] Although much of the business debate over welfare law through the 1920s had focused on pensions, the new federal law leaned heavily on the regulatory potential of the unemployment program. Despite the fact that only Wisconsin had passed an unemployment law before 1935, many more were actively considering legislation (which, in some states, had passed one house or been defeated narrowly). For most, the threat of inconsistent or inequitable state law was enough to inspire support for a federal solution. In turn, while private or state-level unemployment insurance was rare, the regulatory potential of a federal law (which could compel all firms and regions to participate) was considerable. For these reasons, employers applied a decade of lessons learned in administering private and state pensions most vigorously in their demands for federal unemployment law.

55 Wilbur Cohen, "The Swope Plan: A Critical Analysis" (14 September 1934), File 17; "Confidential Report of the Advisory Council to the Committee on Social Security" (18 December 1934), File 6, CES Records; "Report of the Unemployment Insurance Committee to the Industrial Advisory Board" (June 1934), OF 121a, FDR Papers; Senate, *Economic Security Act*, (quote) 3, 22, 126, 162–63; House, *Economic Security Act*, 145–46. The Committee on Economic Security (including Folsom of Eastman-Kodak, Swope of GE, Teagle of Standard Oil, and Leeds of Leeds & Northrup) was an offshoot of NRA industrial advisory boards, the Business Advisory Council, and the Industrial Advisory Board to the President's Organization on Unemployment Relief. See File 19:2, 3, 5, POUR Records; membership lists, File 1:3, Business Advisory Council [BAC] Records, Records of the Department of Commerce (RG 40), National Archives.
56 On agricultural labor, see Lee J. Alston and Joseph P. Ferrie, "Labor Costs, Paternalism, and Loyalty in Southern Agriculture: A Constraint on the Growth of the Welfare State," *JEH* 45 (1985): 95–117; Warren G. Whatley, "Labor for the Picking: The New Deal and the South," *JEH* 43 (1983): 905–29.

Haphazardly and (as it would turn out) ineffectively, the SSA reflected long-standing business concerns. Retailers and consumer-goods firms hoped to buttress aggregate demand.[57] International sectors were willing to exchange wage and welfare concessions for freer trade. And fragmented, labor-intensive sectors pressed for relief from competition, destabilizing levels of unionization, and regional inconsistency in welfare law. "The plea of certain business interests that the time is not ripe [for social security] is a mistaken one," reasoned Swope; "so long as the legislation is applied on a nationwide basis, it makes no difference to industry that unemployment insurance [and pensions] may slightly increase costs." Predictably, the SSA (especially in its pension provisions) also dovetailed with existing company and state plans.[58]

With business largely satisfied with the act's regulatory purposes, debate was confined to two issues: "merit ratings," which would allow firms with established unemployment plans or records of stable employment to opt out of the SSA, and employee contributions to the pension and unemployment programs. Folsom, pioneer of the Kodak and Rochester unemployment plans (and confidant of Senator Wagner) led the charge for some form of merit rating. Others agreed that the act should not "load the cost of seasonal employment upon the companies that have succeeded in stabilizing employment." The CES initially avoided the merit rating issue and concen-

57 The auto industry as a whole was fairly indifferent to the regulatory aspects of federal welfare, but GM executives championed any support of aggregate income that might rekindle the flagging automobile market. An early model for federal welfare was the "Deane Plan," drafted by an executive of GM's consumer financing division (GMAC). Although critics correctly viewed it as an "outright subsidy to consumption," the Deane Plan was widely considered in business and political circles in the early 1930s. See "Report of the Committee on Economic Security," 890ff., File 70, Edwin Witte Papers, State Historical Society of Wisconsin; "Deane Plan," File 28; Alexander Sachs to Donaldson Brown, File 28; "Course of Decline in Employment," File 122; Dahlberg, "Supplementary Report on the Deane Plan," File 123, Alexander Sachs Papers, FDRPL; "Deane Plan," Official File 396; Raskob to Roosevelt (15 December 1933), PPF 226, FDR Papers.

58 Marion Folsom, "Company Annuity Plans and the Federal Old Age Benefit Plan," *Harvard Business Review* 14 (1936): 414–24; NICB, "Company Pension Plans and the SSA," 8, 24; SCC Reports 1935 and 1936, Boxes 28 and 21, Harrington Papers; Don Martin [Ohio Manufacturer's Association] to James Emery (25 September 1935), file 852.1; "Provisions of Company Pension Plans as adjusted to the Social Security Act," File 258, NAM Papers; H.M Forster file, File 56, CES Records; "Memorandum: Conference on Social Security," Advisory Council Subject File 350:8, NRA Records; Witte memorandum of interview with Swope (October 1934), File 21, CES Records; "Preliminary Draft of [CES] Report" (1934), file 201, Witte Papers.

trated its efforts on getting the bill through the House in any form, "since there will ample time to get it fixed up in the Senate." Folsom renewed his efforts while the bill languished between the House and Senate in May. When the Senate passed their version in June, merit ratings were granted by the "Clark amendment," which then became the sticking point in six weeks of Senate-House conference debates. Finally, even Folsom admitted that such a provision was "quite futile," adding that "he would not be interested in attempting to handle his own plan to do the government's job." Perhaps more importantly, private insurers repeatedly reminded Folsom and others that they would have little to do with company plans, which by this time were considered a poor risk. The conference report dropped the Clark amendment.[59]

Business interests also pressed the issue of employee contributions (which employers had introduced as private plans proved costly and the courts strengthened employees' drawing rights). The CES and Business Advisory Council urged employee contributions when early estimates set the cost of Social Security as high as 5 percent of payrolls. Swope and Walter Teagle (of Standard Oil) added that employee contributions would increase benefits and encourage employee loyalty even if they did not ease the employer's costs. Others were opposed or indifferent to employee contributions, in part because they did not bear on the problem of interstate competition, which was central to the entire program, and in part because "contributions by employers are, in the long run, passed on to consumers, while contributions paid by workers . . . cannot be shifted." These were weak objections in the face of an overwhelming push to spread the costs of private welfare to competitors *and* to employees. The final bill entrenched the sharply regressive principle of employee contributions.[60]

The pension and unemployment provisions of the SSA took direct aim at laggard states and firms. Business proponents of the SSA hoped that the

59 Folsom to Wagner (13 March 1934), File 328:2; Thomas Eliot to Wagner (23 June 1935), File 328:20; Folsom to Wagner (13 May 1935), File 328:20, Wagner Papers; (quote)Adams [John Manning Paper] to Edwin Witte (20 November 1934), File 58; Deane [GM] to Arthur Altmeyer (11 November 1934), File 44; Witte to John Andrews (2 April 1935), File 54; (quote) Rulon Williamson to Witte (25 July 1935), File 14, CES Records; Witte, "Organized Labor and Social Security," 252–53.

60 W.E. Woodward to Wagner (7 May 1934), File 382:2, Wagner Papers; BAC, "Report of the Committee on Social Legislation" (10 April 1935), File 17; Swope to Witte (10 December 1934); Teagle to Witte (11 December 1934), File 16; "Statement Concerning the Report of the Committee on Social Legislation" (10 April 1935), File 17; (quote) "Confidential Report of the Advisory Council to the Committee on Economic Security" (18 December 1934), File 6, CES Records.

national payroll tax set up to fund the unemployment program would "stimulate state payroll levies" and "remove the unfair competitive advantage" enjoyed by some (primarily southern) states. The payroll tax was "deposited with the Secretary of Treasury for safekeeping and management," and its proceeds were to be returned to the state upon passage of adequate legislation. In this way, all firms would bear the costs of unemployment insurance, while only those with existing (or frantically legislated) state laws would reap the benefits. State legislators hurried the passage of skeletal legislation in an effort to take advantage of this "taxation angle." As John Emery of the protectionist and southern-dominated National Association of Manufacturers (NAM) complained, the SSA was "intended not to produce revenue, but to produce legislation." The Social Security Administration itself drafted most of the state laws.[61]

The compulsory pension program (funded by employee and employer contributions) was similarly designed to spread the costs of private and inconsistently legislated state pensions among all states and firms. Although the SSA also included welfare provisions unconnected to private labor markets (destitute old-age assistance and aid to dependent children and the blind), debate over the costs and benefits of these programs was largely divorced from consideration of the "business" provisions (unemployment insurance and payroll-financed pensions). Most importantly, financial responsibility for simple relief was left entirely to the states; federal aid encouraged states to channel funds into programs in which matching federal funds were available, but states or firms were not compelled to participate.[62]

Legislators and business interests whose respective states had assumed welfare burdens strongly supported the SSA. As H.W. Story of Milwaukee-based Allis-Chalmers argued, the welfare system needed "some sort of compulsion . . . we are already making contributions in Wisconsin and would

61 (Quote) M. Murray to Witte (19 March 1935), File 1; (quote) "Revised Draft of Final Report" [1935], File 6; J. Clark, "Some Inter-relationships of Federal and State law," File 12, CES Records; "Summary of Federal-State Subsidy Plan" (November 1934), File 2:3, BAC Records; House, *Economic Security Act*, 41, 148–49; Senate, *Economic Security Act*, (quote) 5, 6, 226–37, 926; (quote) Don Martin [Ohio Manufacturers' Association] to James Emery (25 September 1935), File 852.1, NAM Papers; Raymond Atkinson, *The Federal Role in Unemployment Compensation Administration* (Washington, 1941); U.S. Senate, *Arguments in the Cases Arising under the Social Security Act*, S. Doc. 53 (Washington, 1937), 2–17, 36–39, 122–33; Social Security Board, "Draft Bills for State Unemployment Compensation" (January 1936), File 1165:6, PRR Papers.
62 Clarence Heer, "Financing the Social Security System in the South," *SEJ* 4 (1938): 292–94, 299.

like our competitors to do likewise." The congressional delegations of Massachusetts, Michigan, New Jersey, New York, and Ohio – all states with significant pension liabilities – led the fight for a federal law. Indeed, New York State alone was responsible for 53 percent of all pensioners covered under state law, and its annual pension costs were $1.23 per capita, almost twice the state average of $.77. This burden certainly contributed to Senator Wagner's championship of federal welfare. Many midwestern interests (including Robert Wood of Sears and the LaFollettes of Wisconsin), were also dismayed by the deflationary impact of New Deal banking legislation and hoped that "passage of the unemployment bill will be in itself a large inflationary measure, which will . . . depreciate the dollar and lead to its ultimate revaluation." Broader support came from the renewed Democratic Party, which had established a complex power base composed of a rigidly one-party South, disenchanted northern voters, and (most crucially) a badly coordinated coalition of northern industrial interests.[63]

Predictably, business support for the SSA was strongest among profit-anxious, competitive firms that saw federal welfare law as both an extension of ill-fated experiments in welfare capitalism and a pragmatic response to state law they may or may not have supported. Typical was the Wisconsin truck manufacturer who had unsuccessfully opposed his state's welfare laws and, by 1935, was ready to up the ante by supporting a federal law: "Since we are at such a distinct disadvantage with our competitors in other states, you can readily see that Wisconsin manufacturers, doing an interstate business, are more interested to see that this social legislation becomes national in scope rather than restricted only to our particular state." After 1929, support also came from a number of leading employers (including the business members of the CES, all of whom had experimented with private welfare plans in the 1920s) who hoped that federal unemployment insurance would regulate competition, preempt more radical state initiatives, and pre-

63 (Quote) H.W. Story in "National Conference on Economic Security" (November 1934), File 4, CES Records; House, *Economic Security Act*, 77, 192–93; Senate, *Economic Security Act*, 70; *MLR* 37:2 (August 1932), 252, 258–59; Robert LaFollette to Robert Wood [Sears] (5 April 1933); (quote) Wood to LaFollette (7 April 1933), File 9, Robert Wood Papers, HCHPL; LaFollete telegram to Roosevelt (23 February 1933), PPF 1792; LaFollette to Roosevelt (14 January 1935), PPF 6659; Perkins Memo (11 January 1935), PPF 1792, FDR Papers. On the Democrats, see Joel Rogers and Thomas Ferguson, *Right Turn: The Decline of the Democrats and the Future of American Politics* (New York, 1986), 40–50; Richard F. Bensel, *Sectionalism and American Political Development, 1880–1980* (Madison, 1984), 155–73, 317–67; V.O. Key, *Southern Politics in State and Nation* (New York, 1949), 315–84; Tindall, *Emergence of the New South*, 607–49.

serve existing unemployment and pension plans while spreading their costs among competitors. And retailers and some consumer-goods industries had supported state welfare law and, because those programs were threatened by the Depression, pressed for federal action after 1929. Generally, both those that had supported state legislation and those that had found it burdensome supported the federal act.[64]

Business support for the SSA was far from uniform. But business opposition reflected the disparate goals of different industries and firms and not any generic objection to the premises of public welfare. The SSA's strongest opponents were small firms. "It is one thing for Swope, Folsom, Leeds, Lewisohn and me to accept the proposal of a tax on payroll . . . because our companies can absorb the additional expense," admitted Teagle, "but [it is] a horse from a different garage with a great majority of the smaller employers." The SSA inspired spirited debates within the Chamber of Commerce, the NAM, and the NICB, but the ability of smaller and regional firms to deadlock their peers on the issue did little to check business interest in the SSA's passage. The fiscally conservative NICB opposed compulsory federal welfare, but employers among its membership dissented sharply from the board's position. As one Chamber of Commerce director observed, the debate over social security was little more than "an issue between certain [business] factions, particularly in the manufacturing end."[65] As in earlier debates over private and state welfare, the "business" position was characterized by material and competitive anxieties, limited horizons, and a chronic distrust of the political institutions which business consistently relied upon to solve their problems.

Political and economic opposition also came from the South, which feared losing its wage advantage and disrupting the paternalist and racial premises

64 (Quote) Highway Trailer Company to Witte (5 April 1935), File 54, CES Records; Jacoby, "Welfare Capitalism to Welfare State," 4, 14; Edwin Witte, *The Development of the Social Security Act* (Madison, 1962), 50–89.

65 (Quote) Teague to Witte (11 December 1934), File 16, CES Records; "Confidential Memorandum on NICB Conference" (15 October 1934), Post-Presidential Individual File 3848, Hoover Papers; (quote) CoC Proceedings 23/30 (1935), 141, Chamber Papers; on the debate within the chamber, see CoC Proceedings 23/30 (1935), Chamber Papers; *New York Times*, 25 January 1935, 1; on NAM, see "Social Security Legislation," handwritten notes on SSA; Social Security Committee Meeting (25 January 1935), File V:1; Social Security Committee Meeting (16 April 1936), File V:2, NAM Papers. As one example of industry divisions, U.S. Steel (whose competitive position had continued to slip under the NRA) supported the Social Security Act, whereas the association of smaller manufacturers, the National Metal Trades Association, opposed it (Senate, *Economic Security Act*, 869–72).

of the southern political economy ("The average Mississippian," noted the *Jackson Daily News*, "can't imagine himself chipping in to pay pensions for able-bodied Negroes to sit around in idleness"). For one southern executive, the SSA was a tactic of "northern industrialists backed by labor and the President against the South and its industrial development." Senator Harry Byrd (D-Virginia) accused the Roosevelt administration of "coercing the states to do what the Federal Government desires, although the money originally comes from the states." As the Depression persisted, however, the recalcitrance of southern politicos softened. Hard times loosened the ties between southern employers and southern congressional interests, as maximizing the flow of federal relief and ensuring reelection proved more powerful incentives than continued championship of the low-wage economy. Tempted by the partisan coat-tails of the Roosevelt presidency and pressed by local necessity, southern legislators exacted the exemption of agricultural labor and subscribed reluctantly to welfare regulation. Somewhat ironically, the South was so solidly and predictably Democratic that the political costs of pointedly anti-South legislation were minimal.[66]

The South hoped superficial compliance with the SSA would affect industrial competition as little as possible, and most state laws passed hurriedly in 1935 anticipated a constitutional test. Edwin Michael, a Virginia employer, complained to his state manufacturers' association that if the SSA were held unconstitutional, any state that had gone along "would find itself committed to a system of pensions and of taxes developed without reference to its particular needs . . . and probably without corresponding legislation in a number of other states which are business competitors." Conversely, the failure to pass laws might mean that "industries in that particular state, and employers in that particular state [would] suffer" if the SSA was upheld. The administration of the act allayed southern fears. Despite its regulatory pretensions, the SSA did little to transform industrial competition. The exception of agricultural workers from its provisions ensured that reserves of inexpensive labor would remain even as industrial wages were pulled near

66 Tindall, *Emergence of the New South*, 373, 473–91 (*Jackson Daily News* cited, 491), 618; (quote) J. Rogers to R. Graham (18 June 1935), File II:404:4, Westmoreland Papers; Senate, *Economic Security Act*, 2–13, 70–79 (Byrd quote, 70), 122. See also A. Cash Koeniger, "The New Deal and the States: Roosevelt versus the Byrd Organization in Virginia," *JAH* 68 (1982): 876–96; Lee Alston and Joseph Ferrie, "Resisting the Welfare State: Southern Opposition to Farm Security Administration," in *The Emergence of the Modern Political Economy*, ed. Robert Higgs (Greenwich, 1985), 91–114; Gavin Wright, "The Political Economy of New Deal Spending," *Review of Economics and Statistics* 52 (1974): 30–38.

northern standards. And as southern states scrambled to raise revenue for matching federal grants, they relied on a narrow and regressive tax base. While costs to southern industry increased, the SSA actually widened the state-to-state disparity in welfare expenditure.[67] Overall, the funding provisions of the SSA marked a significant retreat from the inconsistently progressive provisions of legislated or impending state laws and did little to stem regional competition.

The combination of scattered business demand for a federal welfare policy and widespread business determination to avoid its costs resulted, as William Leuchtenberg notes, in "an astonishingly inept and conservative piece of legislation."[68] Indeed, the ink was scarcely dry on the SSA's final draft when most business interests began to question its intent and impact. Small and southern business, ably represented by NAM, had consistently questioned the premises of federal welfare law. This sentiment spread quickly after 1935 and by the late 1930s had found a voice among some of the earliest and strongest proponents of federal social security. Business opposition grew with an appreciation of the material and managerial costs of welfare regulation and with the failure of the SSA to provide the market stability it promised. Cutthroat competitors continued to flout federal law; sharp regional wage differentials remained; and in international competition, federal standards became a liability for all firms. In short, the baldly contradictory macroeconomic, regulatory, and fiscal goals (and consequences) of the SSA reflected the immense political power and the chronic shortsightedness and disunity of business interests.

The SSA (now widely considered a monument to antibusiness policy and bureaucratic excess) was, in essence, a business bill. Although spurred in large part by reform and class pressures in the trough of a general depression, the SSA also reflected the efforts of industrial and regional interests to rationalize disparate experiments in state and private welfare and to spread the

---

67 Edwin Michael to Virginia Manufacturers' Association (6 December 1935), File V:341, Westmoreland Papers; Heer, "Financing the Social Security Program in the South," 299; transcript of Hopkins-Morgenthau telephone conversation (8 January 1935), File 3:58–60, Morgenthau Diaries, FDRPL; Patterson, *The New Deal and the States*, 92, 99; B. Guy Peters, "The Development of the Welfare State and the Tax State," in *Nationalizing Social Security in Europe and America*, ed. Douglas Ashford and E.W. Kelley (Greenwich, 1986), 219–43; Mark Leff, "Taxing the 'Forgotten Man': The Politics of Social Security Finance in the New Deal," *JAH* 70 (1983): 359–81; Cox, "The Social Security Act of 1935 and the Geography of the American Welfare State," 5–20.

68 William Leuchtenberg, *Franklin D. Roosevelt and the New Deal, 1932–1940* (New York, 1963), 132.

costs of these experiments among all competing states and firms. "We believe the only way legislation might relieve any competitive conditions," argued a beleaguered New York employer in 1928, "is to have workmen's compensation, health insurance, old age pensions and similar welfare legislation under the jurisdiction of the Federal Government." Federal welfare law would, in turn, "bear most heavily on part-time operators" and force "inefficient producers," as Sidney Hillman noted, "to pay for their reserve labor supply." Swope promised the Senate in 1931 that federal social security legislation would serve "to compel the recalcitrant minority." Wagner concurred three years later that the "chief merit" of the SSA "is that it will exert a profound influence upon the stabilization of industry."[69]

Federal welfare followed the failure of private plans and the distressingly inconsistent policies of individual states. Although New Deal welfare policy would quickly lose credibility under the pressures of chronic regulatory failure, persistent regional competition, and emerging international competition, the disappointment of its proponents should not be confused with opposition to its premises. The misery of the 1930s pressed reformers, voters, politicians, workers, and unions alike to support federal welfare law. But the Social Security Act passed in 1935 was largely the work of a motley coalition of business interests grasping for solutions to the ravages of economic competition and federated economic regulation.

69 "Social Security Act," [Chamber of Commerce] *Washington Review* (22 February 1937); (quote) NICB, *Legislation in New York*, 92; (quote) *ALLR* 23 (1933): 138; Hillman quoted in Nelson, *Unemployment Insurance*, 84; Swope in Senate, *National Economic Council*, 311; Wagner in Senate, *Economic Security Act*, 2.

8. New Deal, Old Deck
Business, Labor, and Politics After 1935

In the months and years after the legislative flurry of 1935, business, labor, and political interests continued to battle over the meaning of the New Deal. In the short term, from 1935 to the onset of World War II, growing business opposition signaled both disappointment with the New Deal's failures and anxiety over its material and managerial costs. This disenchantment was the product not of a fundamental antagonism between private and public interest but of the New Deal's persistent inability to accomplish recovery and orderly competition. In the longer term, through World War II and into the postwar era, the New Deal was recast around new priorities and new circumstances: internationalism, a renewed concern for managerial rights, and the politics and political culture of growth. In this sense, the postwar trajectory of New Deal policies marked less a retreat from than a clarification of their basic premises.

Business and Politics in the Late 1930s

By most estimates, business either opposed the Roosevelt administration from the outset or at least came to bitterly resent its policies by the late 1930s. Colorful illustrations of this theme are sprinkled throughout contemporary and historical accounts: Hanna Coal executive George Humphrey always spelt Roosevelt with a lowercase "r"; dinner guests of banker J. P. Morgan were forbidden to mention the "R" word at all. The easy assumption that (as contemporary magazine articles announced) "Businessmen Fear Washington" or "They Hate Roosevelt," however, makes for poor and inexact history. As the preceding chapters suggest, New Deal policies were essentially business-friendly measures in progressive clothing. Yet at each turn of the New Deal, some business interests were vocal and insistent in their opposition. This basic contradiction, inconsistency, or fickleness deserves explanation. Generally, scholars have confused the question of whether the New Deal served business needs with the question of whether

280

the New Deal did so *successfully*, and they have assumed (in narrowly functional reasoning) that any business opposition can be taken as evidence that
New Deal policies were antibusiness. As I argue below, business-driven
political programs simply failed, in large part because "business" rarely
agreed on the benefits of such programs and almost always agreed that such
programs were too costly.[1]

In its broadest sense, business opposition to politics is generated not by a
natural antagonism but by the fact that business and the state share the task
of economic governance so closely. Although industry leaders and politicians
routinely decry efforts to shift the balance one way or the other, as Charles
Lindblom notes, this conflict is "constrained by their understanding that
they together constitute the necessary leadership for the system" and is
confined to "an ever-shifting category of secondary issues – such as tax rates
and particulars of regulation and promotion of business."[2] Of course, the
culture of the American political economy is largely an exercise in denying
this close and dependent relationship. Even as politics infuse every level of
economic activity, business interests and government officials guard the
myth that such intervention is intended only to "level the playing field," to
restrain "unfair competition," or to ensure that free markets have room to
operate. In this atmosphere, business support for the New Deal could not
survive long. Those whom the New Deal disappointed suddenly saw federal
power as a threat rather than a solution; those whom the New Deal helped
were inclined to take the credit themselves and see politics as a costly obstacle
to further growth and prosperity.

The economic conditions of the 1930s and the political stakes of the New
Deal magnified these tensions. The New Deal's inconsistencies and cross-
purposes reflected the disparate demands of different interests, all of whom
championed their own pet panaceas and opposed or misunderstood others.
Consumerist strategies designed to inflate purchasing power collided with
productionist strategies that inflated prices. Federal wage and welfare stan-

1 Herman Kross, *Executive Opinion: What Businessmen Said and Thought on Economic
Issues, 1920s–1960s* (New York, 1970), 162; W.P. Kiplinger, "Why Businessmen
Fear Washington," *Scribner's* (October 1934): 207–10; Marquis Childs, "They Hate
Roosevelt," *Harper's* (May 1936): 634–42; Donald Brand, *Corporatism and the Rule
of Law: A Study of the National Recovery Administration* (Ithaca, 1988), 125. See
also Ellis Hawley, "A Partnership Formed, Dissolved, and in Renegotiation: Business and Government in the Franklin D. Roosevelt Era," in *Business and Government: Essays in 20th Century Cooperation and Conflict*, ed. Joseph Frese and Jacob
Judd (Tarrytown, 1985), 187–94.
2 Charles Lindblom, *Politics and Markets* (New York, 1977), 179–80.

dards encouraged inflation rather than redistribution. And conservative fiscal policy and anticompetitive regulation pulled the dollar in opposite directions. These dilemmas confounded policymakers, who had neither the institutional experience nor the practical inclination to deal coherently with problems of demand management, industrial regulation, labor law, and fiscal policy. In all, business opposition to the New Deal was only peripherally concerned with the abstract issues of limited government, free markets, or constitutional fealty in which such opposition was invariably couched. Business counted among its ranks political realists, ideological cynics, inveterate optimists, and shortsighted opportunists – an unsettling combination that magnified expectations and frustrations.[3]

Endemic contradictions and changing conditions constantly shifted the balance of business support and opposition. New Dealers were willing to accept a degree of business discontent (which, after all, girded populist images and mass support at election time) but were by no means willing to write off the patronage of important industrial interests in an increasingly "capital-intensive" political universe.[4] And although its policies were staunchly (if not always effectively) probusiness, the Roosevelt administration did not always seek or receive backing from the same firms and industries, which went through cycles of political solicitation, confusion, disenchantment, and accommodation. Many who supported or opposed particular policies made a virtue out of necessity and elaborated or justified their positions with (often misleading) rhetorical flourish. And on the heels of particularly difficult or compromising political decisions, business support often narrowed considerably only to expand or regroup around new issues or realities.

3 See David Vogel, "Why Businessmen Distrust Their State: The Political Consciousness of American Corporate Executives," *British Journal of Political Science* 8 (1978): 45–78.

4 While Depression-era issues encouraged a last gasp of partisan organizing and electoral mobilization, business and political elites had already begun closing the political compass and creating a business- (investment-) dominated political system. After 1950, voter alienation and the costs of mass-media campaigns would exacerbate this class skew in electoral politics. See Walter Dean Burnham, "The Appearance and Disappearance of the American Voter," in *The Current Crisis in American Politics* (New York, 1982), 121–65; Benjamin Ginsberg, "Money and Power: The New Political Economy of American Elections," in *The Political Economy: Readings in the Politics and Economics of American Public Policy*, ed. Thomas Ferguson and Joel Rogers (Armonk, 1984), 167–68; Martin Shefter, "Political Parties, Political Mobilization, and Political Demobilization," in Ferguson and Rogers, *The Political Economy*, 140–48; Thomas Ferguson and Joel Rogers, *Right Turn: The Decline of the Democrats and the Future of American Politics* (New York, 1986), 40–77.

In all, business response to the New Deal was shaped by the uneven impact of New Deal policies, changes in the conditions under which early political deals were first made, and a growing appreciation of the costs of political solutions. More specifically, business opposition to the New Deal can be traced to four sources. First, business-minded regulatory policies failed consistently. Because such experiments entailed financial and managerial sacrifices, few were willing to prolong them if they proved unproductive. Second, as the focus of the National Recovery Act (NRA) narrowed to a more coercive and costly emphasis on labor policy, many firms balked at the implicit threat to managerial power. This was true of those who entirely rejected the premises of New Deal labor policy and of those who accepted the logical link between the NRA and the Wagner Act but resented the subsequent loss of discretion and flexibility. Third, the regional jealousies that inspired New Deal federalism were not easily erased. New federal powers altered but did not erase patterns of interstate and regional competition. And fourth, the central premise of labor-driven regulation – that labor costs would increase across an industry at the expense of marginal producers and consumers – was undermined by the reality and threat of international competition.

Sour Grapes: The New Deal Gets Old

The New Deal did not age well. Most applauded it initially (although few went so far as one executive, who dubbed Roosevelt "the greatest leader since Jesus Christ"). But almost immediately, the economic and administrative chaos of the NRA began to make enemies. As Hoover predicted bitterly and accurately in 1933, support for the New Deal would collapse "when the scared business man beg[an] to see . . . that his high hopes of escape from the Sherman Act into the heaven of assured high profits [was] illusory." Firms and industries had a contingent faith in the NRA and sharply different stakes in its success. While few objected outright to the act, as J.P. Morgan partner Russell Leffingwell noted, most were "subject to repeated disappointments." Business resented the failures rather than the premises of recovery policy. "Business wants the codes, in spite of all the complaining one hears," reasoned a furniture manufacturer in late 1934, adding that "men really want what the codes promise, and kick because the promises have not been kept."[5] Although played up in contemporary and

5 Kroos, *Executive Opinion*, 164 (quote), 178–79; (quote) Hoover to Sen. Simon Fess

historical accounts as a revolt of oppressed consumers and small businesses, this shift in attitude reflected little more than an end to the delusion that business would voluntarily shoulder the costs necessary to bring order to their respective corners of the industrial economy.

Business doubts also reflected fundamentally different political demands and aspirations within and among industries and the increasingly onerous (in light of its absent or elusive benefits) burden of federal regulation. The NRA was an attempt, as Ellis Hawley notes, "to give 'something' to everyone, institutionalize the divisions, and avoid, at least for the time being, a definite commitment." But superficially common goals obscured substantial disagreement. In naive isolation, each NRA code satisfied the demands of leading firms in a particular industry. But together the codes created innumerable problems, including increased prices, contradictory jurisdiction, and inconsistent interpretation. As a chemical executive noted typically, "I have only sympathy for NRA to the extent of the chemical code." The codes also generated opposition within industries. New Deal programs benefited some interests at the expense of others and left the price of organization to be paid by regional or marginal competitors. "Under cover of the national emergency," admitted Teagle of Standard Oil, "interested parties have tried to impose on other members of their industry additional costs and other restrictions to do away with advantages previously held by competitors."[6]

In the long run, both marginal and leading firms balked at the coercion implicit in New Deal policies. The former resented the intent of federal regulation; the latter resented its failures. Business, as Hawley notes, "wor-

(5 July 1933), Post-Presidential Individual [PPI] File 2649, Herbert Hoover Papers, Herbert C. Hoover Presidential Library, West Branch, IA; Broadus Mitchell, *Depression Decade* (New York, 1947), 257–58; Aide Memoire to Telephone Conversation with Leffingwell (17 January 1936), President's Personal File [PPF] 8793, Franklin D. Roosevelt Papers, Franklin D. Roosevelt Presidential Library [FDRPL], Hyde Park, NY; (quote) Alfred Haake, "The NIRA from the Standpoint of Trade Associations and Code Authorities" (1934), File 1644:2, John Raskob Papers, Hagley Museum and Library, Wilmington, DE; Ellis Hawley, *The New Deal and the Problem of Monopoly* (Princeton, 1966), 66–71; miscellaneous correspondence, "Business," Official File [OF] 172:1–3, 7, FDR Papers.

6 Ellis Hawley, "The New Deal and Business," in *The New Deal: The National Level*, ed. David Brody, John Braemen, and Robert Bremner (Columbus, 1975), 60 (quote), 67, 71–72; *NAM Bulletin* (3 November 1933), File 194, National Association of Manufacturers [NAM] Papers, Hagley Museum; Senate, Committee on Finance, *Investigation of the NRA* (Washington, 1935), 1584, 1703–5; (quote) Charles Belknap [Chemical Alliance] to W. Bell [American Cyanamid] (13 March 1934), File 15, DuPont Company Administrative Papers, Hagley Museum; Teagle, "In Retrospect" (13 June 1934), File 1173:6, Pierre S. DuPont Papers, Hagley Museum.

ried constantly about creating an apparatus that might be used against them." Acceptance of the price of federal regulation was always a short-term strategy; as an oil executive explained to Interior Secretary Wilbur in 1929, "What [business interests] want is something of a temporary nature that will pull them out of the hole and then they want to be left alone." Neither Hoover nor Roosevelt, both of whom appreciated the inherent fickleness of business politics, were able to satisfy those who continued to demand regulatory compulsion and those who had tired of federal intervention. In 1933, most accepted Chamber of Commerce Director Silas Strawn's observation that "a planned economy cannot be effective unless the executive is vested with the power to enforce it." Over the next few months, many came also to agree with Strawn's warning that the costs of such power might resemble a "dictatorship such as they have in Russia, Italy and Germany."[7] Business wanted a superhero to swoop down and set things right. What they got was a police force that was neither particularly effective nor likely to abandon the beat in the near future.

The New Deal had a few consistent supporters and a few consistent critics, but most business sentiment reflected a short-term jumble of opportunism, anxiety, and disillusion. The Roosevelt administrations' fiercest opponents after 1935 were, in many cases, those most intimately involved in New Deal circles before 1935. The DuPonts, for example, latched onto the Democratic Party as a vehicle for Prohibition repeal (hoping that a post-Prohibition system of federal liquor taxes would displace corporate and income taxes) and participated enthusiastically in the early New Deal.[8] As the New

---

7 Hawley, "New Deal and Business," 57, 59; Mark Requa to Wilbur (15 May 1929), Presidential File [PF] 217, Hoover Papers; Strawn quoted in Kroos, *Executive Opinion*, 174.

8 Ferguson, "Critical Realignment," 436–42, 456–538; Gerard Colby Zilg, *Du Pont: Behind the Nylon Curtain* (Englewood Cliffs, 1974), 178–79, 188, 195–97, 278–79, 303–5; Jasper Crane to Lamont (27 January 1939), File 2-9, Thomas Lamont Papers, Baker Library, Cambridge, MA; Raskob to James Farley (5 November 1934), PPF 44854, FDR Papers; Robert Burk, *The Corporate State and the Broker State: The Du Ponts and American National Politics, 1925–1940* (Cambridge, 1990), 40–41. Pierre DuPont wrote in 1932 that "if we could get some recognition of the liquor industry that would enable us to subject it to taxation, . . . undoubtedly one-fourth of the national taxes would be obtained from the liquor industry" and that while "efforts to reduce taxation are important, . . . it's much more important to secure reduced taxes through repeal of the [prohibition] amendment by restoring the excise tax on liquor." Four years later, he argued that "the effort [for repeal] should have been directed against XVI [income tax amendment], which I believe could have been repealed with the expenditure of less time and trouble than was required for the abolition of its younger brother." See Irenée DuPont to Hoover (21 March 1921),

Deal stumbled along, the DuPonts and others began to question the rewards of their participation, especially as the scope of federal regulation began actually increasing the tax burden. The DuPonts' growing opposition to the New Deal, soon formalized in the American Liberty League (ALL), clearly rested less on the business versus government dramatics of the ALL platform than it did on the political anxieties and disappointments of leading chemical firms. The ALL was little more than an "ideological smokescreen," as Robert Burk notes, "given the prior willingness of prominent DuPonts to serve on New Deal boards and agencies as long as executive policy had been shaped by them and had met their approval."[9]

In the end, even those who were not slighted or disappointed by the New Deal were likely to add their voices to the chorus of opposition. After scrambling for political solutions to the Depression, those interests that showed any recovery after 1932 or 1935 were quick to disavow political assistance and to accuse the New Deal of obstructing further gains. Like a drunk rescued from the gutter, suggested Robert LaFollette, business resented both the implication that they had needed any help and the fact that their rescuer had found them in such a degraded condition. "As soon as the businessman sees a slight improvement," complained another senator, "he keeps shouting 'the government must get out of business.' Businessmen do nothing but bellyache."[10] The boundary between politics and markets was easily shifted in such a way that successful political solutions were seen as triumphs of the market and market failures were ascribed to political interference. Such willful delusion allowed business and its sympathizers to see the crash as the culmination of political errors, the early NRA as the capstone of self-regulation, and the later NRA as the leading edge of socialism.

As glimmers of recovery broke through in 1936 and 1937, the legislative innovations of 1933–35 were cast aside as relics of a desperate time. "The life preserver which is so necessary when the ship is sinking," observed Harper Silbey of the Chamber of Commerce, "becomes a heavy burden when man is back on dry land." The most tangible target of business outcry

Commerce File [CF] 186, Hoover Papers; Pierre S. DuPont to American Taxpayers League (10 June 1932), (27 January 1930), File 1119; P.S. DuPont to John Pollard (21 March 1932), File 765:1; P.S. DuPont to Alfred Sloan (9 May 1932), File 1173; P.S. DuPont to L.D. Staplin (16 January 1936), File 765:2, Pierre S. DuPont Papers.

9 Burk, *The Corporate State and the Broker State*, 86–149 (quote, 144). The standard history of the American Liberty League is George Wolfskill, *Revolt of the Conservatives* (Boston, 1962).

10 Senator Connally (D-Texas) quoted in George Wolfskill and John A. Hudson, *All but the People: Franklin D. Roosevelt and his Critics* (New York, 1969), 144.

was the cost of New Deal programs, including union wages and taxes. After 1935, organized business made a fetish of "limited government" and "balanced budgets" (catch phrases that served as useful political abstractions for more belligerent positions on social security or workers' rights and obscured the persistence of a regressive tax system). This fiscal conservatism was transparently self-serving; it masked a spate of more specific objections to New Deal policy and a general unwillingness to pay for programs whose benefits were elusive or insufficient. In all, it was the inefficacy of politics, rather than any intellectual objection to political intervention, that caused the hiccup of fierce libertarianism after 1935.[11]

Management Rights and the Labor Problem

With the dissolution of the NRA, industry leaders and the Roosevelt administration scrambled to put together a patchwork of legislation cut to fit the needs of distinct sectors of the industrial economy. This strategy was forced by the legal obstacles raised by the *Schecter* decision and by business dissatisfaction with the NRA. Post-NRA regulatory policies (which included resale price maintenance and "little NRAs" in industries such as trucking, coal, and oil) were more coercive and more discretionary than the industrial codes. Just as the political and economic stakes were considerably greater, so were the prospects for business resistance. And of the costs associated with New Deal policies, the most troubling for business was the problem of labor and labor organization.

New Deal labor law supplemented the NRA's anticompetitive policies with the "police" power of industrial unions. Although many industries and firms supported the Wagner and Social Security Acts, their reasons for doing so were dissimilar and often contradictory. Competitive, labor-intensive firms saw federal labor law as a means of flushing out marginal and regional cutthroat competitors. Less competitive mass-production firms weighed their antagonism toward any form of organized labor against the real threat of genuinely radical unionization and unhappily encouraged efforts to direct the labor movement into business-minded channels. Capital-intensive (often

11 Business response to New Deal fiscal policies is traced in Robert Collins, *The Business Response to Keynes, 1929–1964* (New York, 1981), 24–52 (Silbey quote, 41); and Mark Leff, *The Limits of Symbolic Reform: The New Deal and Taxation, 1933–1940* (New York, 1984). These tensions are still apparent. As John Endean of the American Business Conference argued recently, "What entrepreneurs and businesspeople want most from George Bush isn't red meat, it's consistency" (*Business Week*, 1 June 1992, 43).

internationalist) firms, which stood to bear little increase in labor costs, saw higher wages and union recognition as practical solutions to industrial conflict and the disappearance of mass purchasing power. Others clung to the last point as well, albeit with some cynicism. "The thinking of the employer group," noted one labor economist drily, ". . . might be summarized by saying that they believed strongly in other employers paying high wages."[12]

With starkly different reasons for supporting or opposing elements of the New Deal's stance on labor, employers were extremely sensitive to the form and administration of collective bargaining and welfare law. Because the direct and managerial costs of labor policy were so great, any hint that its various benefits might not be forthcoming provoked a vehement response. And many employers who were threatened by either uniform industry standards or the increased power of labor within their gates objected to labor-driven regulation from the outset. "Loss of control over labor relations [under Section 7a of the NRA] . . . was a bitter pill to swallow," as the editors of *Fortune* observed, "but the coating of price regulation was thick and sweet and the pill went down."[13] After the NRA, with labor policy the sole source of regulation, the pill was even harder to digest.

Even sympathetic employers based their acceptance of New Deal labor policy on different goals, perceptions, and horizons. Few who accepted the immediate utility of union wages as a means of quelling competitive pressures or spurring consumption also accepted any longer-term commitment to workers' rights. As the weight of the Depression began to lift, employers began to rethink their concessions to organized labor. By the later 1930s (and certainly after 1945), the threats of chronic underconsumption, radical unionism, and competitive chaos were less urgent. Yet as employers soon realized, the political and economic power that made it possible for unions to rationalize or organize labor costs also made it difficult to remove or restrain those unions once their organizational utility was exhausted. In the longer run, regulatory policies premised on high labor costs would not survive economic internationalization, and only in instances where the equalization of costs among rival firms overwhelmed issues of global competitiveness were such policies seriously pursued.[14]

A few industries, such as coal (which until very recently faced no international competitive pressures) continued to pursue unionization as a guard

---

12 Don Lescohier quoted in Kross, *Executive Opinion*, 91.
13 "The Trade Association Emerges," *Fortune* 8 (August 1933), 40.
14 On the last point, see Colin Gordon, "Dead on Arrival: The American Health Care Debate," *Studies in Political Economy* 39 (1992): 141–58.

against regional competition and as a substitute for the organization of firms. Some, notably steel and autos, integrated CIO unions into the competitive ethos of their respective industries and pragmatically embraced the regulatory and antiradical potential of conservative industrial unionism. Others, including paragons of corporate liberalism such as GE, followed their superficially conciliatory policies of the 1920s and 1930s with brutal antiunion offensives.[15] Regionally, union strength remained uneven, and unionism in regionally competitive industries (such as textiles) did little to even out state-to-state disparity in labor costs. Accordingly, states moved to unify costs not by supporting federal law but by chipping away at its authority at the state level. In turn, the federal government was pressed to prevent states from jockeying for competitive advantage by undermining the Wagner Act; in 1947, the federal government leveled the playing field again with the Taft-Hartley Act.[16]

In short, many business interests accepted the immediate organizational and regulatory logic of federal labor policy but failed to appreciate its ultimate costs and inflexibility. Many underestimated the impact of unionization on managerial power and, when labor strategies either failed or became unnecessary, found it difficult to backtrack to the golden years of the open shop. And many lost faith in strategies centered on high and uniform labor costs as economic regionalism persisted in the national economy and global competition intruded on nationalist regulation. The competitive and social circumstances under which business accepted the logic of collective bargaining did not last past the late 1930s; the legal and organizational framework of collective bargaining, much to the dismay of business, remained intact well into the postwar era.

15 Colin Gordon, "Pittston and the Political Economy of Coal," *Z Magazine* 3 (February 1990): 95–100, and "Miners' Health Bargain," *Z Magazine* 5 (May–June 1992): 56–57; William Serrin, *The Company and the Union* (New York, 1974), passim; Howell Harris, *The Right to Manage: Labor Relations Policies of American Business in the 1940s* (Madison, 1982), passim; Ronald Schatz, *The Electrical Workers* (Urbana, 1983), 165–243; Herbert Northrup, *Boulwarism: The Labor Relations Policies of the General Electric Company* (Ann Arbor, 1964), passim.

16 Although the Social Security Act owed its existence primarily to nagging inequalities in the burden and administration of state welfare law, federal labor law had no significant precursors in the states. But the Wagner Act became a striking board for restrictive state laws designed to curtail the federal act's guarantees and gain an edge in interstate commerce. See Karl Klare, "Judicial Deradicalization of the Wagner Act and the Origins of Modern Legal Consciousness, 1937–1941," *Minnesota Law Review* 62 (1978): 265–339; Charles Killingsworth, *State Labor Relations Acts* (Chicago, 1948), 1–23; Sanford Cohen, *State Labor Legislation, 1937–1947* (Columbus, 1948), 3–34.

State and Nation: The Persistence of Regionalism

The New Deal broke sharply with the past by attacking the competitive dimensions of federated politics and regionally uneven industrial development. The political economy of federalism distorted the competitive strategies of states, regions, and firms and cut across different industries in different ways. Under pressure of the Depression, industrial and political New Dealers considered regional disparity in labor, welfare, and regulatory law as serious an obstacle to stability and recovery as cutthroat economic competition.

For a variety of reasons, however, New Deal federalism fell short of expectations. While the *Schecter* decision (which reaffirmed state prerogative over intrastate commerce) was a major blow, the coercive economic nationalism pursued by the New Deal and its (primarily northern) business patrons was on shaky legs long before any legal punches were landed. Competition between states and regions encompassed vast differences in economic development; the varying degrees of influence of race, migrant labor, and agriculture on regional labor markets; and a wide range of short- and long-term relationships between business interests and local or state politics. These differences, particularly acute between North and South, could not be erased by legislative fiat. The Roosevelt administration found it exceedingly difficult (indeed impossible) to administer the NRA or its successors in the South without either accepting persistent and flagrant noncompliance or brokering regulatory provisions for southern Democrats in such a way that federal uniformity was abandoned.[17]

Although New Deal policies, including the Wagner, Social Security, and Fair Labor Standards (1938) Acts, closed much of the gap between North and South, states were still free to compete in other areas. State income and consumption taxes undermined the regulatory and redistributive intent of federal law, while state business taxes (or their absence) perpetuated regional competition.[18] In turn, the whims of local politicians, judiciary officials, and

---

17 Philip Wood, *Southern Capitalism: The Political Economy of North Carolina, 1880–1980* (Durham, 1986), 134, 139, 155.

18 Leff, *The Limits of Symbolic Reform*, 48–90; James Cobb, *The Selling of the South: The Southern Crusade for Industrial Development, 1936–1980* (Baton Rouge, 1982). See also Howell Raines, "Alabama Bound," *New York Times Magazine*, 3 June 1990, 40–44, 48, 82, 88, quoting Alabama Republican Chairman Ray Scott: "We do everything but kiss them all over their body from the bottom of their you-know-what to the top of the watchmacallit trying to get these people to come in here and bring another industry in" (40); he notes that "Kimberley-Clark pays 93 cents an acre on

police made the sincere enforcement of federal laws (especially those concerning civil and union rights) less than certain. And the South and Southwest, where supply-side military federalism displaced social federalism in the postwar era, continued to hold out open arms for union-busting emigrés from the North. After flirting with national standards, industry returned to exploiting regional disparity and using the threat of migration to "whipsaw" union demands or wring concessions from northern workers and politicians.[19]

In politics, the New Deal's offensive against the "colonial economy" of the South was unhappily endured by southern politicos only as long as their immediate political and financial dependence on federal relief exceeded their longer-term regional economic strategies. After 1936, the rapprochement between southern congressional Democrats and the Roosevelt administration fell apart, in part because the Congress of Industrial Organizations (CIO) had turned its attention to the mills, factories, and refineries of the industrial South and in part because, at the first hint of recovery, the benefits of federal relief paled beside the threat of federal intervention in southern labor and race relations. New Deal policies were also confounded by the relative health of the South's agricultural industries (textiles and tobacco), which made them less eager to accept federal regulation and its ancillary costs. And World War II erased the fiscal crisis of state and local governments that had made their concession to New Deal federalism necessary and possible.[20]

The persistence of political and economic regionalism sparked growing opposition. Regions, industries, and firms targeted by federal recovery and labor legislation objected to regulatory and fiscal federalism from the outset. Those that stood to gain from the New Deal's economic nationalism resented the ability of regional competitors to maintain political and economic advantages and turned their backs on policies that had not delivered as promised. In the postwar era, business proved willing to overlook the occasional inconvenience of regulatory disparity and inconsistency and fell back to older

the Alabama side and $4.36 an acre in Georgia. . . . From 1901 until the decline of the iron furnaces in the mid-1970s, Alabama property taxes were tailored for United States Steel. Now they are tailored for companies that own pine trees" (44).

19 Kim Moody, *An Injury to All: The Decline of Industrial Unionism* (New York, 1988), 17–40, 95–146; Temporary National Economic Committee, Monograph 26, *Economic Power and Political Pressures* (Washington, 1941), 100.

20 James T. Patterson, *Congressional Conservatism and the New Deal* (Lexington, 1967), 128–63; Edwin Amenta and Theda Skocpol, "Redefining the New Deal: World War II and the Development of Social Provision in the United States," in *The Politics of Social Policy in the United States*, ed. Margaret Weir et al. (Princeton, 1988), 102–3.

patterns of legislative competition, tax mongering, and jurisdictional shop-ping.[21]

National Regulation in an International Economy

Beneath the surface of the New Deal system lay a single, dormant fault line: the threat of international competition. New Deal policies, especially those concerned with labor, were premised on isolation from global markets; with competition confined to domestic markets, regulatory policy simply raised costs for all competing firms and passed the extra burden on to consumers. This reasoning reflected a tradition of industrial policy that had always of-fered high protective tariffs or quotas to any industry with the time or in-clination to ask for them, and it infused New Deal regulatory and labor policies. The Roosevelt administration echoed its Republican forerunners by espousing an international economic platform that encouraged the export of loans and manufactured goods, promoted restrictive international cartels in basic commodities, and resisted the import of anything but cash.[22]

International pressures did not seriously challenge the New Deal's im-plicit nationalism in the 1930s, but there were hints of future problems. While the Depression (which brought with it a destructive pattern of tariff retaliation and competitive currency depreciation) underscored the contra-dictions of protectionism, the triumph of internationalism was still a decade away. During the Hoover years, a smattering of internationalists favored the rapid reconstruction of European industry, lenient reparation demands on Germany, and various institutional safeguards for the free flow and con-vertibility of currencies. But the manufacturing economy remained over-whelmingly protectionist and leery of European competition. Even those who were internationally active preferred the sanctuary of multinational car-tels. Hoover echoed this position, dismissing Wall Street internationalism as a "mental annex to Europe" and doing little to challenge the power of protectionist sentiment in Congress. The Democrats (reflecting both pre-vailing nationalism and the DuPonts' heavy investment in the party's Na-tional Committee) chimed in with a high-tariff platform in 1928.[23]

---

21 The best study is Cobb, *Selling of the South.*
22 E. E. Schattschnieder, *Politics, Pressures, and the Tariff (New York, 1935)*, passim; Melvyn Leffler, *The Elusive Quest: America's Pursuit of European Stability and French Security, 1919–1933* (Chapel Hill, 1979), 274–368; Lloyd Gardner, *Economic Origins of New Deal Diplomacy* (Madison, 1964), 3–35; Frank Simonds, "A New Deal in Foreign Policy?" *Harper's* 166 (April 1933): 1–7; Meeting with Roosevelt (4 January 1937), File 51:16–17, Morgenthau Diaries, FDRPL.
23 Gabriel Kolko, *Main Currents in Modern American History* (New York, 1984), 206–

Few appreciated the complex connections between protectionism and the pursuit of high-wage, inflationary recovery policies. High tariffs made costly regulatory experimentation possible; the possibility of future tariff revision (let alone full-blown free trade) made it risky. The sentiments of John Raskob of GM (perhaps the least dogmatic of the high-tariff Democrats) were typical:

> I believe we must work out a different policy under which American manufacturers will be forced to compete with the world for American as well as export trade, however, giving to those manufacturers the protection necessary to enable them to pay the high wages established in this country, as against the low wages in other countries, and also to protect them against "dumping" and any other advantages which foreignors [sic] may possess and which are beyond the control of American manufacturers to meet without governmental help. If we could get such a tariff policy. I would be in favor of abolishing the Sherman law entirely.[24]

This approach overflowed with contradictions. In its purest form, the internationalist position concentrated on efficient patterns of capital exchange and investment and betrayed little concern for U.S. labor standards or jobs. But the "whatever protection is necessary" notion left the tariff mired in interest-group politics and perpetuated the shortsighted simplicity of the "Open Door," which espoused the virtues of free trade as long as the United States held a clear competitive advantage but closed doors whenever and wherever this advantage was absent or lost.[25]

In all, internationalism was a future problem. The sentiments of Cordell Hull and a few high-tech and banking internationalists did little to encourage

11; Frank Costigliola, *Awkward Dominion: American Political, Economic, and Cultural Relations with Europe* (Ithaca, 1984), passim; Thomas Ferguson, "From Normalcy to New Deal: Industrial Structure, Party Competition, and American Public Policy in the Great Depression," *International Organization* 38 (1984): 41–94; Herbert Hoover, *The Memoirs of Herbert Hoover: The Great Depression, 1929–1941* (New York, 1952), 9; Joseph Brandes, "Product Diplomacy: Herbert Hoover's Anti-Monopoly Campaign At Home and Abroad," in *Herbert Hoover as Secretary of Commerce*, ed. Ellis Hawley (Iowa City, 1972), 185–216; Frank Page [IT&T] to Hoover (16 July 1925), CF 458; Secretary of the Treasury [Mills] to American Legation [The Hague]. (6 January 1930), PF 952; Thomas Lamont to Hoover (25 May 1932), PPF 168, Hoover Papers; Leffingwell, "Debt Suspension Matter" (Memoranda of Conversations between Lamont and Hoover, n.d.), File 98–18; "Confidential Memorandum: The Allied Debt to the United States Government" (1922), File 80–17, Lamont Papers.

24 Raskob to A.H. Geuting (10 November 1932), File 602(12), Raskob Papers.

25 Raskob, "A Democratic Business View of the Tariff," (27 October 1930), File 765(1), Pierre S. DuPont Papers; Gardner, *Economic Aspects of New Deal Diplomacy*, 24–46; Sachs, "Politics, 1932–1933," (n.d.), File 137; Innes-Brown Memo (n.d.), File 35, Alexander Sachs Papers, FDRPL.

global expansion or the political concessions upon which that expansion depended. The U.S. response to the Depression was decidedly protectionist, and the Reciprocal Trade Agreement Act of 1934 formalized collective inaction without any palpable influence on exports or imports. Only the outbreak of World War II gave U.S. planners the opportunity to infuse wartime diplomacy with the conditions for a postwar economic order. Once in place, internationalism clearly undermined the premises of New Deal nationalism. An executive of Vick Chemical complained that although taking wages out of competition and girding aggregate demand had a superficial appeal, "the logical extension of this theory is that you have to carry it all over the world and force every nation to set a floor [under wages]."[26] International competition left employers unable to pass on the costs of mandatory welfare and unionized labor, a condition that had been central to business support for the Wagner and Social Security Acts. Protectionists (no longer able to bury labor costs in tariffs) and internationalists (less and less concerned with domestic conditions) turned their backs on policies they had previously supported.

The New Deal After 1945: Lessons, Limits, Retreats

Our understanding of the postwar fate of the New Deal is colored by two conflicting images. On one hand, the New Deal may be seen as a shortsighted and ultimately capricious set of business policies, making its slow collapse after 1945 hardly cause for complaint. On the other hand, it may be seen as a far-reaching set of labor and social reforms; its collapse, accordingly, marks the loss of at most a golden political age and at least a golden opportunity for substantial and lasting reform. Both views, of course, have their merits. The New Deal's business premises did not prevent workers from pressing their own case and turning the New Deal to their advantage. It is not necessary to view the 1930s through Roosevelt-tinted glasses, in other words, to appreciate the real and potential benefits of new wage, benefit, and labor relations law. And whatever their origins, the National Recovery, Wagner, and Social Security Acts did reach far beyond the Depression decade and continue to frame political debates to the twilight of the twentieth century.

26 Kolko, *Main Currents*, 220–24; Cordell Hull to Roosevelt (28 November 1934); Hull to Roosevelt (28 August 1935), OF 424, FDR Papers; H. Smith Richardson in "Round Table Conference: New Aspects of the NIRA," Chamber of Commerce Proceedings 23/30 (1935), Chamber of Commerce Papers, Hagley Museum.

The question for the postwar era would be whether the future of the New Deal would reflect its considerable promise or its narrow premise.

Business's dissatisfaction with the New Deal had, by the late 1930s, created a potentially explosive political situation. But the growing tension between politics and private interest dissipated quickly with the onset of World War II. As in 1917, the antigovernment mood evaporated with the opportunities of wartime production and profits, especially given the government's willingness to shoulder the costs of conversion and reconversion. But the war effort did much more than temporarily scramble the Roosevelt admin- istration's priorities. While mobilization shuffled the nagging dilemmas of the New Deal behind the artifice of wartime production, it also created a conviction that the solution to the nation's economic woes lay in maintaining those levels of production by other means when the war ended. Postwar pursuit of the politics of growth – a synthesis of domestic concessions and aggressive internationalism – became the means by which the administration would both solicit business support for the war and permanently escape the political and economic impasse of the late 1930s. While a few viewed the war effort as an opportunity to cement and build upon the progressive prom- ise of the New Deal, most saw it as the foundation of a future in which hard choices about regulation and redistribution would no longer be necessary.[27]

Consider the large institutional and intellectual premises of economic pol- icy. The politics of growth, of course, were little more than an absence of serious politics, an abdication of planning to the dubious promise of infinite economic expansion. As became painfully clear in the early 1970s, growth was not self-generated but was an accident of World War II and its after- math. The "American Century" staggered to a halt after barely two decades of increasingly burdensome intervention abroad and commercial Keynesi- anism at home. The costs of empire, which included both ongoing commit- ments and the less tangible pursuit of credibility and prestige, quickly out- stripped the returns. The recovery of old competitors and the emergence of new ones suggested that the pillars of the postwar accord (high-wage busi- ness unionism, military Keynsianism, and meager social policy) were, in fact, serious competitive liabilities. In a political economy driven by constituency

27 Kolko, *Main Currents*, 153–56; Herbert Stein, *The Fiscal Revolution in America* (Chi- cago, 1969), 169–96; Barton Bernstein, "The Automobile Industry and the Coming of the Second World War II," *Southwestern Social Science Quarterly* 47 (1966): 22– 33; Richard Lauderbaugh, *American Steelmakers and the Coming of the Second World War* (Ann Arbor, 1976).

service and supply-side intervention, the pursuit of government-induced growth betrayed not only an infinite potential for systematic corruption and misplaced priorities but also as the century wore on, little guarantee that the health of U.S. firms had much to do with the health of the U.S. economy.[28]

Despite its substantial presence in the postwar political economy, the state proved unwilling and unable to broker among competing interests, let alone adopt any larger prescriptive vision. This reflected the quadrennial myopia of economic politics, abiding faith in the politics of growth, and the monotonous conflation of private and public interest reinforced by the New Deal. After 1945, the federal government abandoned the Depression-era pursuit of national standards and by the 1970s was actively encouraging the states in their "race to the bottom." Various permutations of the "New Federalism" both off-loaded federal responsibilities and discouraged the growth of state governments. The latter were pressed not only by the "fend for yourself" federalism emanating from Washington but also by the devastation of local and state tax bases that followed the "tax revolt" of the late 1970s. Indeed, the limits of U.S. politics emerged clearly in the postwar tax system. As a percentage of national production or income, taxes are lower and less progressive in the United States than in any of its industrialized peers. Willing to tolerate state intervention (especially when it was couched as a guarantee of fair competition or military strength), Americans never proved willing to pay the price.[29]

Although the fiscal crisis of democratic capitalism is a virtually global phenomena of the postwar era, the gap between the demands on government

28 Samuel Bowles, David Gordon, and Thomas Weisskopf, *After the Wasteland: Democratic Economics for the Year 2000* (Armonk, 1990), 23–25; Alan Wolfe, *America's Impasse: The Rise and Fall of the Politics of Growth* (New York, 1981), 13–32; Fred Block, "Mirrors and Metaphors: The United States and Its Trade Rivals," in *America at Century's End*, ed. Alan Wolfe (Berkeley, 1990), 93–101; Charles Maier, *In Search of Stability*, 121–52; Stein, *Fiscal Revolution*, 197–240; Mancur Olson, "Supply-Side Economics, Industrial Policy, and Rational Ignorance," in *The Politics of Industrial Policy*, ed. Claude Barfield and William Schambra (Washington, 1986), 264–69; Aaron Wildavsky, "Squaring the Political Circle: Industrial Policies and the American Dream," in *The Industrial Policy Debate*, ed. Chalmers Johnson (San Francisco, 1984), 33–37.

29 Edward Tufte, *Political Control of the Economy* (Princeton, 1978), 3–64; Joel Rogers and Joshua Cohen, *On Democracy: Toward a Transformation of American Politics* (New York, 1983), 47–87; Thomas Schwartz and John Peck, "Six Profiles of the Changing Face of Fiscal Federalism: An Overview," in *The Changing Face of Fiscal Federalism*, ed. Thomas Schwartz and John Peck (Armonk, 1990), 3–14; Louis Ferleger and Jay Mandle, "Americans' Hostility to Taxes," *Challenge* (July–August 1991): 53–55.

and the willingness to pay for its services has emerged most starkly in the United States. This is in part a reflection of the persistent and fierce individualism that runs through U.S. political culture and in part a reflection of the willingness and ability – so evident in the New Deal – of private interests to duck the costs of public policies. The politics of growth set aside all but the most capricious and opportunistic adaptation of Keynesian ideas to domestic conditions. By the time growth stalled in the early 1970s, its political and intellectual culture made any return to the economic policies of the 1930s unthinkable. Paradoxically, both the postwar boom and its collapse were taken as evidence of the poverty of an activist state. Growth, while it lasted, proved the market could solve all problems. Decline, as it deepened, was taken as evidence that even meager social provisions and economic regulation were bankrupting the country.[30]

Consider industrial policy. In the United States, what passes for industrial policy has never been much more than an ad hoc and accidental consequence of antitrust law and attempts to deal with imperfect competition. As a result, regulation is driven not by any sense of macroeconomic goals (let alone public interest) but by the needs and anxieties and fortunes of "problem" industries – that is, those with the time and resources to make themselves heard. The NRA experience, which starkly illustrated the contradictions and dilemmas of such an approach, was largely taken as evidence that the state could not and should not either impose regulations that some competitors did not want or pursue order in many industries under the aegis of a single law. Accordingly, post-NRA regulatory policy focused even more exclusively on industry-specific initiatives and abandoned any pretense of a coordinated or coherent position regarding industry. Even to the extent that subsequent administrations flirted with variations on Keynesianism, their attention was confined to aggregate problems of fiscal management, capital formation, and patterns of public spending. Industrial policy remained largely an exercise in greasing squeaky wheels, a piecemeal pattern of subsidies and sanctions within given industries.[31]

30 Adam Przeworski and Michael Wallerstein, "Democratic Capitalism at the Crossroads," *democracy* 2 (1982): 52–68; Ira Katznelson, "A Radical Departure? Social Welfare and the Election," in *The Hidden Election: Politics and Economics in the 1980 Presidential Campaign*, ed. Joel Rogers and Thomas Ferguson (New York, 1981), 317–38.
31 Thomas McGraw, "Mercantilism and the Market: Antecedents of American Industrial Policy," in *The Politics of Industrial Policy*, 33–62; Ellis Hawley, " 'Industrial Policy' in the 1920s and 1930s," in *The Politics of Industrial Policy*, 63–86; Hawley, *The New Deal and the Problem of Monopoly*, 481–85; Kathleen Kemp, "Industrial

It is hardly surprising that postwar debates over economic regulation re-
volve around the ability of business either to dominate regulation from the
outset or, given their unique stake and expertise and resources, to "capture"
the regulatory process once it is in place.[32] Yet the very terms of this debate
confuse the industry-specific biases of the U.S. regulatory experience with
the larger philosophical question of whether a state can or cannot direct
markets without messing things up. The dismal record of economic regulation in industry after industry, after all, has less to do with the inherent
qualities of markets or politics than with the discretionary focus of policy
and the willingness to see politics (as in the NRA-era) as the market by other
means. Although academic and political conservatives have largely succeeded
in portraying economic policy as a zero-sum problem of more or less regulation, the reality is more complex. Markets are innately political; the interplay of supply-side economics and industry-specific regulation after 1945
determined not the degree of political intervention but the form it would
take. Even through the carnival of deregulation that began in the mid-1970s
("Don't just stand there," Murray Weidenbaum of the Council of Economic
Advisers directed his staff in 1981, "undo something") the goal was not
more markets and less politics but more political subsidies and fewer political
sanctions.[33]

Cycles of industry-specific regulation and deregulation served as a surrogate for industrial policy. Even the "new social regulation" of the 1960s
and 1970s, despite its pretense of public interest and industry sanctions, only
marginally widened the scope of regulation. Although third parties were able
to make some use of courts and regulatory agencies, their influence was still
constrained by business conditions. And competitive anxieties (especially

Structure, Party Competition, and the Sources of Regulation," in *The Political Economy*, 104–10.

32 The standard conservative view is captured in George Stigler, "The Theory of
Economic Regulation," *Bell Journal of Economics and Management Science* 2 (Spring
1971): 3–21. Other conservatives, especially in the face of the "new social regulation"
of the 1970s, allowed that simple regulatory capture might be qualified by the ways
in which the costs and benefits of regulation were concentrated or diffused, but the
focus on industry-specific policy remained unchallenged. See James Q. Wilson,
"The Politics of Regulation," in *The Politics of Regulation*, ed. James Q. Wilson
(New York, 1980), 357–94.

33 Alan Stone, "State and Market: Economic Regulation and the Great Productivity
Debate," in *The Hidden Election*, 232–59; Olson, "Supply-Side Economics, Industrial Policy, and Rational Ignorance," 264–69; Barry Bluestone and Bennett Harrison, *The Great U-Turn: Corporate Restructuring and the Polarizing of America* (New
York, 1988), 76–108; Weidenbaum quoted in Bowles, Gordon, and Weisskopf, *After
the Wasteland*, 129.

after the mid-1970s) inevitably and successfully identified the costs of regulatory compliance as a serious liability. And as the half-hearted industrial policy debate spilled into the 1980s, conservatives dredged up the NRA experience as evidence that any political solutions were futile. The political culture of regulation continued to conflate business interest with the public interest and to marginalize others (labor, consumers, environmentalists) as presumptively illegitimate "special interests." As long as economic regulation was tied to specific problems of industrial competition and assessed according to its immediately tangible costs and benefits, industrial policy would remain, as Robert Reich suggests, "one of those rare ideas that has moved swiftly from obscurity to meaningless without any intervening period of coherence."[34]

Consider social policy. Since 1935, the U.S. welfare state has moved little beyond the limited premises of New Deal welfare policy. While close to international standards of old-age security and benefits for retired workers, the United States is a serious laggard in family allowances, health coverage, and various forms of public assistance and unemployment insurance. There is little pretense of redistribution; the core federal "welfare" program, Social Security, acts primarily as an income-forwarding machine for the middle class. Indeed, the New Deal distinguished sharply between welfare redistribution and self-funded social security, a bifurcation that persisted after 1945 and was deepened by the reforms of the mid-1960s.[35] The limits of the U.S. welfare state reflect in part the limits of the New Deal, which never saw the federal role as much more than one of evening out a sporadic system of private benefits. Deference to private benefits was, of course, most evident in the persistence of employment-based health insurance, a choice that set the United States apart from all of its industrialized peers. Even relatively generous programs such as unemployment insurance were clearly a product of necessity before 1945 and a tenuous product of prosperity thereafter. With the end of postwar growth, private and public retrenchment and the useful conviction that real security can only come from the market, took hold.[36]

34 Theodore Lowi, *The End of Liberalism* (New York, 1979); Bowles, Gordon, and Weisskopf, *After the Wasteland*, 127–35; David Vogel, "The 'New' Social Regulation in Historical Perspective," in *Regulation in Perspective: Historical Essays*, ed. Thomas McCraw (Cambridge, 1981), 155–85; Otis Graham, *Losing Time: The Industrial Policy Debate* (Cambridge, 1992), 259–64; Reich quoted in McCraw, "Mercantilism and the Market," 33.
35 Theda Skocpol, "America's Incomplete Welfare State: The Limits of New Deal Reforms and the Origins of the Present Crisis," in *Stagnation and Renewal in Social Policy*, ed. Martin Rein (Armonk, 1987), 36–37.
36 Gordon, "Dead on Arrival," 141–45; Alexander Keyssar, "History and the Problem

By international standards, the U.S. welfare system is one of the least developed and one of the most vulnerable to attack. Social Security (encompassing the new benefits instituted in the 1960s), while woefully inadequate by the standards of other industrialized nations, is spuriously attacked as the source of declining productivity and governmental debt – despite compelling evidence that it is *inadequate* social programs that contribute to competitive weakness and that "entitlement" programs (which encompass more than 80 percent of social spending) more than pay for themselves. In turn, the Social Security Act clearly distinguished between maternalist and paternalist (job-related) benefits, and black Americans were systematically excluded by exemptions for agricultural and domestic labor. These conceptual constraints of race and gender not only shaped policy from the outset but became the centerpiece of the social policy debate as postwar economic and demographic change accelerated both the ghettoization of the black working class and the feminization of poverty. As social provision, originally constructed around the needs of white male breadwinners, came under attack, the prominence of women and blacks among welfare recipients infused discussions of social policy with cynical but powerful images of racially pathological poverty and welfare-induced family dissolution.[37]

The U.S. welfare state is also exceptional for its reliance on private benefits. Through the postwar era, employers continued to champion private benefits (usually facilitated by generous tax advantages) as a means of ensuring private control of social spending. Politicians, in keeping with the larger logic of growth, were happy to organize social provision through the workplace. And organized labor increasingly saw workplace benefits, especially pensions, as both a source of organizational power and compensation for the narrowing of collective bargaining after World War II. This was a

---

of Unemployment," *Socialist Review* 19 (1989): 15–34; Robert Haveman, *Starting Even: An Equal Opportunity Program to Combat the Nation's Poverty* (New York, 1988), 103–21.

37 Fred Block, "Rethinking the Political Economy of the Welfare State," in *The Mean Season: The Attack on the Welfare State*, ed. Fred Block et al. (New York, 1987), 109–60; Block, "Mirrors and Metaphors," 98–105; Gwendolyn Mink, "The Lady and the Tramp: Gender, Race, and the Origins of the American Welfare State," in *Women, the State, and Welfare*, ed. Linda Gordon (Madison, 1990), 92–122; Virginia Shapiro, "The Gender Basis of American Social Policy," in *Women, the State, and Welfare*, 41–48; Helen Slessarev, "Racial Tensions and Institutional Support: Social Programs During a Period of Retrenchment," in *The Politics of Social Policy*, 357–79; Heidi Hartmann, "Changes in Women's Economic and Family Roles in Post–World War II America," in *Women, Households, and the Economy*, ed. Catherine Stimpson and Lourdes Beneria (New Brunswick, 1987), 33–64.

relatively happy compromise during the postwar boom, but it became extremely tenuous as soon as the economy began to falter. In the soft coal industry, for example, the Mine Workers traded mechanization and job loss against an industry-wide welfare agreement in 1950. By the 1980s, some firms began questioning their contributions to the welfare plan and demanded concessions. After three years of labor strife, hasty political solutions, and corporate intransigence, the Mine Workers found that their health insurance cards, in the words of *Business Week*, weren't "worth the plastic they're made from." The firms ducking industry standards identified themselves, appropriately enough, as the "Private Benefits Alliance."[38]

As a consequence of the original premises, postwar development, and contemporary political context of its social policy, the United States remains a nation of tremendous wealth and tremendous neglect. The rate of poverty runs consistently twice as high as that of any comparable country (and nearly three times the cross-national averages for children and the elderly). This is largely a reflection of the fact that government programs in the United States have only marginal impact on the incomes of the poor; while other OECD countries average an after-tax-and-transfer poverty reduction of over 16 percent, the reduction in the United States hovers around 6 percent. Indeed, if one takes a bird's-eye view of the federal government's role in the economy, the rapid growth of income transfers as a percentage of federal spending has been almost entirely offset by a uniquely regressive tax system. The government spends more, but the effect on fundamental inequality has been virtually negligible. The basic limits of welfare policy, coupled with an insistence on organizing benefits through the workplace, have created a meager and capricious system of social provision in which the larger fiscal dilemmas of the modern welfare state are magnified and exaggerated.[39]

Finally, consider labor policy and labor relations. While the war effort temporarily calmed managerial anxieties, employers launched a broadside against both the rigidity of wartime labor relations and the legacy of the New

---

38 Beth Stevens, "Labor Unions, Employee Benefits, and the Privatization of the American Welfare State," *Journal of Policy History* 2 (1990): 233–54; Frank Dobbin, "The Origins of Private Social Insurance: Public Policy and Fringe Benefits in America, 1920–1950," *American Journal of Sociology* 97 (1992): 1416–50; Gordon, "Pittston and the Political Economy of Coal," 95–100; *Business Week* cited in Gordon, "Miners' Health Bargain," 56–57.

39 Thomas Smeeding, "Why the U.S. Antipoverty System Doesn't Work Very Well," *Challenge* (January–February 1992): 30–35; Haveman, *Starting Even*, 103–21; Gabriel Kolko, *Wealth and Power in America* (Boston, 1962); Przeworski and Wallerstein, "Democratic Capitalism at the Crossroads," 52–68; Claus Offe, *Contradictions of the Welfare State* (Cambridge, 1985), 147–61, 179–206.

Deal as soon as the guns fell silent. The trajectory of postwar labor relations underscored both the managerial premises of the New Deal's position and the fragility of labor's economic and political power under changing circumstances. The postwar politics of productivity magnified the "responsible" and "job conscious" aspects of the Wagnerian compromise and convinced managers and unions that aggressive internationalism (supplemented by "military Keynesianism" at home) would bring sustained growth and render the thorny redistributional debates of the 1930s obsolete. The Cold War perpetuated both the political culture of the war years and the ideological and institutional concessions of the war effort. Increasingly, the postwar labor relations system (exemplified by the 1948 GM-UAW pact) sanctified the "right to manage" and confined itself to routine contractual details: wages, benefits, seniority, job classification, and grievance procedures.[40]

The adaptation of the Wagner Act to the postwar political economy was sealed by the Taft-Hartley Act of 1947. Yet Taft-Hartley was not so much a retreat from Wagner as it was an evaporation of the circumstances (depression and war) under which concessions made sense to business, and a clarification of the conservative, pragmatic unionism that business had always expected from New Deal labor policy. After 1935, it became clear that the National Labor Relations Board (NLRB) did little more than bring an inherently conservative "court-dominated" tradition of labor policy into the belly of the executive branch. In the long run, federal labor policy would prove as capricious and opportunistic as its private counterparts; witness the candid effort to "zap labor" by administration after administration in the 1970s and 1980s and the unwillingness of the postwar NLRB to constrain antiunion employers or protect workers' rights with any sincerity. The Wagner Act was not a work of philosophy but a means to an end: an economic order characterized by industrial peace, competitive stability, and adequate consumption. In the postwar world, the same goals demanded quite different strategies and priorities. Whether this marked the dismantling of an exceptional legislative moment or the confirmation of its unexceptional premises, the road from Wagner to Taft-Hartley to the present clearly marked the boundaries of labor's political and economic power.[41]

40 Nelson Lichtenstein, *Labor's War at Home: The CIO in World War II* (New York, 1982), 233–45; Harris, *The Right to Manage*, 41–104; Thomas Kochan et al., *The Transformation of American Industrial Relations* (New York, 1986), 21–46.

41 Christopher Tomlins, *The State and the Unions: Labor Relations, Law, and the Organized Labor Movement in America, 1880–1960* (New York, 1985), 247–316; Katherine Van Wezel Stone, "The Postwar Paradigm in American Labor Law," *Yale Law Journal* 90 (1981): 1509–80; Bluestone and Harrison, *The Great U-Turn*, 21–

The Wagner Act (which, as early as 1944, one of Wagner's assistants had dubbed "the ball and chain of the labor movement") both guaranteed and confined workers' rights. Even organized workers, after all, faced a familiar set of material anxieties. Although the CIO accomplished substantial job security, it did nothing to alter the core assumption that the well-being of workers depended upon the success of their employers. Indeed, as the postwar experiences of the automobile and steel industries suggest, the combination of bureaucratic pattern bargaining and growth politics simply magnified the logic of job-conscious, business unionism. Increasingly, postwar labor relations pressed organized workers into discrete and narrowly economistic bargains with industrial employers. By the mid-1950s, as Ruth Milkman notes of the UAW, organized labor was "a staid, bureaucratic institution that concentrated its energies on the increasingly complex technical issues involved in enforcing its contracts and improving wages, fringe benefits, and job security for its members." In all, the New Deal had little to say on larger issues of workers' rights, let alone the relative security of those who remained outside the temporarily privileged core of the industrial economy. "Every worker," as David Montgomery observes, "knows that she or he remains 'under surveillance' on the job and a 'pariah' without one."[42]

The New Deal did not significantly challenge business's privileged position in politics or the private economy and simply recast the fundamental inequity between employer and employee around their organized, rather than individual, interests. In the workplace, the material constraints of job dependency and market competition persisted in new forms. In politics, as Nelson Lichtenstein notes, labor's influence "was reduced to a sort of militant interest group politics" in which a seat on the rocket of postwar growth was more important than the pursuit of workers' rights or workers' control. The New Deal formula, sharply constrained from the outset, was incapable of adjusting to the demographic, economic, and technological change of the postwar era. Labor's clout on the floor of factories and legislatures – softened by Taft-Hartley, the politics of growth, and a necessary but debilitating pursuit of business unionism – disappeared with the illusion of permanent growth in the early 1970s. The postwar economy was not a rocket but a roller coaster, and organized labor was pressed to accept the logic of pro-

52; Joel Rogers, "Divide and Conquer: Further 'Reflections on the Distinctive Character of American Labor Laws,' " *Wisconsin Law Review* 1 (1990): 1–147.

42 Morton Stavis quoted in Tomlins, *The State and the Unions*, 251; Ruth Milkman, "Labor and Management in Uncertain Times," in *America at Century's End*, 131–38 (quote, 135); David Montgomery, "American Workers and the New Deal Formula," in *Workers' Control in America* (New York, 1979), 154.

ductivity on the downside as well. Business unionism, as the modern working class has discovered, is little comfort in hard times. The concessionary bargaining of the 1980s testified to the limits of the New Deal system, or at least to the degree to which it had bet its future on the politics of growth.[43]

The collapse of organized labor narrowed not only the compass of workplace politics but also the possibilities and aspirations of the larger political culture as well. In 1945, the labor movement claimed enough of the private economy and the Democratic party to exert a potentially unprecedented influence in national politics. Yet as careful observers noted at the time, labor's new prominence was misleading and undeniably tenuous. And by the 1980s, organized labor had settled to the status of just another "special" interest, no more important than hog farmers or health insurers. The panacea of growth and the logic of business unionism imprisoned not only organized labor but also the future of social policy and the premises of state intervention in all aspects of economic life. For some, the New Deal stretched the acceptable boundaries of politics; an exceptional response to exceptional circumstances, it was never meant to imply a fundamental overhaul of the economic order. For others, the promise of New Deal always outstripped its results; it was (or should have been) the framework upon which the nation could build an economic democracy equal to its political traditions.

In the end, the dubious legacy of the New Deal reflects both postwar conditions (which confused political solutions with a tenuous prosperity) and the premises of the New Deal itself (which saw economic and political equity as by-products of business-driven reform). Through the 1980s and early 1990s, the economy has slipped into patterns of speculative uncertainty and market stagnation eerily reminiscent of the late 1920s. Global interdependence, rapid technological change, and deindustrialization, however, have distorted the political response. Just as the New Deal gave way to the politics of growth, the politics of growth have given way to the politics of the lowest common denominator. Business has haphazardly pursued a political climate that sees government as little more than an institutional consumer, the costs of government as an unnecessary burden, and international

43 Rogers, "Divide and Conquer," 103–47; Montgomery, "New Deal Formula," 156–61; Moody, *An Injury to All*, 41–70, 95–219; Nelson Lichtenstein, "From Corporatism to Collective Bargaining: Organized Labor and the Eclipse of Social Democracy in the Postwar Era," in *The Rise and Fall of the New Deal Order*, ed. Steve Fraser and Gary Gerstle (Princeton, 1989), 122–52 (quote, 123); Charles Heckscher, *The New Unionism: Employee Involvement in the Changing Corporation* (New York, 1988), 23–33, 40–44, 55–81.

competition as an escape from the notion that economic interests bear any responsibility for the health of national economies. Politically unorganized and economically insecure, working people have borne the burden of the twisted political priorities exemplified (but certainly not initiated) by recent administrations.[44]

In this respect, appeals for a revival of the political and social values of the New Deal should not be taken lightly or uncritically. The coercive federal legislation of the 1930s and the laissez-faire opportunism of the present are two sides of the same coin. The former reflected business strategies in a destructively competitive national industrial economy; the latter reflects business strategies in a complex and competitive global economy. Although the "progressive" legislation of the 1930s always had the potential to redress gross disparities in political power, wealth, and economic rights, its origins and subsequent interpretation have adhered to prevailing business demands. The creation of a truly democratic polity and a truly democratic economy depend upon the pursuit of radically different public policies that take the political empowerment of women and men seriously, rather than relying on mass abstention in elections between two business-dominated parties, and that take the economic rights of working people seriously, rather than ex-tending and withdrawing such rights at the whim of business conditions and business demands.

44 See Joshua Cohen and Joel Rogers, " 'Reaganism' After Reagan," *The Socialist Register* (1988): 392–403.

Bibliographical Essay

The New Deal has been the object of numerous specialized studies, but there have been few efforts to assess its overall importance in light of both the full archival record and the interpretive insights of other disciplines. The following highlights some of the more important or influential sources on the origins, history, and legacy of the New Deal. A full list of archival sources follows this essay; a complete list of sources consulted or cited can, of course, be found in the notes to each chapter.

William Leuchtenberg's *Franklin Roosevelt and the New Deal* (1963) is easily the best of an extensive, but interpretively thin, library of narrative or biographical approaches. Early critical overviews, such as the introduction to Howard Zinn's *New Deal Thought* (1966) or Barton Bernstein's "The New Deal: The Conservative Achievements of Liberal Reform," in *Toward A New Past: Dissenting Essays in American History,* ed. Barton Bernstein (1968) contain important insights but are quite dated. Fortunately, the poverty of synthetic New Deal research is relieved somewhat by the interpretive wealth of more specialized studies. Certainly all scholarly roads to the New Deal still pass through Ellis Hawley's magisterial *The New Deal and the Problem of Monopoly* (1966), a sweeping yet nuanced account of the contradictions of the New Deal's economic program. I have also benefited from efforts to build upon Hawley's insights, including Robert Himmelberg, *The Origins of the National Recovery Administration* (1976), and Hawley's own essays on the 1920s. And, more importantly, I have drawn extensively from efforts to link the NRA debacle with the labor policy of the "second" New Deal; see especially Stanley Vittoz, *New Deal Labor Policy and the American Industrial Economy* (1987), and Grant Farr, *Origins of Recent Labor Policy* (1959). A wider focus on the industrial politics of the New Deal can be found in Thomas Ferguson, "From Normalcy to New Deal: Industrial structure, party competition, and American public policy in the Great Depression," *International Organization* 38 (1984), and in Gabriel Kolko's brief but provocative account of the New Deal in his *Main Currents in Modern American History* (1984).

307

The opening chapter ("Rethinking the New Deal") is largely an effort to bring insights from other disciplines to bear on the historical problem of the New Deal. On problems of "rational choice" and collective action, see Mancur Olson, *The Logic of Collective Action* (1965); Russell Hardin, *Collective Action* (1982); and the work of Jon Elster, especially *Ulysses and the Sirens* (1979), *Nuts and Bolts for the Social Sciences* (1989), and the opening chapters of *Making Sense of Marx* (1985). My understanding of "democratic capitalism" leans heavily on Adam Przeworski, *Capitalism and Social Democracy* (1986); Charles Lindblom, *Politics and Markets* (1977); Lindblom, "The Market as a Prison," *The Journal of Politics* 44 (1982); Joel Rogers, "Divide and Conquer: Further 'Reflections on the Distinctive Character of American Labor Laws,'" *Wisconsin Law Review* (1990); and Joel Rogers and Joshua Cohen, *On Democracy* (1984). On economic competition, see Joe Bain, *Barriers to New Competition* (1956); Josef Steindl, *Maturity and Stagnation in American Capitalism* (1976); Naomi Lamoreaux, *The Great Merger Movement in American Business, 1895–1904* (1985); and especially the work of John Bowman, including *Capitalist Collective Action: Competition, Cooperation and Conflict in the Coal Industry* (New York, 1989); "The Logic of Capitalist Collective Action," *Social Science Information* 21 (1982); and "Politics of the Market: Economic Competition and the Organization of Capitalists," *Political Power and Social Theory* 5 (1985). Problems of economic federalism, routinely detailed in the political record, business press, and private correspondence of the 1920s and 1930s, have received relatively little scholarly attention. Exceptions include William Graebner, "Federalism in the Progressive Era," *Journal of American History* 64 (1977); David Brion Robertson, "The Bias of American Federalism," *Journal of Policy History* 1 (1989); Aaron Wildavsky, "Federalism Means Inequality: Political Geometry, Political Sociology, and Political Culture," in *The Costs of Federalism*, ed. Robert Golembiewski and Aaron Wildavsky (1983); and my "New Deal, Old Deck: Business and the Origins of Social Security, 1920–1935," *Politics and Society* (1991). My interest in unpacking the logic of business and politics in the 1930s was, in part, sparked by Theda Skocpol's important essay, "Political Response to Capitalist Crises: Neo-Marxist Theories of the State and the Case of the New Deal," *Politics and Society* 10 (1980), and by the ongoing debate over the nature of the state, nicely summarized in Martin Carnoy, *The State and Political Theory* (1984).

Chapter Two ("Competition and Collective Action") is based largely on an extensive and very uneven corpus of corporate and industrial histories – most of which betray little interest in any larger political and social context.

This said, even impressionistic and celebratory accounts of one man's or one firm's entrepreneurial genius (which dominate the scholarship on U.S. industrial capitalism) contain important information on business conditions and strategies. More critical (and useful) accounts include Norman Nordhauser, *The Quest For Stability: Domestic Oil Regulation, 1917–1935* (1979), and William Robbins, *Lumberjacks and Legislators: Political Economy of the U.S. Lumber Industry, 1890–1940* (1982). In many respects, contemporary scholarship – such as Carroll Daugherty, *The Economics of Iron and Steel* (1937); Myron Watkins, *Oil: Conservation or Stabilization?* (1936); and various articles in the *Southern Economic Journal, Journal of Political Economy, American Economic Review,* and *Fortune* – are better than anything that has been written since. Some of the best recent scholarship on U.S. industry comes via labor history, such as Steve Jeffreys, *Management and Managed: Fifty Years of Crisis at Chrysler* (1986); *On the Line: Essays in the History of Auto Work,* ed. Nelson Lichtenstein and Stephen Meyer (1989); and Ronald Schatz, *The Electrical Workers: A History of Labor at General Electric and Westinghouse, 1923–1960* (1983). Important perspectives on the wider competitive environment included the work of Bowman, Steindl, and Himmelberg listed above and Michael Bernstein's *The Great Depression: Delayed Recovery and Economic Change in America, 1929–1939* (1987), an incisive portrait of the interwar economy. The private and published reflections of the Temporary National Economic Committee, the Federal Trade Commission, the Commerce Department, and the National Recovery Administration were quite useful. The archival record of important firms and industries is not extensive, and many collections that are open to researchers offer a great deal of managerial minutiae and very little in the way of a broader strategic or political perspective. Exceptions include the papers of John Raskob, Thomas Lamont, Alexander Sachs, and the DuPonts, as well as Herbert Hoover's Commerce Files.

Chapter Three ("Workers Organizing Capitalists") uses both old and new scholarship to explore the logic of interwar labor relations. Many readers will recognize the influence of institutional economists, including Lloyd Ulman, *Rise of the National Trade Union* (1955); Sumner Slichter, *Union Policies and Industrial Management* (1941); Jesse Carpenter, *Competition and Collective Bargaining in the Needle Trades, 1910–1967* (1972); Morton Baratz, *The Union and the Coal Mines* (1955); and Harry Millis, ed., *How Collective Bargaining Works: A Survey of Experience in Leading American Industries* (1942) – all of whom suggested how and why some workers and employers would concede to variants of regulatory unionism. Their insights, and those

of numerous union or industry histories, take on fresh meaning against recent explorations of the "material bases of consent," which see the emergence of "job-conscious" unionism less as a simple reflection of cultural and labor exceptionalism than as a consequence of the strategic logic of specific industries and institutional biases of democratic capitalism. See the work of Rogers, Przeworski, Vittoz, Farr, and Bowman cited above, as well as Steve Fraser, "Dress Rehearsal for the New Deal: Shop Floor Insurgents, Political Elites, and Industrial Democracy in the Amalgamated Clothing Workers," in *Working Class America*, ed. Michael Frisch and Daniel Walkowitz (1983). For the larger managerial perspective, see Sanford Jacoby, "American Exceptionalism Revisited: The Importance of Management," in *Masters to Managers: Historical and Comparative Perspectives on American Employers*, ed. Sanford Jacoby (1991). The latter half of Chapter Three, like Chapter Two, uses a mix of business history, contemporary journalism, and archival sources (especially internal NRA research) to document patterns of labor relations in a variety of industrial settings.

Chapter Four ("The Limits of Associationalism") turns to the problem of business organization, picking up on the organizational problems suggested in Chapters Two and Three and exploring the more abstract logic and dilemmas of business collective action suggested in Chapter One. Interwar trade associations have received a great deal of scholarly and contemporary attention; see especially Himmelberg (cited above); James Fickle, *The New South and the "New Competition": Trade Association Development in the Southern Pine Industry* (1980); Louis Galambos, *Competition and Cooperation: The Emergence of a National Trade Association* (1966); Ellis Hawley, "Three Facets of Hooverian Associationalism: Lumber, Aviation, and Movies, 1921–1930," in *Regulation in Perspective*, ed. Thomas McGraw (1981); Temporary National Economic Committee, *Trade Association Survey* (1941); and Simon Whitney, *Trade Associations and Industrial Control* (1934). On the peculiar logic of business organization, see Olson (cited above); Edgar Heermance, *Can Business Govern Itself?* (1933); Philippe Schmitter and Donald Brand, "Organizing Capitalists in the United States: The Advantages and Disadvantages of Exceptionalism" (unpublished, 1979); and Robert Brady's classic *Business as a System of Power* (1943). The literature on "peak" associations is relatively thin; I have relied on a few articles [Richard Gable, "Birth of an Employers' Association," *Business History Review* 33 (1959); Allen Wakstein, "The NAM and Labor Relations in the 1920s," *Labor History* 10 (1969); Philip Burch, "The NAM as an Interest Group," *Politics and Society* 4 (1973); H. M. Gitelman, "Management's Crisis of Confidence and the

Origin of the National Industrial Conference Board," *Business History Review* 58 (1984)]; and, more importantly, the publications and private papers of the organizations themselves. The Conference Board, the Chamber of Commerce, and NAM have extensive collections; the records of the Special Conference Committee are scattered throughout the Harrington, Raskob, and DuPont papers.

Chapter Five ("The National Recovery Act") stresses the links between the competitive and organizational strategies outlined in the early chapters and the regulatory innovation of the New Deal. My account of the NRA draws on Himmelberg and Hawley (previously cited), as well as Donald Brand, *Corporatism and the Rule of Law: A Study of the National Recovery Administration* (1988), and Bernard Bellush, *The Failure of the NRA* (1975). But I found that the central problems of compliance and enforcement came across most forcefully in the NRA's private and public postmortem – especially Senate Committee on Finance, *Investigation of the National Recovery Administration* (1935), Leverett Lyon, *The National Recovery Administration* (1935), the unpublished code histories, the compliance division's industry reports, and two exhaustive internal reports: Committee of Industrial Analysis, "Report on the Results and Accomplishments of the National Recovery Act" (1937), and a Division of Industrial Economics Staff Study (1936). Also important were contemporary and historical accounts of the experience of particular industries, such as Daugherty (cited above); Sidney Fine, *The Automobile under the Blue Eagle* (1963); and George Galloway, ed., *Industrial Planning under Codes* (1935).

Chapter Six ("The Wagner Act"), which argues that New Deal labor policy reflected long-standing patterns of industrial labor relations and the failure of the NRA, draws upon many of the same sources as Chapters Two and Five, particularly the private and political reflections on the meaning of unionism under the NRA. The ways in which private interests (documented in the Raskob, Sachs, Harrington, NAM, and NICB Papers) understood the relationship between the NRA and the Wagner Act were especially revealing. By 1935, of course, the influence of politics and a new legal and institutional culture of labor relations were also crucial; see Christopher Tomlins, *The State and the Unions* (1985); Peter Irons, *New Deal Lawyers* (1982); Howell Harris, "The Snares of Liberalism? Politicians, Bureaucrats, and the Shaping of Federal Labor Relations Policy in the United States, ca. 1915–1947," in *Shop Floor Bargaining and the State: Historical and Comparative Perspectives*, ed. Jonathan Zeitlin and Stephen Tolliday (1985); and David Plotke, "The Wagner Act, Again: Politics and Labor, 1935-1937," *Studies in Amer-*

ican Political Development 3 (1989). In turn, the willingness and ability of workers to take matters into their own hands was constantly changing the political and managerial atmosphere; see Irving Bernstein, *The New Deal Collective Bargaining Policy* (1950); Michael Goldfield, "Worker Insurgency, Radical Organization, and New Deal Labor Legislation," *American Political Science Review* 83 (1989); and Lizabeth Cohen, *Making a New Deal: Industrial Workers in Chicago, 1919–1939* (1991). For the meaning of the new labor relations across the industrial economy, see Ferguson, Vittoz, and Farr (all previously cited). Penetrating overviews of New Deal labor policy include David Montgomery, "American Workers and the New Deal Formula," in Montgomery, *Workers' Control in America* (1979); Melvyn Dubofsky, "Not So 'Turbulent Years': A New Look at the 1930s," in *Life and Labor: Dimensions of American Working Class History,* ed. Charles Stephenson and Robert Asher (1986); Michael Goldfield, Theda Skocpol, and Kenneth Finegold, "Explaining New Deal Labor Policy," *American Political Science Review* 84 (1990); and the early chapters of Howell Harris, *The Right to Manage: Industrial Relations Policies of American Business in the 1940s* (1982); and Nelson Lichtenstein, *Labor's War at Home* (1982).

Chapter Seven ("The Social Security Act") reaches back into the 1920s, drawing upon industry histories and contemporary surveys of welfare policy. See especially Bryce Stewart, *Unemployment Benefits in the United States* (1930), Murray Latimer, *Industrial Pension Systems in the United States and Canada* (1931), NICB, *Industrial Relations Programs in Small Plants* (1929), and various issues of *The Bulletin of the Bureau of Labor Statistics* and *American Labor Legislation Review.* The scholarship on "welfare capitalism" includes Stuart Brandes, *American Welfare Capitalism, 1880–1940* (1970); David Brody, "The Rise and Decline of Welfare Capitalism," in Brody, *Workers in Industrial America* (1980); Gerard Zahavi, *Workers, Managers, and Welfare Capitalism: The Shoeworkers and Tanners of Endicott Johnson, 1890–1950* (1988); Rick Halpern, "The Iron Fist and the Silk Glove: Welfare Capitalism in Chicago's Packinghouses, 1921–1933," *Journal of American Studies* 26 (1992); Daniel Nelson, *Unemployment Insurance: The American Experience* (1969); and Sanford Jacoby, *Employing Bureaucracy: Managers, Unions and the Transformation of Work in American Industry* (1985). My attempt to link the Social Security Act to the legacy of welfare capitalism and the parallel creation of a "regulatory" labor relations system is, in some respects, a response to the provocative (but, I think, mistaken) work of Theda Skocpol and her students on the origins of the U.S. welfare state; see especially Theda Skocpol and John Ikenberry, "The Political Formation of

the American Welfare State," *Comparative Social Research* 6 (1983); and Ann Orloff, "The Political Origins of America's Belated Welfare State," in *The Politics of Social Policy in the United States,* ed. Margaret Weir (1988). Although the links between federal welfare law, the legacy of the NRA, and the larger organizational logic of New Deal federalism and labor policy are rarely touched upon in conventional histories of social security, they are ably documented in the private considerations of key business interests (see particularly the Leeds & Northrup, Pennsylvania Railroad, Harrington, NICB, and National Civic Federation Papers), in political records (see especially the papers of Edwin Witte, the President's Organization on Unemployment Relief, and the Committee on Economic Security), and in the public record [see Senate Committee on Finance, *Economic Security Act* (1935)].

Chapter Eight ("New Deal, Old Deck") examines the logic of business opposition to the New Deal, and the longer-term prospects for the "New Deal System." My analysis of business opposition is based largely on private and public discontent with failed New Deal policies. On business dissent, see Ellis Hawley, "A Partnership Formed, Dissolved, and in Renegotiation: Business and Government in the Franklin D. Roosevelt Era," in *Business and Government: Essays in 20th Century Cooperation and Conflict,* ed. Joseph Frese and Jacob Judd (1985); Hawley, "The New Deal and Business," in *The New Deal: The National Level,* ed. David Brody et al., (1975); Mark Leff, *The Limits of Symbolic Reform: The New Deal and Taxation, 1933–1940* (1984); and David Vogel, "Why Businessmen Distrust Their State: The Political Consciousness of American Corporate Executives," *British Journal of Political Science* 8 (1978). For the legacy of the New Deal through 1945 and beyond, I have drawn upon a number of specialized and synthetic surveys of the modern U.S. political economy. See, in addition to work previously cited, Samuel Bowles et al., *After the Wasteland: Democratic Economics for the Year 2000* (1990); Thomas Kochan et al., *The Transformation of American Industrial Relations* (1986); Alan Wolfe, *America's Impasse: The Rise and Fall of the Politics of Growth* (1981); Adam Przeworski and Michael Wallerstein, "Democratic Capitalism at the Crossroads," *democracy* 2 (1982); Fred Block et al., *The Mean Season: The Attack on the Welfare State* (1987); Theda Skocpol, "America's Incomplete Welfare State: The Limits of New Deal Reforms and the Origins of the Present Crisis," in *Stagnation and Renewal in Social Policy,* ed. Martin Rein (1987); Ruth Milkman's and Fred Block's essays in *America at Century's End,* ed. Alan Wolfe (1990); and Nelson Lichtenstein's essay in *The Rise and Fall of the New Deal Order,* ed. Steve Fraser and Gary Gerstle (1989).

Manuscript Collections

Baker Library, Harvard University, Cambridge, MA
   Henry S. Dennison Papers
   A. Lincoln Filene Papers
   Louis E. Kirstein Papers
   Thomas W. Lamont Papers

Federal Records Center, Suitland, MD
   Petroleum Administration for War (RG 232)

Franklin D. Roosevelt Presidential Library, Hyde Park, NY
   Adolph Berle Papers
   Morris L. Cooke Papers
   Katherine Ellickson Papers (microfilm)
   John H. Fahey Papers
   Leon Henderson Papers
   Hugh Johnson Papers
   Gardiner C. Means Papers
   Henry J. Morgenthau Diaries
   Franklin D. Roosevelt Papers
   Alexander Sachs Papers

Hagley Museum and Library, Wilmington, DE
   American Iron and Steel Institute (vertical file)
   Chamber of Commerce Papers
   Irenée DuPont Papers
   Pierre S. DuPont Papers
   DuPont Company Administrative Papers
   Willis Harrington Papers
   Archibald Johnson Papers
   Leeds & Northrup Papers (microfilm)
   Lukens Steel Papers
   National Industrial Conference Board Papers
   National Association of Manufacturers Papers

National Industrial Leather Association Papers
Pennsylvania Railroad Papers
John J. Raskob Papers
Sun Oil Papers
Westmoreland Coal Papers

Herbert C. Hoover Presidential Library, West Branch, IA
Herbert C. Hoover Papers
Edward E. Hunt Papers
Nathan MacChesney Papers
Lewis L. Strauss Papers
Ray Lyman Wilbur Papers
Robert E. Wood Papers

Littauer Library, Georgetown University, Washington, DC
Robert F. Wagner Papers

National Archives, Washington, DC
Bureau of Foreign and Domestic Commerce (RG 151)
Department of Commerce (RG 40)
National Labor Relations Board (RG 25)
National Recovery Administration (RG 9)
President's Organization on Unemployment Relief (RG 73)
Social Security Administration (RG 47)

New York Public Library, New York, NY
National Civic Federation Papers

State Historical Society of Wisconsin, Madison, WI
Arthur J. Altmeyer Papers
William M. Leiserson Papers
Edwin Witte Papers

Index

317